Using the IBM Personal Computer:

Organization and Assembly Language Programming

Using the IBM Personal Computer:

Organization and Assembly Language Programming

Mark A. Franklin

Departments of Electrical Engineering and Computer Science
Washington University
St. Louis, Missouri

HOLT, RINEHART AND WINSTON
New York   Chicago   San Francisco   Philadelphia
Montreal   Toronto   London   Sydney   Tokyo
Mexico City   Rio de Janeiro   Madrid

The cover illustration is the additive color model from Miles Color Art, Tallahassee, Florida prepared using the digital facsimiles process (patent pending), Center for Color Graphics, Florida State University, Tallahassee, Florida.

IBM ® is a registered trademark of International Business Machines Corporation.

Address correspondence to:
383 Madison Avenue, New York, NY 10017
First distributed to the trade in 1984 by Holt, Rinehart and Winston general book division.

Library of Congress Cataloging in Publication Data

Franklin, Mark A., 1940–
    Using the IBM Personal Computer

    Bibliography: p.
    Includes index.
    1. IBM Personal Computer. 2. IBM Personal Computer—
Programming. 3. Assembler language (Computer program
language) I. Title. II. Title: The I.B.M. Personal
Computer.
QA76.8.I2594F73 1985   001.64   84-10865
ISBN 0-03-062862-8 (pbk.)

ISBN 0-03-062862-8

Printed in the United States of America

Published simultaneously in Canada

4 5 6   039   9 8 7 6 5 4 3 2 1

CBS COLLEGE PUBLISHING
Holt, Rinehart and Winston
The Dryden Press
Saunders College Publishing

Contents

v

Preface

This book is intended for those who seek to go beneath the exterior view presented by higher-level computer languages, and understand the operation of the IBM Personal Computer (PC) at a deeper level. Accordingly, the book focuses on the architecture and operation of the IBM PC and its machine and macro assembly languages. In addition, we explore the operating system and BIOS (Basic Input/Output System) facilities available at the assembly language level, and we present techniques for interfacing assembly language programs with those written in higher-level languages. Included is all the essential material necessary to program effectively in assembly language.

The Intel 8088 Microprocessor provides the core computing engine for the IBM PC; consequently, the book contains a great deal of material on the operation of this powerful 16-bit microprocessor. A thorough understanding of this material provides a sound basis for understanding the operation of many contemporary computers.

There are numerous practical situations where knowledge of machine organization and assembly language programming is necessary or even essential. These situations generally require that more control be exerted over the internal operations of the computer than is typically afforded by higher-level languages. Such control, for example, may be needed to achieve maximum speed. A higher-level language may be adequate from a logical point of view, but the programs generated may be too slow for the application in question. Close control over the computer at the assembly language level can often exploit the computer's resources in a more efficient manner. Toward this end, special attention is devoted (Chapter 11) to the problem of interfacing assembly language routines with higher-level-language routines. This allows use of the simpler and more powerful programming constructs available in higher-level languages for most programming activity while using assembly language programs for time-critical sections.

Assembly language programming is also needed when close control over standard input/output devices is required, or when special input/output devices are to be interfaced to the computer. Chapter 10 covers the operation and control of several standard devices using BIOS.

Moreover, special applications sometimes require that modifications or additions be made to the computer's overall control program or operating system. Such modifications typically must be done at the assembly language level. Techniques for implementing such adjustments are discussed in Chapter 9, which contains a review of the disk operating system's function calls and their use.

Although the book centers on the IBM PC, the bulk of the material also applies to the IBM PC*jr* and IBM PC/XT computers. All of these systems use the Intel 8088 Microprocessor and therefore employ the same machine and assembly languages. By the same token, the book also can be used to learn assembly language programming on the host of compatible computers now available. This includes systems based on the Intel 8086 Microprocessor, which is faster than the Intel 8088 but functionally identical to it.

This text supports a comprehensive introductory course on computer organization and assembly language programming for people with some background in higher-level-language programming and general notions relating to algorithms and programs. There is no hardware or logic design background required, and any material needed in this area is contained in the text. The book can be used in a formal course setting or as a guide for self-study. Numerous examples are provided in the text, and each chapter concludes with a summary of the main points and a set of problems to help reinforce the material. To take full advantage of the material, an IBM Personal Computer (or compatible equivalent) should be available. The best way to learn assembly language, or for that matter any programming language, is to work problems and write, debug, and run programs.

The book is divided into two major parts: Part I, Chapters 1 through 7, contains basic material on computer organization, operation, instruction set, and assembly language which is needed to write assembly language programs. Part II, Chapters 8 through 11, contains advanced material on macros, interrupts, and DOS (Disk Operating System) and BIOS facilities, with the concluding chapter dealing with higher-level-language–assembly language interfacing techniques. Skill in assembly language programming can be achieved by concentrating initially on Part I, after which more specialized material in Part II can be acquired as needed. Once the language and its associated facilities have been mastered, the book will continue to serve as a useful reference.

I am grateful to my colleagues at Washington University and elsewhere for their support in this endeavor. Particular thanks goes to Sy Pollack for his cheerful encouragement and careful reading of the book, to Tom Patterson for his help in developing and debugging example programs, to Howard Bomze for his close reading of Chapters 9 and 10, and to my brother David for his steadfast optimism that it would get done. My thanks also to CBS Educational Publishing and to the CBS book reviewers who made many valuable suggestions. Finally, I want to thank my wife, children, and friends who had to put up with my replies of the form, "I'm sorry, I have to go work on the book," but nevertheless remained faithful.

The book is dedicated to my wife, Barbara, and to my parents, Jack and Celia Franklin, without whose understanding and help this would not have been possible.

Part

I
The
Basics

1

Introduction and Overview

Development of the Large Scale Integration and Very Large Scale Integration (LSI and VLSI) of digital circuits has dramatically lowered the price and increased the performance of computers. This effect, coupled with a large and favorable market response, has resulted in what is called "the personal computer." Computers in this class are *personal* in at least two senses. First, they are inexpensive enough so that many "persons" can now afford to purchase one for themselves. Second, the expectation is that they will often be used in ways determined primarily by the individual user. Their low cost is giving users increased freedom to explore new application areas ranging from use as very smart terminals to dedicated use as processors for a host of other applications.

Often the computer is purchased and used as a packaged, or "turnkey," system where both the hardware and software have been tailored to an application of interest. Dedicated word processing systems fall into this category. In many situations users will program applications for themselves in higher-level languages such as BASIC, FORTRAN, or PASCAL. Such languages significantly ease the task of programming and should be used whenever possible. Use of these languages allows one to concentrate

3

principally on the logical requirements of the problem at hand rather than on questions related to the details of a particular computer's design.

In some situations, however, there will be a desire, or need, to go beneath the language exterior which higher-level languages present. One may want to discover how the computer is designed at a deeper level than is available to the higher-level-language programmer and determine the capabilities available when programming at this more "basic" assembly and machine language level. Moreover, there is a certain satisfaction which results from a more detailed understanding of a machine, especially one as generally important and progressively invasive as a computer. Though referred to as a *personal computer*, the IBM PC is prototypical of many contemporary computers in terms of its organization and capabilities. Consequently, an understanding of its operation provides a broad insight into the architecture and operation of computers.

There are many practical situations where a detailed understanding of the machine's organization and instructions is necessary. These situations generally require that more control be exerted over the internal operations of the computer than is typically afforded by higher-level languages. Such control may be needed to achieve high speed. A higher-level language may be able to do the job from a logical point of view, but the code it generates may be too slow for the application in question. Close control over the computer at the assembly language level may allow one to exploit the computer more efficiently.

Direct control may also be required when special input or output devices are interfaced with the computer. While many higher-level languages provide for control of such standard devices as printers, these languages are generally inadequate when nonstandard devices are used or nonstandard operations are to be performed. For example, although the IBM PC BASIC language (1)* includes commands for control of such devices as the joystick, speaker, and video display, these are not typically supported by the FORTRAN and PASCAL languages. Separate assembly language routines can, however, be written for controlling these devices, and these routines in turn may be accessed from FORTRAN and PASCAL programs. In Chapter 11 the problems of interfacing assembly language routines with high-level-language programs are considered in some depth.

Finally, some adventurous souls will want to modify an existing operating system (i.e., the control program under which other programs are typically run) or perhaps even design their own. This usually requires knowledge of the inner workings of the computer and operating system, and an ability to control both hardware and software resources at the assembly language level.

This book presents the logical and functional organization of the IBM PC and computer programming of the PC at the assembly language level. The emphasis is on both achieving a basic understanding of this computer and providing material of direct use to the practitioner who needs more detailed control of the PC to satisfy program speed-up or special peripheral requirements. A brief overview of the book and the general approach taken to present this material may be found in the Preface.

---

*Numbers in parentheses refer to works listed in the References at the end of the book.

1.1 COMPUTER ORGANIZATION

The basic general-purpose digital computer can be viewed functionally as having the five hardware components shown in Figure 1-1. The larger box at the top of the figure includes the arithmetic/logic (execution unit) and control units (bus interface unit), which together constitute the microprocessor heart of the IBM PC. This microprocessor, fabricated as a single semiconductor chip, is produced by the Intel Corporation. It is discussed further in Section 1.2.

The central function of a computer is to manipulate and operate on data. The data may be in the form of numerical data, or operands, upon which some arithmetic operation is to be performed (e.g., addition) or character information which is to be manipulated in some fashion (e.g., sorting). In any case, the functional unit which operates on the data is the *Arithmetic/Logic Unit* (ALU). Since the ALU can perform a variety of operations (e.g., addition, subtraction, logical **AND**, etc.), a *control unit* must be present to select the particular ALU action to be taken at any given instant. The control unit, in turn, is directed by information which is held in the computer's *memory unit*; it has the added responsibility of directing the removal of, or *fetching*, this information from the memory unit. The information consists of sequences of commands called *instructions*. While some of these instructions direct the ALU, others relate to such general control functions as where the next sequence of instructions of

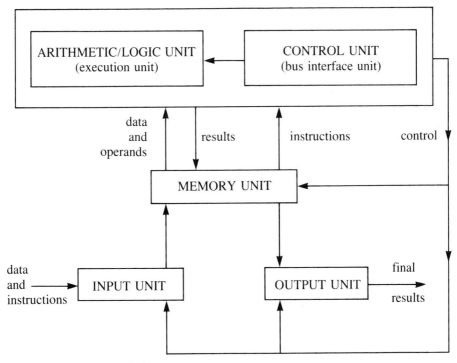

Figure 1-1   The basic digital computer.

interest is located in memory. Performing the operations specified in an instruction is referred to as *executing* the instruction.

Certain sequences of instructions are treated as a group because they encompass some broad purpose (e.g., obtaining the arithmetic average of a group of numbers). Such a sequence is called a *program*, and because these instructions are stored in memory (whose contents can be changed) computers of this type are called *stored-program computers*. Programs and data are entered into the memory unit through the *input unit*. (e.g., a keyboard). In general, the programs in memory can be changed by entering different information via the input unit. This ability to change the program in memory, and thus the set of instructions which directs the computer's operation, has led to use of the term *software* to designate the set of programs available to a given computer. This contrasts with the *hardware* (e.g., the ALU), whose characteristics remain relatively fixed over long periods of time.

The results of instruction execution (e.g., the arithmetic average obtained) at some point will move from the ALU to the memory, and then from the memory to the *output unit*, where it will be available to the user. This completes the cycle from input to output.

1.1.1 Memory Unit

The *memory unit* holds both instructions to be processed by the control unit and data to be processed by the ALU. The unit itself is a group of electronic devices which can be viewed as consisting of thousands of switches, with each switch set in one of two positions, or states. Each switch is said to be in either the "1" state or the "0" state, and the information associated with such a two-state *binary* device is referred to as *1 bit* of information. The physical mechanism used to implement these switches varies. The states in the computer's *main memory* (i.e., the memory that holds data or instructions that will soon be needed by the control unit or ALU), for example, often correspond to the presence or absence of an electric charge at designated points on specially prepared semiconductor material. In addition to main memory, computer systems often have *secondary*, or *auxiliary*, memory such as disks or tape drives. These memories are used to store programs and data which are either not currently being used, or are too large to fit into main memory all at once. With such secondary devices, switch states typically correspond to an orientation associated with a magnetic material. Though generally larger in size than the main memory, secondary memories are usually slower by several orders of magnitude. Thus a floppy, or flexible, disk might take 300 ms (milliseconds; a ms equals 0.001 second) and a hard-disk unit 50 ms to access a given piece of information, while a semiconductor main memory might require only 0.5 μs (microseconds; a μs equals 0.000001 second).

Bits are normally aggregated into 8-bit groupings called *bytes*. Memory may be viewed as consisting of an ordered sequence of bytes. This ordering permits one to identify particular bytes in memory by assigning an integer (referred to as an *address*) to each byte. Figure 1-2 shows a 1,048,576-byte (2^{20} bytes, or 1 megabyte) memory. In the example, memory address 0 contains the bit pattern 00101001 while the highest address in memory, 1,048,575, contains the pattern 11001010.

memory contents	memory address
11001010	1,048,575
10100101	1,048,574
• • •	• • •
11101000	2
00000000	1
00101001	0

Figure 1-2   A 1-megabyte memory.

Capabilities for both writing into and reading from memory are necessary in order to execute new programs or manipulate data. Such a memory is referred to as a *read/write memory* (RWM), although the term *random access memory* (RAM) is also commonly used. There are situations, however, when it may be preferable to have portions of memory (or even the entire memory) contain fixed bit patterns which can only be read. This might be reasonable, for instance, in a dedicated application where the program being executed doesn't change. Such a memory is called a *read-only memory* (ROM), and once it has been programmed (i.e., its contents set), it is not easily changed. This avoids the problems associated with losing programs in memory perhaps because of equipment malfunction (e.g., loss of power), and the associated problems of reloading lost programs. The programs which control standard input and output functions in the IBM PC (called *BIOS*), for instance, are kept in a ROM.

1.1.2 Control Unit

From Figure 1-1 it is clear that the control unit serves as the principal manager of information transfer and manipulation in the computer. Its primary functions are

 1. Fetching instructions from memory
 2. Interpreting or decoding instructions
 3. Performing memory address calculations
 4. Fetching any necessary operands
 5. Directing the ALU to perform required operations
 6. Routing results to their proper destinations

To perform these functions, instructions must provide four items of information to the control unit. These are

1. The operation to be performed
2. The source location(s) of any required operands
3. The destination location(s) of any generated results
4. The location of the next instruction to be executed

This information is encoded as an instruction having a specified number of bits (typically an integer multiple of 8), and the particular encoding style is referred to as the *instruction format*. For example, consider the *two-address* instruction format shown symbolically below.

OPERATION CODE	OPERAND 2 ADDRESS	OPERAND 1 ADDRESS

The *operation code*, or *op code*, is a particular bit combination which, when *decoded* by the control unit, specifies the operation to be performed. The two operands used in the operation are found at the addresses specified. The destination address of the result of the operation is implied in this case, and is taken to be the same address as the operand 2 address. Thus, operand 2 is destroyed as a result of executing the instruction. The address of the next instruction to be executed is also implied. Since instructions which are to be executed in sequence are generally stored in the memory unit in successive memory locations, the implied next instruction in this case would be located at the next higher memory address after the currently executing instruction.

To make this example more explicit, consider one form of the 16-bit integer **ADD** instruction available on the IBM PC.

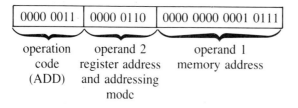

0000 0011	0000 0110	0000 0000 0001 0111
operation code (ADD)	operand 2 register address and addressing mode	operand 1 memory address

The operation code is the first byte of the instruction and the particular bit pattern shown indicates that a 16-bit **ADD** operation is to take place. The second byte specifies where the operands are to be found and how their addresses are to be calculated (referred to as the *addressing mode*). In this case operand 2 is in a special 16-bit memory location found in the ALU and referred to as the *AX accumulator* or *AX register*. The third and fourth bytes specify an address in the memory unit. The contents at this address (0000 0000: the least significant address bits, and 0001 0111: the most significant address bits), and the next higher address correspond to operand 1. The results of the addition are placed in the AX register with its previous contents being destroyed. The instruction itself would appear in memory as follows:

	memory contents	memory address
INC (INCrement) AX	01000000	4004
ADD instruction	00010111	4003
	00000000	4002
	00000110	4001
	00000011	4000

In the example above, the **ADD** instruction begins at location 4000. After the **ADD** instruction is completed, the implied next instruction to be executed is the next sequential instruction in memory. In this case it is an increment instruction which results in a 1 being added to the AX register.

The IBM PC has an extensive set of about 100 instructions and a varied set of instruction formats and addressing methods. These are considered in depth in Chapters 3 through 6.

1.1.3 Arithmetic/Logic Unit

Once the control unit indicates to the ALU which operation is to take place, and ensures that the operands are available, the ALU takes over and performs the designated operation. As will be discussed in Chapters 4 through 6, a wide variety of operations are possible including all of the normal arithmetic operations (e.g., addition, subtraction, multiplication, and division) and logical operations (e.g., **AND, OR, NOT**, and exclusive or, **XOR**).

In addition to having the logical hardware to perform various operations, the ALU has grouped with it a set of special memory locations, or registers. Their addressing scheme is separate from that of the main memory unit, and they are typically faster to access than main memory. In addition, some of these registers also have unique operational properties. The AX register discussed in the example above is one of eight general-purpose registers available in the IBM PC for storage of intermediate results and for special processing tasks.

The ALU also includes a *flag*, or *status*, register. Certain bits in this register indicate when special conditions have occurred in the ALU. For instance, if the result of an addition operation is zero, then the *zero flag* is set to 1; otherwise it is set to 0. This flag corresponds to a particular bit in the flag register, and instructions are provided to examine and test this bit. The flag register and the general registers are discussed further in Chapter 3.

Table 1-1   Intel 8088 Features

Direct memory addressing capability	1 megabyte
Internal datapath width	16 bits
External datapath width	8 bits
System clock rate (on IBM PC)	4.77 MHz
Instruction time (16-bit register, register integer **ADD**)	0.63 μs.
Number of basic instructions	about 100
Total number of instructions (includes 8- / 16-bit, and various address modes)	about 300
Number of addressable 16-bit I/O ports	32,000
Number of general-purpose 16-bit registers	8
Number of 16-bit memory segmentation registers	4
Number of pins on the chip	40
Size of the microprocessor package	$0.54 \times 2.0''$

Other features
- **a.** Stack and interrupt instructions
- **b.** Multiply/divide operations on 8-/16-bit integers
- **c.** Operations on packed and unpacked BCD numbers
- **d.** Move, scan, and compare string operations
- **e.** Byte translation operations
- **f.** Multiprocessor synchronization instructions

Intel support chips used in the IBM PC
- **a.** Intel 8284 Clock Generator and Driver
- **b.** Intel 8288 Bus Controller
- **c.** Intel 8259 Programmable Interrupt Controller
- **d.** Intel 8237 Programmable DMA Controller
- **e.** Intel 8253 Programmable Interval Timer
- **f.** Intel 8255 Programmable Peripheral Interface
- **g.** Intel 8087 Numeric Data Processor (optional)

1.1.4 Input and Output Units

The input and output (I/O) units provide the mechanisms for transmitting instructions and data to and from the computer. In a broad sense, the I/O system consists of three interacting facilities: First, there are the physical I/O units themselves. Typical user-oriented input units are keyboards, light pens, and joysticks. Some user-oriented output units are video monitors and display terminals, printers, plotters, and speech synthesizers (i.e., units that allow the computer to "talk"). In addition there are storage units (disk and tape drives) which can operate in either input or output mode.

Second, there is the manner in which the units are connected to and controlled by the computer. Generally, a separate device called an I/O control unit (also called a peripheral adapter or controller) is present for each type of I/O unit to provide a connection and control capability. Such adapters are available for nearly all I/O units of interest. One of their roles is to help enforce a common logical and electrical framework for interfacing peripherals to the computer.

Third, there are the procedures and instructions available to the programmer for interacting with these adapters and, through them, with the I/O devices themselves. These, and related issues, are considered in Chapter 10.

1.2 THE INTEL 8088 MICROPROCESSOR

To take advantage of the cost/performance benefits associated with the use of VLSI technology, designers of the IBM PC chose to implement the core computing engine (i.e., the control and arithmetic/logic units) with a single high-performance microprocessor chip. The particular microprocessor selected was the *Intel 8088* (also referred to as the *iAPX 88*; see references 2 and 3). In addition, a range of related Intel chips were used to implement input/output control. Some general characteristics of the microprocessor chip, and thus of the IBM PC, are given in Table 1-1.

While a detailed examination of the Intel 8088 chip structure is beyond the scope of this book, some general comments about its organization and relationship to the functional units described in the previous section are appropriate. Consider Figure 1-3, which uses Intel's nomenclature to designate the principal parts of the Intel 8088.

The microprocessor chip can be viewed as being divided into an Execution Unit (EU) and a Bus Interface Unit (BIU). The EU corresponds to the ALU unit described earlier with the AX register included as one of the general-purpose registers shown. The purpose of the flag register was discussed earlier. The BIU corresponds to the control unit with some additional components to be described below. Buses correspond to parallel information transmission paths along which operands, results, instructions, or control information may flow.

The BIU determines instruction and data memory addresses necessary for proper operation. It interfaces with data, address, and control buses external to the chip, which are in turn connected to main memory and various special I/O chips. Information external to the microprocessor is thus transmitted via the BIU.

The BIU keeps track of the instructions it has fetched from memory using the *instruction pointer* register (called the *program counter* in other processors). As instruc-

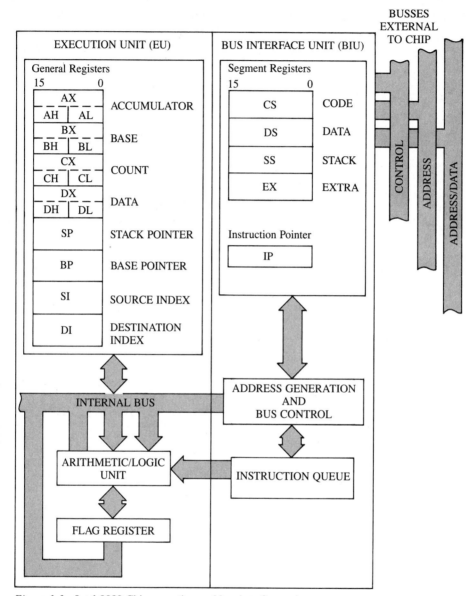

Figure 1-3 Intel 8088 Chip execution and bus interface units.

tions are fetched, they are placed in the *instruction queue*, whence they are decoded and ALU operation directed.

One interesting feature of this design is that the BIU continuously attempts to keep its instruction queue filled. Thus, in parallel with ALU execution, the BIU tries to remove the next sequential instruction from memory and place it in the queue, where it will be ready when the current ALU operation is complete. This overlapping of BIU and EU operation enhances performance by attempting to remove delays associated with instruction fetching. Of course, if the ALU requires operands from memory to perform its current operation, then operand fetches take precedence over additional instruction fetches. In addition, if the next instruction required is not the next sequential instruction in memory, then the BIU effectively clears its instruction queue and then restarts the fetching and queue filling process from the correct memory location.

The segment and general purpose registers shown in Figure 1-3 are discussed in detail in Chapter 3, where we shall consider memory addressing modes and general register functions. Finally, it should be pointed out that the 8088 is one of a family of microprocessor chips produced by Intel. Table 1-2 summarizes some of their capabilities. All of the processors listed have 16-bit-wide internal datapaths and operations.

The Intel 8086 microprocessor is functionally identical to the 8088 (i.e., the same programs will run on both microprocessors); however, it has somewhat higher performance because of the presence of a larger instruction queue and a wider external datapath (16 versus 8 bits). The larger instruction queue permits the 8086 to prefetch a greater number of instruction bytes than is possible with the 8088, thus further reducing delays associated with instruction fetching. The wider external datapath also reduces data transmission delays by permitting the fetching of 2 bytes rather than one in a single memory cycle. The upward-compatible 80188 and 80186 microprocessor chips achieve still higher performance by having higher clock rates and by adding 10 new instructions to the basic instruction set. Significant cost reductions also are achieved when using these newer chips since an interrupt controller, a timer, a clock, and two DMA (Direct Memory Access) channels are all contained on the same chip as the processor itself. These facilities require separate chips with the current IBM PC (see Table 1-1). The 80286 microprocessor chip has a still-higher clock rate (10 MHz). It is also upward-compatible with the 8086/88 and 80186/88. Though it doesn't contain the interrupt controller, timer, clock, and DMA channels present on the 80186/88 chips, it does include memory management facilities to aid in memory protection and support virtual memory operations. These facilities are needed to effectively design multiuser, time-shared operating systems. These chips may well be used in the development of the next generation of IBM PCs. Note, though, that the basic processor architecture (i.e., the organization of Figure 1-3) and instruction set are the same for all these microprocessors, and thus the bulk of the material presented in this book applies to them as well as the 8088 and current IBM PC. For more information on the 80186/88 microprocessor chips see reference 2.

1.3 SOFTWARE ORGANIZATION

1.3.1 Software Design and Development

Design and development of effective software systems of any reasonable size is a complex task akin in style and organizational requirements to any substantial engineering endeavor. This process can be viewed as consisting of the following five steps (4):

1. **Requirements Specification:** This step concerns defining just what problem is to be solved. It involves an in-depth needs analysis and specification. In simple

Table 1-2   The Intel 8086/88 Microprocessor Family

Microprocessor	External Datapath	Instruction Queue Length	Maximum Clock Rate	Other Features
iAPX 8088 (IBM PC)	8 bits	4	5 MHz	See Table 1-1.
iAPX 8086	16 bits	6	5 MHz	Functionally identical with the 8088 but 10 to 20% more powerful.
iAPX 8086-2	16 bits	6	8 MHz	Identical to 8086 but with higher clock rate.
iAPX 80186	16 bits	6	8 MHz	Runs all 8086/8088 software. Has 10 new instructions. Contains integrated clock generator, programmable interrupt controller, programmable timer, and Direct Memory Access (DMA) controller. About twice as powerful as the standard iAPX 8086.
iAPX 80188	8 bits	4	8 MHz	Functionally identical to the 80186. Somewhat lower performance because of smaller instruction queue and external datapath.
iAPX 80286	16 bits	6	10 MHz	Upward software compatibility with the 8086/88 and 81086/88 processors. Contains added memory management instructions and facilities. Up to 6 times the power of the 8086.

situations this may seem obvious. However, when dealing with groups and organizations, even the simplest tasks, if not defined precisely, may cause subsequent problems. A document developed jointly by the ultimate system users (customers) and the software developers, stating needs and requirements, will avoid unnecessary misunderstandings and clarify objectives of the software development task. The document itself may include a user's manual, input and output specifications, and performance requirements.

2. **Design:** This step involves the actual software design. It includes investigating and analyzing alternative methods for satisfying the requirements specification of step 1, and designing the data and control structures to be used. The algorithms to be used are specified at this point. Experience has shown that an effective way to deal with complexity is to follow a "divide and conquer" strategy. Partitioning the system into modules, which can be designed and implemented on an individual basis, uses such an approach and is an important part of this design step. While the most common method of partitioning a system calls for each module to implement a complete function, a number of other strategies have been suggested (5, 6).

3. **Implementation:** Implementation involves coding the individual modules defined in step 2 in the selected programming language(s), and developing the associated program documentation. This book is concerned primarily with this implementation phase, where implementation is in the IBM PC's assembly language.

4. **Check-out and certification:** No matter how much care is taken, design or implementation errors will inevitably occur, and a debugging and check-out phase will be needed. Some of the errors found will be confined to a particular module (e.g., an instruction in the module doesn't work quite the way the programmer anticipated). Others will concern communications between modules. Still others may relate to basic systems assumptions (e.g., assumed properties of the input data are not always true). To build confidence in the final software product, separate testing and check-out procedures should be done at the module, subsystem, and system levels. In some situations formal certification tests will be specified during the initial requirements phase. These must now be satisfied for the system to be accepted by the final user or customer.

5. **Maintenance:** Maintenance involves making changes in an operational system. These changes may be necessary because errors or bugs have been discovered after the system has been delivered, or because new features are to be added to the system. Provisions for easing the maintenance burden on large systems (over a system's lifetime, maintenance costs are often comparable to design and development costs) should be made during the design and implementation steps. Adequate documentation is essential here, as well as built-in programming aids and test modes which read out critical registers and areas of memory, and allow for easy insertion of test data.

Notice that creating and maintaining proper documentation, though not presented as a separate step, is a vital and continuing concern throughout the life cycle of a software system. The process of developing software systems following structured or engineered procedures is referred to as *software engineering*. Because of the high costs associated with producing reliable and maintainable software systems, interest in this area has grown and the reader is directed to references 4, 7, 8, 9, and 10 for more material on this topic.

1.3.2 Software Environment and Tools

Design and development of software systems occurs within a software environment that contains various "tools" which aid in performing the tasks described above. We focus here on certain common tools useful in implementation and check-out. Many of the key tools are provided as part of the *operating system* used on the computer. This system is itself a general program whose main functions are as follows:

1. Resource allocation (e.g., memory management)
2. Input/output control and communication with the outside world (e.g., send a character out to the printer)
3. Job and task scheduling and execution (e.g., select the program to be executed next and initiate execution)
4. Command interpretation (e.g,. interpret the user command to list files present on a designated disk)
5. Information protection (e.g., protect one user's file from inadvertent destruction by another user)
6. Utility, tool, and software resource access (e.g, provide user access to an assembler)

In a general way, the operating system attempts to provide the user with a "friendly" and efficient environment in which to develop and execute programs, and control and allocate system (hardware/software) resources. A variety of competing operating systems are available for the IBM PC, both from the manufacturer and from independent vendors. Most provide certain basic tools and utilities. Some of these must be purchased separately and they are typically designed to be used with a particular operating system (and its particular data and control structures). The principal tools found in most operating system environments are are follows:

1. **Editor:** Allows you to create, edit, and manipulate text files.
2. **File Handler:** Allows you to copy, rename, delete, display, and print existing files and file directories.
3. **Higher-Level-Language Compilers and Interpreters:** Allows you to express algorithms and develop programs in a higher-level language, and provides facilities for executing (after compilation or interpretation) these programs.
4. **Assembler:** Allows you to express algorithms in a mnemonic form close to the computer's machine language, and provides facilities for direct translation into bit-level machine instruction representation.
5. **Linker:** Allows you to bring together modules derived from compilers, assemblers, and program libraries which are to be executed as a single unit, and ensures that various common memory address references in different modules are resolved properly. The output of the linker is a file containing machine instructions which can be loaded into memory and executed.
6. **Loader:** Allows you to load files (typically produced by the linker) into memory and execute them.
7. **Debugger:** Allows you to load files into memory; examine and change flags, memory, and register contents; execute single instructions; control program execution by enforcing breaks when specified memory addresses are referenced; and translate memory bit sequences of 1s and 0s into assembly language mnemonics. Some debuggers also provide a simple built-in assembler. Functions are oriented toward close user interaction with an assembly language program which is being debugged.

While we will only discuss the assembler in depth, all the tools listed above (except for 3) are needed to develop, execute, and debug assembly language programs. A higher-level-language compiler (FORTRAN, PASCAL) or interpreter (BASIC) is also needed for the exercises of Chapter 11, Higher-Level-Language Interfacing. The reader who intends to attempt the exercises at the ends of the chapters and actually run some programs should therefore begin to read the manuals associated with these tools.

1.3.3 Algorithm Development and Documentation

Consider the following problem: Develop (design) and implement an algorithm to sum all positive integers found in a sequential set of memory locations (i.e., an integer array).

Although the problem statement appears to be fairly clear, more information is needed to perform this task properly. Most of this information would be collected during the Requirements Specification step discussed earlier. Some of the questions which must be answered are

a. How is the array loaded into memory and where is it located?

b. How large is the array or how can its length be determined?

c. How large are the integers in the array (e.g., how many bits long) and how are integer numbers represented (i.e., representation of positive and negative numbers)?

d. What should be done with the result?

e. Is the program to be developed as a stand-alone program or is it to be a module (procedure or subroutine) which will be called upon by some other program module?

f. If it is to be a callable module, then what are the mechanisms and protocols to be used in passing information between modules?

g. Are there any performance constraints on execution speed or memory space?

For illustration purposes say that we are developing a stand-alone program which is to operate on a fixed array 10 bytes long. For simplicity we shall assume that the array will be defined as part of the program and does not need to be read in from some external device or created by another program module. Each array element is a positive or negative integer whose maximum absolute value is 12. Negative integers may be distinguished from positive integers by the presence of a 1 in the leftmost bit. The result is to be placed in the 8-bit AL register (i.e., the rightmost 8 bits of the AX general register) and then displayed in IBM PC symbolic form (see Table 10-6) on the system monitor screen. Execution speed is of prime importance so the algorithm is to be implemented in assembly language.

The design process in this case is simple and is not considered here. The algorithm itself is documented below, first in a pseudo-higher-level-language form sometimes referred to as *structured English*, and then in a graphical form using standard flowchart notation. One or the other should be used to document the algorithm selected.

As with many contemporary higher-level languages, the descriptive format above is *block structured*, with blocks of related statements enclosed between **BEGIN/ END**

```
PROGRAM ISUM1
; program to sum positive integers in an array of length ten
NUMSET is a byte array of 10 integers whose contents is
        1, 2, -3, -4, 5, 6, -7, -8, 9, 10
BEGIN
set AL register to 0
FOR I: = 1 TO 10 DO
        BEGIN
        IF ( element I in NUMSET is positive )
        THEN ( add element I of NUMSET to AL )
        ELSE ( do nothing )
        END
display the contents of AL on the monitor
END     ISUM1
```

Figure 1-4 The **ISUM1** algorithm structure.

declarations. Such structuring is a convenient way of modularizing a program. An interesting feature of the IBM PC is that some of this block structured spirit has been designed into the organization of the microprocessor. This will be seen in Chapter 3 in the discussion of processor segmentation features.

The **FOR** statement above indicates that the **BEGIN-END** statement group which follows is to be executed 10 times with the index I being incremented by 1 on each execution. Thus all the elements of the **NUMSET** array are sequentially selected. The **IF-THEN-ELSE** construct checks each array element and, if positive, adds it to AL. On completion of the **FOR** loop, the contents of AL is displayed.

Flowcharts are constructed by connecting certain basic symbols with directed lines to indicate the sequence of operation and flow of control in an algorithm or program. Some of the standard flowchart symbols are given in Figure 1-5.

The flowchart for **ISUM1** is given in Figure 1-6. **NUMSET** again designates the array of 10 integers of interest. The CX register is used to control the loop iteration. Although loop control could be achieved by monitoring the I variable, the Intel 8088 gives the CX register special properties oriented toward this function. This will be considered later.

Notice that in terms of control flow, the flowchart presented is fairly detailed. The operation of the **FOR** loop and the **IF-THEN-ELSE** constructs are explicitly shown, and actual operations (i.e., addition) on various registers are indicated. Indeed, this could well represent program documentation as opposed to algorithm documentation and, as shown in the next section, implementing the corresponding assembly program from this flowchart is relatively straightforward.

1.3.4 Assembler Preliminaries

Figure 1-7 is a complete assembly language program which implements the processing described in the previous section. Detailed elements of this program will be considered

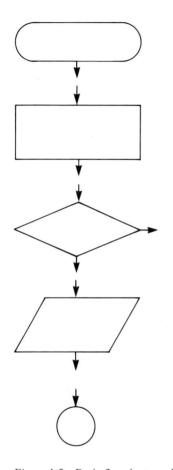

TERMINAL: Indicates start, end, or interruption of algorithm or program flow.

PROCESS: Indicates processing activity. Execution of a task, function, or group of instructions might be represented with this symbol.

DECISION: Indicates a decision point in the algorithm or program. Program flow direction and control can be shown with this symbol.

INPUT/OUTPUT: Indicates communication with input or output devices.

CONNECTOR: A unique identifier is typically placed with the connector circle. It indicates that the flowchart continues in another place, perhaps on another page, where another connector with the same identifier is found.

Figure 1-5 Basic flowchart symbols.

in later chapters; at this point, however, some general observations can be made. First note that each line in the program represents one of the following three items:

1. An instruction to be executed by the computer.
2. A command (i.e., a pseudo-operation) to the assembler to perform a task, or take note of some input statement condition (e.g., there are no more statements in the program).
3. A comment provided by the programmer for documentation purposes which has no effect on actual program operation. Any text on a line which follows a semicolon is a comment.

Lines that are not comments are typically divided into four fields. The leftmost field may contain a name or label which identifies the line in the program and directly relates to a memory address to be assigned by the assembler. Proceeding to the right, the next field indicates what action is to be taken (e.g., **ADD**). This is followed by a

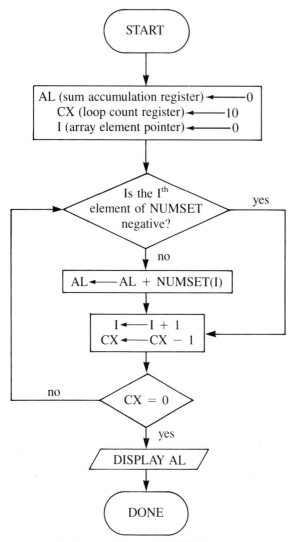

Figure 1-6 Program flowcart for **ISUM1.**

field specifying the operand(s) to be used. Finally a comment may be present which explains the intent of the line. The purpose of the assembler is to translate this assembly language representation into a correct sequence of 1s and 0s which correspond to the machine language representation of the specified actions.

Observe that the program is divided into three blocks, or segments, with each block beginning with a **SEGMENT** statement, and ending with a **ENDS** (**END** Segment) statement. The first segment, **DSEG**, contains the pseudo-operation statements **DB** (Define Byte) and **DW** (Define Word), which direct the assembler to reserve and initialize certain memory locations. The **DB** statement, for instance, defines an array

```
; ***   PROGRAM FOR SUMMING POSITIVE NUMBERS   ***
; ***        A BYTE ARRAY OF TEN NUMBERS       ***
;
DSEG      SEGMENT      ; begin data segment
NUMSET    DB      1, 2, -3, -4, 5, 6, -7, -8, 9, 10   ; data
TEN       DW      10              ; array length
DSEG      ENDS                    ; end data segment
;
SSEG      SEGMENT STACK           ; begin stack segment
          DW      256 DUP (?)     ; define 256 word stack
SSEG      ENDS                    ; end stack segment
;
CSEG      SEGMENT                 ; begin program segment

SUM1      PROC    FAR             ; define FAR PROCedure
          ASSUME  CS: CSEG, DS: DSEG, SS: SSEG
;         INITIALIZE STACK AND LOAD SEGMENT REGISTER (S)
;
SUM:      PUSH    DS              ; stack <--- return segment address
          XOR     AX, AX          ; AX <--- 0
          PUSH    AX              ; stack <--- return offset address
          MOV     AX, DSEG
          MOV     DS, AX          ; load Data Segment register
;         PERFORM SUMMATION OPERATION
;
          MOV     AL, 0           ; AL accumulates sum
          MOV     SI, 0           ; SI is index into NUMSET
          MOV     CX, TEN         ; CX gets array length
SLOOP:    CMP     NUMSET [SI], 0  ; check for number < 0
          JL      NXTNUM          ; jump if number < 0
          ADD     AL, NUMSET [SI] ; add array element to AL
NXTNUM:   INC     SI              ; increment array pointer
          LOOP    SLOOP           ; get next element if CX .ne. 0
;
;         DISPLAY AL AND TERMINATE PROGRAM
;
          MOV     DL, AL          ; load DL with display character
          MOV     AH, 2           ; load AH for operating system
                                  ; display character function call
          INT     21H             ; interrupt for function call
          RET                     ; FAR RETurn to operating system
;
SUM1      ENDP
CSEG      ENDS                    ; end of code segment
          END     SUM
```

Figure 1-7 Assembly language program for **ISUM1**.

of 10 integers (each integer takes 1 byte of memory) and initializes the array with the indicated decimal values. **NUMSET**, the first word on the **DB** statement line, is a *label* and represents the memory address where the first byte (containing the number 1) of the array is stored. When accessing elements in the array, **NUMSET** can be used as a starting address to find all the other array elements. The label **DSEG** designates the starting address for all the statements grouped together in that segment.

The second segment, labeled **SSEG**, defines an area of memory referred to as a *stack*. Stacks, discussed in Chapter 4, have special properties and associated instructions. The third segment, **CSEG**, contains the program instructions which are placed within a **FAR** procedure named **SUM1**. Procedures, also discussed in Chapter 4, begin with a **PROC** statement and end with an **ENDP** statement. By defining the program to be a procedure, and initially setting up the stack properly, return of control to the operating system on program termination can be simply effected by executing a **RET** (**RET**urn) instruction. The three instructions which immediately follow the comment **INITIALIZE STACK AND LOAD SEGMENT REGISTER(S)** perform this stack manipulation. The **ASSUME** statement and the instructions **MOV   AX,DSEG** and **MOV   DS,AX** relate to initialization of the segment registers and will be considered in Chapter 3.

The eight instructions which follow the comment **PERFORM SUMMATION OPERATION** are the core instructions which implement the desired algorithm. The first three **MOV** (**MOV**e) instructions load the AL, SI, and CX registers with the values 0, 0, and 10, respectively. These registers are in the set of general-purpose registers found in the computer's execution unit (see Figure 1-3). The **CMP** (**C**o**MP**are) instruction compares an integer taken from the **NUMSET** array with the number 0. The particular integer accessed is determined by the addressing mode specified in the **CMP** instruction. In this case the mode (**NUMSET[SI]**) indicates that an address is to be formed by adding the value found in the SI register with the address value designated by the label **NUMSET**. Thus, different array elements can be accessed by changing the contents of SI.

As a result of the **CMP** instruction, bits in the flag register are set (see Figure 1-3). Since the array value was compared to 0, these bits can be used to determine whether the integer selected was positive or negative. This is done with the **JL** (**J**ump if **L**ess) instruction. If the integer was negative, then the next instruction executed is the one found at the address specified by the label **NXTNUM** (i.e., there is a "jump" to the instruction at **NXTNUM**). If the integer is positive, then it is added into the register AL as indicated in the **ADD** instruction. In both cases the **INC** (**INC**rement) instruction at **NXTNUM** is executed. This instruction adds 1 to the SI register so that it can be now be used to point to the next integer in the **NUMSET** array.

The **LOOP** instruction effectively implements the higher-level **FOR** instruction and thus permits easy implementation of loops. Every time the **LOOP** instruction is executed, the CX register is automatically decremented by 1 and then tested. If CX is not equal to zero, then the next instruction executed is the one at the label specified (in this case **SLOOP**). Thus, since CX was initially loaded with the value 10, 10 loop iterations will be performed.

After performing these iterations, the instructions following the **DISPLAY AL AND TERMINATE PROGRAM** are executed. These instructions use certain facilities provided by the IBM Disk Operating System (DOS, see Chapter 9). DL and AH are part of the general-purpose register set. The contents of AL are displayed by first moving them into DL (**MOV   DL,AL**). The value, 2, indicating an operating system function display request, is then loaded into AH (**MOV   AH,2**). The **INT** (**INT**errupt) instruction now shifts control to the operating system program which performs the display operation and then returns to the **SUM1** procedure, where execution continues with the next instruction. The actual display is determined by translating the integer in DL into its corresponding display symbol (see Table 10-6). The final **RET** (**RET**urn) instruction transfers control back to the operating system. The operating system now notifies the user that the system is now available for other processing requests.

The final **END   SUM** pseudo-operation statement tells the assembler that there are no more assembly language statements to be processed and that program execution is to begin with the instruction labeled **SUM**.

1.3.5 The Overall Implementation Process

The overall assembly language program implementation process is illustrated in Figure 1-8. The name given beneath each tool and the file output names correspond to those available with the IBM DOS. Clearly other editors, assemblers, and entire operating systems can be used. Equivalent basic tools will be present in these environments.

The assembly language program to be implemented is typically entered into the system using an editor. The editor creates a file for the text (e.g., **PROG.ASM**). This is used as input into the assembler, which in turn may produce up to three new output files. The principal file thus produced contains a machine language translation of the assembly language input (e.g., **PROG.OBJ**). The bit patterns associated with the operation codes and addressing modes used are contained in this file. Most memory addresses, however, have yet to be assigned at this point. There are two reasons for this. First, the area of memory where the program is to reside has not yet been determined. Second, there may be address references to other assembly modules. These modules, assembled at a different time, may contain variables or procedures used by the module being currently assembled. These references are later resolved during the link process. However, at this point during the assembly process, memory references within (local to) the module being assembled are developed on a relative basis, and any references external to the current module are left unresolved.

Two other files may be produced by the assembler at the option of the user. The first, a listing file (e.g., **PROG.LST**), contains each original assembly language line input supplemented by line number. In addition, for those lines which are assembly language instructions, the bit patterns and relative addresses assembled from the instruction are provided. Lines showing pseudo-operations which define or reserve memory locations include the bit patterns associated with these definitions. Any errors found during the assembly process are also reported in this file. The second file, a cross-reference

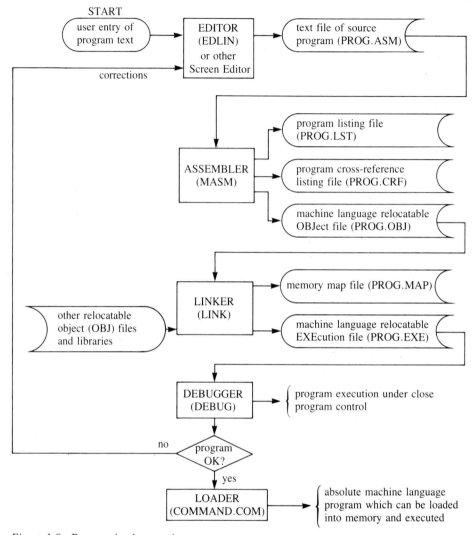

Figure 1-8 Program implementation process.

file (**PROG.CRF**), provides a list of all labels used in the program, and the listing file line number(s) where they appear. Both files contain useful information necessary in the debugging process.

The object module produced by the assembler, along with any other object modules which are referenced, are submitted to the linker, whose main function is to combine these separate modules into a single module, and resolve any cross-references among the modules. This single module (e.g., **PROG.EXE**) typically contains the machine language bit patterns for the entire program to be loaded into memory for execution. Depending on the linker program, the user may influence where the final module is to be loaded into memory. In the IBM DOS, for instance, the user may specify whether it is to be eventually loaded into the high or low end of memory. Absolute memory locations are still not assigned since what is high or low memory depends on the amount of memory available, and possibly on the operating system version being used. Thus, the principal output of the linker is a single relocatable object module. As a secondary output useful in debugging, the linker can also produce a memory map file (**PROG.MAP**) which indicates where various program modules will be located in memory relative to each other.

At this point the debugger program may be used to load the **EXE** module and execute it under close programmer control. For instance, the debugger permits one to execute the program one instruction at a time (called *one-stepping*), examining registers and memory locations after each instruction execution. This sort of technique is often needed to find the various errors which crop up during program implementation.

Finally, the program may be loaded and executed using the operating system's loader. The loader will take the output of the linker, load the program into memory, and then transfer control to it. Program operation now commences. Note that since loaders are used so often (i.e., all of the implementation tools discussed above had to be loaded), they are often combined with the operating system command processing structure. Thus, it is usually not necessary to load and run the loader explicitly. Often all that is necessary is to give the name (it may have to have a particular extension such as **EXE**) of the program to the operating system and loading and execution will begin automatically.

1.4 SUMMARY

This chapter has introduced the basic organization and operation of the IBM PC, the tasks associated with assembly language program development, and the PC assembly language itself. The PC uses a powerful microprocessor chip, the Intel 8088, which has 16-bit internal pathways, the capacity to address 1 megabyte of memory, an extensive set of instructions and addressing modes, and reasonably fast instruction execution times (e.g., a 16-bit register-to-register integer **ADD** takes about 0.63 μs). The assembler permits one to develop low-level machine language programs using a convenient set of mnemonics to represent basic machine instructions and memory address references. It also has powerful program development aids (e.g., *macros*, considered in Chapter 8) which are useful when implementing large software systems. The presence of editor, linker, debugger, and loader programs allows one to complete the assembly language software development task more conveniently.

EXERCISES

1.1 How many two-state binary devices (or bits of information) are needed to uniquely represent each letter of the English alphabet? If, instead of using binary memory devices, a three-state trinary device were available, how many of these devices would be needed to uniquely represent each letter?

1.2 How many bits are necessary to uniquely address each byte of a 1-megabyte memory (i.e., the maximum address space of the Intel 8086/88)?

1.3 Consider the program given in Figure 1-7.

   a What are the contents of the AL, SI, and CX registers after the third iteration through the loop defined by **SLOOP**? After the seventh iteration?

   b Answer **a** above with the **DB** statement changed to read:

         NUMSET   DB   1, -2, 2, -9, 6, -6, 5, -5, 10, 9

   c What is the contents of the DL register after execution of the instruction **MOV   DL,AL**? Assume the **DB** statement first is as given in Figure 1-7, and then as given above in **b**.

1.4 In specifying the problem of Section 1.3.3, it was stated that array elements were to have a maximum absolute value of 12. What problems might occur if this were changed to say a maximum absolute value of 20?

1.5 Consider the problem of sorting an array of positive integers to produce a new array which is in ascending numerical order.

   a Develop a "Requirements Specification" document for this problem. Make your own reasonable assumptions about various problem details.

   b Develop an algorithm to solve this sorting problem and document the algorithm using a "Structured English" format as shown in Figure 1-4.

1.6 Say that in a certain application program, a typical instruction execution takes 2 μs (2×10^{-6} second), while accessing and reading a record from disk takes on the average 100 ms (100×10^{-3} second). The application program in question sequentially reads and processes 1000 records from the disk. If each record processing requires 100 instructions, how long does it take to run the application program ? To speed up such application programs two options have been suggested. The first is to purchase a disk which is twice as fast. The second is to somehow increase the clock rate on the computer to effectively halve the instruction execution time. If these each have the same cost, which one should be chosen and why?

1.7 In Section 1.1.2 a two-address instruction format was presented. In a similar manner a three-address and a one-address format can be designed as shown below.

OPERATION CODE	OPER. 2 ADDR.	OPER. 1 ADDR.	RESULT ADDR.

   example: ADD A,B,C   (C)◄——(A) + (B)

OPERATION CODE	OPER. 1 ADDR.

   example   ADD A   (REGISTER)◄——(REGISTER) + (A)

In the three-address machine, the addresses of the operands and the result are specified explicitly. The notation (X) indicates "contents of memory location X." In the one-address machine, the second operand is considered to be present in a fixed register which has been previously loaded using another instruction (**LOAD REGISTER**), and the result of the operation is placed in that same register. The register must be unloaded (**STORE REGISTER**) to place the result in a memory location. Say that the operation code takes 1 byte of memory, and operand addresses each take 2 bytes of memory. Compare the memory requirements of the one-, two-, and three-address machines specified in computing the following set of expressions (i.e., some short source program):

$$(X) \leftarrow (A) + (B) \cdot (C)$$
$$(Y) \leftarrow (F) + (G)$$
$$(Z) \leftarrow \frac{(Y)}{(X)}$$

Begin by writing a program to perform the above operations for each of the three machines.

1.8 Referring to Problem 1.7, say that each instruction fetch takes one time unit, and each memory operand fetch and deposit (i.e., placing a result into a memory location or storing a register into memory) also takes one time unit (ignore time for fetching operands located in registers). Compare the three addressing schemes in terms of the time required to execute the program given in Problem 1.7.

1.9 Within the bus interface unit in Intel 8088 there is an instruction queue which can hold up to 4 bytes of the instruction stream. In the Intel 8086 this queue can hold up to 6 bytes. Explain how increasing the size of this queue can increase the effective instruction processing rate of the microprocessor. What happens as this queue is further increased?

1.10 Implement, debug, and run the **ISUM1** problem given in Section 1.3.3 in one of the higher-level languages available on your IBM PC.

1.11 Lipow (11) indicates that the number of programming faults or errors per line of code (fault rate) can be predicted by the expression

$$\frac{N}{P} = A + B \cdot \ln P + C \cdot (\ln P)^2$$

P is the number of lines of executable source code in a program, and N is the total number of faults predicted. A, B, and C are constants which are dependent on the programming language used. For an assembly language program approximate values are $A = 0.001184$, $B = 0.0009749$, and $C = 0.00001855$. For a higher level language the values are $A = 0.005171$, $B = 0.002455$, and $C = 0.00004638$.

Assuming that it takes 4 times as many lines of code to implement an algorithm in assembly language versus a higher-level language, compare the number of program faults which will occur in each case over a range of programs having 100 to 10,000 lines of higher-level-language code.

1.12 Apply the expression of Problem 1.11 and make a fault comparison for the **ISUM1** program given in Figure 1-7, and developed in Problem 1.10.

1.13 Use the editor on your system to create a text file for the **ISUM1** program given in Figure 1-7. Assemble the program and obtain listing and cross-reference files. Learn how to display these files on your terminal and examine their contents.

    a From the listing file determine how many bytes of memory the **ISUM1** program requires.

    b What is the binary representation for **INC   SI**?

    c What is the average instruction length for instructions in **ISUM1**?

    d What use can be made of the cross-reference file?

1.14 Link the object program obtained in Problem 1.13 and obtain the execute and map files for **ISUM1**. Run the program and record the symbol displayed. Check this by determining the correct answer and using Table 10-6.

1.15 How can the **DB** statement be changed if one wanted the sum to result in displaying the dollar, $, symbol?

1.16 Run the debug program for your system. Load your **ISUM1** execution module with debug.

    a Display the registers and see if the IP (Instruction Pointer) points to the first executable instruction of your program.

    b Dump the memory contents starting at the CS:IP address found in **a**. Compare the contents of memory with the binary representations found in the listing file.

    c Use the one-step or trace function of the debug program to execute **ISUM1** instructions one at a time, examining the various registers used to determine if the program is operating properly. Note that AL and DL are the lower 8 bits of the AX and DX registers. If needed, read ahead in Chapter 2 for information on hexadecimal numbers.

    d Run the entire program and see if the correct answer is obtained.

1.17 Design and document an experiment to determine the execution times for **ISUM1**, first when implemented in assembly language, and second when implemented in the higher-level language used in Problem 1.10. Execute the experiment and compare the running time results.

1.18 Taking into account the relative number of lines of code needed for assembly versus higher-level-language programs (say 4 to 1), the number of programming errors one can expect (see Problems 1.11 and 1.12), and the relative speeds one can expect (see Problem 1.17), discuss the advantages and disadvantages of using assembly language versus higher-level languages in those applications where both can functionally perform the required task. What information is needed to quantify this comparison and how would it be used?

2

Data
and
Number
Representation

As indicated in Chapter 1, the fundamental unit of information in a computer is the bit, and each bit can be thought of as being in either in the 1 state or the 0 state. While operations on single bits are possible, most computer operations deal with aggregations of bits that can be accessed, operated on, and interpreted as a group. Interpretation in this context relates to what meaning we assign to a bit grouping. Does a particular set of bits represent an integer, a floating-point number, a letter, or perhaps some other symbol? This chapter deals with several common ways of interpreting bit groupings.

Note that the question of interpretation says nothing about how one actually places a group of bits into the computer's memory so that they can be subsequently operated on by an assembly program. This operational question clearly must be dealt with if one is to be able to use the computer. The DOS Macro Assembler provides facilities for loading memory with user-designated values. These are referred to as *data pseudo-operations* (or *data pseudo-ops* for short). Such operations reserve space in memory and may also be used to load that memory space initially with user-specified values. The operations are "pseudo" because they are directed toward the Macro Assembler providing a service (in this case reserving and initializing memory) and not toward the actual production of machine instructions. Pseudo-operations will be considered in detail in Chapters 7 and 8.

2.1 BITS, BYTES, WORDS, AND DATA PSEUDO-OPERATIONS

The most important bit groupings in the IBM PC are the *byte* (8 bits) and the *word* (16 bits, or 2 bytes). Their importance derives from the fact that the Intel 8088's processor instructions, datapaths, and memory organization are oriented toward working with bit groups of these sizes. Many processor instructions, for instance, operate on either bytes or words, and the internal datapaths in the processor are one word wide. Of critical importance, however, is that memory is organized so that bits are arranged as successive bytes, and that bytes and words (pairs of bytes) can be accessed (addressed) with single operations. Accessing groups of bits in a single parallel operation is significant from a performance point of view. Indeed, one common measure of computer power is the number of bits that can be accessed from memory simultaneously.

The assembler data pseudo-ops which allocate storage for bytes and words are **DB** (**D**efine **B**yte) and **DW** (**D**efine **W**ord). Consider for example the assembly language segment shown below.

```
DB  ?
DW  ?
```

The first of these statements reserves a byte of storage in memory, while the second reserves a word of storage. There are two things to note about this segment. First, there is no specification here of how the bits in the defined byte and word should be set. Indeed, the question mark indicates that the initial values for these bits are undefined. Second, there is no identifier that an assembly language program can associate with the byte and word thus defined. Ordinarily these storage locations would be defined with some purpose in mind which typically would require that a name or label be associated with them. For instance, if the byte to be defined is labeled **SMALL_INTEGER** and the word is labeled **AN_INTEGER**, then we would have the labeled data pseudo-ops

```
SMALL_INTEGER    DB  ?
AN_INTEGER       DW  ?
```

The byte and word above can now be referred to in a program by their respective labels. For some programs this may be just what is needed; however, in other situations it may be desirable to have specific initial values in these locations. For instance, **SMALL_INTEGER** and **AN_INTEGER** may be integer constants needed for some calculation. This initial loading can be done easily by appending the data definition statement with the initial value desired for that storage location.

```
SMALL_INTEGER    DB    00110101B
AN_INTEGER       DW    0101011111001101B
```

The sequence of 1s and 0s represent the bit settings for the defined byte and word. Note that the sequence is terminated with the letter B. This indicates to the assembler that the number preceding it is to be interpreted as a *binary* number. Binary and other number systems are discussed in the next section. For the moment, however, this number can be considered merely as a sequence of bit settings. The figure below shows how the byte and word defined above would reside in memory as bytes placed as successive memory addresses.

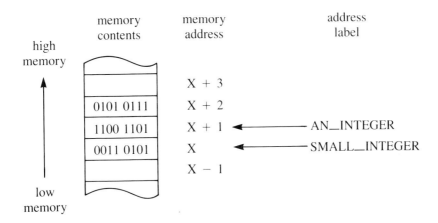

Notice that **SMALL_INTEGER**, having been defined first, is at a lower memory position than **AN_INTEGER**. **AN_INTEGER** begins at memory location X + 1, with the *low-order byte* (the rightmost 8 bits) occupying the memory address X + 1 and the *high-order byte* (the leftmost 8 bits) occupying the address X + 2. Remember, this only represents the initial storage allocation. Once execution of the assembly language program begins, the contents of these memory locations can be changed by the program as needed.

The approach to defining the initial contents of bytes and words given above is somewhat awkward. Writing down and keeping track of strings of 1s and 0s is tedious and prone to error. In the next section a more concise method will be presented for entering initial data. First, however, let us complete our discussion of various bit aggregates which can be defined using the assembler's data pseudo-ops. These are presented in Table 2-1 below. Entries in the rightmost column represent common interpretations given to the designated group of bits. The **DD, DQ,** and **DT** pseudo-ops operate in a similar fashion to the **DB** and **DW** pseudo-ops already considered. Thus, to reserve and initialize the contents of 4 consecutive bytes of memory the following statement might (unfortunately) be used.

    LONGCONST   DD   00110111101000001110110110101101B

Note that while one may reserve memory locations using the pseudo-ops of Table 2-1, the operating system will normally determine what actual physical memory addresses correspond to the reserved locations. Not all of memory is available for user programs and data storage; some is needed by the operating system, some is allocated to system ROM which contains the BASIC language interpreter and BIOS (Basic/Input Output

Table 2-1 Basic Storage Allocation Units and Data Pseudo-operations

	NUMBER OF			DATA	DATA
	BITS	BYTES	WORDS	PSEUDO-OP	TYPE
BYTE	8	1		DB	byte integer byte offset ASCII code
WORD	16	2	1	DW	word integer word offset
DOUBLE WORD	32	4	2	DD	short integer short real
QUADWORD	64	8	4	DQ	long integer long real
TENBYTE	80	10	5	DT	temporary real packed decimal

System) programs, and some is reserved for video display purposes. This is shown in Appendix A, which contains a "memory map" for the IBM PC operating under the DOS 2.1 operating system.

2.2 NUMBER REPRESENTATION

2.2.1 Number Systems

We consider now the question of representing positive numbers in different number systems. In everyday life the decimal, or base-10, number system is generally used. A positive integer in this system is represented as a summation of multiples of powers of 10. Thus, the number 4305 in the decimal number system is equal to

$$4 \cdot 10^3 + 3 \cdot 10^2 + 0 \cdot 10^1 + 5 \cdot 10^0$$

More generally a positive integer is defined by a sequence of digits:

$$\underbrace{d_n}_{\text{MSD}} d_{n-1} d_{n-2} \cdots d_2 d_1 \underbrace{d_0}_{\text{LSD}}$$

where the value of the integer is given by

$$d_n \cdot b^n + d_{n-1} \cdot b^{n-1} + d_{n-2} \cdot b^{n-2} + \cdots + d_2 \cdot b^2 + d_1 \cdot b^1 + d_0 \cdot b^0 \quad (2\text{-}1)$$

b is the *base*, or *radix*, of the number system; d_0, the rightmost digit, is referred to as the *least significant digit* (LSD); and d_n, the leftmost digit, is referred to as the *most significant digit* (MSD). This is an example of a *positional number system* (i.e., the position of the individual digits determines the power of b by which each digit is multiplied).

Table 2-2   Decimal, Binary, Octal, and Hexadecimal Integers

Decimal	Binary	Octal	Hexadecimal	Decimal	Binary	Octal	Hexadecimal
0	0	0	0	16	10000	20	10
1	1	1	1	17	10001	21	11
2	10	2	2	18	10010	22	12
3	11	3	3	19	10011	23	13
4	100	4	4	20	10100	24	14
5	101	5	5	21	10101	25	15
6	110	6	6	22	10110	26	16
7	111	7	7	23	10111	27	17
8	1000	10	8	24	11000	30	18
9	1001	11	9	25	11001	31	19
10	1010	12	A	26	11010	32	1A
11	1011	13	B	27	11011	33	1B
12	1100	14	C	28	11100	34	1C
13	1101	15	D	29	11101	35	1D
14	1110	16	E	30	11110	36	1E
15	1111	17	F	31	11111	37	1F

Four number systems are of particular relevance when discussing and programming computer systems: binary (base 2), octal (base 8), decimal (base 10), and hexadecimal (base 16). Table 2-2 gives the first 32 positive integers in each of these systems.

In the case of the hexadecimal system, the letters A through F are used to represent the decimal values 10 through 15 since only 10 number characters are available in our common English symbol set.

The development above is adequate if only positive integers are required. To represent fractional values expression (2-1) must be expanded to include negative exponents. Thus a number having a fractional part is represented by the set of digits

$$d_n \, d_{n-1} \, d_{n-2} \cdots d_2 \, d_1 \, d_0.d_{-1} \, d_{-2} \, d_{-3}$$

$$\underbrace{\uparrow}_{\text{radix point}}$$

The integer and fractional parts are separated by a dot referred to as the *radix point* (or the decimal point in the familiar base-10 system). The value of the number including its fractional part is given by

$$\overbrace{d_n \cdot b^n + d_{n-1} \cdot b^{n-1} + \cdots + d_1 \cdot b^1 + d_0 \cdot b^0}^{\text{integer part}}$$

$$\underbrace{+ \, d_{-1} \cdot b^{-1} + d_{-2} \cdot b^{-2} + \cdots}_{\text{fractional part}} \qquad (2\text{-}2)$$

The base *b* is now raised to positive powers to obtain the integer part of the number and negative powers to obtain the fractional part of the number. Table 2-3 gives fractional values that can be obtained with 3 bits.

Table 2-3 Decimal, Binary, Octal, and Hexadecimal Fractions

Decimal	Binary	Octal	Hexadecimal
.000	.000	.0	.0
.125	.001	.1	.2
.250	.010	.2	.4
.375	.011	.3	.6
.500	.100	.4	.8
.625	.101	.5	.A
.750	.110	.6	.C
.875	.111	.7	.E

2.2.2 Number System Conversion

Given a positive number expressed in a particular number system b, the next question is how to obtain the corresponding number (i.e., the number of equal value) in some other number system c. If c, the target system, is base 10, then simple application of Equation (2-2) will yield the answer. For example, interpret **SMALL_INTEGER**, defined with a data pseudo-op in Section 2.1, as a binary integer. Its decimal value is

$$0 \cdot 2^7 + 0 \cdot 2^6 + 1 \cdot 2^5 + 1 \cdot 2^4 + 0 \cdot 2^3 + 1 \cdot 2^2 + 0 \cdot 2^1 + 1 \cdot 2^0 = 53$$
$$= 53D$$

To represent a number explicitly we shall normally append to it a letter designating one of the four bases of principal concern to us here. Thus D stands for decimal, or base 10, in 53D above; and in a similar manner, B, O or Q, and H, respectively, will be used to represent numbers in the Binary, Octal, and Hexadecimal systems. Any number where the base is not explicitly indicated is taken to be base 10. This is also the notation used by the assembler; thus the three data pseudo-ops given below are equivalent and result in the same storage allocation and initialization.

```
SMALL_INTEGER     DB      00110101B
SMALL_INTEGER     DB      53
SMALL_INTEGER     DB      53D
```

EXAMPLE 2-1   Convert 136.75Q to base 10.

ANSWER

$$1 \cdot 8^2 + 3 \cdot 8^1 + 6 \cdot 8^0 + 7 \cdot 8^{-1} + 5 \cdot 8^{-2} = 94.953125D$$

Thus

136.75Q = 94.953125D

There remains the general problem of converting a number from one arbitrary base to another. Initially we will restrict ourselves to positive integers. Say that X is an integer in the base-b number system and we want to obtain the number Y in the base-c number system. The number Y will be composed of the digits $y_n \, y_{n-1} \cdots y_1 \, y_0$ and X can be expressed in terms of these digits as

$$X = y_n \cdot c^n + y_{n-1} \cdot c^{n-1} + \cdots + y_1 \cdot c^1 + y_0$$

where the expression is evaluated using base-b arithmetic. Now divide X by c.

$$\frac{X}{c} = (y_n \cdot c^{n-1} + y_{n-1} \cdot c^{n-2} + \cdots + y_1 \cdot c^0) + \frac{y_0}{c}$$

$$= Q_1 + \frac{y_0}{c}$$

The terms within the parentheses are multiples of powers of c and hence are evenly divisible by c. The number y_0, on the other hand, is a number less than c and hence represents the remainder of the X/c division. Thus, the first digit in Y is the remainder obtained by dividing the source number X by the target number base c. Having obtained y_0, the next digit y_1 can be computed by dividing Q_1 by c. Following the same reasoning, the remainder will now equal y_1. The process is continued until a quotient equal to zero is produced. Some examples below illustrate this procedure.

EXAMPLE 2-2 **a** Convert 53D to base 8.

ANSWER

$$\frac{53}{8} = 6 + \frac{5}{8} \longrightarrow \qquad y_0 = 5$$

$$\frac{6}{8} = 0 + \frac{6}{8} \longrightarrow \qquad y_1 = 6$$

$$53D = 65Q$$

b Convert 53D to base 16.

ANSWER

$$\frac{53}{16} = 3 + \frac{5}{16} \longrightarrow \qquad y_0 = 5$$

$$\frac{3}{16} = 0 + \frac{3}{16} \longrightarrow \qquad y_1 = 3$$

$$53D = 35H$$

c Convert 53D to base 2.

ANSWER

$$\frac{53}{2} = 26 + \frac{1}{2} \qquad \longrightarrow \qquad y_0 = 1$$

$$\frac{26}{2} = 13 + \frac{0}{2} \qquad \longrightarrow \qquad y_1 = 0$$

$$\frac{13}{2} = 6 + \frac{1}{2} \qquad \longrightarrow \qquad y_2 = 1$$

$$\frac{6}{2} = 3 + \frac{0}{2} \qquad \longrightarrow \qquad y_3 = 0$$

$$\frac{3}{2} = 1 + \frac{1}{2} \qquad \longrightarrow \qquad y_4 = 1$$

$$\frac{1}{2} = 0 + \frac{1}{2} \qquad \longrightarrow \qquad y_5 = 1$$

$$53D = 110101B$$

The data pseudo-op for **SMALL_INTEGER** can now be written in the following additional equivalent forms.

```
SMALL_INTEGER    DB    65Q
SMALL_INTEGER    DB    35H
```

Note in the above examples, all arithmetic was done in the base-10 system since the source number was a base-10 number. In general, arithmetic must be done in the source number's base. While we haven't discussed arithmetic operations in nondecimal number systems, the general concepts used in decimal operations apply. The principal difference is that for each number system a new set of arithmetic tables (e.g., multiplication table) must be used.

The conversion procedure described above is a general one and can be used for arbitrary integer number conversions. A shortcut, however, is available when converting a binary number to either an octal or hexadecimal number, or converting an octal or hexadecimal number to a binary number. The basis for the shortcut is that both the numbers 8 and 16 are powers of 2. To begin with, one must know the binary-to-octal, octal-to-binary conversions involving 3 bits (i.e., 000B = 0Q, 001B = 1Q, 010B = 2Q, . . . , 110B = 6Q, and 111B = 7Q), and the binary-to-hexadecimal, hexadecimal-to-binary conversions involving 4 bits (i.e., 0000B = 0H, 0001B = 1H, 0010B = 2H, . . . , 1110B = EH, and 1111B = FH). These may be found in Table 2-2.

For binary-to-octal or binary-to-hexadecimal conversion the procedure is as follows. Divide the binary number into groups of 3 (for octal) or 4 (for hexadecimal) bits starting with the rightmost, or least significant, bit. Now replace each group with the corresponding octal or hexadecimal digit. The resultant octal or hexadecimal number is the converted number. It is a simple exercise for the reader to determine why this procedure works.

EXAMPLE 2-3   Convert the 16-bit binary number 0101011111001101B to octal and then to hexadecimal.

ANSWER

   To solve this problem, segment the binary number into groups of 3 bits each and assign the corresponding octal number to each group.

0	101	011	111	001	101	binary number
0	5	3	7	1	5	octal number

Thus

   0101011111001101B = 53715Q

Segmenting the binary number into groups of 4 bits each and assigning the corresponding hexadecimal number to each group yields

0101	0111	1100	1101	binary number
5	7	C	D	hexadecimal number

Thus

   0101011111001101B = 57CDH

To go from octal or hexadecimal back to binary, simply make the appropriate substitution of the binary equivalent for each digit and the corresponding binary number is obtained.

   The conversion methods considered thus far handle only positive integers. The method given below deals with positive fractions. Let X now be a fraction represented in the base-b number system. We would like to obtain the corresponding fraction Y in the base-c number system where Y is composed of the digits $y_{-1} y_{-2} \cdots y_{-m}$. The number X can be expressed in terms of these digits as

$$X = y_{-1} \cdot c^{-1} + y_{-2} \cdot c^{-2} + \cdots + y_{-m} \cdot c^{-m}$$

where the expression is evaluated using base-b arithmetic. Multiply X now by c.

$$c X = y_{-1} + (y_{-2} \cdot c^{-1} + \cdots + y_{-m} \cdot c^{-m+1}) = y_{-1} + F_1$$

The terms within the parentheses are all fractional values since y is a digit in the base-c number system. The first term, however, is an integer; hence the first digit of Y can be obtained by multiplying X by c and retaining the integer part of the result. The second digit of Y can now be computed in a similar manner by multiplying F_1 by c and once again retaining the integer part. When the fractional value becomes zero, then the process terminates. Note that termination can't be guaranteed.

EXAMPLE 2-4   Convert .609375D to base 4.

ANSWER

$$(4)(.609375) = 2.4375 \longrightarrow y_{-1} = 2$$
$$(4)(.4375) = 1.75 \longrightarrow y_{-2} = 1$$
$$(4)(.75) = 3.00 \longrightarrow y_{-3} = 3$$

$$.609375D = .213 \text{ (base 4)}$$

2.2.3 Signed Numbers

This section considers methods for representing and manipulating negative numbers. Given a word length, the representation question can be viewed as a problem of effectively assigning all possible combinations of bit patterns to a range of positive and negative numbers.

Say that we were dealing with a computer whose word length were 4 bits. With 4 bits we can obtain 16 (2^4) bit combinations; and thus if we were considering only positive numbers, we could represent the integers 0 through 15. Some of these combinations, however, must now be used to represent negative numbers. In order to achieve a balanced system, about half of the available combinations should be positive integers and half negative. One choice might be to represent the numbers 0, 1 through 7, and -1 through -7. The next question is just how to assign the 4 bits to the selected numbers. Consider the assignment given below.

Table 2-4   A Signed-Magnitude Number Representation

Decimal Number	Bit Assignment	Decimal Number	Bit Assignment
$+0$	0000	-0	1000
$+1$	0001	-1	1001
$+2$	0010	-2	1010
$+3$	0011	-3	1011
$+4$	0100	-4	1100
$+5$	0101	-5	1101
$+6$	0110	-6	1110
$+7$	0111	-7	1111

This assignment has some nice properties. First, 0 and the positive numbers 1 through 7 are represented in a natural manner as binary integers. Second, if one forgets about the most significant bit for a moment, the negative numbers are also standard binary numbers. Third, by examining the most significant bit it is easy to distinguish between positive and negative numbers. Effectively, we have a 3-bit number representation with one bit, the most significant one, designating the sign of the number. For obvious reasons this is referred to as a *signed-magnitude* representation and it corresponds closely to the method we normally use for representing negative numbers (i.e., the MSB corresponds to a minus or a plus sign). While it is certainly possible to design logic to perform arithmetic with such an assignment, it turns out that overall the logical operations required are generally simpler with other somewhat different schemes. Note, for instance, that with a signed-magnitude representation, logic must be provided for both addition and subtraction. Furthermore, to determine the sign of the result of an operation, in some cases the relative magnitude of the operands are needed. Finally the existence of two types of 0s is inconvenient.

Consider next what are referred to as the *2's complement* and *1's complement* assignment schemes, which are shown below for the case of a 4-bit word.

With the 2's complement scheme there is only a single representation for 0 and, as before, both schemes permit the most significant bit to be used to determine the sign of the number. The 2's complement scheme is an example of a *radix-complement* number system, while the 1's complement scheme is an example of a *diminished radix–complement* number system.

Table 2-5   2's Complement and 1's Complement Number Representation

Binary	2's Complement	1's Complement		Binary	2's Complement	1's Complement
0000	0	+0		1000	−8	−7
0001	+1	+1		1001	−7	−6
0010	+2	+2		1010	−6	−5
0011	+3	+3		1011	−5	−4
0100	+4	+4		1100	−4	−3
0101	+5	+5		1101	−3	−2
0110	+6	+6		1110	−2	−1
0111	+7	+7		1111	−1	−0

In radix-complement number systems the negative of a number can be obtained by performing the following operation:

$$X* = b^n - |X|$$ (2-3)

where X is the original number, b is the radix, or base, of the number system being used, n is the number of digits being used to represent the number, and $X*$ is the negative of X. $X*$ is called the *b's complement of X*. The vertical bars $|\ |$ indicate that the absolute value operation is performed.

The negative of a number in the diminished radix-complement system is obtained as follows:

$$X* = b^n - 1 - |X|$$ (2-4)

Again X is the original number, b is the radix, n is the number of digits being used, $X*$ is the negative of X, and $X*$ is called the *(b-1)'s complement of X*.

EXAMPLE 2-5   Find the 2's complement of 6 (0110B). Assume that numbers are 4 bits in length.

ANSWER

$$X* = 2^4 - |6| = 10000B - 0110B = 1010B$$

Note that $1010 + 0110 = 0000$ if the carry out of the MSD is discarded. Find now the 1's complement of 6.

$$X* = 2^4 - 1 - |6| = 10000B - 0001B - 0110B = 1001B$$

EXAMPLE 2-6   **a** Find the 10's complement of the decimal number 235. Assume that numbers are three digits long.

ANSWER

$$X* = 10^3 - |235| = 765$$

b Find the 9's complement of 235.

ANSWER

$$X* = 10^3 - 1 - |235| = 764$$

Note that $235 + 764 = 999$, which is -0 in this system.

While Equations (2-3) and (2-4) yield the correct values for the complement numbers, they do not immediately reveal how easily one can obtain the complement with very little logical complexity. The example below demonstrates this.

EXAMPLE 2-7 **a** Find the 2's complement of 6 assuming a word length of 4 bits.

ANSWER

$$6 \longrightarrow 0110 \longrightarrow \text{invert} \longrightarrow 1001$$
$$\text{add } 1 \longrightarrow \underline{0001}$$
$$\text{2's complement} \quad 1010$$

b Find the 2's complement of -6.

ANSWER

$$-6 \longrightarrow 1010 \longrightarrow \text{invert} \longrightarrow 0101$$
$$\text{add } 1 \longrightarrow \underline{0001}$$
$$\text{2's complement} \quad 0110$$

c Find the 1's complement of 6.

ANSWER

$$6 \longrightarrow 0110 \longrightarrow \text{invert} \longrightarrow 1001 \longleftarrow \text{1's complement}$$

d Find the 1's complement of -6.

ANSWER

$$-6 \longrightarrow 1001 \longrightarrow \text{invert} \longrightarrow 0110 \longleftarrow \text{1's complement}$$

Thus, to find the 2's complement of a number, merely invert the bits and add 1. To find the 1's complement, just invert the bits. Given the ability to easily find the negative of a number, the operations of addition and subtraction on positive and negative numbers are straightforward.

Consider first 2's complement operations. Addition of numbers is performed in the usual manner, irrespective of sign. Thus

$$
\begin{array}{ll}
+3 \quad 0011 & -2 \quad 1110 \\
\underline{+4 \quad 0100} & \underline{+5 \quad 0101} \\
+7 \quad 0111 & +3 \quad \boxed{1} \; 0011
\end{array}
$$

$$\underbrace{\phantom{+3 \quad \boxed{1} \; 0011}}_{\text{discard carry out}}$$

$$
\begin{array}{ll}
-3 \quad 1101 & +5 \quad 0101 \\
\underline{-2 \quad 1110} & \underline{-7 \quad 1001} \\
- \quad \boxed{1} \; 1011 & -2 \quad 1110
\end{array}
$$

$$\underbrace{\phantom{- \quad \boxed{1} \; 1011}}_{\text{discard carry out}}$$

Subtraction is performed by taking the 2's complement of the subtrahend and then performing addition. Thus

```
+3      0011 ───────────────────────────→  0011
-(+4)   0100 ──────→ 2's complement ──────→  1100
─────                                        ─────
-1                                           1111
```

```
+7      0111 ───────────────────────────→  0111
-(+2)   0010 ──────→ 2's complement ──────→  1110
─────                                        ─────
+5                                        [1] 0101
                                          ‿‿‿‿‿‿‿‿
                                          discard carry out
```

In the 1's complement case, addition is performed in the normal manner with one slight complication. When a carry-out is produced from the most significant digit, a 1 is added to the result. If there is no carry, normal addition is performed.

```
+3      0011           +5      0101
+4      0100           -7      1000
─────   ─────          ─────   ─────
+7      0111           -2      1101
```

```
-2      1101           -3      1100
+5      0101           -2      1101
─────   ─────          ─────   ─────
     [1] 0010               [1] 1001
        ↳0001                  ↳0001
        ─────                  ─────
+3      0011           -5      1010
```

Subtraction in the 1's complement case is performed by taking the 1's complement of the subtrahend and then performing addition. Note that a 1 must be added in if a carry out is produced. Thus

```
+3      0011 ───────────────────────────→  0011
-(+4)   0100 ──────→ 1's complement ──────→  1011
─────                                        ─────
-1                                           1110
```

```
+7      0111 ───────────────────────────→  0111
-(+2)   0010 ──────→ 1's complement ──────→  1101
─────                                        ─────
                                          [1] 0100
                                             ↳0001
                                             ─────
                                             0101
```

While both the 2's complement and 1's complement schemes are logically simple and roughly of equivalent logical complexity, the tendency has been toward use of 2's complement systems in current computer designs. The Intel 8088, and thus the IBM PC, uses 2's complement forms when dealing with signed numbers. A variety of instructions and features are present which exploit this form.

For instance, the **NEG**ate instruction is provided in the IBM PC to obtain the 2's complement of a given integer. The program fragment below illustrates its use.

```
CON_BYTE    DB      2AH         ;Initialize location CON_BYTE
                                ;with 0010 1010.
            NEG     CON_BYTE    ;Take the 2's complement of the
                                ;contents of location CON_BYTE.
                                ;After the instruction is
                                ;executed CON_BYTE contains D6H.
```

The **NEG**ate instruction is denoted by the mnemonic **NEG**. A semicolon tells the assembler program that the remaining text in the line represents comments provided by the programmer for his or her own documentation and clarification purposes. Finally, the assembler recognizes that the **NEG** instruction refers to a byte and not a word, because **CON_BYTE** has been defined as a byte in the data pseudo-op which preceded it. The fragment below shows **NEG**ate operating on a word.

```
INI_SUM     DW      B57DH
            NEG     INI_SUM     ;Result in INI_SUM is 4A83H
```

Addition, subtraction, multiplication, and division instructions will be considered in depth in Chapter 5. The program fragment below illustrates some of the simpler arithmetic instructions provided.

EXAMPLE 2-8   Add 1BF2H to 47BBH. Subtract 7F25H from the result. The final result should be in the 16-bit register AX.

ANSWER

```
WORD_ONE    DW      1BF2H
WORD_TWO    DW      7F25H
            MOV     AX, WORD_ONE    ; (AX) <--- (WORD_ONE)
            ADD     AX, 47BBH       ; (AX) <--- (AX) + 47BBH
            SUB     AX, WORD_TWO    ; (AX) <--- (AX) − (WORD_TWO)
```

The instructions illustrated above operate either on bytes or words. One question of concern is what happens when the result of an operation on two numbers doesn't fit in the allocated number of bits. For example, consider the following byte additions.

0111 0101	1100 1010
0100 0001	1001 0110
1011 0110	1 0110 0001

Notice that in the first case two positive numbers are added and the result is a negative number. In the second case, two negative numbers are added and the result (i.e., the lower-order 8 bits) is a positive number. In both cases the problem is that we have exceeded the range of allowable integers within the 8-bit, 2's complement number definition. The condition above is referred to as *overflow*, and a bit indicator, the OF bit or flag, is present in the computer to note when this condition has occurred. Since this typically represents an error condition, instructions (**J**ump on **O**verflow:**JO** and **J**ump if **N**o **O**verflow:**JNO**) are provided to test whether the OF flag has been set, and if it has been set (or not set), to transfer control to another part of the program where error conditions are handled.

EXAMPLE 2-9   Add 10 to the 16-bit register AX and test for overflow. If overflow has occurred, then transfer control to the instruction located at **OVRERR**.

ANSWER

```
ADDTEN:     ADD     AX,  10      ;main program begins
            JO      OVRERR       ;IF  (OF=1)  GO  TO  OVRERR
                         .

            {main program}
                         .

                                 ;main program ends
OVRERR:                          ;overflow error routine
                         .

            {overflow routine}
                         .
                                 ;overflow routine ends
```

AX is one of a number of 16-bit registers which are available in the Intel 8088. These registers can be addressed explicitly, and they possess certain special properties which will be discussed in the next chapter. In the example above, AX can just be considered as a 16-bit storage location. Transfer of control under this error condition can also be achieved using the computer's *interrupt* facilities, as will be seen in Chapters 4 and 9.

While detecting overflow can prevent undesirable errors from propagating, there is still the question of how to deal with numbers which require more bits than are available in a single word. The next section examines this question.

2.2.4 Range, Precision, and Floating-point Numbers

In order to distinguish between number range and precision, consider a hypothetical computer with an 8-bit word size. Clearly, with a single word, only 256 numbers can be represented exactly. One choice might be the positive integers 0 through 255. If we now wanted to represent the number 12.375, we would have to approximate it, and would probably do so with the number 12. This represents what is referred to as a *rounding* operation, and it arises because of the finite number of bits allocated for number representation. In this case, if we could increase the word size to 11 bits, having 8 bits for the integer part and 3 bits for a fractional part, then the number 12.375 could be represented exactly while the number *range* (0 to 255) would be preserved. The number 12.34 couldn't be represented exactly; however, it could be approximated by 12.375, and the approximation would be better than the 8-bit case since there are now 3 more bits available. Thus, adding precision requires more bits if number range is to be preserved.

Another approach to the above problem would be to change the range associated with the initial 8-bit word. Instead of representing positive integers from 0 to 255, represent only numbers over the range 0 to 31. Since only 5 bits are required for this, the three remaining bits could be used to represent 3-bit fractional values over this more limited range. Thus, number precision can be increased by sacrificing number range. It all depends upon how you want to use your bits.

Now suppose that we are dealing with the basic IBM PC, where 8-bit bytes and 16-bit words represented in 2's complement form can be processed as whole units by the various arithmetic instructions provided. Thus, for example, a single **ADD** instruction can perform addition on either bytes or words (or even a mixture of the two). Consider the situation where a full 16-bit word does not provide sufficient range or precision in a particular application. In terms of range, with 16 bits and 2's complement notation, the range of a number X is: $-2^{15} = -32,768 \leq X \leq +32,767 = 2^{15} - 1$. Say that a double word of 32 bits is adequate for the application in question (i.e., $-2^{31} \leq X \leq +2^{31} - 1$). How can we do addition or subtraction on double words when only 8- and 16-bit addition and subtraction are provided by the basic computer? One approach is to do two successive 16-bit additions or subtractions, first on the lower 16 bits of the operands, and then operating on the upper 16 bits of the operands. The only problem with this solution is that any carry or borrow which needs to propogate from the lower 16 bits to the upper 16 bits must be preserved.

Provisions have been made in the computer to handle this situation. First, any arithmetic operation which results in a carry out of (or borrow into) the most significant bit of the result will result in the setting of a flag or special testable bit in the computer. Like the overflow flag, the *Carry Flag,* CF, can be tested by various instructions (**J**ump if **C**arry:**JC** and **J**ump if **N**o **C**arry:**JNC**). Furthermore, special addition and subtraction instructions (**AD**d with **C**arry:**ADC** and **S**u**B**tract with **B**orrow:**SBB**) have been provided to use this carry bit when adding or subtracting numbers involving multiple bytes. Thus **ADC** adds both the two operands specified and the carry bit to produce the addition result. This is shown in the example below.

Note that in several places the address of the high-order 16 bits has been obtained by use of a simple arithmetic expression (e.g., **AINTEGER + 1**). Note also that this approach can be used to perform addition on integers having an arbitrary number of bytes. Finally, since the question of handling numbers whose range is very large arises in many applications, provision has been made to add onto the basic Intel 8088 and IBM PC a special-purpose processor oriented toward performing arithmetic on large numbers. This unit is called the *Intel 8087 Numeric Data Processor* and is described in reference 12. With this unit, for instance, double-word addition (short-integer addi-

EXAMPLE 2-10   Add the two double words located at **AINTEGER** and **BINTE-GER**. Place the result in **CINTEGER**.

ANSWER

```
AINTEGER    DD    ?                ;contents initially undefined
BINTEGER    DD    ?                ;contents initially undefined
CINTEGER    DD    ?                ;contents initially undefined
                                   ;will hold addition result
            MOV   AX, AINTEGER     ;(AX) <--- (low order 16 bits
                                   ;         of AINTEGER)
            ADD   AX, BINTEGER     ;(AX) <--- (AX) + (low order
                                   ;       16 bits of BINTEGER)
                                   ;The carry bit may be set.
            MOV   CINTEGER, AX     ;(CINTEGER) <--- (AX),
                                   ; store low order result.
            MOV   AX, AINTEGER+1   ;(AX) <--- (high order 16 bits
                                   ;         of AINTEGER). MOV
                                   ;instructions do not affect
                                   ;status bits such as CF.
            ADC   AX, BINTEGER+1   ;(AX) <--- (AX) + (high order
                                   ;16 bits of BINTEGER) + carry.
                                   ;A check could be done here to
                                   ;determine if the double word
                                   ;range has been exceeded.
            MOV   CINTEGER+1, AX   ;(CINTEGER) <--- (AX),
                                   ; store high order result.
```

tion) of the sort shown in Example 2-10 can be performed with a single machine instruction.

Depending on number range and precision requirements, one can continue to increase the number of bytes representing a program's data and variables. A point comes, however, when adding more bits to increase numerical precision may be only of marginal use. Of more importance, in certain applications, is the ability to deal with a very large number range. While this can be done by increasing word length (i.e., each additional bit adds a factor of 2 to the range), a more effective use of bits can be achieved by using a different number format.

This number format, referred to as *real* or *floating point*, consists of two principal parts: an exponent and a *mantissa* (or fractional part). The general format is as follows:

s1	exponent	s2	mantissa

s1	$xN \ldots x1x0$	s2	$yM \ldots y1y0$

s1 and s2 are sign bits for the exponent and mantissa, respectively. Assume for this discussion that all numbers use sign-magnitude representation. If there are M + 1 bits used for the mantissa, and N + 1 bits for the exponent, then the number given above equals

$$+/-(.yM \cdots y1y0) \cdot 2^{+/-(xN \cdots x1x0)}$$

The choice of + or − depends on the values of s1 and s2.

Consider, for example, a 16-bit number with M = 8 and N = 4. The range of this number is roughly $-2^{31} \le X \le +2^{31}$ since the 5 bits used for the exponent can represent a number whose maximum magnitude is $2^5 - 1$. Note that if the 16-bit word were used to represent a number in the standard format described before, then given that 9 bits are used for the fractional part of the number, the range of the resulting number would be $-2^6 \le X \le +2^6 - 1$, considerably less than with the floating-point format.

Specific implementations for floating-point representations often vary from this format. Reference 13 presents some alternative formats and discusses some of the intricacies associated with floating-point data representation. For efficiency reasons, and also to conform to the proposed IEEE standard on floating-point notation (14, 15), real-number formats on the IBM PC differ slightly from the general format given above. Two IBM PC real formats are shown below. Each utilizes a different number of bits, and the one employed will depend on precision, range, and memory requirements of the application program involved. Arithmetic instructions oriented to these formats are available when the Intel 8087 Numeric Data Processor is present. Otherwise separate programs (usually written in assembly language) must be developed for operating on these formats.

SHORT REAL | s | exponent | mantissa |

bit position 31   23   0

LONG REAL | s | exponent | mantissa |

bit position 63   52   0

The short and long real formats are often called *single precision* and *double precision* formats. The s above is the sign of the mantissa part of the number. The mantissa itself is taken to be in *normalized form*. A real number is in normalized form when its mantissa has been shifted left until it has the form 1.xx⋯xx (i.e., the mantissa is a number between 1 and 2). Of course, when this is done, the exponent must be properly adjusted by decreasing its value by 1 for every left shift taken. Since the leftmost bit after normalization is always a 1, there is really no need to keep it around. Thus in the above formats this leftmost 1 is not explicitly maintained.

Table 2-6   Biased Exponent Form For Short Real Numbers

Exponent Value	Value + Bias	Biased Exponent Form
+ 0	If s = 0 and mantissa = 00 ⋯ 00	0000 0000
− 0	If s = 1 and mantissa = 00 ⋯ 00	0000 0000
DENORMALS	mantissa ≠ 00 ⋯ 00	0000 0000
− 126	− 126 + 127 = 1	0000 0001
− 125	− 125 + 127 = 2	0000 0010
⋮	⋮	⋮
− 2	− 2 + 127 = 125	0111 1101
− 1	− 1 + 127 = 126	0111 1110
0	0 + 127 = 127	0111 1111
+ 1	+ 1 + 127 = 128	1000 0000
+ 2	+ 2 + 127 = 129	1000 0001
⋮	⋮	⋮
+ 127	+ 127 + 127 = 254	1111 1110
+ ∞	If s = 0 and mantissa = 00 ⋯ 00	1111 1111
− ∞	If s = 1 and mantissa = 00 ⋯ 00	1111 1111
INDEFINITE	If s = 1 and mantissa = 10 ⋯ 00	1111 1111
NAN	mantissa ≠ 00 ⋯ 00 or 10 ⋯ 00	1111 1111
	NAN = Not A Number	

The exponent is stored in *biased exponent* form. The bias is 127 (7FH) for a short real number and 1023 (3FFH) for a long real number. To understand the use of this bias consider the 8-bit exponent of a short real number. With 8 bits, 256 numbers can be represented. Divide up this number space as shown below in Table 2.6.

Delaying for the moment discussion of the special exponent values in which all 1s or all 0s are present, it is obvious from the table how one obtains the biased exponent for an exponent value in the range − 126 to + 127. But why is this form used? The reason is that with this form it is easy to determine which of two exponents is larger. All one has to do is to perform bit pair comparisons starting with the leftmost bit. As long as the bits are equal, move right to the next bit pair. When the bits differ, then the exponent containing the 1 is the larger of the two. Knowing which of two exponents is larger, the difference between the two can be obtained, and the exponents can be equalized by appropriate shifting of a single operand mantissa. This operation is generally performed prior to doing the various arithmetic operations. If the Intel 8087 Numeric Data Processor is present, then it is done automatically by this unit when one of its real-number arithmetic instructions is executed; otherwise it is done by the system's software.

The special values at the top and bottom of Table 2-6, in conjunction with facilities available in the Intel 8087, provide programmer control over extreme situations such as overflow (exceeding the maximum expressible floating-point number), underflow (falling below the minimum expressible floating-point number), and certain invalid operations (e.g., divide by zero). As shown in the table, infinity values are represented. These values may be produced by the Intel 8087 when overflow conditions result from some operation. DENORMALS are those numbers whose magnitudes are too small to be represented in normalized format with the most negative exponent available (i.e., -126 for short real, and -1022 for long real), but are representable in an unnormalized form. Thus, for example, the number $1.0010110 \cdots 00 \cdot 2^{-129}$ is smaller than can be handled in a short real normalized format. The number can, however, be represented as $.0010010110 \cdots 00 \cdot 2^{-126}$. Such a number would be stored with a mantissa of $.0010010110 \cdots 00$ and an exponent of $00 \cdots 00$. Notice that it is readily distinguishable from true zeros, and from the smallest normalized numbers that can be represented. An attempt to operate on a DENORMAL number is a special condition indicated in the Intel 8087 by the "denormalized" flag. If an operation results in a number whose exponent is less than -126 (short real) or -1022 (long real), an underflow condition exists and the Intel 8087 sets an underflow flag. This may result in an interrupt, or the 8087 may attempt to produce a DENORMAL number having the maximum exponent possible. The special INDEFINITE value is produced by the Intel 8087 when certain invalid operations are attempted, for instance, dividing zero by zero. A complete list of these invalid operations is given in reference 12. Finally, there are a group of bit combinations available which may be used and interpreted at the discretion of the programmer. These are referred to as NANs (Not A Number). Within the Intel 8087 storage registers, all these special number representations have tags associated with them so that they can be processed properly by the processor.

EXAMPLE 2-11 Obtain the short real biased exponent normalized form for the decimal number 200.625 (2.00625E2 in scientific notation). Thus, obtain the binary form that would result from the following data definition statement:

```
SHT_RCONST      DD      2.00625E2
```

ANSWER

Convert first 200 and then .625 to their binary equivalents. Following the procedures of Section 2-3, one obtains

$200 = 11001000B$ and $.625 = .101B$

Thus

$200.625 = 11001000.1010B$

Obtain the normalized form of the binary number.

$11001000.1010 = 1.10010001010 \ E111$

Change the exponent E111 to biased form by adding the bias 7FH.

$$111 + 1111111 = 10000110$$

Thus

$$200.625 = 1.10010001010 \text{ E}10000110 \text{ (normalized short real form)}$$

The format in memory would be

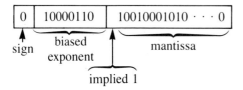

and it would be laid out in memory as

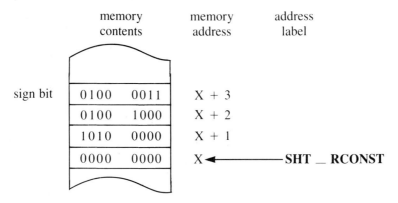

We are now in a position to compare the range and precision available with the various standard number formats used on the IBM PC and Intel 8088. This is done in Table 2-7.

The integer and short and long real formats have already been discussed. The temporary real format is one which is used primarily within the Intel 8087 Numeric Data Processor. It permits representation of numbers with very large range and high precision. It is particularly useful in iterative scientific calculations where problems with round-off errors arise, or where calculations involve small differences in large numbers which subsequently are used in, say, division operations. For completeness its format is given below.

TEMPORARY REAL	s	exponent	1	mantissa

| bit position | 79 | | 64 | 63 | | 0 |

Table 2-7 Range and Precision of Data Formats
(integer range assumes 2's complement forms)

DATA FORMAT	# BITS	# SIGNIFICANT		APPROXIMATE DECIMAL RANGE
		BITS	DECIMAL DIGITS	
byte integer	8	8	2–3	$-128 \leq X \leq +127$
word integer	16	16	4–5	$-32{,}768 \leq X \leq +32{,}767$
short integer	32	32	9–10	$-2\text{ E }9 \leq X \leq +2\text{ E }9$
long integer	64	64	18–19	$-9\text{ E }18 \leq X \leq +9\text{ E }18$
short real	32	24	6–7	$+1.2\text{ E }-38 \leq \mid X \mid \leq$ $+3.4\text{ E }38$
long real	64	53	15–16	$+4.2\text{ E }-307 \leq \mid X \mid \leq$ $+1.7\text{ E }308$
temporary real	80	64	19	$+3.4\text{ E}-4932 \leq \mid X \mid \leq$ $+1.2\text{ E }4932$
packed decimal	80	—	18	$-99\cdots 99 \leq X \leq 99\cdots 99$ $\uparrow\_\_18 \text{ digits }\_\_\uparrow$

In this case the bias for the exponent is 16383 (3FFFH). Note also that for this format the 1 in the leftmost position of the normalized mantissa is not implied but is explicitly maintained in the normalized number representation.

2.2.5 Binary-Coded Decimal (BCD) Numbers

Another positional number scheme often used is the BCD, or Binary-Coded Decimal, system. Its use is especially common in applications requiring exchange of numerical information between the computer and various peripheral devices. The standard 4-bit BCD code uses the ordinary binary representations for the decimal numbers 0 through 9; i.e., $0000 = 0, 0001 = 1, 0010 = 2, \ldots$, and $1001 = 9$. The other six possible combinations of 4 bits, namely, 1010, 1011, 1100, 1101, 1110, and 1111, are not allowed. In effect, these patterns are wasted.

A multiple-digit number in the BCD system is simply a string of BCD digits interpreted as a normal base-10 number. For instance, consider the following bit string which has been divided up into 4-bit subgroups.

BCD Number	0100	1001	0101	0011
Decimal Number	4	9	5	3

Thus, the decimal equivalent of a BCD integer is obtained by starting with the rightmost bit, forming 4-bit groups, and writing down the decimal equivalent for each group. The reverse is done to obtain the BCD equivalent of a decimal number.

Since, in the BCD system, we are maintaining the common base-10 system by merely encoding the digits in a specified manner, both fractional and signed numbers are dealt with in the standard manner. When dealing with fractional numbers, a decimal point position is established, and numbers must be manipulated in a manner consistent with regard to that position. Signed BCD numbers may be handled by using a sign-magnitude approach, in effect using a single designated bit to represent the + or − sign. This format is used by the Intel 8087 and will be discussed later in this section.

BCD numbers are stored in two principal ways. These are referred to as the *packed* and *unpacked* formats and are shown below.

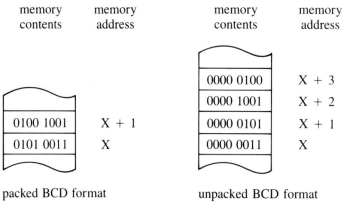

packed BCD format   unpacked BCD format

In packed format, two BCD digits are stored per byte with the more significant digit placed in the leftmost 4 bits. In the unpacked format a single BCD digit is stored per byte in the low-order 4 bits. The upper 4 bits are unused but must be set to zero to ensure proper operation of certain Intel 8088 and IBM PC instructions.

One concern here is just how to perform arithmetic on BCD numbers. Consider adding the two BCD digits 1001 and 0011. Straightforward binary addition would yield 1100. However, this is not a valid BCD digit. To get around this problem one can add a correction factor of 0110 (6) to the result of the binary addition. 1100 + 0110 = 1 0010 (12D), which is the correct answer. The correction factor is not added in all the time. It should be added in only when the result of the digit pair addition is greater than 9, or when a carry-out is produced by the addition.

Standard binary subtraction of BCD numbers may also produce an incorrect result. To adjust for this, 0110 must be subtracted from the BCD digit pair difference if the result is greater than 9, or if a borrow was needed.

The Intel 8088 and IBM PC handle BCD addition and subtraction operations by providing special *adjust* instructions which are used after regular binary addition or subtraction instructions to provide the correction required. For unpacked BCD numbers the instructions **AAA** (ASCII Adjust for Addition) and **AAS** (ASCII Adjust for Subtraction) are provided, while for packed BCD numbers the instructions **DAA** (Decimal Adjust for Addition) and **DAS** (Decimal Adjust for Subtraction) are used. Details of these instructions, the associated correction processes, and material on BCD multiplication and division are found in Chapter 5.

Just as with standard binary integers, there is often a need for BCD numbers which have large range and/or high precision. While such numbers can be processed in a manner similar to the multiple-byte operations discussed in Example 2-10, programs to perform these operations can be very time-consuming. With this in mind, the Intel 8087 Numeric Data Processor includes an instruction (**FBLD**) for converting a standard BCD format, called the *packed decimal* format, to the temporary real format discussed in Section 2.2.4. Once in this temporary real format, all of the floating-point instructions available with this unit can be used. When the required floating-point operations have been completed, another instruction (**FBSTP**) converts the floating-point format back into the BCD packed decimal format. The packed decimal format is given below and is the last entry in Table 2-7.

PACKED DECIMAL | s | ------ | D17 | D16 | D15 | · · · | D3 | D2 | D1 | D0 |

bit position 79   72   0

Each of the 18 digits is a 4-bit BCD number, with the most significant digit being D17. The s is the sign bit (0 = positive, 1 = negative). Bits 72 through 78 are unused. Clearly, even if the Intel 8087 is not present, this format can and should be used as a standard with any BCD arithmetic programs. This will make both BCD data structures and programs compatible with others that become available, and also permit the Intel 8087 to be used effectively at a later date if it becomes part of your system.

2.3 ALPHANUMERIC CHARACTER REPRESENTATION

Much of the data which must be processed by computers are not numeric in form. Information such as names, addresses, and titles may contain alphabetic characters, numeric symbols, and special symbols (e.g., ;, :, =, +, etc.). These are referred to as *alphanumeric* characters. Over the years, standards have developed which specify the bit encodings associated with various alphanumeric character sets. For instance, on many IBM computers the EBCDIC (Extended Binary Coded Decimal Information Code) is used. For the PC, IBM chose to use the widely accepted ASCII (American Standard Code for Information Interchange) code as the basis for encoding alphanumeric characters.

The ASCII code contains 7 bits and thus can be used to represent 128 (2^7) characters. As shown in Table 2-8, each bit pattern is associated with a letter (uppercase or lowercase), a digit (0,1, . . . ,9), a special symbol, or a control character (e.g., SOH, STX, etc., discussed later in this section).

Several points should be noted about this table. First, the sequences of letters (either uppercase or lowercase) and integers correspond to ASCII codes which are naturally increasing binary sequences (i.e., A = 1000001, B = 1000010, C = 1000011, etc.). Second, the integers are encoded so that their lower-order (rightmost) 4 bits

Table 2-8   The ASCII Code

$b_3b_2b_1b_0$	000	001	010	011	100	101	110	111
0 0 0 0	NUL	DLE	SP	0	@	P	`	p
0 0 0 1	SOH	DC1	!	1	A	Q	a	q
0 0 1 0	STX	DC2	"	2	B	R	b	r
0 0 1 1	ETX	DC3	#	3	C	S	c	s
0 1 0 0	EOT	DC4	$	4	D	T	d	t
0 1 0 1	ENQ	NAK	%	5	E	U	e	u
0 1 1 0	ACK	SYN	&	6	F	V	f	v
0 1 1 1	BEL	ETB	'	7	G	W	g	w
1 0 0 0	BS	CAN	(	8	H	X	h	x
1 0 0 1	HT	EM	)	9	I	Y	i	y
1 0 1 0	LF	SUB	*	:	J	Z	j	z
1 0 1 1	VT	ESC	+	;	K	[	k	{
1 1 0 0	FF	FS	,	<	L	\	l	|
1 1 0 1	CR	GS	-	=	M	]	m	}
1 1 1 0	SO	RS	.	>	N	^	n	~
1 1 1 1	SI	US	/	?	O	–	o	DEL

correspond to the BCD digit representations discussed in the previous section. Thus, ASCII digits can be used in unpacked BCD arithmetic operations. The higher-order (leftmost) 3 bits of the ASCII digits are 011. These bits do not interfere with the unpacked BCD correction operations **AAA** (**A**SCII **A**djust for **A**ddition) and **AAS** (**A**SCII **A**djust for **S**ubtraction). However, they should be set to zero before multiplication or division operations are performed.

When placing ASCII data in memory it is natural to use a single byte for each character, that is, to use an 8-bit byte to store a 7-bit character code. Rather then waste this eighth bit, it is put to use in two different ways. First, IBM has extended the ASCII code (referred to as *extended ASCII*) by using this eighth bit to represent an additional 128 characters. This permits a host of special display characters such as horizontal and vertical lines, Greek characters, playing card suits, and funny little faces to be represented. These characters are shown in Table 10-6, where their use is discussed in conjunction with video display techniques.

Second, the eighth bit is often used as a *parity* bit to aid in the detection of errors which may occur during data transmission. For instance, when data is transmitted over telephone lines, there is the possibility of corruption by electrical noise. The value of

Table 2-9 ASCII Control Character

NUL	Null	DLE	Data Link Escape
SOH	Start of Heading	DC1	Device Control 1
STX	Start of Text	DC2	Device Control 2
ETX	End of Text	DC3	Device Control 3
EOT	End of	DC4	Device Control 4
	Transmission		
ENQ	Enquiry	NAK	Negative Acknowledge
ACK	Acknowledge	SYN	Synchronous Idle
BEL	Bell	ETB	End of Transmission
			Block
BS	Backspace	CAN	Cancel
HT	Horizontal	EM	End of Medium
LF	Line Feed	SUB	Substitute
VT	Vertical Tab	ESC	Escape
FF	Form Feed	FS	File Separator
CR	Carriage Return	GS	Group Separator
SO	Shift Out	RS	Record Separator
SI	Shift In	US	Unit Separator
SP	Space	DEL	Delete

bit 8, when used as a parity bit, is determined in one of two ways. If *even parity* is used, then the bit is established so that the number of the 1 bits in any ASCII character is an even number. If *odd parity* is used, then the opposite is true.

For example, the ASCII representation for the letter A is 100 0001. If even parity is used, the 8-bit ASCII code would be 0100 0001 while odd parity would make the code 1100 0001. Consider now what would happen if even parity were used, the letter A were sent over some transmission medium, and a single bit in A were corrupted by noise. Suppose bit 2 were changed so that the character received was 0100 0101 (i.e., the letter E). The receiver of this character, having the ability to add up the number of 1 bits and determine that an odd number was present, and knowing that even parity was in use, would conclude that a transmission error occurred. At this point various higher-level error recovery protocols would come into play and the receiver would likely request a retransmission of the information. This parity bit is automatically generated and checked when data transmission uses the standard IBM PC Asynchronous Communication Adapter, and associated BIOS routines (See section 10.4).

A final point to be noted about the ASCII code concerns the characters found in the leftmost columns of Table 2-8. These are control characters and their abbreviated meanings are given in Table 2-9 below.

These control characters are used in a variety of ways. One use is in the higher-level communications protocols mentioned in the previous paragraph. For instance, if a parity error was detected, a message containing the control character NAK might be returned indicating that the message is to be repeated. Another use of these characters is in controlling peripheral devices such as printers where LF (Line Feed) and CR (Carriage

Return) have direct meaning. A complete discussion of these characters and their uses can be found in reference 16.

Finally, there is the question of placing ASCII characters into the computer's memory. We have already discussed the data pseudo-op **DB** (DefineByte), in Section 2-1. This can be used directly to allocate and initialize storage to particular ASCII values. For instance, the ASCII character A can be placed in location **LETA** as follows:

```
LETA        DB      41H
```

The sequence ABCD can be placed at location **LETABCD** with

```
LETABCD     DB      41H, 42H, 43H, 44H
```

The same allocations can be accomplished somewhat more easily using the quote feature of the assembler. Thus

```
LETA        DB      'A'
LETABCD     DB      'ABCD'
```

The assembler does this by locating symbols or symbol sequences found in quotes and automatically translating them to their ASCII equivalents.

The duplicate feature of the assembler can also be used to initialize memory with repeated strings of ASCII characters. For example:

```
HEADING     DB      3 DUP 'NAME   NUMBER   PRICE      ',13,10
```

This statement will place in memory the ASCII equivalents of the character sequence **NAME NUMBER PRICE** three successive times. The last sequence is followed with the carriage return and line feed characters.

2.4 SUMMARY

In the IBM PC, bit aggregations of 8(byte), 16(word), 32(doubleword), 64(quadword), and 80(tenword) bits are used to represent a variety of number and character types. The basic IBM PC provides arithmetic instructions for directly operating on 8- or 16-bit operands. The Intel 8087 Numeric Data Processor, if present in your IBM PC, permits direct operation on larger numbers covering double word (short integer) and quadword (long integer) operands. Signed numbers are represented in the 2's complement number system.

To further extend the range and precision of numbers permitted, floating-point (real) formats are defined. These include short (mantissa = 23 bits, exponent = 8 bits) and long (mantissa = 52 bits, exponent = 11 bits) real formats which use biased exponent and sign-magnitude mantissa forms. A super range and precision format, the temporary real format (mantissa = 64 bits, exponent = 15 bits), is also defined. This format is often used to hold intermediate results when critical sequences of calculations are being performed where numerical errors must be minimized. Within the Intel 8087, these formats can be operated on directly; however, even without the presence of this numeric processor, these formats should be used to provide compatibility with available floating-point software routines.

In the IBM PC provision has also been made to handle both packed and unpacked binary-coded decimal (BCD) numbers. Various "adjust" instructions are available to correct the results of standard arithmetic instructions to the requirements of BCD arithmetic. A large-range (18 decimal digits) packed decimal format is also defined and may be translated directly into floating-point format with the Intel 8087.

In addition to processing numbers, computers must be able to manipulate and represent a variety of other symbols such as letters and special characters. Such symbols may be represented in the standard fashion using the 7-bit ASCII code (Table 2-8). The IBM PC also utilizes an 8-bit extended ASCII code which contains the 7-bit ASCII code as a subset. This extended ASCII code has bit patterns for a variety of special characters including Greek symbols and vertical and horizontal lines one character in size. In communications applications, the standard 7-bit ASCII code is often augmented with an eighth bit referred to as a parity bit. This bit is used detecting errors which may have occurred during data transmission.

Finally, assembler commands for reserving and initializing IBM PC memory are provided through use of "data pseudo operations." Data pseudo-operations corresponding to all of the number and character formats described above are available and are defined in Table 2-1.

EXERCISES

2.1 Convert the following binary numbers to their decimal equivalent:

    a 11010   **c** 0.1101

    b 111011   **d** 1101.00111

2.2 Convert the following hexadecimal numbers to their decimal equivalent:

    a 3A8   **c** D9.7E

    b 0.F2A   **d** 3FFF.ABCD

2.3 Convert the following decimal numbers to their hexadecimal equivalent:

    a 42   **c** 39.725

    b 93   **d** 32767.255

2.4 Convert the following decimal numbers to their octal equivalent:

    a 77   **c** 256

    b 16378.255   **d** 1024.56

2.5 Convert the following hexadecimal numbers to their octal equivalent:

    a 3FH   **c** F1AD.3BH

    b D3FCH   **d** A39B.84H

2.6 Convert the following octal numbers to their hexadecimal equivalent:

    a 144   **c** 234.76

    b 277.4023   **d** 10075.270

2.7 Convert the following octal numbers to their decimal equivalent:

    a 101   **c** 2000.77

    b 320.02   **d** 4107.0123

2.8 Convert the following numbers from one base to another as indicated:

    a 255(base 6) = ? (base 7)

    b 1024.35(base 8) = ? (base 3)

2.9 Show the contents of the memory locations corresponding to the following memory initialization:

```
CONSTANT    DB      01100101B
LABEL       DW      0111101010111101B
```

2.10 Write the 2's and 1's complements for the following 16-bit hexadecimal numbers:
  a 3FFD   **c** FF9A
  b 34B0   **d** 70FF

2.11 Assume that subtraction is performed by taking 2's complement of the subtrahend and then performing addition. Perform the following computation showing the binary operations involved. The numbers given are all hexadecimal.
  a ED89 − FD76   **c** F98C − E98D
  b 34D8.EF − 34A9.DE

2.12 Find out the contents of the register AX after the execution of the following program fragment.

```
CAT     DW      2BAFH
DOG     DW      A441H
BIRD    DW      289AH
        MOV     AX,     CAT
        ADD     AX,     BIRD
        SUB     AX,     DOG
```

2.13 Assume that the memory addresses are given in hexadecimal. Find out the contents of the memory location GIRL and GIRL + 1 after the execution of the following program fragment:

```
BOY1    DW      204AH
BOY2    DW      B9E2H
GIRL    DW      ?
        MOV     AX,     BOY2
        MOV     GIRL,   BOY1
        ADD     AX,     GIRL
        MOV     GIRL,   AX
```

2.14 Write, in octal, the contents of the memory locations defined in the following initialization:

```
WORD1   DW      3A3BH
WORD2   DW      FEEEH
WORD3   DD      20FD4ABEH
BYTE1   DB      7FH
BYTE2   DB      EFH
```

2.15 Suppose that a real number is stored using the short real format shown below. Give the numbers decimal equivalent.

```
31              23                      0
┌───────────────┬──────────────────────┐
│ 1 00010111    │ 101110001 · · · 0     │
└───────────────┴──────────────────────┘
```

Note that the exponent is in the biased exponent form (bias $= 127$).

2.16 Write the following decimal numbers in a short real normalized format or a short real unnormalized format (if it can't be represented in normalized format):

    a $3.5 \cdot 2^{123}$ **e** $10234.45 \cdot 2^{-129}$

    b $2.95 \cdot 2^{33}$ **f** 2^{-126}

    c $8.13 \cdot 2^{-33}$ **g** $1.0000000025 \cdot 2^{-127}$

    d $3.24 \cdot 2^{-135}$

2.17 Write the following decimal numbers in BCD form.

    a 2390   **c** 9009

    b 2777   **d** 4080

2.18 Write the following numbers in BCD form and then perform the indicated BCD computation. Show how the correction operation comes into play.

    a $2395 - 2296$ **c** $1777 - 1790$

    b $3498 + 2432$

2.19 Write the following numbers in a packed BCD format:

    a $9.8234 \cdot 10^{12}$ **c** $1.345090 \cdot 10^{16}$

    b $3.9084 \cdot 10^{17}$

Note that in certain cases the number must be truncated or rounded before it is stored in the packed BCD format

2.20 Refer to Table 2-7. What would be the consequences of adding 2 more bits to the short real format? How should these bits be added? To the mantissa, the exponent or both? Rewrite the table line for the short real format.

2.21 State how to distinguish a positive zero and a denormalized real number if both numbers are stored in a short real format.

2.22 State how to distinguish a NAN from an infinity ($+ \infty$ or $- \infty$).

2.23 During a computation, an intermediate result will be denormalized if it is less than the smallest representable number in that format (i.e., $1.2 \cdot 2^{-126}$ for the case of a short real format). A DENORMAL is produced in order to continue the computation. What are the advantages and disadvantages of the denormalization?

2.24 One of the merits of the instruction set of 8087 is that a user may continue his or her computation even if an unexpected intermediate result like $+\infty$ or $-\infty$ occurs in the computation. Give a real-world example to show the use of this feature.

2.25 Say that numerical output can be presented in either decimal or hexadecimal forms. Under what circumstances would one choose one form over the other?

3

Computer
Organization
I

This chapter focuses on the organization of memory, the registers, and the available instruction formats and addressing modes, and how all of these items fit together in an operational computer.

3.1 MEMORY ORGANIZATION

3.1.1 The Memory Space

The memory on the Intel 8088 and IBM PC can be as large as 1 megabyte (1,048,576D or 100000H bytes). Thus, 20 bits are required to identify each byte in the entire memory. This memory (address) space is viewed as being broken up into *segments* which are 64 kilobytes, or 64K (65536D or 10000H bytes), in length. A *segment base address* is an address within the 1-megabyte range where a segment begins. If segments were allowed to begin at any arbitrary address, then segment base addresses would have to be 20 bits in length. Consider, however, what occurs when segment boundaries are restricted to multiples of 16. Every 20-bit segment base address would have its lower-order 4

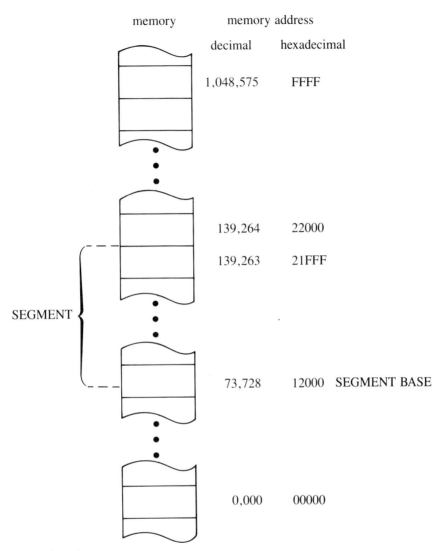

Figure 3-1 A memory segment.

bits equal to 0. Consequently, these four 0s can be implied and only 16 bits need be provided for segment base address specification. Figure 3-1 shows a segment beginning at address 1200(0)H and ending at 21FFFH. The 0 in the parentheses indicates that this is an implied 0.

Consider now the problem of addressing a location in the 1-megabyte memory. Say that the memory location of interest is 20F2AH. This just happens to be within the segment defined in Figure 3-1. One way of describing this location is to specify first the segment base address, 1200(0)H, and then an offset address into the 64 kilobyte segment, 20F2AH − 1200(0)H = EF2AH. This pair, the segment base address (e.g., 1200H) and the offset address (e.g., EF2AH), is often referred to as the *logical* address as opposed to the actual, real, physical, or *absolute* memory address (e.g., 20F2AH). Given a logical address, the absolute memory address can be obtained by shifting the 16-bit segment base address left 4 bits to obtain a 20-bit address, and then adding it to the offset address. This is shown below.

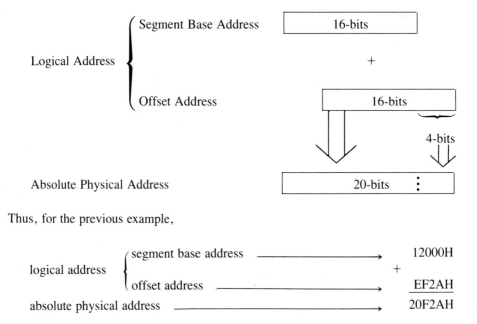

Thus, for the previous example,

$$\text{logical address} \begin{cases} \text{segment base address} & \longrightarrow \quad 12000\text{H} \\ & \qquad\qquad\qquad\qquad + \\ \text{offset address} & \longrightarrow \quad \underline{\text{EF2AH}} \end{cases}$$

absolute physical address $\longrightarrow$ 20F2AH

Since this 4-bit left shift and add operation is often used, it would be convenient to have a shorthand operator notation to designate its occurrence. The character pair " + ' " will be used for this purpose. Thus, 1200H + ' ER2AH = 20F2AH. Notice that there are many ways of specifying the same address by using different combinations of segment base addresses and offset addresses. Figure 3-2 shows the absolute address 20F2AH formed as logical addresses (1200H,EF2AH) and (1880H,872AH).

3.1.2 The Segment Registers

Within the Bus Interface Unit (BIU) part of the Intel 8088 (see Figure 1-3) are four 16-bit registers referred to as the *segment registers* and a single 16-bit register called the *instruction pointer* register. These registers and their names are shown in Figure 3-3.

Segment registers provide the segment base address part of a logical memory address. This, together with an appropriate offset, can then be used to form an absolute memory address. Thus, these four segment registers, when loaded with the proper values, potentially can address a quarter of a megabyte of memory. The presence of four segment registers permits certain of these registers to be used for specialized memory addressing functions and provides the user with a high level of flexibility in

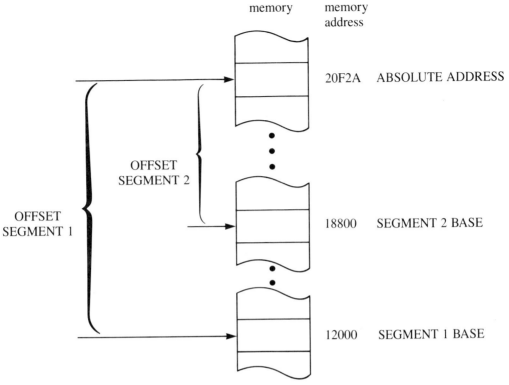

Figure 3-2 Logical-to-absolute address mapping.

partitioning and organizing memory for use in a modular manner. In general, segment register usage in forming logical addresses is as follows:

1. CS (CODE SEGMENT)—Used when referencing memory for fetching instructions. The offset is taken from the IP register.
2. DS (DATA SEGMENT)—Used when referencing memory for fetching or storing data operands. The offset is the result of an *effective address* calculation. In many cases, this effective address is determined by the addressing mode and operand address of the instruction being executed, in conjunction with the contents of one or more general registers. Effective address calculations are considered in Section 3.2, where we discuss addressing modes.

    There are four exceptions to use of the DS register when referencing data operands. For completeness these are given here even though some of the terms used are to be explained in later sections.

a. Stack operand references use the SS register (see 3 below).
b. The destination string in a string instruction uses the ES register (see 4 below).
c. The SS register is used for any operand references where the effective address calculation utilizes the BP general register.

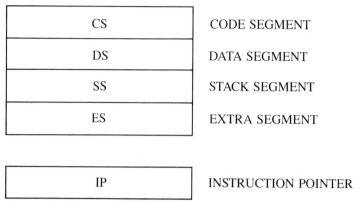

CS	CODE SEGMENT
DS	DATA SEGMENT
SS	STACK SEGMENT
ES	EXTRA SEGMENT

IP	INSTRUCTION POINTER

Figure 3-3   The segment registers and instruction pointer.

      d. An operand reference (other then *b* above) may use a specific segment register when that register is explicitly requested through use of a segment override byte (to be discussed below).

3. SS (STACK SEGMENT)—Used when referencing memory locations as part of a stack operation (Section 4.1). In this case, the offset is taken from the SP (Stack Pointer) general register (Section 4.1). SS is also used in any memory reference which employs the BP (Base Pointer) general register in developing an effective address. In this case the offset is the effective address which has been calculated.

4. ES (EXTRA SEGMENT)—Used when referencing memory locations which are the destination operands of a string instruction (Section 6.3). The offset is taken from the DI (Destination Index) general register.

The above discussion indicates normal or default segment register usage. In certain situations, this can be overridden if a special byte called the *segment override byte* is placed immediately before the instruction whose segment usage is to be altered. This is discussed further in Section 3.2.2.8.

3.1.3 Instruction Fetching and the Instruction Pointer

Reexamining the operation of the BIU (Figure 1-3), the instruction fetching sequence can now be seen in terms of the CS establishing a base address for a 64-kilobyte segment within which current instructions are to be obtained. The *Instruction Pointer* (IP) provides the offset for the specific instruction byte to be fetched. Each byte, when fetched, is put into the instruction queue, from which it is taken in turn by the execution unit. As the instruction bytes are removed, the IP register is incremented, and the next byte is fetched.

    As long as instructions follow one another sequentially in memory and are sequentially executed, the process of incrementing IP to obtain the next instruction offset proceeds smoothly. What happens though when it is necessary to execute instructions which are out of sequence with the currently executing instruction? To do this a **JMP** (Ju**MP**) instruction might first be executed. This instruction directs the computer to continue executing instructions but from a nonsequential location in memory. As a result of the jump instruction, first the queue is reset (i.e., effectively cleared). If the jump is to an instruction which resides in the current code segment (called an *intra*-segment or **NEAR** transfer), the IP register is then reset with the offset address of this instruction. If the jump is to an instruction outside the current code segment (called an *inter*segment or **FAR** transfer), then the CS register is reset with the segment base address and the IP register is reset to the offset address of this instruction. The new values of IP and CS are contained in the **JMP** instruction itself (Section 4.3).

The first byte of the instruction which was jumped to is now fetched and passed to the EU. Subsequent sequential instruction bytes are then fetched when possible in an attempt to keep the instruction queue full. The process continues until the next **JMP** instruction is encountered, at which time the IP and possibly CS registers are again reset.

3.1.4 Segmented Memory

The presence of four separate and independent segment registers provides the programmer with great flexibility in managing memory resources. Since segment registers can be loaded with simple **MOV** instructions, a programmer easily can change the area of memory from which code, operands, stack data, and string data are fetched. This enhances the recommended programming practice of placing data, stack, and instruction program elements in separate memory areas. It also enables one to easily reload these program elements into different memory areas depending on the current operating environment. This latter capability is particularly important in multiprogramming environments where data and code blocks from several programs are continually swapped in and out of memory as the demand for new program blocks evolves.

In general, segments may be nonoverlapping or overlapping, with several parts of physical memory being associated with the same segment register at different times during a programs execution. In Figure 3-4*a* there are four nonoverlapping segments. Figure 3-4*b* shows DS and ES segments overlapping and indicates that two portions of memory are associated with SS at different times. By permitting overlapping segments, memory can be used more efficiently. For instance, say that the Extra Segment is associated with string storage and only requires 4 kilobytes. There is no reason to waste the remaining 60 kilobytes of the ES. Starting the Data Segment within the ES, but after the 4 kilobyte string area (see Figure 3-4*b*), uses the memory more efficiently.

As a simple example of segmenting memory consider the **ISUM1** program which was discussed in Section 1.3. The program is divided into three program segments: a segment labeled **DSEG** to be used for data, a segment labeled **SSEG** to be used for a stack, and a segment labeled **CSEG** to be used for instructions (ES is not used). Each of these program segments is defined by a **SEGMENT-ENDS** assembler pseudo-operation pair. These pairs associate each instruction, variable, and label with a particular program segment label (i.e., **CSEG, DSEG,** or **SSEG**). In the case of the **SSEG** segment, the keyword **STACK** has been added to indicate that the memory locations

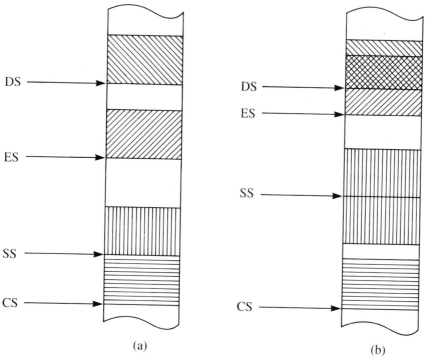

Figure 3-4 Nonoverlapping and overlapping memory segments.

associated with this segment are to be used for the system stack. That is, the operating system will utilize this area for its required stack operations. Note that even though the **ISUM1** program performs no stack operations directly, the assembler and operating system necessitate a system stack definition. Note also that we have shifted somewhat what is meant by the term *segment*. Initially, the term was used to indicate a 64-kilobyte block of memory. Now it is used to indicate a program module, instructions, or data which may be as large as 64 kilobytes. That is, a "program segment" fits within a "memory segment."

At this point, with the exception of the **SSEG** segment definition, there is no indication which segment register is to be used with the defined segments. The **ASSUME** pseudo-operation connects the program segment definitions with particular segment registers. Thus, for instance, **DS:DSEG** indicates that the data defined in the program segment labeled **DSEG** is to be accessed using the DS segment register.

The segment registers themselves still must be loaded. Just what values are loaded is dependent in part on how the linker and loader have assigned the program segments to memory locations, and on how the segment registers have been initialized during the loading process. Typically, the CS register will be loaded with the proper base address so that, in conjunction with the IP register, the program's first executable instruction will be referenced. This instruction is known to the assembler from the **END** statement of the main code segment. In the case of the **ISUM1** program, this statement is **END SUM**, where **SUM** is the label of the first instruction to be executed. This information is passed to the linker and then the loader. The SS and SP registers will also be properly loaded if a run time stack segment (e.g., **SEGMENT STACK**) is defined in the program. Other segment registers must be explicitly loaded by the programmer. In the **ISUM1** program this is done for the data segment register with the instructions **MOV   AX,DSEG** and **MOV   DS,AX**.

The MAP listing for the **ISUM1** program (generated by the linker) can be used to determine where these segments are relative to each other (Table 3-1). The listing also indicates the number of bytes in each defined segment. Numbers under Start and Stop indicate beginning and ending relative addresses. It is clear that the linker has allocated the **CSEG** segment to memory locations below **DSEG**, and that the **DSEG** segment, in turn, has been allocated to locations below **SSEG**.

Table 3-1   MAP Listing for The **ISUM1** Program

Start	Stop	Length	Name
00000H	00028H	0029H	CSEG
00030H	0003BH	000CH	DSEG
00040H	0023FH	0200H	SSEG

3.2 ADDRESSING MODES AND EFFECTIVE ADDRESS CALCULATIONS

The effective address is calculated from information present in the instruction currently being executed and often also from information found in the general registers located in the execution unit. Just how this calculation is performed depends on the *addressing mode* specified by the instruction. The next sections discuss the general registers, addressing modes, and effective address calculation. Use of the override segment byte to countermand default segment register usage is also considered.

3.2.1 The General Registers

Within the execution unit part of the Intel 8088 (Figure 1-3) are eight 16-bit registers referred to as the *general registers*. These registers and their names are shown in Figure 3-5.

Note that the general registers are divided into two groups, a *data group* and a *pointer* and *index group*. As implied by their names, the data group usually holds data operands needed by the various data operation instructions (the BX register is also used in effective address calculations for some addressing modes). In some cases, specific registers in the data group are designated for certain operations. For instance, the AX register must hold one of the operands when an integer word-multiply instruction is executed. The double-word result is placed in AX (low-order word) and DX (high-order word). Note also that each register in the data group can be considered as consisting of a single 16-bit word, or two 8-bit bytes, a high (H) order byte and a low (L) order byte. Data-oriented instructions can usually operate on either byte or word data

high byte   low byte

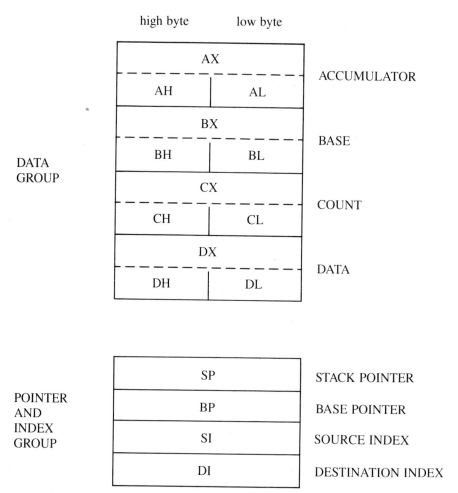

Figure 3-5   The general registers.

and are thus designed to use either an entire register or byte components as operands. For example, the program segments in Figure 3.6 add the contents of a memory word (or byte) located at label **ALPHA** to the contents of CX (or CL) and place the result in CX (or CL).

Notice that when writing the assembly language mnemonics for the **MOV** and **ADD** instructions, it is not necessary to designate them as being word or byte instructions. The assembler program recognizes whether a word or byte instruction is intended by determining the operand *type* (see Problem 3-8).

The pointer and index group usually are used in addressing functions by holding information needed for effective address calculations. They may also hold information required for performing a variety of string and stack operations. Table 3-2 indicates some of the special and instruction-implied uses associated with the general registers.

```
; Word Addition                |    : Byte Addition
ALPHA   DW      360            |    ALPHA  DB      360
BETA    DW      45             |    BETA   DB      45
        MOV     CX, BETA       |           MOV     CL, BETA
        ADD     CX, ALPHA      |           ADD     CL, ALPHA
```

Figure 3-6 Word and byte operations.

Table 3-2 General-Register Usage

Register	Subregister	Usage
AX		Word-multiply and -divide and I/O instructions.
	AL	Byte-multiply and -divide, I/O, translate, and decimal arithmetic instructions.
	AH	Byte-multiply and -divide instructions.
BX		Based addressing modes (use DS register as default segment register). Translate instruction.
CX		String and loop instructions.
	CL	Rotate and shift instructions.
DX		Word-multiply and -divide and I/O instructions.
SP		Stack-oriented addressing modes (use SS register as segment register).
BP		Based addressing modes (use SS register as segment register).
SI		String-oriented instructions.
DI		String-oriented instructions

3.2.2 Addressing Modes

There is a rich variety of addressing modes available on the IBM PC. These modes ease the programming task by permitting access to data and input/output ports in a natural and efficient manner. This section presents these modes and provides examples of their use.

3.2.2.1 Register Addressing   For many instructions, operands can be held in any of the segment and general registers. Depending upon the particular instruction involved,

Instruction: ADD CX,DX

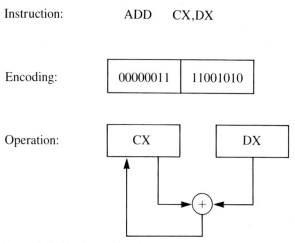

Figure 3-7 Register addressing.

Instruction: ADD AL,6

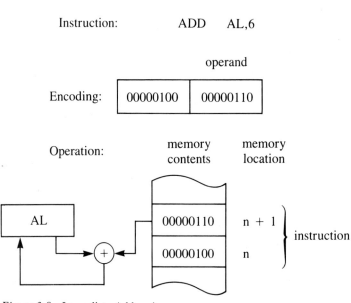

Figure 3-8 Immediate Addressing.

registers may provide either or both source operands, and may be designated as the destination for instruction results. Since there are a limited number of registers, only a few bits are required within an instruction to specify the register(s) to be used. Instructions which fetch all their operands from registers thus tend to be shorter in length. They also will tend to execute the fastest since their operands are present within the execution unit and no time is spent fetching operands from memory. A register-to-

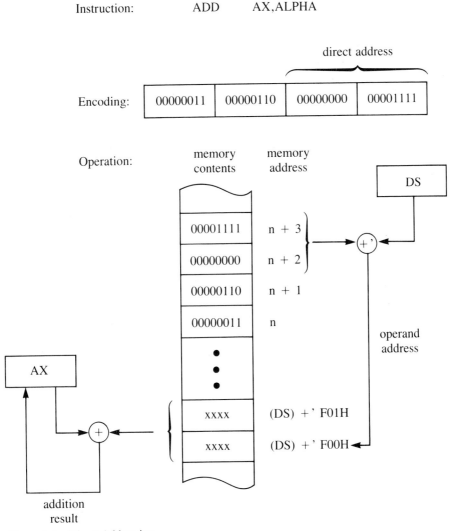

Instruction: ADD   AX,ALPHA

Encoding:

| 00000011 | 00000110 | 00000000 | 00001111 |

Operation:

Figure 3-9 Direct Addressing.

register **ADD** operation is shown in Figure 3-7. The contents of CX are added to DX with the result stored in CX.

3.2.2.2 Immediate Addressing

With immediate addressing, the operand (i.e., the immediate operand) is stored along with the instruction in memory. That is, the operand "immediately" follows the instruction in memory and is fetched from memory as part of the instruction fetch process. Being part of the instruction, the immediate operand enters the execution unit through the instruction queue. This reduces the time required

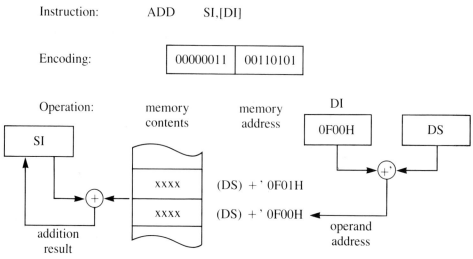

Instruction: ADD   SI,[DI]

Encoding: | 00000011 | 00110101 |

Figure 3-10   Indirect Addressing.

to fetch the operand, thereby reducing execution time. In the example in Figure 3-8, the decimal integer 6 is added to the AL register with the result being placed in AL.

Note that if an immediate word operation were indicated, the low-order byte of the immediate operand would precede the high-order byte in memory.

3.2.2.3 Direct Addressing

As the name implies, the effective address of the operand is taken directly from the appropriate field in the instruction. In the example in Figure 3-9, the contents of the word starting at location **ALPHA [ALPHA = (DS) + ' 0F00H]** are added to the contents of AX and the result placed in AX.

The + ' operation above corresponds to absolute address calculation discussed in Section 3.1.1. This involves shifting the segment base address left 4 bits, and then adding it to the offset, or effective, address to obtain the absolute address.

3.2.2.4 Indirect Addressing

With direct addressing, the effective address was contained in an address portion of the instruction. With indirect addressing, the effective address is found in either the DI, SI, or BX register. That is, the address is not found "directly" in the instruction, but "indirectly" by accessing a register. In the example in Figure 3-10, DI contains the address 0F00H. The contents of the word starting at location (DS) + ' 0F00H are added to the contents of SI with the results stored in SI.

3.2.2.5 Based Addressing

Either the BX or BP registers may be designated as base registers in calculating the effective address of an operand. In both cases the contents of the designated base register are added to a displacement address (8 or 16 bits)

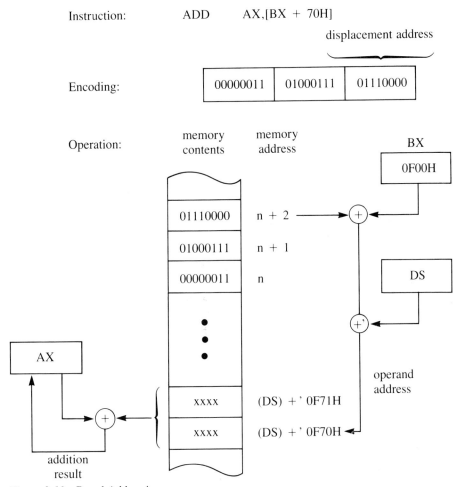

Instruction: ADD   AX,[BX + 70H]

displacement address

Encoding: | 00000011 | 01000111 | 01110000 |

Operation:

memory contents / memory address

Figure 3-11   Based Addressing.

contained in the instruction to form the effective address. A key difference in selecting BX or BP, however, relates to the default segment register used to calculate the absolute address once the effective address has been obtained. The use of BP directs the bus interface unit to use the SS register, while the default segment register used with BX is the DS register. That is, BP (Base Pointer) is normally used to point to the top of a stack and thus typically uses the stack segment register (see Section 4.1).

In Figure 3-11, BX contains the base address F00H. The operand of interest is at F70H (relative to DS) and it is to be added to the contents of AX with the result returned to AX.

Based addressing is a powerful approach to accessing data which are structured in a regular manner. The example presented below illustrates this.

EXAMPLE 3-1   Consider a company that manufactures 256 different items. As part of its on-line information system it stores 128 bytes of information in the IBM PC's memory related to each item. Each 128-byte block contains such information as item name, description, selling price, discount rates, and number in stock. Assume that the blocks are placed sequentially in memory starting at an address labeled **ITEM**. The first block corresponds to the item with identification number (ID) 1, the second to the item with ID 2, etc. Byte number 8 in each block (byte number 0 is the first byte of the block) is the number of units of that item currently in stock. The data structure is shown in Figure 3-12.

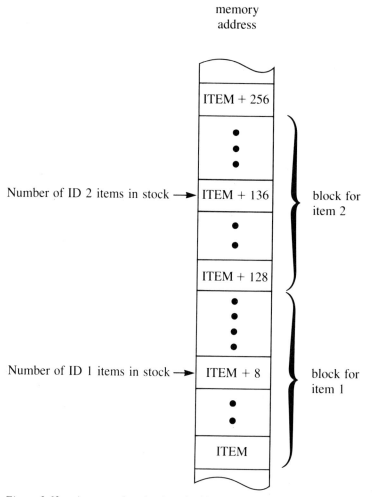

Figure 3-12   An example using based addressing.

Given an item ID in AL, write a procedure to determine how many such items are available in stock. Place that value in AH. A procedure is a program which can be "called" by another program in a structured manner (Section 4.2).

ANSWER

```
DATA_SEG        SEGMENT                         ;begin data segment
ITEM            DB          32768 DUP (?)       ;item data
DATA_SEG        ENDS                            ;end data segment
;
STAK_SEG        SEGMENT STACK                   ;begin stack segment
                DW          128 DUP (?)         ;128 word stack
STAK_SEG        ENDS                            ;end stack segment
;
PROC_SEG        SEGMENT                         ;begin procedure seg.
                ASSUME   CS: PROC_SEG, DS: DATA_SEG
                PUBLIC   STOCK
STOCK           PROC     FAR                    ;activated by inter-
                                                ;segment call
BEGIN:          MOV      DI, DATA_SEG
                MOV      DS, DI                 ;initialize data seg.
                PUSH     BX                     ;save call routines BX
                PUSHF                           ;register and flags
; **** PROCEDURE BODY START ****
                LEA      BX, ITEM               ; (BX) <--- Offset addr.
                                                ;of Item block area
                DEC      AL                     ; (AL) <--- Item - 1
                MOV      CL, 128                ; (CL) <--- Block Size
                MUL      CL    ; (AX) <---(Item -1) * Block Size
                ADD      BX, AX                 ;  (BX) <--- address of
                                                ; requested block
                MOV      AH, [BX + 8]           ;get byte   8 of block
; **** PROCEDURE BODY FINISH ****
                POPF                            ;restore calling rou-
                POP      BX                     ;   tines flags and BX
                RET                             ;return from procedure
STOCK           ENDP                            ;end procedure "STOCK"
PROC_SEG        ENDS                            ;end procedure segment
                END
```

Figure 3-13 Program for Example 3-1.

The program of Figure 3-13 includes a number of features we shall discuss later in the text. For the moment, however, focus on the instructions contained in the procedure body. The first instruction (**LEA**) loads the starting offset address of the entire block data structure (**ITEM**) into BX. The second instruction (**DEC**) decrements AL. Since AL contains the ID , and the lowest ID is 1, decrementing AL allows us to identify the block beginning at **ITEM** with ID 1. The **MOV   CL,128** instruction loads the block size into CL. The **MUL** instruction creates the offset from **ITEM** to the beginning of the block associated with ID. The 16-bit result of the multiplication is found in AX. Adding AX to BX (which contains the address of **ITEM**) now places the address of the 128-byte block corresponding to the item of interest into BX. The **MOV   AH,[BX + 8]** uses the based addressing mode to select out byte 8 and place its contents into AH.

3.2.2.6 Indexed Addressing   The SI and DI registers are referred to as *index* registers. With indexed addressing, the effective address is calculated as the sum of the contents of an index register with a displacement field (8 or 16 bits) contained in the instruction. This is illustrated in Figure 3-14, where the contents of memory location **ARRAY** + 70H (relative to DS) is added to the contents of DX with the result returned to DX. SI initially contains 70H and the address of **ARRAY** is 0F00H.

Index registers are typically used when accessing elements in an array where the displacement address sets up a starting address and the index register points to the element in the array to be accessed.

3.2.2.7 Based-Indexed Addressing   Direct addressing uses the displacement field to form an effective address. Based and indexed addressing each add to the displacement field the contents of the base and index register, respectively, to form an effective address. With based-indexed addressing the contents of both the base and index registers are added to the displacement field to form an effective address. By having two address components contained in two separate registers, the programmer has a powerful tool for accessing complex data structures.

Consider the data structure presented in Example 3-1. Say that each block contains within it an array of byte integers. The array begins at byte 32 of the block (the first byte is byte 0) and is of length 10. The elements within each array are to be added together. One way of organizing access to these array elements is to use the base register BX to hold the starting address of the block being accessed, set the displacement field to point to byte 32 in the block, and have an index register (SI) point to the particular array element to be added. If the elements are to be added to the AX register, then the **ADD** instruction in Figure 3-15, which uses based-indexed addressing, might be employed. BX contains the address **ABLOCK** and SI contains the array element offset address **AELEMENT**.

3.2.2.8 Segment Override   Section 3.1.2 discussed the use of segment registers in calculating absolute memory addresses. Default segment register usage was indicated. In certain situations, this default usage can be overridden by preceding the instruction whose usage is to be altered with a *segment override byte*. For instance, calculation of the absolute address for **TEN** in the instruction **MOV   CX,TEN** would normally use the DS register. If one wanted to use the SS register, then the instruction would be preceded with the segment override byte 36H. The assembler can be instructed

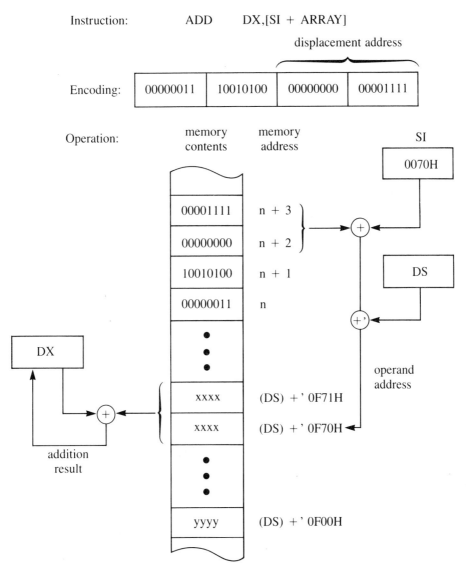

Figure 3-14 Indexed addressing.

to automatically insert this override byte by writing the above instruction as **MOV   CX,SS:TEN**. The form **SS:TEN** will be recognized by the assembler and cause it to place the byte 36H in memory immediately prior to the **MOV** instruction.

There are three situations where the segment register is fixed and cannot be overridden: (*a*) Instruction fetching must use the CS register. (*b*) Stack operations must use the SS register. (*c*) The string destination in string operations must use the ES register. The segment override byte for all other cases is as follows: For ES use: 26H; CS use: 2EH; SS use: 36H; DS use: 3EH.

Instruction: ADD   AL,[BX + SI + 32]

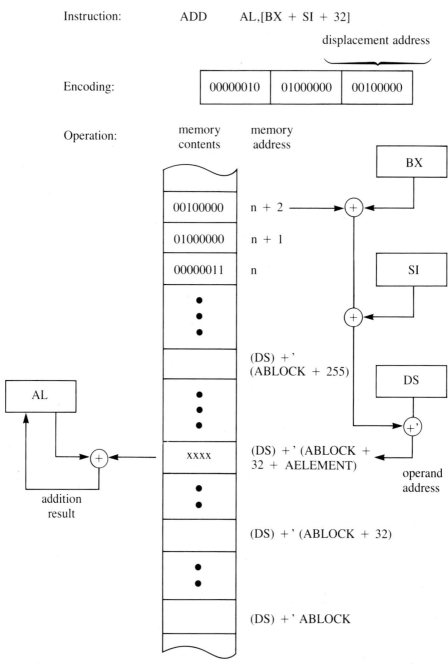

Figure 3-15 Based-indexed addressing.

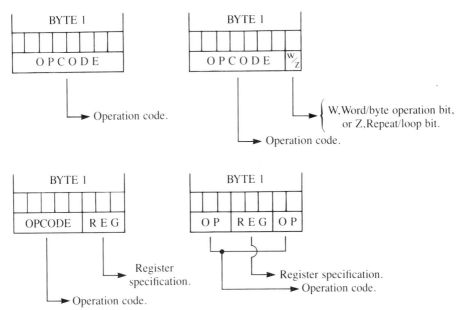

Figure 3-16   Varieties of single-byte instruction formats.

3.3 INSTRUCTION FORMATS AND ENCODING

The IBM PC uses instruction formats varying in length from 1 to 6 bytes. Generally, one need not be concerned with instruction format details since the assembler automatically produces the correct format and associated bit patterns from the assembly language program representation. During debugging, however, it sometimes is necessary to examine the exact formats and bit patterns of particular instructions. Moreover, in those situations where efficiency is important, a knowledge of the computer's instruction formats and encoding aids in determining the most efficient addressing modes. Figures 3-16, 3-17, and 3-18 present the major instruction formats available. Shaded portions of the instruction indicate that for certain formats these bytes may not be present. The entire set of instruction formats is given in Appendix B.

Consider first the single-bit indicators W,S,D,V, and Z. These are summarized in Table 3-3. W (bit 0 in byte 1 of many instructions) indicates whether the operation is a word or byte operation. Thus, for example, the immediate instructions *ADD AL,6* and *ADD AX,6* are encoded as 0406H and 050600H, respectively. The S bit is used in immediate instructions where a word operation is indicated by W = 1; however, only a byte of data is provided with the instruction. When this situation occurs (W = 1 and S = 1), the 8-bit immediate operand is treated as the lower-order 8 bits of a word operand with the sign bit extended to the higher-order byte of the word at the time addition takes place. For example, consider an immediate add instruction where S = W = 1 and the 8-bit immediate operand equals 9AH. In this situation since the sign bit equals 1 (i.e., the immediate operand is a negative 2's complement number),

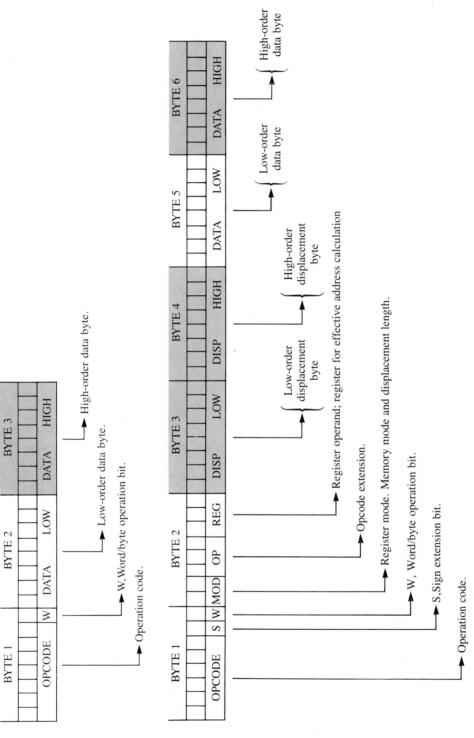

Figure 3-17 Varieties of immediate addressing mode instruction formats.

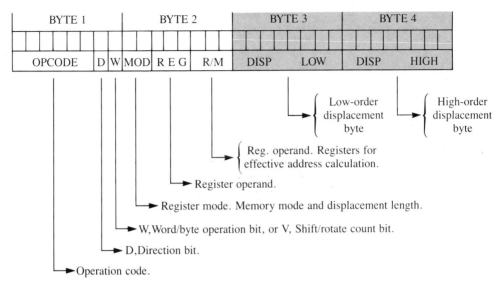

Figure 3-18 Other instruction formats.

the immediate operand is considered to be FF9AH when addition takes place. If W = 1 and S = 0, then all 16 bits of the immediate operand must be provided.

The D bit indicates the "direction" of the instruction operation. Many instructions can be viewed as having one or two "source" fields, and a single "destination" field. The **ADD** instruction, for instance, has two source operand fields and a destination field. The following options are available for **ADD** instructions not employing immediate addressing (Figure 3-17).

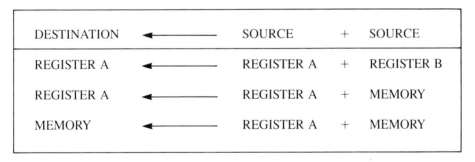

Notice that in every case at least one register must be specified. The D bit indicates whether the register specified in the REG position of the instruction byte is to be a source or destination.

For example, consider the instruction **ADD   AX,ALPHA** where **ALPHA** is the address 0F00H. This is encoded as 0306000FH (see Section 3.2.2.3) with D = 1, indicating that AX will contain the result of the addition. The instruction **ADD ALPHA, AX** is encoded as 0106000FH with D = 0, indicating that the contents of memory location **ALPHA** (relative to DS) will contain the result.

Table 3-3 Single-Bit Encoding

Field Bit	Value	Function
W	0	Instruction operates on byte data
	1	Instruction operates on word data
S	0	No sign extension
	1	Sign-extend 8-bit immediate data to 16 bits if W = 1
D	0	Instruction source is specified in REG field
	1	Instruction destination is specfied in REG field
V	0	Shift/rotate count is one
	1	Shift/rotate count is specified in CL register
Z	0	Repeat/loop while zero flag is clear
	1	Repeat/loop while zero flag is set

The V bit is used in conjuntion with shift and rotate instructions (see Section 6.2.2). With V = 0, the number of bit positions shifted or rotated is 1, while with V = 1 the number is specified in the CL register.

The Z bit is used in conjunction with the repeat and loop instructions. Looping or repeating with a string instruction can be made conditional on the value of the zero flag in the flag register. With the **LOOPZ** (or **LOOPE**) instruction, for instance, Z = 1, and looping continues as long as the contents of CX is not equal to zero and the zero flag is set. With **LOOPNZ** (or **LOOPNE**) Z = 0, and the looping condition requires that CX not be zero, and that the zero flag be clear. This behavior is explained in detail in Section 4.3.3.

Several of the instruction formats contain a 3-bit register (REG) field. The particular register designated can be determined from Table 3-4. Consider, for example, the instruction **ADD   AX,[BX + 70H]** (see Section 3.2.2.5). The first byte of the instruction has W = 1. The second byte of the instruction is encoded as 01000111 with the register bits being 000, thereby specifying the AX register.

The final instruction fields to be explained are the R/M and MOD fields, which together specify an addressing mode. Table 3-5 indicates how these fields are interpreted. Notice that all of the addressing modes other than the immediate mode are

Table 3-4 Register (REG) Field Encoding

Reg	W = 0	W = 1	Reg	W = 0	W = 1
000	AL	AX	100	AH	SP
001	CL	CX	101	CH	BP
010	DL	DX	110	DH	SI
011	BL	BX	111	BH	DI

Table 3-5 Addressing Mode Fields Encoding

R/M	MEMORY MODES MOD = 00	MOD = 01	MOD = 10	REGISTER MODE MOD = 11 W = 0 REGISTER	W = 1 ADDRESSING
	BASED-INDEXED ADDRESSING				
000	[BX+SI]	[BX+SI+D8]	[BX+SI+D16]	AL	AX
001	[BX+DI]	[BX+DI+D8]	[BX+DI+D16]	CL	CX
010	[BP+SI]	[BP+SI+D8]	[BP+SI+D16]	DL	DX
011	[BP+DI]	[BP+DI+D8]	[BP+DI+D16]	BL	BX
	INDIRECT ADDRESSING	INDEXED ADDRESSING			
100	[SI]	[SI+D8]	[SI+D16]	AH	SP
101	[DI]	[DI+D8]	[DI+D16]	CH	BP
		BASED ADDRESSING			
111	[BX]	[BP+D8]	[BX+D16]	BH	DI
	DIRECT ADDRESSING				
110	[D16]	[BP+D8]	[BP+D16]	DH	SI

specified by using this table. The immediate mode is specified with the instructions op code field. This can be seen by examining Appendix B.

Consider again the **ADD   AX,[BX + 70H]** discussed above. The displacement 70H can be represented in 8 bits; hence the notation D8 is used to denote its presence in the instruction. The entry **[BX + D8]** occurs in Table 3-5 with R/M = 111 and MOD = 01. The format for byte 2 of the instruction as shown in Figure 3-18 is MOD,REG,R/M, which translates to the encoding 01 000 111.

Notice that three of the modes (00,01,10) are memory modes; that is, one of the operands is taken from memory. The bracket notation [ ] indicates that an effective address is calculated and used to locate the operand in memory. In the register mode both the source and destination are registers. Thus encoding the instruction **ADD   CX,DX** requires that W = 1, and with D = 1, the remaining fields would be encoded as REG = 001, R/M = 010 and MOD = 11.

3.4 THE FLAG REGISTER

The Intel 8088 and IBM PC have a special 16-bit register referred to as the *flag* or *status* register. Six of these bits, called *status flags*, are used to indicate that certain conditions have occurred as a result of executing certain instructions. That is, these conditions are *flag*ged. For example, if the the result of an arithmetic operation is negative, then this condition is flagged by setting the sign bit. Status flags can be tested, set, and reset under program control, and thus the occurrence of one or more conditions can be used to control program branching and flow.

Three of the bits in this register, called *control flags*, are used to control certain operations of the processor. For instance, one bit is assigned to enabling or disabling processor interrupts. The remaining 7 bits are currently unused. Figure 3-19 shows flag register bits and their names and abbreviations. Table 3-6 contains some instructions which test, set, or clear the various flags. The complete set of conditional jump instructions is given in Table 4-3.

3.4.1 Status and Control Flags

The general use of the status and control flags is given below.

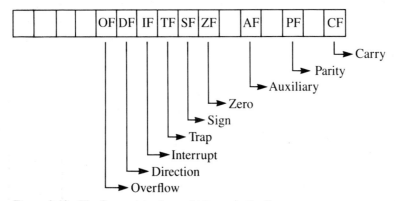

Figure 3-19   The flag register (unused bits normally 0).

Table 3-6 Some Flag-Related Instructions

Flag	Some Related Instructions
CF	**JNC**—Jump if no carry.
	JC—Jump if carry.
	STC—Set carry flag.
	CLC—Clear carry flag.
	CMC—Complement carry flag.
OF	**JNO**—Jump on no overflow.
	JO—Jump on overflow.
ZF	**JNZ (JNE)**—Jump if not zero. (Jump if not equal.)
	JZ (JE)—Jump if zero. (Jump if equal.)
SF	**JNS**—Jump if no sign. (If positive.)
	JS—Jump on sign. (If negative.)
PF	**JNP (JPO)**—Jump if no parity. (Jump if parity odd.)
	JP (JPE)—Jump on parity. (Jump if parity even.)
DF	**CLD**—Clear direction flag.
	STD—Set direction flag.
IF	**CLI**—Clear interrupt flag. (Disable.)
	STI—Set interrupt flag. (Enable.)

3.4.1.1 Carry Flag (CF)   The CF flag is set if there has been a carry out of, or borrow into, the most significant bit of the result (either 8 or 16 bit) of an operation. An example of this was given in Section 2.2, where the problem of adding multibyte (multiword) operands was considered. In this situation the flag typically is used in conjunction with the **ADC** (**AD**d with **C**arry) instruction, which allows the carry conveniently to be added into the next byte (or word) of a multibyte (or multiword) addition. In a similar manner, multibyte (multiword) subtraction can be effected using the **SBB** (**Su**btract with **B**orrow) instruction. The CF may also be used to isolate bits in a word or byte with the shift or rotate instructions available. For instance, the instruction **RCL** (**R**otate through **C**arry **L**eft) rotates a byte or word operand left through the carry flag a number of times, where this number is either 1 or is specified in the CL register. This is shown in Figure 3-20 for the case of **RCL   AL,CL**, where CL contains the number 3, AL initially contains 57H, and CF is set at 1.

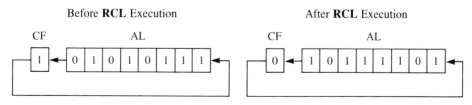

Figure 3-20   Shifting into the carry flag.

3.4.1.2 Auxiliary Carry Flag (AF) Consider the low-order 4 bits of a byte (or lowest 4 bits of a word). An operation which results in a carry out of, or borrow into, these low-order 4 bits causes the auxiliary carry flag to be set to 1. If no carry out, or borrow into, occurs, AF is set to zero. This capability is needed when performing multiple-digit arithmetic operations on BCD numbers (see Section 2.2.5) and is used by the various decimal-adjust instructions such as **DAA** (**D**ecimal-**A**djust for **A**ddition) and **DAS** (**D**ecimal-**A**djust for **S**ubtraction).

3.4.1.3 Overflow Flag (OF) An overflow occurs when an arithmetic operation results in the range of a signed number being exceeded. For instance, byte addition of the positive 2's complement numbers 01001010 and 00111000 results in 10000010, which is a negative number. Similarly, the addition of the two negative numbers 11010000 and 10001001 yields a positive number and sets OF. If an overflow does not occur, then OF is set to 0. Note that while OF can be tested using the **JNO** and **JO** instructions, an internal interrupt also can be generated on an overflow condition by use of the **INTO** (**INT**errupt if **O**verflow) instruction.

3.4.1.4 Zero Flag (ZF) The ZF is set to 1 if the result of an operation is a zero. If not, it is set to 0. Note the ZF is tested during operation of certain string instructions as indicated in Table 3-3 and is used to control the length of the string operated on.

3.4.1.5 Sign Flag (SF) The SF is set equal to the value of the high-order bit of the result of an operation. When dealing with 2's complement numbers, this bit corresponds to a 1 if the number is negative, and a 0 if it is positive. Thus SF indicates the sign of the result.

3.4.1.6 Parity Flag (PF) Consider the low-order 8 bits of a data operation result. If there are an even number of 1s present in this low-order byte, the PF is set to 1. An odd number of 1s sets it to 0.

3.4.1.7 Direction Flag (DF) The DF is used in conjunction with string operations. Such operations typically use the SI register as an offset pointing to a source operand address, and the DI register as an offset pointing to a destination operand address. These offsets either are incremented or decremented during string processing. When incremented, the string is processed from a low memory address up to a high memory address. When decremented, it is processed from a high memory address down to a low memory address. If the DF is set to 1, decrementing occurs; if it is set to 0, incrementing occurs.

3.4.1.8 Interrupt Flag (IF) The IF is used to enable (i.e., permit) or disable (i.e., prohibit) external interrupts which arrive on the Intel 8088 INTR line from interrupting the execution unit (see Section 4.3.4). Such interrupts can be used by external devices to signal the execution unit that a task has been completed, or a condition has occurred.

The interrupts are called *maskable* because the IF can be used to "mask" their occurrence. This is in contrast with external interrupts which arrive on the NMI (Non-Maskable Interrupt) line and are always enabled.

3.4.1.9 Trap Flag (TF)   Interrupts also can be generated internally under program control. One way of doing this is to set the TF to 1, which in turn puts the processor in *single-step* mode. In this mode, an internal interrupt will be generated after each instruction. This is a useful debugging technique because control is returned to the programmer after each instruction execution. The programmer can examine the state of the computer, determine the effects of the instruction's operation, and decide whether the program is operating as intended. This, indeed, is what occurs when using the trace command in the DOS debug facility.

Notice in Table 3-6 that there are no instructions to set and clear TF directly. The flag is set and cleared by operating on bit 8 of the word in the system stack which corresponds to a saved flag register. This word is loaded into the flag register from the stack on execution of the **IRET** (Interrupt **RET**urn) instruction. The details of this process are explained in Sections 9.1 and 9.2.1.2.

In addition to the flag-specific instructions noted in Table 3-6, two instructions which place the contents of the flag register on the stack and load the flag register from the stack should be noted. These are **POPF** (**POP F**lags off stack) and **PUSHF** (**PUSH F**lags onto stack). The flag register is also placed on the stack when either an internal interrupt [as result of executing the **INT** (**INT**errupt) instruction], or an external interrupt occurs. The flag register is also loaded from the stack on execution of the **IRET** instruction.

3.5 SUMMARY

The memory on the IBM PC can be as large as 1 megabyte, thereby requiring 20 bits for each *absolute physical address*. Such addresses are formed from *logical addresses*, which consist of two 16-bit parts. The first is a *segment base address*, while the second is an *offset address*. The absolute physical address is obtained by shifting the segment base address left four bit positions, and then adding it to the offset address. The segment base address is stored in one of four registers referred to as the *code*, *data*, *stack*, and *extra* segment registers. Different segment registers are used when forming addresses during different computer operations. Thus, the code segment register is typically used when forming addresses needed for fetching instructions, while the data segment register is typically used when forming addresses needed for fetching data.

During instruction fetching, the offset address is obtained from the 16-bit *instruction pointer*. The contents of this register are incremented appropriately during execution of each instruction so that the next instruction will be fetched from the proper location. Program branching or jumping will also require that the instruction pointer be loaded with a new offset address. In addition, if the jump address is outside the range of the current code segment register, the segment register will have to be reloaded as well.

When fetching data, the offset address is determined by the *addressing mode* of the instruction being executed. Determining the offset address from an instruction's addressing mode, operand address information, and possible register information is referred to as *effective address calculation*.

When accessing data, the data segment register generally is used in forming the segment base address. Other segment registers may be used by explicitly prefacing the instruction with a *segment override byte*. In certain addressing modes and situations, however, a specific segment register other than the code segment register automatically will be used by the bus interface unit in determining the absolute physical address. For instance, the stack segment register must be used whenever the BP (Base Pointer) register is used in an effective address calculation.

The BP register is one of eight *general registers* available in the IBM PC. Four of these, the *accumulator*, the *base*, the *count*, and the *data* registers are called the *data group*, while the *stack pointer*, *base pointer*, *source index*, and *destination index* are referred to as the *pointer and index group*. The data group typically is used to store data being processed by the various instructions, while the pointer and index group typically is used to aid in various address calculations. All the registers can be explicitly addressed, thereby enabling them to be accessed and operated on in a general manner. Many of the registers are implicitly addressed during certain operations. Some of these implicit uses are summarized in Table 3-2. In addition to their implicit use, the pointer and index group registers, and the BX register, are associated with specific addressing modes and participate in effective address calculations.

The instructions themselves are encoded in a variety of formats ranging from 1 to 6 bytes in length. This variety permits efficient encoding of many commonly used instructions, while at the same time preserving a diversity of addressing modes and instruction types.

A *flag register* is present in the IBM PC to indicate when certain conditions have occurred as a result of instruction execution, and to permit the programmer to exercise control over certain operating functions. *Status bits* in the flag register indicate such conditions as carry and overflow, while *control bits* in the flag register, for instance, enable or disable the occurrence of interrupts and traps. Special instructions are present to set, clear, and test these bits.

EXERCISES

3.1 Run the **ISUM1** program given in Chapter 1 using your operating system's **DEBUG** facility. Determine how to set up program breakpoints. Set up breakpoints for before and after execution of the **CMP** instruction. Check the flags when both negative and positive numbers are compared to zero. Determine what the **CMP** instruction does to these flags. What flags are set to indicate a negative value has been encountered?

3.2 Change the **DB** statement in **ISUM1** to

```
NUMSET   DB   9, 10, 11, 12, 13, 14, 15, 16, 17, 18
```

Run **ISUM1** under your system's **DEBUG** facility. When does the OF flag get set and why?

3.3 Modify the **ISUM1** program to check for even parity on members of the **NUMSET** array. Change the **DB** statement to

NUMSET   DB   1, 3, 3, 2, 5, 5, 4, 7, 9, 9

Use the **JP** (**J**ump on **P**arity), **JPE** (**J**ump if **P**arity **E**ven), **JNP** (**J**ump if **No** **P**arity), or **JPO** (**J**ump if **P**arity **O**dd) instructions to check PF flag. Determine the number of parity errors that have occurred. If a parity error occurs, then display the character E on the screen and an integer indicating the number of such errors.

3.4 The Intel 8086/88 has four segment registers. What performance gain might accrue if the microprocessor were redesigned to have eight or sixteen segment registers? Give an example where having more segment registers might be a benefit.

3.5 It has been proposed that segment addresses always begin on multiples of 256 (rather than 16). How many bits of segment register storage would be saved if this were done? What are the system performance implications of such a change?

3.6 It has been proposed that a future microprocessor design have segments which are 128 kilobytes in length rather than the current 64 kilobytes. What are the implications of this change from the point of view of the microprocessor design, and from the point of view of systems programming and performance.

3.7 Determine whether each group of three logical addresses (i.e., segment base address, offset address) corresponds to the same absolute (physical) address.

a (34C5, 0100)   (34B5, 0110)   (2725, 0EA0)
b (4BC5, 01FE)   (4AFE, 0210)   (4C00, 00FE)
c (04C5, 00FF)   (04A5, 012F)   (04E5, FF10)
d (04B5, 01FE)   (03A4, 030F)   (0503, 01B0)
e (2283, 000F)   (201D, 0275)   (211F, 0173)

3.8 Consider the program segments of Figure 3-6. What happens if operands of mixed types are used. That is, for the left program replace the statement **MOV CX,BETA** by **MOV CL,BETA**. For the right program, replace **BETA DB 45** with **BETA DW 45**. Try this out using the assembler at your disposal. Explain the results. Examine the bit pattern for the **MOV** instructions generated by the correct programs and determine where they differ.

3.9 Give the encoding for the following two **ADD** instructions:

ADD   AX, BX   and   ADD   BX, AX

3.10 Indicate the assembly language instructions which would generate the following encoded **MOV** instructions. Indicate in words the addressing mode corresponding to each instruction.

a 8B 07   **e** 8B 47 04
b 8B 00   **f** 8B 05
c 8B 42 02   **g** B8 24 10
d 8B C3   **h** A1 24 AF

3.11 Translate the following assembly language **ADD** instructions into their machine language equivalents.

a ADD AX, CX

b ADD AX, [BX]

c ADD BX, 1024H

d ADD CX, [AX + 10]

e ADD AL, [BP+SI+2]

f ADD DL, [SI+8]

g ADD DX, NAME (**NAME** is a label whose relative address is 256.)

h ADD NAME, DX

3.12 Design and document an algorithm to translate an arbitrary **ADD** instruction into its binary machine language equivalent. Use the structured English style presented in Chapter 1.

3.13 For each of the following word addition and subtraction operations indicate the contents of the CF, AF, OF, ZF, SF, and PF flags after the operation has been completed. Assume the carry bit is set to zero before the operation has begun.

a F24F + A3F4

b F24F − F24E

c 1000 + E14B

d 0899 + EEEE

e 8000 − FFFF

f EFFF + 0001

g FAC2 + 053D

h 5857 + A7AA

3.14 Determine the assembly language instructions which generated each of the following sequence of bits. You may use the unassemble feature (reverse assemble) available in the debugging facility of most operating systems, or you may do it manually using the material in the Appendices.

a	b	c
50	8D 16 0040	B9 000A
B0 A0	B4 0A	BE 0000
F6 E6	CD 21	8B 16 0000
32 F6	BB 0001	A1 0002
D0 E2	32 ED	F7 B4 0004
03 D0	8A 8F 0040	89 84 0018
81 C2 8000	BE 0040	89 94 0020
58	BF 0090	46
8B DA	F3 A4	E0 EA
26 88 07		

3.15 The compare instruction subtracts two operands and causes the various status flags to be set. Given that a compare instruction has been performed, indicate how the SF and OF flags can be used together to determine if one operand was *less than* the other.

3.16 As in Problem 3.15, assume that a compare instruction has just been executed. Indicate what flags would be tested and how they would be tested to determine if one operand was *less than or equal to* the other.

3.17 Determine the segment register used in accessing the operands in each of the following instructions:

a 88 46 00

b 3E 8B 03

c A3 D2 07

d 36 8E 84 10 17

4

Program Control
and
Decision Making

This chapter begins by considering the stack and procedure features, two crucial facilities required to produce structured programs and programming systems effectively. These features are supported on the IBM PC by a number of functions built into the hardware.

The second part of this chapter reviews the transfer and control instructions available on the IBM PC. While some of these have already been introduced, this section provides a complete discussion. Assembly language notation and mnemonics are used whenever possible to provide an informal introduction.

4.1 STACKS

A stack is a data structure where items are stored and retrieved in a *Last-in First-Out* (LIFO) manner. For instance, if the data items are the characters N I G O L where L is stored first, O second, G third, I fourth, and N last, then on retrieval from the stack, N comes out first, I second, and so forth. Such a data structure is very useful in computer operations ranging from arithmetic expression evaluation to procedure parameter passing. Indeed, an entire class of computer architectures has been designed based on the use of stacks, and related stack operations (17, 18). While the IBM PC is not a classical stack machine, it does have important stack features which are essential to general system operations, and to the development of most assembly language programs.

A stack on the IBM PC is a set of consecutive memory locations up to 64K (64 kilobytes) in length; that is, a stack is associated with a segment. While a programmer may define many stacks, at any point in time the *current stack* is defined by the contents of the stack segment (SS) and stack pointer (SP) registers. The SS register contains the base address of a 64K segment within which the stack resides. The SP register contains an offset from the base address which defines the *Top of Stack* (TOS). The TOS location contains the last data item to be placed on the stack.

Given that SS and SP have been properly initialized, there are two principal operations performed on stacks: A **PUSH** operation places an item on the stack; a **POP** operation removes an item from the stack. These operations are implemented by **PUSH** and **POP** instructions. Their characteristics are given in Table 4-1. The notation (X) means "the contents of X," while ((X)) means "the contents of the memory location pointed to by the contents of X."

Consider the stack operations shown in Figure 4-1. In (*a*) the SS register contains 00B0H and the SP register contains 00A5H. As indicated, the data items most recently pushed on the stack are in the lowest memory addresses. As data items are pushed on the stack, the stack grows downward in memory toward the address contained in the SS register. A wraparound occurs when an attempt is made to push an item on the stack when SP contains a zero offset. In Figure 4-1, (*b*) shows the contents of the stack

Table 4-1   Stack Operations

Operation	Action	Explanation
PUSH SOURCE	$(SP) \leftarrow (SP) - 2$	SP is decremented by 2. The stack expands by 2 bytes and a new TOS location is established.
	$((SP)) \leftarrow (\textbf{SOURCE})$	The data item located at **SOURCE** is placed at the new TOS location.
POP DESTINATION	$(\textbf{DESTINATION}) \leftarrow ((SP))$	The data item located at the TOS is placed at the **DESTINATION**.
	$(SP) \leftarrow (SP) + 2$	SP is incremented by 2. The stack contracts by 2 bytes and a new TOS location is established.

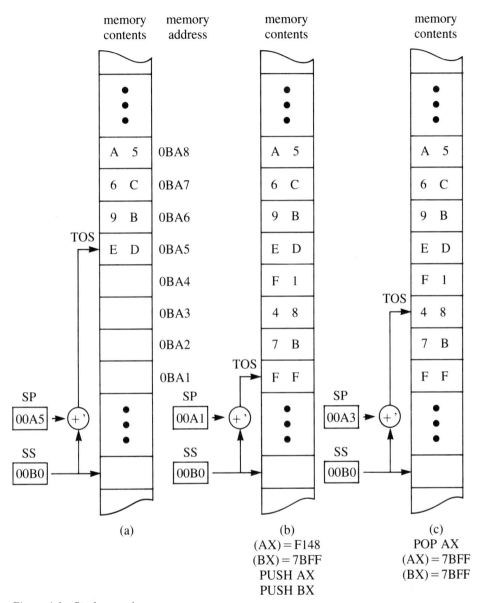

memory   memory   memory   memory
contents address   contents   contents

A 5	0BA8	A 5	A 5
6 C	0BA7	6 C	6 C
9 B	0BA6	9 B	9 B
E D	0BA5	E D	E D
	0BA4	F 1	F 1
	0BA3	4 8	4 8
	0BA2	7 B	7 B
	0BA1	F F	F F

TOS

SP
00A5

SS
00B0

SP
00A1

SS
00B0

SP
00A3

SS
00B0

(a)

(b)
(AX) = F148
(BX) = 7BFF
PUSH AX
PUSH BX

(c)
POP AX
(AX) = 7BFF
(BX) = 7BFF

Figure 4-1 Stack operations.

after the execution of two **PUSH** instructions, with (*c*) showing the stack after subsequent **POP** operation. Notice that items are not actually removed from the stack (i.e., destroyed) when a **POP** operation occurs; only the contents of SP change, and the stack values are copied into the designated destination.

Special versions of these instructions, **PUSHF** (**PUSH** Flags) and **POPF** (**POP** Flags), also are available to store the contents of the flag register on the stack, and to restore the flag register from the stack. This is useful for saving and restoring the flag register on entering and leaving procedures (see Example 3-1).

While the **PUSH** and **POP** instructions allow access to the stack in a LIFO manner, it is often useful to access values of the stack using standard addressing mechanisms, without being constrained by the LIFO ordering. This is of particular importance when the stack is used as a temporary storage area for holding parameters that are to be passed between programs or procedures. One of the most convenient techniques makes use of the BP register. Recall that in operand references where the effective address calculation involves the BP register, the SS is used as the default register to determine the absolute address. Thus, to perform operations directly on values held in the stack, the contents of SP could be moved into BP, and then based or based-indexed addressing modes (using BP) could be used to access the stack. For example, the following instruction sequence moves the contents of the fourth word from the TOS into AX (the TOS position is the first word):

```
MOV BP, SP
MOV AX, [BP + 8]
```

Note that in a similar fashion an override byte can be used to designate the SS register as the segment register to be used in situations where it is not the default.

4.2 PROCEDURES

Effective use of procedures is a key element in writing programs which are well organized, structured, easily understood, and testable. A procedure, sometimes called a *subroutine*, is a body of code whose execution can be started from various places in a program. This is very handy if the same sequence of instructions is required in a number of places. Rather than replicate the sequence of instructions every time it is needed, a single copy of the sequence can be defined as a procedure and "called" whenever needed. Thus, whenever the sequence is to be executed, a special type of program transfer is made, the procedure is executed, and then control returns to the program that initiated the transfer (i.e., the "calling program"). This is illustrated in Figure 4-2, where the program **MAIN** is shown to call a procedure **STAT** 2 times. **STAT**, for example, might be a procedure to calculate statistical values (e.g., mean, variance, etc.) associated with a set of numbers and return the calculated values to **MAIN**.

Use of procedures also helps to create well designed programs. One element in this process involves dividing programs up into modules, each handling a particular function, and each large enough to be useful, yet small enough to be comprehensible (6, 10). A natural way to implement such modules is to construct them as procedures. Further structure can be added to the program development process by organizing modules in a hierarchical fashion. For example, say that the **STAT** procedure of Figure 4-2 performs a number of separate functions. These functions can also be made into procedures which are themselves called by the procedure **STAT**. This idea of procedures calling other procedures is referred to as *nesting procedures* and is illustrated in Figure 4-3 where **STAT** calls the procedures **MEAN** and **AUTO**. Finally, there are situations

memory

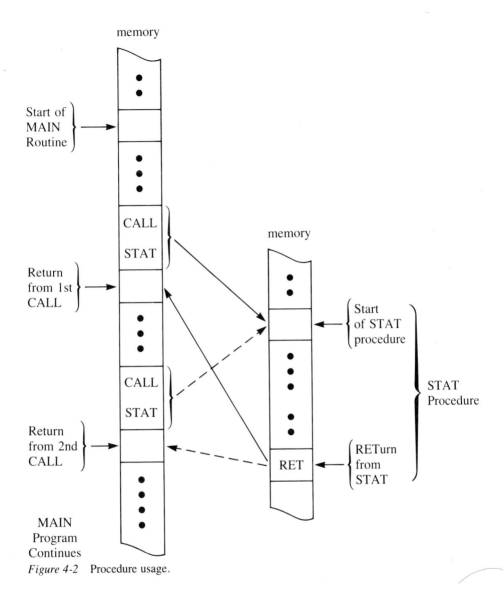

Figure 4-2 Procedure usage.

where it is useful to have procedures call themselves in what is referred to as a **RECURSIVE** manner. This is considered at the end of the chapter, in Section 4.4.

4.2.1 Procedure Calls and Returns

The **CALL** instruction transfers control from the executing program to the called procedure. The instruction is similar to the **JMP (JuMP)** instruction (see Sections 3.1.3 and 4.3) in that both instructions break sequential execution flow, and cause it to

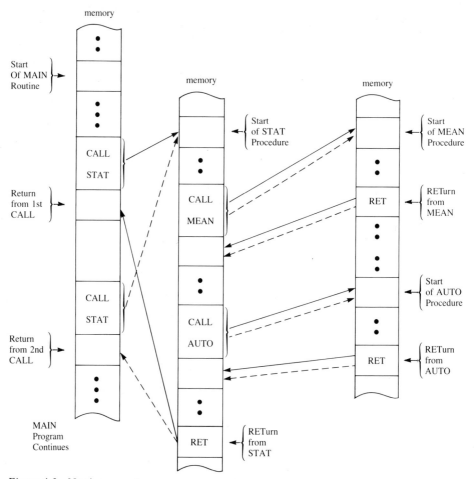

Figure 4-3 Nesting procedures.

continue at some designated target location. It differs from the **JMP** instruction in that the **CALL** saves the address of the instruction to which the procedure is to return, while the **JMP** does not.

The **CALL** instruction (and the **JMP** instruction) comes in two varieties. If the procedure being called is located within the current code segment (*intrasegment*), it is referred to as a **NEAR** procedure; if not (i.e., if *intersegment*), it is a **FAR** procedure. A **CALL** instruction to a **NEAR** procedure need only modify the IP so that it contains the correct offset to the procedure entry point. A **CALL** to a **FAR** procedure must modify both the IP and the CS registers to ensure proper procedure entry.

Consider a **CALL** instruction to a **NEAR** procedure using the direct addressing mode. The instruction format in this case is 3 bytes long, with the first byte specifying the opcode, and the second and third bytes containing a signed 16-bit integer. This integer specifies the difference between the offset of the procedure entry point address and the offset of the **CALL** instruction itself. On executing the **CALL** instruction, this difference is added to the contents of IP to create the offset of the procedure address. The use of a difference permits the development of *position-independent code* (also called *dynamically relocatable*): If the code is moved in its entirety from one part of memory to another without changing the *relative* position of any of its components, it will still execute properly.

CALL instructions to **FAR** procedures which use direct addressing must be concerned with both the IP and CS registers. The **CALL** instruction in this case is 5 bytes long, with the first byte specifying the opcode, the second two bytes specifying the offset of the procedure, and the last two bytes specifying the CS address of the procedure. In this case the offset in the second two bytes is loaded directly into IP, and the contents of the last two bytes are loaded into CS. Relative offsets were not used here because code blocks which reside in different segments will generally not preserve their relative positions when moved around in memory.

CALL instructions to **NEAR** procedures can use all the other addressing modes (except immediate) indicated in Appendix C. In the register mode, for instance, the **CALL** instruction specifies a register containing the offset address to be placed in IP (not the offset difference). In the indirect mode, the **CALL** instruction specifies a register containing a memory address. The two bytes at the memory address referenced contain the 16-bit procedure offset address to be placed in IP.

CALL instructions to **FAR** procedures also can use a variety of addressing modes (except immediate and register). In the indirect mode, for instance, the **CALL** instruction specifies a register containing a memory address. In this case the memory address referenced is the first byte of a double-word block. The first word contains the procedure offset, which is placed in IP, and the second contains the procedure's segment base address which is loaded into the CS register.

The discussion above indicates how the address of the procedure is established in IP and CS on executing a **CALL** instruction. It is also necessary to save the return address of the calling routine so that on completing the procedure the calling routine can be restarted at the correct location. The stack is used for this purpose. The **CALL** instruction first adjusts IP to point to the next sequential instruction that follows it. If the call is to a **NEAR** procedure, the contents of IP now is pushed on the stack, **IP** is next adjusted to point to the procedure, and then execution continues at the procedure entry point. If the call is to a **FAR** procedure, the contents of CS and then IP are pushed

Table 4-2 The **CALL DESTINATION** Instruction

Near Call	Far Call
(SP) ◄——— (SP) − 2 ((SP) + 1 : (SP)) ◄——— (IP) (IP) ◄——— Destination offset or offset difference	(SP) ◄——— (SP) − 2 ((SP) + 1 : (SP)) ◄——— (CS) (CS) ◄——— Destination segment (SP) ◄——— (SP) − 2 ((SP) + 1 : (SP)) ◄——— (IP) (IP) ◄——— Destination offset

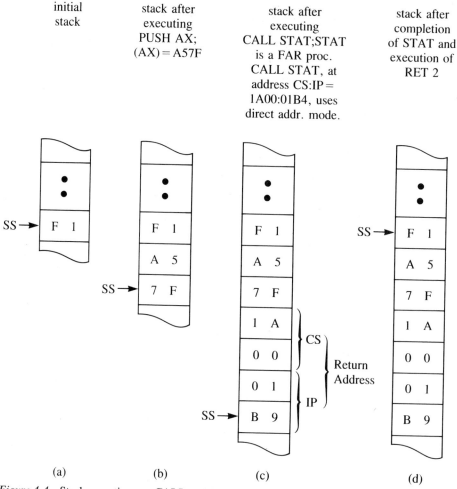

initial stack

stack after executing PUSH AX; (AX) = A57F

stack after executing CALL STAT;STAT is a FAR proc. CALL STAT, at address CS:IP = 1A00:01B4, uses direct addr. mode.

stack after completion of STAT and execution of RET 2

(a)   (b)   (c)   (d)

Figure 4-4   Stack operations on **CALL** and **RET**urn.

on the stack, IP and CS are now loaded to point to the procedure, and then execution continues. Table 4-2 summarizes this process. Figure 4-4 illustrates stack operations resulting from a **FAR** procedure call.

On completing the procedure, a return to the calling routine is performed by executing a **RET** (**RET**urn) instruction. The **RET** instruction restores the IP and CS (for **FAR** procedures) registers by popping the stack and loading these registers with the popped values. Just as there are **NEAR** and **FAR** types of **CALL** instructions, there are **NEAR** and **FAR** types of RET instructions. A **NEAR RET** instruction will pop the stack and adjust only the IP register, while a **FAR RET** instruction will pop the stack and load both the IP and CS registers. It should be clear that it is important to use a **NEAR RET** with a **NEAR CALL**, and a **FAR RET** with a **FAR CALL**. Otherwise the stack will not necessarily contain the correct values for IP and CS. The assembler will normally take care of this automatically.

One final point should be noted regarding the **RET** instruction. A variant of this instruction permits one to add a 16-bit integer to the contents of SP after the IP (for **NEAR** returns) has been popped, or after the IP and CS (for **FAR** returns) have been popped, from the stack. Stack entries can thus be discarded on returning to the calling program. The form of this **RET** instruction is

    RET value

Thus, for example, the instruction **RET   2** pops the stack to set up the return address and then adds 2 to the contents of SP (Figure 4-4*d*). The next section illustrates how this is handy when parameters are passed to and from procedures.

4.2.2 Procedure Parameter Transfer

Procedures often perform tasks that require input data from the calling routine, and they produce results for delivery back to that routine. Clear specification of this transfer process is critical if programs produced by a number of different individuals are to use the procedure effectively. There are three principal methods used in passing data. These are outlined in Table 4-3.

Table 4-3   Procedure Parameter Passing Methods

1. REGISTER METHOD

Approach: General-purpose registers are used to hold the information to be passed. The registers may hold the parameters themselves, or they may hold the addresses of where parameters or parameter lists (arrays) are located in memory.

Advantages: It is easy to pass a small number of parameters. When used to pass arrays of data by passing base addresses, no additional memory is allocated for the data.

Disadvantages: There are a limited number of general-purpose registers available. If these are used by the calling routines for special purposes, they will have to be saved and restored on calling and returning from the procedure.

2. STACK METHOD

Approach: A stack, either the system stack or some other commonly accessed stack, is used to store the parameters, parameter lists, or addresses for parameters or parameter lists.

Advantages: Placing and removing the information on a stack is simple, involving **PUSH** and **POP** commands. Once the procedure is done, and the calling routine has removed any passed information from the stack, the memory allocated for this purpose (i.e., stack elements) is returned to the common memory pool.

Disadvantages: Care must be taken to make sure the stack is cleared properly, and that the stack pointer is at the correct position so that return addresses are accessed properly on executing the **RET** instruction.

3. POST-CALL MEMORY METHOD

Approach: The parameters, parameter lists, or parameter list addresses are stored in the memory locations located immediately after the procedure **CALL** instruction.

Advantages: It is easy for the procedure to determine the location of the parameters, since the return address which is stored on the stack is the memory location directly after the **CALL** instruction.

Disadvantages: It is generally not good practice to mix code and data in the same area in memory. The use of data and code segment registers is intended to encourage this separation. In addition, a fixed amount of memory must be allocated for passing this information, and unlike the stack method, it cannot be easily released for other use on completion of the procedure.

Methods 1 and 2 are generally preferred. Method 1 is convenient when a limited number of parameters or parameter addresses are passed, and when speed is important. Method 2 is more general in scope, and is often used when a broad parameter passing method is to be established across a range of programs and procedures. For example, method 2 generally is employed when assembly language subroutines or procedures are embedded in higher-level language programs (see Chapter 11). Methods 1 and 2 are illustrated in Examples 4-1 and 4-2, respectively.

EXAMPLE 4-1   For certain problems involving simulation and gaming, it is often necessary to generate random integer numbers. The procedure **IRAND1** generates a single positive 8-bit random integer using a shift-register random number generation technique (19). The technique is very fast if the random number to be produced is only a few bits in length. In Chapter 11 it is used as part of a stock market simulation example. It is used in this 8-bit example primarily for demonstration purposes. Figure 4-5 illustrates the basic idea behind shift-register random number generators.

Operation of the random number generator begins with the one-time placement of an initial seed integer in the 16-bit register shown in Figure 4-5. An exclusive **OR** operation is then performed on bits 1 and 2 of the register. The result is a 1 if only one of the two bits is a 1; otherwise, it is a 0. This result is shifted into the most significant bit of the register with other bits in the register being shifted right one position. The rightmost bit is lost in this process. After performing this process 8 times, a pseudo random number is produced in the lower-order byte of the register.

IRAND1 is a procedure which generates a random 8-bit integer using the approach described above. It is called by the program **MAIN1**, which, in this example, merely takes the random integer and displays it on the terminal screen. **MAIN1** makes 40 calls on **IRAND1**, displaying each random character in turn as it is received. The character is passed from **IRAND1** to **MAIN1** using the AL register. **MAIN1** performs the display function by placing the character in DL, loading AH with 2, and then calling a DOS

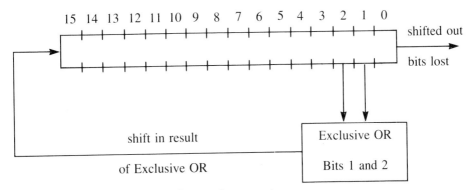

Figure 4-5 Feedback register random number generator.

display routine using the **INT** 21H instruction (see Chapter 9). Notice that **MAIN1** does not require a data segment since all of its operations are register-based.

It is often necessary to generate several random numbers and place them in an array. The procedure **IRANDN** shown in Example 4-2 calls **IRAND1** (which already

```
EXTRN    IRAND1: FAR      ;EXTRN tells the assembler that IRAND1 is a
         ; symbol defined in another module which has the attribute FAR
STAK         SEGMENT  STACK   ;define stack segment STAK
             DW 64 DUP (?)    ;Define 64 word stack
STAK         ENDS             ;end stack segment STAK
;****                 MAIN1 PROGRAM              ****
MAIN1CODE    SEGMENT          ;define code segment MAIN1CODE
MAIN1        PROC    FAR ;MAIN1 program is itself a procedure
             ASSUME CS:MAIN1CODE, SS:STAK
             PUSH    DS       ;Set up
             XOR     AX,AX    ;       MAIN1 for
             PUSH    AX       ;           return to DOS
;
             MOV     CX,40    ;Set loop counter = 40
RLOOP:       CALL    IRAND1   ;Get 8-bit random number
             MOV     DL,AL    ; (DL) <--- random integer in (AL)
             MOV     AH,2     ;Set AH for character display
             INT     21H      ;call DOS display function
             LOOP    RLOOP    ;loop 40 times
;
             RET              ;return to operating system
MAIN1        ENDP             ;end of procedure MAIN1
MAIN1CODE    ENDS             ;end code segment MAIN1CODE
             END MAIN1
;
;****               END OF MAIN1 PROGRAM                ****
;
```

```
; ****                    IRAND1  PROCEDURE                    ****
IRAN_DATA    SEGMENT                      ; define data segment
SEED         DW        231H               ; random # generator seed
IRAN_DATA    ENDS                         ; end of data segment
;
IRAN_SEG     SEGMENT
IRAND1       PROC      FAR
             ASSUME    CS: IRAN_SEG, DS: IRAN_DATA
             PUBLIC    IRAND1        ; Assembler command making symbol
   ;  IRAND1 available to other programs being linked together.
             PUSH      CX                 ; Save caller's CX
             PUSH      DX                 ; Save caller's DX
             MOV       AX, IRAN_DATA
             MOV       DS, AX             ; Set our DS
             MOV       AX, SEED           ; Get seed
             MOV       CX, 8              ; # bits to be generated
;
NEXT:        XOR       DX, DX             ; clear DX
             TEST      AX, 02             ; is bit 1 = 1 ?
             JZ        BIT1E0             ; if bit 1 = 0,  (DL) <--- 0
             MOV       DL, 1              ; if bit 1 = 1,  (DL) <--- 1
BIT1E0:      TEST      AX, 04             ; is bit 2 = 1 ?
             JZ        BIT2E0             ; if bit 2 = 0,  (DH) <--- 0
             MOV       DH, 1              ; if bit 2 = 1,  (DH) <--- 1
BIT2E0:      XOR       DL, DH   ; DL(bit 0) <--- XOR of AX(bits 1, 2)
             SHR       DL, 1              ; carry flag <--- DL(bit 0)
             RCR       AX, 1              ; rotate AX moving the carry
                                         ; flag into the high bit of AX
             LOOP      NEXT               ; loop 8 times until CX = 0
;                                  ; new 8-bit random number now in AL
             MOV       SEED, AX  ; current random # becomes new seed
             POP       DX                 ; restore caller's DX register
             POP       CX                 ; restore caller's CX register
             RET                          ; Intersegment return to MAIN1
IRAND1       ENDP                         ; end procedure IRAND1
IRAN_SEG     ENDS                         ; end codes segment IRAN_SEG
; ****        END OF  PROCEDURE  IRAND1                       ****
             END
```

exists and thus needn't be rewritten or debugged) a number of times to generate several random numbers. The number of random numbers and the address of the array into which they are to be placed is passed to **IRANDN** from the **MAIN2** routine through use of the system stack. This illustrates the stack method of passing parameters. **MAIN2** calls **IRANDN**, and **IRANDN** in turn calls **IRAND1**. This illustrates the idea of *procedure nesting*. Notice that the storage and access of return addresses which occurs when issuing **CALL** and **RET** instructions works perfectly well with nested procedures (see Problem 4- 6).

EXAMPLE 4-2 Procedures for generating enough random numbers to fill up an array **R_ARRAY** are given below. **MAIN2** calls **IRANDN**, passing it the address and length of **R_ARRAY**. **IRANDN** in turn calls **IRAND1** a number of times, each call resulting in the generation of a single random number. Note in **IRANDN** how BP is used to access the parameters on the stack without disturbing the stack pointer.

```
;****                        MAIN2 PROGRAM                      ****
EXTRN      IRANDN: FAR
R_DATA          SEGMENT                 ;define data segment RDATA
R_ARRAY         DB      10 DUP (?)      ;array for random integers
RDATA           ENDS                    ;end data segment definition
;
STAK            SEGMENT STACK           ;define stack segment STAK
                DW      64 DUP (?)      ;stack of 64 words
STAK            ENDS                    ;end stack segment definition
;
MAIN2_SEG       SEGMENT                 ;define MAIN2_SEG code segment
MAIN2           PROC    FAR             ;MAIN2 is itself a procedure
                ASSUME  CS:MAIN2_SEG, DS:RDATA, SS:STAK
START:          MOV     AX, STAK        ;set up stack
                MOV     SS, AX          ;          segment register
                MOV     AX, RDATA       ;set up data
                MOV     DS, AX          ;          segment register
;****                        BODY MAIN2 PROGRAM                 ****
                MOV     AX, SIZE R_ARRAY ;SIZE is an assembler command
                                         ;returning the size of R_ARRAY
                PUSH    AX               ;stack <--- size of R_ARRAY
                MOV     AX, OFFSET R_ARRAY ;OFFSET is an assem. command
                                         ;returning address of R_ARRAY
                PUSH    AX               ;stack <--- address of R_ARRAY
                CALL    IRANDN           ;CALL procedure IRANDN
                RET                      ;return to program which calls MAIN2
MAIN2           ENDP                     ;end procedure MAIN2
MAIN2_SEG       ENDS                     ;end code segment MAIN2_SEG
                END     START
;****                        END OF MAIN2 PROGRAM               ****
                END
;****                        BEGIN IRANDN PROCEDURE             ****
EXTRN      IRAND1: FAR
IRANDN_SEG      SEGMENT                  ;define code segment IRANDN_SEG
IRANDN          PROC    FAR              ;define FAR procedure IRANDN
                ASSUME  CS: IRANDN_SEG
                PUBLIC  IRANDN
```

```
               PUSH    BP              ;save caller's BP
               MOV     BP,SP           ;use BP later to access stack
               PUSH    BX              ;save caller's BX
               PUSHF                   ;save flags for MAIN routine
;****                   PROCEDURE  BODY                    ****
               MOV     CX,[BP + 8]    ;CX holds size of R_ARRAY
               MOV     BX,[BP + 6]    ;BX holds offset of R_ARRAY
               MOV     DI,0           ;DI holds index into R_ARRAY
NEXT:          CALL    IRAND1          ;generate one random integer
               MOV     [BX + DI],AL   ;random integer ---> R_ARRAY
               INC     DI              ;increment R_ARRAY index
               LOOP    NEXT            ;LOOP until CX = 0
;****              RESTORE  REGISTERS  AND  RETURN          ****
               POPF                    ;restore caller's flag register
               POP     BX              ;restore caller's BX register
               POP     BP              ;restore caller's BP register
               RET     4               ;discard parameters and return
IRANDN         ENDP                    ;end of IRANDN procedure
IRANDN_SEG     ENDS                    ;end IRANDN_SEG code segment
;****              END  OF  IRANDN  PROCEDURE              ****
               END
```

4.3 INSTRUCTIONS TO TRANSFER PROGRAM CONTROL

Transferring control from one portion of a program to another is a central feature of most programs. In a well designed program the complexity of such transfers is kept at a minimum, and, when needed, transfers are performed in as straightforward and structured a manner as possible. The IBM PC provides a variety of program transfer instructions. They are listed in Table 4-3 along with their assembler mnemonics and, for conditional transfers, the table includes flags tested by the transfer instruction.

4.3.1 Unconditional Transfers

The unconditional transfers **CALL** and **RET**urn were discussed in the last section on procedures. The jump instruction (**JMP**) is similar to the **CALL** except that no return address is stored on the stack. In both cases a direct addressing form of the instruction is available when intrasegment transfers are required. Such a transfer is implemented by using 2 bytes in the instruction to specify a relative displacement from the current offset address. The displacement word is given as a 2's complement integer which represents the difference between the offset of the instruction following the **JMP** instruction, and the offset of the transfer location. By using a 2's complement number for the displacement, both positive and negative displacements of up to 32 kilobytes may be specified. Thus, from a given address, a 64-kilobyte address space (i.e., a full segment) can be reached. This is illustrated in the following examples.

Table 4-3 Program Transfer Instructions

<table>
<tr><td colspan="3" align="center">Unconditional Transfers</td></tr>
<tr><td>CALL</td><td></td><td>Call a procedure</td></tr>
<tr><td>RET</td><td></td><td>Return from a procedure</td></tr>
<tr><td>JMP</td><td></td><td>Jump</td></tr>
</table>

	Conditional Transfers	
	Flags Tested	Jump If . . .
JA/JNBE	(CF or ZF) $= 0$	above/not below or equal
JAE/JNB	CF $= 0$	above or equal/not below
JB/JNAE/JC	CF $= 1$	below/not above nor equal/carry
JBE/JNA	(CF or ZF) $= 1$	below or equal/not above
JE/JZ	ZF $= 1$	equal/zero
JG/JNLE	((SF xor OF) or ZF) $= 0$	greater/not less nor equal
JGE/JNL	(SF xor OF) $= 0$	greater or equal/not less
JL/JNGE	(SF xor OF) $= 1$	less/not greater nor equal
JLE/JNG	((SF xor OF) or ZF) $= 1$	less or equal/not greater
JNC	CF $= 0$	no carry
JNE/JNZ	ZF $= 0$	not equal/not zero
JNO	OF $= 0$	not overflow
JNP/JPO	PF $= 0$	no parity/parity odd
JNS	SF $= 0$	no sign/positive
JO	OF $= 1$	overflow
JP/JPE	PF $= 1$	parity/parity even
JS	SF $= 1$	sign

	Iteration Controls
LOOP	Loop while CX not equal 0
LOOPE/LOOPZ	Loop while CX not equal 0 and ZF $= 1$
LOOPNE/LOOPNZ	Loop while CX not equal 0 and ZF $= 0$
JCXZ	Jump if CX is zero

	Interrupts
INT	Interrupt
INTO	Interrupt if overflow
IRET	Interrupt return

EXAMPLE 4-3 An intrasegment **JMP** instruction using the direct addressing mode is located at offset address A000H. The jump is to specify a transfer to address 4000H. Determine the displacement word used with this jump instruction.

ANSWER

The **JMP** instruction in this addressing mode is 3 bytes long with the first byte used for the opcode and next 2 bytes used for the displacement. IP therefore contains A003H as the jump instruction is being executed. Subtracting 4000H from A003H yields 6003H. A negative displacement from the current IP location is needed for transfer to 4000H. Taking the 2's complement of 6003H yields the displacement 9FFDH.

EXAMPLE 4-4 Assume an intrasegment **JMP** instruction as in Example 4-3. The **JMP** is to specify a transfer to address 1000H. Determine the displacement word used with this jump instruction.

ANSWER

Subtracting 1000H from an IP address of A003H yields 9003H. This is greater than 32 kilobytes; hence, unlike Example 4-3 above, with 16 bits we cannot form a negative displacement from IP to reach 1000H. However, if the segment address space is viewed as circular with the address 0000 following FFFF, then a positive displacement from A003H can reach 1000H. The displacement from A003H to 0000 is 5FFDH (i.e., 10000H − A003H). Adding the displacement from 0000 to 1000H yields a total displacement of 6FFDH. This can be verified by adding 6FFDH to A003H and discarding the carry-out from the high-order digit.

A short form of the jump instruction (**SHORT JUMP**) is also available for those situations where the transfer location is within −128 and +127 bytes of the instruction following the **JMP**. The relative displacement requires only a single byte rather than the 2 bytes needed for the 32K displacement. The assembler can be directed to produce a short **JMP** instruction by including the word **SHORT** in the instruction. For example, the instruction **JMP SHORT LABEL** tells the assembler to produce a short **JMP** instruction to the address specified by **LABEL**.

EXAMPLE 4-5 An intrasegment **JMP** instruction using the direct address mode is located at A000H. The **JMP** is to specify a transfer to address A080H. Determine the displacement used with this jump instruction.

ANSWER

Being within +128 of the jump instruction (plus 2), a short jump may be used. The short jump is 2 bytes long with one byte being used for the op code, and one byte for the displacement. Adding 2 to the **JMP** instruction address and subtracting it from A080H yields a displacement of 7EH.

In addition to storing a displacement directly with the instruction, intrasegment **Ju**MPs and **CALL**s can also be made using the nonimmediate addressing modes specified in Appendix B. These modes, and the various intersegment addressing modes, are the same for the **JMP** and **CALL** instructions.

4.3.2 Conditional Transfers

Section 3.4 discussed the flag register and the meaning the various flag or condition bits present in that register. The conditional transfer instructions test these bits and perform a jump if the designated condition is present; otherwise the next instruction in sequence is executed. The conditions tested by each jump instruction are specified in Table 4-3. Flag bits may be set and cleared in several ways. First, flag instructions such as **STC** (**S**et **C**arry Flag) and **CLC** (**CL**ear **C**arry flag) are available to set and clear selected flags directly. Second, instructions such as **CMP** (**C**o**MP**are), **CMPS** (**C**o**MP**are String), and **TEST** are present to set flags as result of comparing two or more operands. In the typical sequence, the compare instruction is followed by a conditional jump instruction. Thus, for instance, two operands located in registers **AX** and **BX** can be compared (e.g., **CMP   AX,BX**) and then a conditional jump used to test for operand equality (e.g., **JE   NEXT**). Finally, most instructions set or clear various flags as a result of the instruction operation. The flags affected with each instruction execution are specified in Appendix C.

While many of the conditional transfer instructions are straightforward, one point requires clarification. Notice that there are some instructions which use the terms *above* and *below*, while some use the terms *greater* and *less*. The difference between these terms relates to whether one is dealing with unsigned integers, or 2's complement numbers. Consider the two numbers 0000 0101 and 1111 1011. When interpreted as unsigned integers, the second is "above" the first (251 versus 5). On the other hand, when interpreted as 2's complement numbers, the first is "greater" than the second ($+5$ versus -5). That is, the terms *above* and *below* refer to the relation between two unsigned numbers, while *greater* and *less* concern the relation between two signed numbers. Assuming that a **CMP** instruction is executed prior to issuing a conditional jump, the reader should examine the flag bits set by the **CMP** instruction and then tested for various conditional jump instructions to become acquainted with their operation (see Problem 4-9).

Several points should be noted concerning specification of the transfer address in a conditional jump instruction. First, only the direct addressing mode is available. Second, the addressing information contained in the instruction represents a difference between the **JMP** instruction offset address (actually the offset address of the sequentially executed instruction following the **JMP**) and the transfer location offset address. Third, this difference is specified as an 8-bit 2's complement integer, thus permitting transfer within the current segment, over a -128 to $+127$ byte range. That is, all conditional jump instructions are **SHORT** jumps. While this restricts the jump transfer range, it forces position-independent coding in conditional transfers. In addition, the use of an 8-bit displacement saves a memory byte with this frequently used instruction group.

4.3.3 Iteration Control

Many important algorithms and programs use iteration. That is, they involve repeated execution of some sequence of instructions (called the *iteration sequence*), until some terminating condition occurs. Of course, if that condition never comes to pass, we then have the classic "endless loop" error. Since iteration constructs are used frequently, it is important that iteration control mechanisms be efficient. Consider a program in which there is an instruction sequence which is to be repeated 100 times before executing the subsequent portion of the program. One way of controlling such a loop is to

1. Set up a counter which is initialized to 100.
2. Decrement the counter each time the repeated instruction sequence is completed. (Note that when the result of a **DEC**rement instruction is zero, the ZF will be set to 1.)
3. Use the conditional jump **JNZ** to test the ZF for occurrence of the final iteration. If the final iteration has not taken place, jump back to the beginning of repeated sequence.

As shown in Figure 4-6*a*, this looping construct uses standard move, decrement, and conditional jump instructions. The Intel 8088 also provides some special iteration instructions which aid in implementing loops more efficiently. These instructions (**LOOP**, **LOOPE/LOOPZ**, and **LOOPNE/LOOPNZ**) share several characteristics. First, they typically are used as the last instruction in the iteration sequence as shown in Figures 1-7 and 4-6*b*, and in Example 4-1. Second, they use CX as a counter, decrement CX by 1 on execution, and use the CX = 0 condition for iteration control (in two cases along with another condition). Third, if continued iteration is warranted, control is transferred to a location specified by a **SHORT** label. As with the conditional jump instructions, a short label is a 8-bit 2's complement number which permits transfer over a -128-to-$+127$ byte range relative to the location of the **LOOP** instruction itself. Loop instructions are thus position-independent and require only 2 bytes.

The basic **LOOP** instruction decrements the CX register by 1, and if CX is not zero, transfers control to the target address. If **CX** equals zero, the next instruction in sequence is executed. In addition to testing the CX register for zero, the **LOOPE** (**LOOP** while Equal)/**LOOPZ** (**LOOP** while Zero), and **LOOPNE** (**LOOP** while Not Equal)/**LOOPNZ** (**LOOP** while Not Zero) instructions also test the value of the ZF flag. In the first case, transfer occurs if CX is not zero and if the ZF flag is 1. In the second case, transfer occurs if CX is not zero and if the ZF flag is 0. The three loop instructions are summarized in Table 4-4.

The ability to control loop transfer on the ZF flag is an added programming convenience. For example, say that the instruction sequence to be repeated processes a

```
            .                      .              ;program body
            .                      .
        MOV CX,100             MOV CX,100         ;(CX) <--- iterations
START:                    START:                  ;begin iteration sequence
            .                      .
            .                      .
        REPEATED              REPEATED
        INSTRUCTION           INSTRUCTION
        SEQUENCE              SEQUENCE
            .                      .
            .                      .              ;end iteration sequence
        DEC  CS
        JNZ  START            LOOP   START         ;test for repeat condition
                                                   ;if condition unsatisfied
                                                   ;jump to start
            .                      .              ;program continues
            .                      .
            .                      .
            .                      .

          (a)                    (b)
```

Figure 4-6   Iteration control (loop 100 times).

line of alphanumeric characters which have been read from a terminal and stored in memory. Each loop iteration processes one character in the line. The line may have a maximum length which could be stored in CX, or it may be terminated before that maximum has been reached by making the last valid character a termination character (e.g., carriage return). On comparing each character encountered with the termination character, the ZF flag can be set or reset and the **LOOPNE** instruction can be used for iteration control (see Problem 4.10).

One other instruction in the iteration control group is **JCXZ** (**J**ump if **CX** is **Z**ero). Again, a short-label is supplied with **JCXZ** to allow transfer of control over a -128 to $+127$ byte range on the condition CX $= 0$. Unlike the other loop instructions, CX is not altered by **JCXZ**. This instruction is useful in conditional bypassing of loops.

Table 4-4   Loop Instructions

Instruction	CX Action	Test Condition for Transfer
LOOP	CX $\leftarrow$ CX $- 1$	CX .NE. 0
LOOPE/LOOPZ	CX $\leftarrow$ CX $- 1$	(CX .NE 0) and (ZF .EQ. 1)
LOOPNE/LOOPNZ	CX $\leftarrow$ CX $- 1$	(CX .NE. 0) and (ZF .EQ. 0)

Note that examining the condition CX = 0 before entering a loop is equivalent to testing whether the loop is to be executed zero times.

4.3.4 Interrupts (An Introduction)

In the same spirit as procedure calls, jump, and conditional jump instructions, interrupts alter sequential instruction flow, causing a transfer to some target location. Such a transfer can be initiated in three ways:

1. By executing the interrupt instruction (**INT**). This is called a *software interrupt* since its origin is a program instruction. Many operating system functions and system supplied input/output programs are called using software interrupts.
2. In response to some exceptional condition whose origins are principally within the IBM PC (e.g., divide by zero). This is called an *internal hardware interrupt*.
3. In response to a signal activated by an external device (e.g., a key has been struck on the keyboard). This is called an *external hardware interrupt*.

Unlike calls and jumps, interrupt transfer addresses are held in locations in lower memory with different locations allocated to different types of interrupts. Thus, when an interrupt occurs, the appropriate location in lower memory is automatically accessed and used to reset the CS and IP registers. As with the **CALL** instruction, the stack is used to store the return address of the program which was interrupted. In addition, the contents of the flag register are also saved on the stack.

The program to which control has been transferred is often referred to as the *interrupt service routine*. This routine performs those tasks associated with the particular interrupt which has occurred (e.g., identify the key which has been struck and store its code in a specified location). When this routine has completed, the **IRET** (Interrupt **RET**urn) instruction is typically executed. This instruction is comparable to the **RET** instruction used when returning from a procedure. The instruction retrieves address and flag information from the stack; resets the IP, CS, and flag registers; and transfers control back to the interrupted program. Since interrupts represent a somewhat more advanced topic, detailed explanations and usage are presented in Chapters 9 and 10.

4.4 RECURSIVE PROCEDURES

A procedure that calls itself is referred to as a *recursive procedure*. This is a special form of the nested procedure which was discussed earlier, in Section 4.2. Recursive procedures are useful because certain algorithms can be simply expressed in a recursive manner. Consider, for example, the problem of calculating the factorial of a positive integer. The factorial of a positive integer N is defined to be:

$$N! = N \cdot (N - 1) \cdot (N - 2) \cdot \ \cdots \ \cdot 2 \cdot 1 \qquad \text{for all } N > 0$$

This can be expressed recursively as:

$$N! = N \cdot (N - 1)! \qquad \text{where } 0! = 1, \text{ for all } N > 0$$

That is, $N!$ is defined in terms of $(N - 1)!$. $N!$ may now be obtained by first recursively expanding the factorial expression, and then performing successive multiplications as shown below for the case of 4!. Each line may be viewed as a program or procedure level with the top line corresponding to the calling program and the lower lines corresponding to successive procedure calls. The recursive procedure calls correspond to the left part of the diagram while procedure returns correspond to the right part.

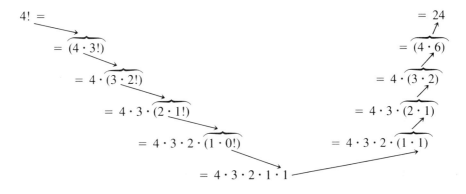

Consider now a procedure **FACT** (Figure 4-7), which is to be used in a recursive factorial calculation. There are two variables of interest here. The first is the integer N. The main calling routine initially pushes N onto the stack and then calls **FACT**. **FACT** recursively calls itself, decrementing N and pushing it onto the stack prior to each call. This is typical of recursive procedures where local variables are passed by storing them on the stack. In the case of the **FACT** procedure, this continues until N equals zero.

Once this occurs, the second variable of interest comes into play. This is referred to as the *partial product*. When the N equals 0 condition has been detected, this partial product is set to 1. On each subsequent return from **FACT** a new partial product is formed (e.g., 1·1, 2·1, 3·2, 4·6, etc.) and passed to the next higher level **FACT** procedure. This partial product could also be passed using the stack; however, in the

```
BEGIN PROCEDURE FACT
    save registers on the stack;
    access stack and obtain N;
    IF N = 0
            PARTIAL PRODUCT <--- 1;  GO TO EXIT
    ELSE
            N <--- N-1;  PUSH N onto stack;
            CALL FACT;
            retrieve N from stack;
            PARTIAL PRODUCT <--- PARTIAL PRODUCT * N;
EXIT:   restore registers;
    RETURN discarding local parameter N;
END PROCEDURE FACT
```
Figure 4-7 Recursive factorial algorithm.

```
;****                    FACT PROCEDURE              ****
;    FACT TAKES THE FACTORIAL OF A POSITIVE NUMBER N.
;    PRIOR TO CALLING FACT, N (A WORD) MUST BE PUSHED
;    ONTO THE STACK. N! IS RETURNED IN AX.
;
FACTSEG SEGMENT                  ;beginning of code segment
FACT PROC     FAR                ;beginning of FAR procedure
        FACT     PUBLIC
        ASSUME   CS:FACTSEG      ;no data segment needed
        PUSH     BP              ;save caller's BP
        MOV      BP,SP           ;[BP+X]  mode will be used to access stack
        PUSH     BX              ;save caller's BX
        MOV      BX,[BP + 6]       ;(BX) <--- N
        CMP      BX,0            ;is N = 0 ?
        JNZ      NXTCALL         ;if N .NE. 0, go to NXTCALL
        MOV      AX,1            ;if N = 0, partial product <--- 1
        JMP      SHORT EXIT      ;exit from procedure
NXTCALL: DEC      BX             ;if N .NE. 0, N <--- N - 1
        PUSH     BX              ;PUSH N - 1 on stack
        CALL     FACT            ;recursive call of FACT,
                                 ;on return AX has PARTIAL PRODUCT
        MOV      BX,[BP + 6] ;(BX) <--- current N
        MUL      BX              ;(DX,AX) <--- N* partial product,
                                 ;assume max. factorial of 64k,
                                 ;(AX) <--- new partial product
EXIT POP      BX                 ;restore caller's BX and BP
        POP      BP
        RET      2               ;return, discard 1 parameter
FACT ENDP                        ;end FACT procedure
FACTSEG ENDS                     ;end FACTSEG code segment
```

implementation shown in Figures 4-7 and 4-8 it is passed using the AX register. Note that while **FACT** is illustrative of a recursive procedure, in this case, it is a very inefficient way to calculate factorials (see Problem 4-14). There are, however, many problems, particularly in the area of data structure manipulation, which are simply expressed and reasonably efficient when solved in a recursive manner (20).

4.5 SUMMARY

Stacks up to 64 kilobytes in length are supported in the Intel 8088. The *Stack Segment* (SS) register contains the base address of a 64K segment within which the stack resides. Many stacks may exist in memory at the same time with the program loading the SS register as necessary prior to operation on the stack of interest. The *Stack Pointer* (SP) register contains an offset from the base address which defines the *Top Of Stack* (TOS) address and this address contains the last data item placed on the stack. Various instructions such as **PUSH** and **POP** (i.e., place/remove an item on/

from the stack) are available to operate on stacks and modify the SP register appropriately. Operations on stacks can also be made directly using the BP register in effective address calculation.

To provide for program clarity and structure it is often useful to partition a program into blocks of code which represent functional modules. Such code modules may be required at different points in the program. *Procedures*, or *subroutines*, provide a mechanism for defining such modules, for permitting a module to be initiated from different points in a program, and, on completion of module execution, for returning to the initiating program. The **CALL** instruction is available to transfer control to and begin execution of a procedure, and the *return* instruction (**RET**) is used to return from a procedure to the calling program. Both instructions use the stack to store and restore critical procedure and calling program addresses. **PUSH** and **POP** instructions can be used to store and restore other registers. Section 4.2.2 considers methods for passing and returning information between calling programs and procedures.

The IBM PC and Intel 8088 have a wide variety of instructions. These instructions may be partitioned into six main groups. The first group contains instructions which allow *transfer* of *program control*. That is, they permit a break in the normal sequential execution of instructions. In this group are the unconditional (e.g., **CALL**, **RET**, and **JMP**) and conditional (e.g., **JA**, **JAE**, etc.) transfer, iteration control (e.g., **LOOP**, **LOOPE**, **LOOPNE**, and **JCXZ**), and interrupt (e.g., **INT**, **INTO**, and **IRET**) instructions. The next chapter considers instructions available for performing arithmetic.

EXERCISES

4.1 Indicate the contents of SS, SP, and the TOS position after each instruction in the program segment given below is executed. Assume: **STACK_SEG** has address 04B5, **DATA_SEG** has address 04E5, **CALL SUB1** is a far call, **SUB1** has address 04F0:0000, DX = 04E5, and **SUB1** only changes contents of AX.

```
PUSH   DS
SUB    AX, AX
PUSH   AX
MOV    AX, STACK_SEG
MOV    SS, AX
MOV    AX, DATA_SEG
MOV    DS, AX
CALL   SUB1
MOV    DS, AX
```

4.2 Consider the example of Figure 4-1. After how many successive **POP** operations would a stack "underflow" condition occur (i.e., although the stack is empty, you are attempting to remove an item)? After how many successive **PUSH** operation would a stack "overflow" occur (i.e., you are attempting to push an item onto a full stack)?

4.3 Show that using a 16-bit 2's complement offset difference as the second two bytes in a **CALL** instruction (direct addressing, **NEAR** procedure call) allows one to call a procedure located anywhere in the current code segment, independent of where in the segment the **CALL** instruction is located.

4.4 Modify the program **IRAND1** of Example 4-1 so that it produces a single random bit whenever it is called. Modify the calling program **MAIN1** so that it checks the random bit produced and displays a T (display code 54H) if it is a 1, and an F (display code 46H) if it is a 0. Have **MAIN1** produce 60 random bits. Assemble, link, and execute the program.

4.5 Determine the first four random integers generated in Example 4-1.

4.6 For Example 4-2, trace the stack contents as it changes from just before the initial call of **IRANDN** from **MAIN2** to just after the final return back to the **MAIN2** routine. Draw a stack and indicate its contents after each major stack contents change.

4.7 For each of the program fragments below (see Figure 1-7 and Example 4-1) indicate the coding of the conditional branch instruction.

a
```
NEXT:   TEST   AX, TEST00
        JNZ    NT00
        SHR    AX, 1
        LOOP   NEXT
        JMP    DONE
NT00:   TEST   AX, TEST01
```
b
```
SLOOP:   CMP   NUMSET[SI], 0
         JL    NXTNUM
         ADD   AL, NUMSET[SI]
NXTNUM:  INC   SI
```

4.8 Which flags are set when the operations indicated are performed on the given operands. Assume that all flags are initially cleared, that AX = 00A0H, BX = 0, and that (**MEM_WORD**) = 00A1H.

a ADD	**AX,MEM_WORD**		**e ADC**	**AX,MEM_WORD**	
b SUB	**AX,MEM_WORD**		**f DAA**		
c MOV	**AX, −2**		**g DEC**	**BX**	
d MUL	**AX,MEM_WORD**		**h RCR**	**MEM_WORD,1**	

4.9 Say that the instruction **CMP   AX,BX** is executed followed by a conditional jump. For each of the situations below indicate what flags are set as a result of the **CMP** instruction, and whether a transfer to the jump address takes place.

a AX = 05H BX = FBH **JA**	**e** AX = 0 BX = FOH **JNA**
b AX = 05H BX = FBH **JG**	**f** AX = 2 BX = 2 **JZ**
c AX = FOH BX = EFH **JNBE**	**g** AX = A0H BX = A1H **JNAE**
d AX = 0 BX = FOH **JLE**	**h** AX = A0H BX = A1H **JNLE**

4.10 Say **ARRAY** is the starting location of an 80-byte array of alphanumeric characters. **ARRAY** may not be completely filled with valid characters. In this case, the last valid character is followed by a carriage return character (0DH). Write a program fragment to increment each valid character in **ARRAY** by 1. Demonstrate in your program the use of a loop-type instruction which tests both CX and ZF.

4.11 Say that an intrasegment **JMP** instruction using the direct addressing mode is located at address 1000H. What displacement value should be used for each of the following transfer addresses.

   a F000H   **b** 1F00H   **c** 6FFFH   **d** 0100H

4.12 A Fibonacci number FIB(N) is defined for all N greater or equal to 1 as follows:

$$FIB(1) = FIB(2) = 1$$
$$FIB(N) = FIB(N - 2) + FIB(N - 1) \qquad \text{for } N > 2$$

Write a recursive procedure for calculating the FIB(N). Clearly define all local variables and how they are placed on the stack. Begin with a higher-level description of the algorithm similar to that shown in Figure 4-7 and then write the assembly language procedure.

4.13 Consider the recursive routine **FACT** given in Figure 4-8. For the case of $N = 4$, draw a diagram showing how the contents of the stack evolves as **FACT** is recursively executed. In particular, show the contents of the stack immediately prior to each **FACT** call, and immediately after execution of each **RETurn** instruction.

4.14 Write a procedure **FACTNR** which calculates the factorial of an integer N in a nonrecursive manner. Assume that N is a word which has been pushed onto the stack prior to calling **FACTNR**, and that N! is returned in register AX. Compare **FACT** and **FACTNR** in terms of execution speed.

4.15 Write a program which displays the binary value found in register AL. Use the general DOS function called by the **INT**   **21H** instruction. This should be preceded by the instruction **MOV**   **AH,2**, which selects the display function, and an instruction which moves a display value into DL. The display value for 0 is 30H and for 1 is 31H. Debug and test this program by placing some test values in AL.

4.16 Using the routine of Problem 4.15, write a program to test the procedure **FACT**, and display the binary value for N!.

5

Arithmetic
Instructions

Performing arithmetic operations quickly and efficiently is often a principal motivation
behind computer usage. The IBM PC and Intel 8088 provide a group of 20 instructions
to perform arithmetic operations on both binary integer and decimal numbers. These
instructions may be divided into four groups corresponding to the four basic arithmetic
operations: addition, subtraction, multiplication, and division. On another basis, these
instructions can be viewed as being divided into those performing binary integer operations, and those performing decimal (packed BCD and unpacked BCD or ASCII)
operations. Floating-point operations are not supported directly in the basic processor
and must be implemented either in software, or by adding the Intel 8087 Numeric
Processor to the system. Tables 5-1, 5-2, and 5-3 summarize the various arithmetic
instructions available.

5.1 INTEGER ADDITION AND SUBTRACTION

The **ADD** (**ADD**ition) instruction performs normal addition of two signed or unsigned
binary integers which may be bytes or words. Since a limited number of bits are used

Table 5-1 Integer Arithmetic Instructions*

ADDITION	**ADD**	dest,src†	**ADD**: (dest) ← (dest) + (src). The src and dest can be two registers, a memory and register, a register and memory, or an immediate operand and a register or memory.
	ADC	dest,src	**AD**d with **C**arry: If CF = 0, then **ADD** as above. If CF = 1, then (dest) ← (dest) + (src) + 1.
	INC	dest	**INC**rement: (dest) ← (dest) + 1. The operand may be in either a register or memory.
SUBTRACTION	**SUB**	dest,src	**SUB**tract: (dest) ← (dest) − (src). The src and dest can be two registers, a memory and register, a register and memory, or an immediate operand and a register or memory.
	SBB	dest,src	**S**u**B**tract with **B**orrow: If CF = 0, then **SUB** as above. If CF = 1, then (dest) ← (dest) − (src) − 1.
	DEC	dest	**DEC**rement: (dest) ← (dest) − 1. The operand may be in either a register or memory.
	NEG	dest	**NEG**ate: (dest) ← 0 − (dest). The operand, located in either a register or memory, is subtracted from 0 thus forming its 2's complement.
	CMP	dest,src	**C**o**MP**are: set flags ← (dest) − (src). As with **SUB** except that the operand result of subtraction is not saved. Only the flag setting results are preserved.
MULTIPLICATION	**MUL**	src	**MUL**tiplication (Unsigned): If src is byte: (AH,AL) ← (src) · (AL). If src is word: (DX,AX) ← (src) · (AX). (AH,AL) and (DX,AX) are double-length results of multiplication in the byte and word cases. If the upper half of the result is not equal to zero then CF and OF are set. The source operand can be either in a register or in memory.
	IMUL	src	Integer **MUL**tiplication (Signed): As with **MUL** except that signed multiplication takes place.

Table 5-1 continued

DIVISION	**DIV**	src	**DIV**ision (Unsigned):
			If src is byte: Quotient, Remainder
			  ← (AL,AH)/src, (AL) ← Quotient, (AH)
			  ← Remainder.
			If src is word: Quotient, Remainder
			  ← (DX,AX)/src, (AX) ← Quotient, (DX)
			  ← Remainder.
			If the quotient exceeds the capacity of AL or AX,
			then both quotient and remainder are undefined
			and a type 0 interrupt is generated. The source
			operand can be either in a register or in memory.

	IDIV	src	Integer **DIV**ision (Signed): As with **DIV** above except that a signed division takes place. If the quotient exceeds the maximum positive or negative number permitted, then quotient and remainder are undefined and a type 0 interrupt is generated.

*All instructions operate on either byte or word operands.

†dest = destination; src = source.

(8 or 16) in the operation, care must be taken so that the result does not exceed the permissible number range. In the unsigned case, additions resulting in an integer greater than 255 for byte operands or 65535 for word operands cause the CF flag to be set, indicating an out-of-range situation. In the signed case, the range extends from -128 to $+127$ for byte operations, and $-32{,}768$ to $+32{,}767$ for word operations. Addition results out of these ranges cause the OF flag to be set. Of course, these flags can be tested with various conditional jump instructions. Note that there are cases where both CF and OF are set (see Problem 5-2).

As indicated in Section 2.2.4, number range can be extended by representing integers with a multiple number of words, and by properly operating on these multi-precision representations. The **ADC** (**AD**d with **C**arry) instruction is provided to facilitate multiple word addition by performing normal byte or word addition, and then adding a 1 to the result if CF is set. Example 2-10 illustrates this process.

The **SUB** (**SUB**traction) instruction performs normal subtraction of two binary integers which may be signed or unsigned bytes or words. The CF flag in this case is

Table 5-2 Sign-Extension Instructions

CBW	Convert **B**yte to **W**ord: The sign of the byte in AL is extended to AH. That is, the leftmost bit of AL is extended throughout AH.
CWD	Convert **W**ord to **D**ouble word: The sign of the word in AX is extended to DX. That is, the leftmost bit of AX is extended throughout DX.

Table 5-3 Decimal Arithmetic Instructions

ADDITION	**AAA**	**A**SCII **A**djust for **A**ddition: (AL) is modified so that it contains a valid unpacked decimal (ASCII) number. Flags AF and CF are updated appropriately.
	DAA	**D**ecimal **A**djust for **A**ddition: (AL) is modified so that it contains a valid packed decimal number. Flags AF and CF are updated appropriately.
SUBTRACTION	**AAS**	**A**SCII **A**djust for **S**ubtraction: If AL contains the result of subtracting two unpacked decimal digits, executing **AAS** modifies (AL), if required, so that it contains a valid unpacked decimal digit.
	DAS	**D**ecimal **A**djust for **S**ubtraction: If AL contains the result of subtracting two packed operands, executing **DAS** modifies AL so that it contains valid packed decimal digits.
MULTIPLICATION	**AAM**	**A**SCII **A**djust for **M**ultiply: If AX contains the result of multiplying two unpacked decimal operands, executing **AAM** modifies AX so that AH and AL each contain valid unpacked decimal digits.
DIVISION	**AAD**	**A**SCII **A**djust for **D**ivision: Executing **AAD** prior to dividing two unpacked decimal operands modifies (AL) so that the resulting quotient in AL will be a valid unpacked decimal digit.

set if the subtraction results in a borrow into the leftmost bit of the result. Subtraction is performed by taking the 2's complement of the subtrahend, and then performing addition. By examining the carry-out of the result's leftmost bit the occurrence of a borrow can be determined: No carry-out indicates that a borrow occurred (CF is set to 1), while the presence of a carry-out indicates a borrow did not occur (CF is set to 0). That is, CF is set to the complement of the carry-out bit. This is shown below in Example 5-1.

EXAMPLE 5-1

```
     38                                              0000 0000 0010 0110
  −  24    0000 0000 0001 10000 → 2's comp →         1111 1111 1110 1000
  ──────                                        [1]  0000 0000 0000 1110
     14
                                                     └─→ CF = 0 (no borrow)
```

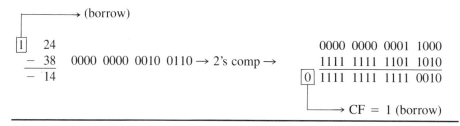

The **SBB** (**S**u**B**tract with **B**orrow) instruction is available to deal with extended precision operands. In this situation, the **SBB** instruction is successively executed on each byte or word pair of the extended precision representation starting with the least significant operand pair. Each execution performs a normal subtraction; however, if the CF flag has been set, indicating that a borrow has occurred, then a 1 is subtracted from the result.

Since adding or subtracting 1 from an operand is a frequent programming operation, **INC**rement and **DEC**rement instructions have been provided to perform this efficiently. In both cases there is a single-byte encoding for incrementing or decrementing a register as well as a 2-byte general form for operands in memory.

Two other instructions are classed with the integer subtraction group. The first is **NEG**ate, which forms the 2's complement of an operand located either in a register or in memory. Thus **NEG   AX** replaces the contents of the word in AX with its 2's complement. Note that the 2's complement representation is not entirely symmetric in that there is one more negative integer than positive integer over the defined range (i.e., for bytes, -128 to $+127$; for words, $-32,768$ to $+32,767$). Performing a **NEG** operation on the most negative integer is therefore a special case which results in no change in the operand and in the OF flag being set.

The final instruction in the integer subtraction group is the **C**o**MP**are instruction. Executing **CMP** results in the source operand being subtracted from the destination operand as in a normal subtraction; however, the result is lost and does not replace the destination operand. The various condition flags are set, and this is the reason for using the instruction. **CMP** is generally followed by a conditional jump instruction which tests these flags. Thus, if two operands are the same, a subtraction will set the ZF flag; this condition could be tested by the **JE** instruction. Note that a 2-byte short form of the instruction is present when comparing an operand with the accumulator.

5.2 INTEGER MULTIPLICATION AND DIVISION

The addition and subtraction instructions work equally well on signed and unsigned integers. Signed and unsigned multiplication and division, however, requires different algorithms, and hence different instructions must be used in each case. The **MUL** and **DIV** instructions are used for unsigned multiplication and division, while the **IMUL** and **IDIV** instructions are used for signed multiplication and division.

Since multiplication of byte operands may yield a 16-bit result, and multiplication of word operands may yield a 32-bit result, provision for differences in operand and result lengths are built into the instruction's operation. In byte multiplication, one byte operand is found in AL while the other is found at the source location. The product is placed in AX, with AL containing its lower-order byte and AH containing its higher-order byte. In word multiplication, one word operand is found in AX while the other is found at the source location. The product's higher- and lower-order words are placed in the double word formed by DX and AX, respectively. This applies to both unsigned (**MUL**) and signed multiplication (**IMUL**). Note also that if the higher-order result is zero (i.e., AH or DX = 0), then the CF and OF flags are cleared to 0; otherwise, they are set to 1. The next section considers using sign-extension instructions to aid in the problem of multiplying a word by a byte.

The division instruction (**DIV**), in a sense, is the inverse of the multiplication instruction. The dividend is assumed to be a double-length operand as if it were a product of some previous multiplication. That is, in the case of byte division, the dividend is the word operand located in AX while the divisor is the byte found at the source location. For word division, the dividend is the double word DX:AX while the divisor is the word found at the source location. The quotient and remainder results are found in AL and AH (for byte division), and in AX and DX (for word division).

The same placement of operands and results also holds for signed division (**IDIV**). In this case, however, on nonintegral divisions, the quotient is truncated toward 0 so that the remainder has the same sign as the dividend. For instance, $+15/-4$ could yield either -3 with R $= +3$, or -4 with R $= -1$; however, the division algorithm selects the first result.

Finally, any division whose result exceeds the capacity of the quotient register will cause a type 0 interrupt. For **DIV** that maximum is 255 and 65,535 for byte and word division, respectively. For **IDIV** the maximum is $+/-127$ for byte division and $+/-32,767$ for word division. A type 0 interrupt results in the flag register being pushed on the stack and then cleared, the CS and IP registers being pushed on the stack, and the words located at memory locations 2 and 0 being loaded into CS and IP, respectively. That is, a **FAR** jump is initiated with CS and IP being loaded from the lowest two words in memory. This is a powerful mechanism which was provided to permit graceful recovery from range violations stemming from division (e.g., divide by zero) operations. A user-provided error recovery routine whose address has been loaded into locations 2 and 0 can thus be automatically invoked when such divide errors occur. (This mechanism is discussed more fully in Chapter 9.)

5.3 SIGN EXTENSION

Table 5-2 outlines the operation of the two sign-extension instructions Convert **B**yte to **W**ord (**CBW**) and Convert **W**ord to **D**ouble word (**CWD**). The **CBW** instruction tests the leftmost bit of AL. If it is a 1 (i.e., AL contains a negative number), then AH is set to FFH; otherwise, it is set to 00H. Thus, the sign of AL is "extended" into AH. In a similar manner, the **CWD** instruction extends the sign of AX into the DX register. These instructions are of particular use when it is necessary to perform signed multiplications and divisions on mixtures of byte and word operands. Take, for instance, the case where a byte operand located in AL is to be multiplied by a word operand found in memory. The **IMUL** instruction assumes that the entire AX register contains a valid operand. In order to ensure that this is true, one could test the sign of the operand in AL and then, depending on the result, load AH with FFH or 00H. The single-byte instruction **CBW** performs this operation.

Consider next the situation where the result of signed multiplication having byte-length operands is to be used as the dividend in a signed division having a 16-bit divisor. Since the **IDIV** instruction uses the double word dividend DX,AX when operating on a word divisor, the multiplication result located in AX must be extended to the double word DX,AX. In order to ensure that DX has the proper sign extension the **CWD** instruction can be executed prior to executing **IDIV**.

5.4 ASCII AND DECIMAL ADDITION AND SUBTRACTION

In Section 2.2.5 the BCD (Binary-Coded Decimal) number scheme was defined. Unfortunately, ordinary binary arithmetic operations, in general, produce incorrect results when applied to BCD numbers. While hardware logic and corresponding BCD instructions could have been designed to perform BCD arithmetic directly, the designers of the Intel 8088 chose instead to utilize the arithmetic instructions available for unsigned binary integers and to provide special adjust instructions which, when used in conjunction with standard integer arithmetic instructions, produce correct BCD results.

Consider first the addition operation. There are three possible outcomes when performing ordinary binary addition on BCD integers.

1. The result is correct (e.g., 0010 + 0011 = 0101).
2. The result is incorrect with an invalid BCD integer being produced (e.g., 0111 + 0011 = 1010). The number 1010, while a valid binary integer, is an invalid BCD integer (i.e., it is out of the BCD digit range 0 to 9).
3. The result is incorrect. However, the lower-order result digit is a valid though incorrect BCD integer (e.g., 1001 + 1000 = 0001 0001).

Condition 2 above can be corrected by detecting when any result digit is greater than 1001 (9D) and then adding in an adjustment factor of 0110 (6D) to that digit. In the example above, 1010 is greater than 1001. Adding in the adjustment factor 0110 yields 0001 0000 (10D), which is the correct result.

Condition 3 can't be detected in the same way since each resulting digit is a valid BCD integer. Notice, however, that in this case a carry was generated out of the least significant digit. If the adjustment factor 0110 is added in when such a carry is generated, then a correct result is produced. The AF flag indicates the presence of such a carry. In the example above adding in the adjustment factor 0110 to 0001 0001 yields 0001 0111 (17D), which is the correct result. That is,

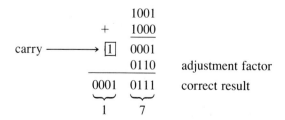

The out of range and carry tests discussed above can be used to perform multiple precision BCD arithmetic, as indicated in Example 5-2.

EXAMPLE 5-2   Add the two numbers 6783 and 3492 using their BCD equivalents in the addition.

ANSWER

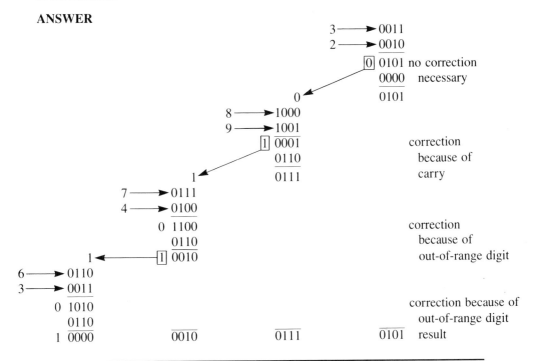

There are two addition adjustment instructions available on the Intel 8088, one dealing with unpacked BCD integers (i.e., a byte contains a single BCD digit in its lower-order 4 bits), and one dealing with packed BCD integers (i.e., a byte contains two BCD digits). Unpacked BCD integers are also referred to as *unpacked decimal* or simply *ASCII* integers. Packed BCD integers are also referred to as *packed decimal* or just *decimal* integers.

The ASCII Adjust for Addition (**AAA**) instruction operates on the result of adding two unpacked decimal digits, where that result is located in the least significant nibble of AL. If the contents of AL are greater than 9, or if the AF flag has been set, the adjustment factor 0110 is added to the least significant nibble of AL, the most significant nibble is cleared to zero, a 1 is added to AH, and the CF and AF flags are set to 1.

The Decimal Adjust for Addition (**DAA**) instruction operates on the results of adding two packed decimal operands, where the results are located in AL. If the least significant nibble of AL is greater than 9, or if the AF = 1, the adjustment 0110 is added to AL and AF is set to 1. Next, if the most significant nibble of AL is greater than 9, or if the CF = 1, 60H is added to AL and CF is set to 1. In this way both the upper and lower nibbles of the packed decimal number are corrected in a single instruction.

In a similar manner, corrective instructions are available to adjust the results of packed and unpacked decimal subtraction to yield the proper BCD numbers. The **A**SCII **A**djust for **S**ubtraction (**AAS**) instruction is used after subtraction of unpacked BCD digits. The **D**ecimal **A**djust for **S**ubtraction (**DAS**) is used after subtraction of packed BCD digits. In general, an adjustment factor of 0110 is subtracted from the results of a BCD subtraction if this result is greater than 9, or if a borrow was needed. Testing for these conditions and performing the adjustment, if necessary, is done by the **AAS** and **DAS** instructions, which should follow directly after the **SUB** or **SBB** instruction employed.

5.5 ASCII MULTIPLICATION AND DIVISION

Adjusting the results of binary multiplication of BCD digits, though possible (see reference 21), is considerably more complicated than with addition or subtraction. For the case of packed decimal numbers, the complexity necessitates extensive additional hardware. For this reason the Intel 8088 designers decided not to provide hardware support for either packed decimal multiplication or division (where equivalent hardware complexity would also be required). If multiplication or division of packed decimal numbers is necessary, then one approach is to first translate the packed numbers into either unpacked BCD or binary representations, use the instructions available for these forms, and then translate back into the packed form.

Unpacked decimal, or ASCII, multiplication is supported with the **A**SCII **A**djust for **M**ultiply (**AAM**) instruction. Consider the multiplication of the two unpacked decimal numbers 7 (0000 0111) and 8 (0000 1000). Standard binary multiplication yields the 16-bit result 0000 0000 0011 1000, while the correct packed decimal result is 0000 0101 0000 0110. Consider now what happens if the binary result, 56, is divided by 10. The quotient, 5, is the correct higher-order BCD digit, while the remainder, 6, is the correct lower-order BCD digit. Following this approach, an algorithm for correcting a binary result located in AX is as follows:

$$\text{QUOTIENT, REMAINDER} \leftarrow \frac{(AX)}{10}$$
$$(AH) \leftarrow \text{QUOTIENT}$$
$$(AL) \leftarrow \text{REMAINDER}$$

This is exactly the operation of the **AAM** instruction. Notice that the upper-order 4 bits of the unpacked decimal numbers to be multiplied must be zero for correct operation. One way of doing this is to use the **AND** instruction to be discussed in Chapter 6.

Algorithms for multidigit unpacked decimal multiplication can now be developed in a straightforward, though somewhat involved, manner. One approach is to follow the same general algorithm used when manually multiplying two multidigit numbers. Notice that after multiplication correction, AH contains the carry digit normally added into the result of the next digit multiplication. After adding in this digit, the **AAA** instruction can then be used to correct the addition result (see Problem 5-8). Morse (reference 21) gives one algorithm for multiplying a multidigit multiplicand with a single-digit multiplier.

In the cases of addition, subtraction, and multiplication, the approach in dealing with packed and unpacked decimal numbers was to perform the operation in question using the standard binary instructions, and then correct the results with an adjust instruction. In the case of division, adjustment is performed prior to use of the standard **DIV** instruction by using the **AAD** (ASCII **A**djust for **D**ivision) instruction. The adjustment transforms the dividend, a two-digit unpacked decimal number located in AH and AL, into its binary equivalent, which is placed into the single-byte register AL. This is done by multiplying (AH) by 10D, adding it to (AL), placing the result in AL, and then clearing AH. The divisor, a single-digit unpacked decimal number, is already its own binary equivalent and needn't be adjusted. Thus, once the dividend is adjusted, the standard **DIV** instruction can be used with the resulting quotient appearing in AL and the remainder in AH.

Note that if the dividend is an arbitrary pair of digits, there is no guarantee that the result of the adjustment and subsequent division operations will be a valid unpacked decimal digit. For instance, if the dividend is 23 (AH = 0000 0010, AL = 0000 0011), then executing **AAD** results in AH = 0000 0000 and AL = 0001 0111. If the divisor is 2, then the results of the **DIV** operation is a quotient of 11D (AL = 0000 1011) and a remainder of 1 (AH = 0000 0001). Clearly the quotient is not a legal unpacked decimal digit. Of what use then is the **AAD** instruction? Consider the example division of a multidigit dividend (5037) by a single digit divisor (6) as given below. R stands for Remainder and Q for Quotient.

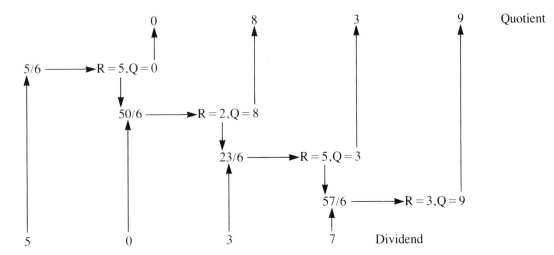

In standard long division, one first performs the division 5/6. The result is 0 with a remainder of 5. The division 50/6 is performed next with this yielding the valid decimal digit 8 and a remainder of 2. The 2 is used along with the dividend digit 3 to form 23 and then to divide 23/6. This yields the valid decimal digit 3 and a remainder of 5. The subsequent division 57/6 yields 9 with a final remainder of 3. Notice that each partial division involves a two-digit dividend and a single-digit divisor, and that the result of the division is always a valid decimal digit. **AAD** instruction is thus well suited to this type of division process. Its use is shown in Example 5-3.

EXAMPLE 5-3 A 10-digit unpacked decimal number (the dividend) is stored in a byte array. The high-order nibble of each digit is assumed to be zero. SI has been loaded to point to the most significant digit in the array which corresponds to the byte with the lowest address. The divisor is a single unpacked decimal digit located in DL. The results of division, also an unpacked decimal number, are to be stored in a byte array. The most significant digit in this array is pointed to by DI. Once again the most significant digit corresponds to the byte in the array with the lowest address. The program fragment below performs the required division, leaving the final remainder in AH.

```
        MOV     AH, 0       ; (AH) <--- 0
        AND     DL, 0FH     ;Clear upper 4-bits of divisor
        MOV     CX, 10      ; (CX) <--- 10, load byte counter
ADIV:   MOV     AL, [SI]    ; (AL) <--- dividend digit
        AAD                 ;Adjust for division.
        DIV     DL          ; (AH,AL) <--- (AH,AL)/(DL) ,
                            ; (AL) <--- QUO, AH ← REM
        MOV     [DI], AL    ;Store one QUOtient digit.
        INC     SI          ; (SI) <--- next dividend digit addr.
        INC     DI          ; (DI) <--- next quotient digit addr.
        LOOP    ADIV        ;DEC CX, IF CX .NE. 0 GO TO ADIV
```

Situations where both the divisor and dividend are multidigit unpacked decimal numbers are more complex. A straightforward (though time-consuming) approach is to perform division by successive subtraction of the divisor from the dividend. An algorithm for the long division process can be developed by starting with the most significant dividend digits and keeping track of the number of subtractions needed. Another approach is to begin by converting the unpacked decimal dividend and divisor into binary numbers, use the standard **DIV** instruction, and then convert the binary result back into unpacked decimal. The range of unpacked decimal numbers which can be handled with this latter approach, of course, is limited (see Problem 5-10).

5.6 SUMMARY

The IBM PC and Intel 8088 provide a variety of *arithmetic* instructions for operation on integer and decimal numbers. Addition (**ADD**, **ADC**, and **INC**), subtraction (**SUB**, **SBB**, **DEC**, **NEG**, and **CMP**), multiplication (**MUL** and **IMUL**), and division (**DIV** and **IDIV**) instructions are provided to support operations on signed and unsigned byte and word integers. Multiple precision operations are supported with the **AD**d with Carry (**ADC**) and **S**u**B**tract with **B**orrow (**SBB**) instructions. Corresponding instructions for unpacked (**AAA**, **AAS**, **AAM**, and **AAD**) and packed (**DAA** and **DAS**) decimal numbers are present. Related instructions to permit sign extension from byte to word (Convert **B**yte to **W**ord, **CBW**), and word to double word (Convert **W**ord to **D**ouble word, **CWD**) enhance mixed byte and word, and word and double-word, operations.

EXERCISES

5.1 Consider the instruction **ADD   AX,BX**. Give examples of the contents of AX and BX such that the results of executing the **ADD** instruction set OF and CF as follows:
   a CF = 0, OF = 0   **c** CF = 0, OF = 1
   b CF = 1, OF = 0   **d** CF = 1, OF = 1

5.2 Verify that on subtraction (**SUB**) a borrow can be detected by noting whether a carry-out occurs when the minuend is added to the 2's complement of the subtrahend. If a carry occurs, there is no borrow (hence CF = 0). If it doesn't occur, there is a borrow (hence CF = 1). Give two examples.

5.3 Perform the addition of the following multiple precision BCD numbers. Add the numbers digit by digit using standard binary addition and add in the adjustment factor where necessary. Show your steps and indicate where adjustment was necessary.
   a 6348 + 5837   **c** 4279 + 8133
   b 3495 + 6775   **d** 1234 + 9876

5.4 Use the data directive statements discussed in Chapter 2 to define the numbers of Problem 5.3a as packed and then unpacked decimal integers. Write two programs to perform the addition indicated—first on the packed and then on the unpacked integer representations.

5.5 Perform the subtraction of the following multiple precision BCD numbers. Subtract the numbers digit by digit using standard binary subtraction, and subtract the adjustment factor where necessary. Show your steps and indicate where the adjustments take place.
   a 5283 − 3992   **c** 5432 − 3456
   b 4928 − 3939   **d** 7254 − 8323

5.6 Use the data directive statements discussed in Chapter 2 to define the BCD numbers of Problem 5.5a as packed and then unpacked decimal integers. Write two programs to perform the subtraction indicated first on the packed and then on the unpacked integer representations.

5.7 Consider the algorithm used for correcting the results of unpacked decimal multiplication. Explain why this algorithm doesn't work on packed decimal data.

5.8 Consider the problem of multiplying two multidigit unpacked decimal numbers.
   a Develop an algorithm using the structured English form of Chapter 1 to multiply a four-digit unpacked decimal multiplicand with a single-digit unpacked decimal multiplier.
   b Following *a*, develop a procedure to perform the specified multiplication. The multiplicand and results are to be located in byte arrays labeled **MCAND** and **MRESULT**, respectively. The multiplier is to be located in a byte labeled **MPLIER**.
   c Develop another algorithm for the case of multiplying two 4-digit unpacked decimal numbers.

5.9 Consider Example 5-3. Say that SI points to an array containing the decimal number 2873657391, and that DL contains the digit 5. Indicate the contents of

AH, AL, CX, and the address pointed to by DI after execution of the following instructions. Do this for the first four iterations through the loop.

```
MOV    AL, [SI]
AAD
DIV    DL
MOV    [DI], AL
```

5.10 Consider the problem of dividing a multidigit unpacked decimal dividend by a multidigit unpacked decimal divisor. Say the algorithm to be used is to first convert the dividend and divisor into binary numbers, then use the **DIV** instruction, and finally convert the result back into an unpacked decimal digit string.

a What range of unpacked decimal multidigit dividends and divisors can be handled with this approach?

b Write a program to convert a 4-digit unpacked decimal integer into its binary equivalent.

c Write a program to convert a 16-bit binary number into its unpacked decimal equivalent.

5.11 Redo Problem 5.10*b*—only this time take the unpacked decimal integer to be six digits in length.

5.12 Consider the problem of multiplying two unsigned double-word (double precision) integers. Let H1 and L1 be the values of the high and low words, respectively, for the first integer. H2 and L2 are the values of the high and low words for the second integer. The multiplication can be performed as follows:

$$
\begin{array}{r}
H1 \cdot 2^{16} \qquad\qquad + L1 \\
\times \quad H2 \cdot 2^{16} \qquad\qquad + L2 \\
\hline
L2 \cdot H1 \cdot 2^{16} \qquad\qquad + L2 \cdot L1 \\
H1 \cdot H2 \cdot 2^{32} + \quad L1 \cdot H2 \cdot 2^{16} \qquad\qquad \\
\hline
H1 \cdot H2 \cdot 2^{32} + (L2 \cdot H1 + L1 \cdot H2) \cdot 2^{16} + L2 \cdot L1
\end{array}
$$

Write a procedure (**DMULT**) to perform multiplication of two unsigned double precision numbers. Assume that the calling program passes operand and result addresses by pushing them on the stack immediately prior to calling **DMULT**. The instruction sequence is **PUSH OPER1, PUSH OPER2, PUSH RESULT, CALL DMULT**.

5.13 Write a procedure to perform the operations given below on 2-digit packed BCD integers found in A and B, and the single-digit unpacked BCD integer found in C.

a $Y \leftarrow (A + 10) - B$

b $Y \leftarrow (A + B) \cdot C$

Clearly define where operands and results are stored, how information is passed to your procedure, and what is the algorithm employed.

6

Other
Internal
Operations

Four other broad instruction groups are available on the IBM PC and Intel 8088 in addition to the program control transfer and arithmetic instruction groups considered in the previous two chapters. These include instructions to facilitate data transfer within the processor and between the processor and external devices (data transfer instructions); instructions to process information at the bit level (bit-manipulation instructions); instructions to operate on blocks of bytes or words which are laid out in memory in a sequential manner (string instructions); and instructions which provide a set of miscellaneous processor control and external device synchronization capabilities (processor control instructions). The operations of these groups are covered in this chapter.

6.1 INSTRUCTIONS FOR DATA TRANSFER

A central operation performed in all programs is the movement of information both within the processor itself (i.e., within and between processor memory and registers) and between the processor and external devices. Table 6-1 lists and briefly explains those data transfer instructions available in the IBM PC and Intel 8088.

Table 6-1 Data Transfer Instructions

GENERAL PURPOSE	**MOV**	dest,src	**MOV**e: Move a word or byte from the source to the destination. The source and destination can be two registers, register and memory, memory and register, or immediate data and register or memory.
	PUSH	src	**PUSH**: Decrement SP by 2, and transfer a word from the source to the stack. The source can be either a register or a memory.
	POP	dest	**POP**: Transfer a word from the stack to the destination, and then increment SP by 2. The destination can be either a register or memory.
	XCHG	dest,src	e**XCH**an**G**e: Exchange the word or byte at the source with the word or byte at the destination. The source and destination can be two registers, or a register and memory.
	XLAT	src-table	Trans**LAT**e: The byte in AL is used to index into a translation table starting at (BX). The byte found at ((BX)+(AL)) is placed in AL. The assembler uses the operand (src-table) to determine if the table is in the current segment.
ADDRESS OBJECT	**LEA**	dest,src	**L**oad **E**ffective **A**ddress: Transfer the offset of the source to the destination. The source is a memory operand and the destination is a 16-bit general register.
	LDS	dest,src	**L**oad **D**ata **S**egment register: The source is a double memory word holding an offset and segment address. The segment address is loaded into DS and the offset is loaded into the 16-bit general register given by the destination.
	LES	dest,src	**L**oad **E**xtra **S**egment register: As in **LDS** above, except that the segment address is loaded into ES.
FLAG TRANSFER	**LAHF**		Load **AH** from **F**lags: Certain flag register bits are loaded into AH where (AH) = (SF):(ZF):(X):(AF):(X):(PF):(X):(CF), X bits are undefined.
	SAHF		**S**tore **AH** in **F**lags: Certain AH bits are loaded into the flag register. This is the reverse of **LAHF** above. The X bits are ignored.

	PUSHF		**PUSH F**lags onto stack: Decrement SP by 2 and transfer the flag register to the top word on the stack.
	POPF		**POP F**lags off stack: The flag register is loaded from the word at the top of the stack. SP is then incremented by 2.
INPUT/ OUTPUT	**IN**	acc,port	**IN**put byte or word: A byte or word is transferred from an input port to AL or AX. The port number may range from 0–255 (uses immediate 8-bit integer) or from 0–64K (uses a 16-bit integer specified in DX).
	OUT	port,acc	**OUT**put byte or word: A byte or word is transferred from the accumulator (AL or AX) to an output port. The port number is specified as above in **IN**.

6.1.1 General-purpose Transfers

There are seven basic types of **MOV** instructions and a variety of possible addressing modes. This leads to a large array of **MOV** instructions ranging from 2 to 6 bytes in length. **MOV** instruction encodings, given in Appendix B, reflect an attempt at efficient encodings for the most commonly used **MOV** instructions. Fortunately, the programmer is generally shielded from this complexity by the assembler, which develops the correct type and encoding from the information provided in the assembly program. **MOV** instructions permit a byte or word to be transferred between registers, from a register to memory, from memory to a register, or from an immediate location to a register or memory. Notice that it is one of a small number of instructions which can operate on segment registers, and provides the principal means for loading and storing these registers. Only the code segment register cannot be loaded directly with either a **MOV** or a **POP** instruction. The reason for this is that loading CS effectively constitutes a jump because it changes the contents of the segment register used (with IP) in determining the next instruction fetch address. When executing the **MOV** instruction, however, the next instruction to be processed is assumed to be the next sequential instruction in memory. A jump in this circumstance, therefore, does not generally make any sense, and such a **MOV** or **POPS** instruction has undefined consequences when attempted. This type of error typically is caught by the assembler during the assembly translation process.

The **PUSH** and **POP** instructions have already been discussed in the context of the stack operations of Section 4.1 and are not pursued here. The exchange instruction, **XCHG**, permits two registers, or a register and memory, to swap words or bytes. A single byte form of the instruction is available for word exchanges between a register and the accumulator.

The translate instruction, **XLAT**, is one of the more interesting instructions in the general-purpose transfer group. Its main use is to facilitate translation from one code to another. A translation table up to 256 bytes in length must be specified by the user prior to use of the instruction (say, by initializing a table through use of a data definition statement). The table is organized so that each code byte to be translated corresponds to an index into the table. This index points to the translated byte. During program execution, when a byte is to be translated, the starting address of the table is loaded into BX, the byte to be translated loaded into AL, and the **XLAT** instruction executed. This results in the translated byte being placed into AL. Example 6-1 illustrates this process with a program to translate an Excess-3 to Gray code.

EXAMPLE 6-1   BCD coding scheme was discussed earlier as one method for representing numbers. The Excess-3 and Gray codes are two other approaches to number representation. Table 4-6 gives the single-digit encoding for each of the two codes. An Excess-3 digit is formed by taking a standard binary code and adding 3 to each value (i.e., 0000 → 0011, 0001 → 0100,...). The Excess-3 code is an example of a **self-complementing** code. Notice that the complement of an Excess-3 digit corresponds to that digit's 9's complement. The Gray code has the property that only a single-bit changes between sequential values.

Table 6-2   Excess-3 and Gray Codes

Decimal Digit	Excess-3	Gray	Decimal Digit	Excess-3	Gray
0	0011	0000	5	1000	1110
1	0100	0001	6	1001	1010
2	0101	0011	7	1010	1011
3	0110	0010	8	1011	1001
4	0111	0110	9	1100	1000

The program fragment below translates an Excess-3 code byte found in location **XBYTE** into its corresponding Grey code representation. The translation table is defined with a DB data definition statement in terms of Excess-3 offsets which yield the corresponding Gray code. Only the lower-order 4 bits of each byte are used.

```
        .
        .
        .
XTABLE  DB      FFH,FFH,FFH,00H,01H,03H,02H  ;translation table
        DB      06H,07H,0AH,0BH,09H,08H ; first 3 entries unused.
        ; value of Excess-3 code is an index into this table.
XBYTE   DB      ?                       ;byte to be translated
        .
        .
        MOV     AL,XBYTE
```

```
MOV     BX, OFFSET XTABLE     ; OFFSET is an assembler
                              ;  pseudo-op giving the
                              ;  offset of XTABLE
XLAT    XTABLE                ; The translated result
                              ;  is found in AL.
  .
  .
```

6.1.2 Address Object Transfers

It is often necessary to know the address of a data structure or object, rather than its value. In Example 6-1 above, the **XLAT** instruction requires that the offset of the translation table be loaded into BX. In Example 4-2, the address of an array was passed as a parameter to a procedure. This latter idea of passing addresses of arrays and structures as parameters rather than the values in the structures themselves is an important programming technique which often improves both execution efficiency and program clarity. Three address object instructions are provided to aid in implementing this idea.

The first **LEA** (**L**oad **E**ffective **A**ddress) transfers the effective address of a memory operand defined in the source field to the 16-bit register (general, pointer, or index) defined in the destination field. In Example 4-2, the offset of array (**R_ARRAY**) is to be pushed on the stack for passage as a parameter to a procedure (**IRANDN**). In the example this is done with the two instructions:

```
MOV     AX, OFFSET R_ARRAY
PUSH    AX
```

The operator **OFFSET** in this situation directs the assembler to determine the offset of R_ARRAY prior to execution, and uses this value as an immediate operand in the **MOV** instruction. Another way of doing this is to use the **LEA** instruction. In this case the instruction sequence would be

```
LEA     AX, R_ARRAY
PUSH    AX
```

In the above situation there is no apparent gain from using the **LEA** instruction. If the memory location whose offset is desired changes during program execution, however, (e.g., R_ARRAY[DI]) then use of the **LEA** instruction is required since the assembler can only know the initial value of the offset.

Say that the segment base address and offset (i.e., logical address) of a data object has been stored in memory as a double-word sequence with the lower-addressed word containing the offset, and the higher-addressed word containing the segment base address. The **LDS** (**L**oad **D**ata **S**egment register) instruction permits this logical address to be loaded into two registers; the segment base address being loaded into DS, and the offset address being loaded into a 16-bit destination register (general register, pointer, or index). The data object can now be addressed with DS containing the correct value, and the offset being available in a register for, say, indexed addressing. The **LES** (**L**oad **E**xtra **S**egment register) operates in the same manner except that the segment base address is placed in the ES register.

6.1.3 Flag Transfers

The **PUSHF** (**PUSH F**lags) and **POPF** (**POP F**lags) instructions permit the flag register to be saved on and restored from the stack. This is useful when entering and returning from procedures where critical flag values needed by the calling routine must be preserved. The flags are stored in two successive stack bytes where the higher- and lower-addressed bytes contain the left and right bytes, respectively, of the flag register (Figure 3-19). The **LAHF** (**L**oad **AH** from **F**lags) and **SAHF** (**S**tore **AH** from **F**lags) instructions load and store five specific flag register bits to and from AH. These instructions are available to support certain Intel 8080 features in the Intel 8088, and are not of direct concern to us here.

6.1.4 Input/Output Transfers

There are a variety of ways to interface peripheral devices with the IBM PC and Intel 8088 (2, 12, 22). One approach utilizes the **IN** (**IN**put) and **OUT** (**OUT**put) transfer instructions. The **IN** instruction permits up to 64K input ports to be addressed. On execution, either a byte or a word is transferred from the addressed input port to AL or AX. In a similar fashion, on executing the **OUT** instruction either a byte or a word is transferred to the addressed output port from AL or AX. Each instruction has two forms. In the first, the fixed-port format, the port to be addressed is specified by an 8-bit address which is located in the instruction itself (e.g., **IN   AL,PORT**). With this form, up to 256 ports can be addressed. Since the writing of self-modifying programs is discouraged, this address, once set in the instruction, is "fixed." In the second form, the variable-port format, the port address is specified by a 16-bit address located in DX. In this case up to 65K port addresses can be specified, and the address itself can be modified by performing operations on DX (e.g., **IN   AL,DX**). This is handy in situations where the same operations are to be performed on a number of ports (e.g., polling ports). Here a common procedure can be established with the port number (to be placed in DX) being modified with each procedure call.

6.2 BIT MANIPULATION INSTRUCTIONS

This section considers instructions which permit direct manipulation of individual bits within bytes and words. These instructions divide into two broad groups: the logical group and the shift/rotate group. Tables 6-3 and 6-4 list and briefly explain these instruction groups.

6.2.1 Bit-Oriented Logic

The first four logic instructions (**AND, TEST, OR,** and **XOR**) require a pair of operands (bytes or words). These may be taken from two registers, memory and a register,

Table 6-3   Bit-Manipulation Instructions

AND	dest,src	Logical **AND**: (dest) ← (dest) **AND** (src). The source and destination can be two registers, memory and register, register and memory, or an immediate operand with either a register or memory. The resulting bit positions are 1 only where corresponding bit positions in both operands are 1. Otherwise they are 0.
TEST	dest,src	**TEST**: (dest) **AND** (src). As with the **AND** instruction except that the result is lost. Used to set flags. Logical equivalent of the **Co**MP**are** instruction.
OR	dest,src	Logical Inclusive **OR**: (dest) ← (dest) **OR** (src). Source and destination locations as with **AND**. The resulting bit positions are 1 if either or both corresponding operand bit positions are a 1. Otherwise they are 0.
XOR	dest,src	**EX**clusive **OR**: (dest) ← (dest) **XOR** (src). Source and destination locations as with **AND**. The resulting bit positions are 1 only if the corresponding operand bit positions are different. Otherwise they are 0.
NOT	dest	Logical **NOT**: (dest) ← **NOT** (dest). The operand can be located either in a register or in memory. Each operand bit position is inverted (i.e., takes the 1's complement).

a register and memory, or an immediate operand and a register or memory location. In addition, with all four instructions CF and OF are cleared and AF is undefined after execution. The remaining flags are set according to the result of the logical operation.

The **AND** instruction performs a logical **AND** of the corresponding bits in the source and destination, placing the result in the destination location. This is useful when it is necessary to clear or mask particular bits in an operand. For instance, when performing various unpacked decimal operations, it is necessary that the high-order 4 bits of the byte operands be cleared. To perform this operation on AL one could execute the instruction **AND   AL,0FH**.

The **TEST** instruction is the logical equivalent to the **Co**MP**are** instruction discussed earlier. With **TEST**, the **AND** operation is performed; however, the result is not saved. The instruction thus serves only to set flags. This instruction can be used to determine the presence or absence of particular bits in an operand. For instance, say that one wants to establish whether bit 2 or bit 3 in AL is set. This can be done with the instruction **TEST   AL,0CH** followed by a conditional branch which tests ZF. If either bit 2 or bit 3 in AL is set, the result will be other than zero.

The **OR** and **XOR** instructions perform the inclusive and exclusive **OR** functions, respectively. **OR** is useful in setting particular bits. For example, **OR   AL,0FH** ensures that the 4 least significant bits of AL are set (other bits are unaffected). **XOR** is useful in complementing particular bits. For example, **XOR   AL,30H** complements bits 4 and 5 of AL. **XOR** can also be used in clearing registers. For example, **XOR   AL,AL** clears the AL register.

OR and **XOR** are often used in the general situation when selected bits must be set, some operation performed, and then the same bits cleared. This occurs, for exam-

Table 6-4 Bit-Manipulation Shift/Rotate Instructions

SAL **SHL**	dest,count dest,count	Shift Arithmetic Left / SHift logical Left: The destination operand may be either in memory or in a register. The operand is shifted left by the amount specified by count. Zeros are shifted into the rightmost bit position with the leftmost bit being successively shifted into CF. Count may be 1, or the value contained in CL. In this latter case, CL must be loaded with desired value and the assembly format becomes **SAL** dest,CL. **SAL** and **SHL** are equivalent assembly mnemonics.
SHR	dest,count	SHift logical Right: The destination operand may be either in memory or in a register. The operation is shifted right by the amount specified by count. Zeros are shifted into the leftmost bit position with the rightmost bit position being successively shifted into CF. The count value is determined as in **SAL/SHL** above.
SAR	dest,count	Shift Arithmetic Right: The destination operand may be either in memory or in a register. The operand is shifted right by the amount specified by count. The leftmost bit position (i.e., the sign bit) is replicated with each shift, with the rightmost bit position being successively shifted into CF. The count value is determined as in **SAL/SHL** above.
ROL	dest,count	ROtate Left: The destination operand may be either in memory or in a register. The operand is rotated left by the amount specified by count. The leftmost bit is successively rotated into both the right-most bit and CF, with the other bits being shifted left accordingly. The count value is determined as in **SAL/SHL** above.
ROR	dest,count	ROtate Right: The destination operand may be either in memory or in a register. The operand is rotated right by the amount specified by count. The rightmost bit is successively rotated into both the leftmost bit and CF, with the other bits being shifted right accordingly. The count value is determined as in **SAL/SHL** above.
RCL	dest,count	Rotate through Carry Left: The destination operand may be either in memory or in a register. CF becomes a 1-bit extension to the operand. This extended operand is rotated left by the amount specified by count. CF is successively rotated into the rightmost bit of the operand with the leftmost bit being shifted into CF, and the other bits being shifted left accordingly. The count value is determined as in **SAL/SHL** above.
RCR	dest,count	Rotate Right through Carry: As in **RCL** except that rotation is to the right instead of the left.

ple, when certain bits must be set in an external peripheral device register to initiate an action, and then later these same bits must be cleared to terminate the action. The following code sequence performs these operations on bits 1 and 2 of port 61H (port 61H is used in controlling the speaker on the IBM PC; see Section 10.6).

```
IN    AL, 61H    ; (AL) <--- port 61H
OR    AL, 03     ; set bits 1 and 2 to initiate action,
                 ; leave other bits undisturbed
OUT   61H, AL    ; port 61H <--- (AL),
                 ; initiate peripheral action

      .          ; action takes place
      .
      .

IN    AL, 61H    ; (AL) <--- port 61H
XOR   AL, 03     ; clear bits 1 and 2 to terminate action,
                 ; other bits left undisturbed
OUT   61H, AL    ; port 61H <--- (AL),
                 ; terminate peripheral action
```

The **NOT** instruction differs from other logical instructions in that it has a single operand, and has no effect on the flags. If AX originally contained 0F0FH, the instruction **NOT**   **AX** would invert all the bits in AX, resulting in its contents being changed to F0F0H.

6.2.2 Shift and Rotate

All seven shift/rotate instructions operate on a single byte or word operand which may be located in memory or in a register. They have the option of shifting/rotating either a single position (count = 1), or a multiple number of positions ranging up to 255 [count = (CL)]. This is determined by the v bit (see Figure 3-18) in the first byte of the instruction. With v = 0 the shift/rotate count is 1. With v = 1, the shift/rotate count is determined by the contents of CL. Figure 6-1 illustrates the operation of these instructions. The isolated bit off to one side in each case represents CF.

The shift instructions may be used to multiply or divide an operand by a power of two. For instance, shifting an operand to the right one bit position halves the number, while shifting to the left one bit doubles the number. The **SHL** and **SHR** instructions may be used in this way for unsigned integers. For signed integers, however, shifting right to divide by a power of two requires that the sign bit be preserved during the shifting process. The **SAR** instruction replicates the sign bit when shifting right, thus permitting division by shifting for signed numbers. Since there is no difference between signed and unsigned integers when shifting left to multiply by a power of two, a single shift instruction (though having two mnemonics: **SHL** or **SAL**) is provided. Note that on left shifting with a count of 1, the OF bit is set if the operation caused the value of the most significant bit to change. Note also that with signed numbers, division by a power of two using a shifting method may yield results which differ from those obtained employing the signed division instruction **IDIV**. This is due to the way the **IDIV**

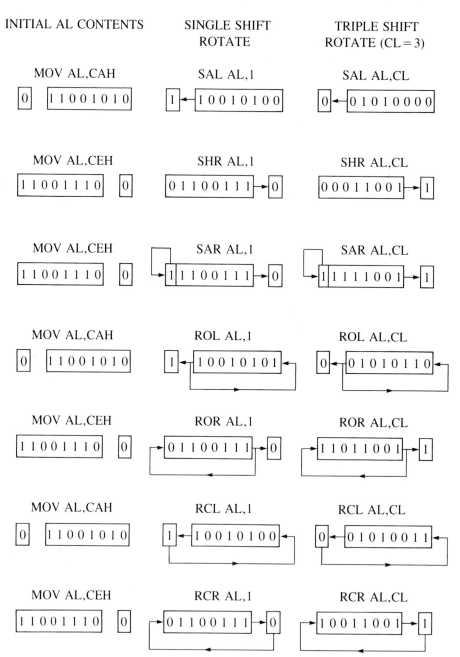

Figure 6-1 Shift/rotate instructions.

instruction truncates nonintegral quotients and handles remainders (see Section 5.2 and Problem 6.6).

The rotate instructions provide a means of shifting bits right or left with the bits shifted off one end of the operand reentering on the other end. This is often termed a *circular shift*. With the **RCL** (**R**otate through **C**arry **L**eft) and **RCR** (**R**otate through **C**arry **R**ight) instructions, CF acts as an extra bit effectively extending the length of the operand. The instruction can be used to isolate individual bits in CF for testing, or to rearrange bit positions in an operand, as needed in a variety of applications (see Example 4-1).

6.3 STRING INSTRUCTIONS

It is often necessary to operate on blocks of bytes or words laid out in memory in a sequential manner. For instance an editor program typically deals with blocks of ASCII characters. Such blocks are referred to as *strings*, and since operations on strings are found in many applications, the Intel 8088 includes a set of string instructions which permit such operations to be performed efficiently. These operations have a number of common properties which are illustrated in the next section by considering the simple problem of moving a string from one section of memory to another. Table 6-5 summarizes the operation of the string instructions.

6.3.1 String Moves and Repeats

Suppose that the contents of **ASTRING**, whose length is 100 bytes, are to be moved into **BSTRING**, also 100 bytes, as shown in Figure 6-2.

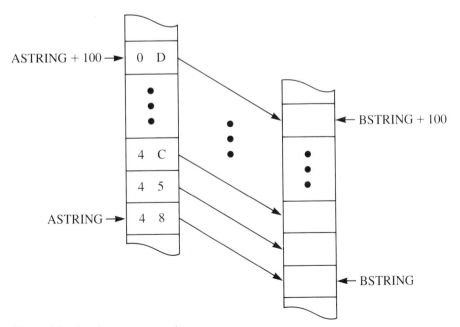

Figure 6-2 A string-move operation.

Table 6-5   String Instructions

MOVS dest-str,src-str **MOVSB**; **MOVSW**	**MOV**e String: **MOV**e **B**yte String; **MOV**e **W**ord String: The byte or word at address (SI) is moved to address (DI). The segment used with SI is the data segment, and that used with DI, the extra segment. Then, if DF = 0, (SI) ← (SI) + Q and (DI) ← (DI) + Q; if DF = 1, (SI) ← (SI) − Q and (DI) ← (DI) − Q. Q = 1 for byte moves, Q = 2 for word moves. Byte or word moves can be requested explicitly using **MOVSB** and **MOVSW**, respectively. With the **MOVS** form, the assembler selects a byte- or word-move operation.
CMPS dest-str,src-str **CMPSB**; **CMPSW**	**CoMP**are String: **CoMP**are **B**yte String; **CoMP**are **W**ord String: The byte or word at address (DI) is subtracted from that at (SI). The result is lost; however, flags are set. See **MOVS** for segment use, (SI) and (DI) modification, and alternative forms.
SCAS dest-str **SCASB**; **SCASW**	**SCA**n String: **SCA**n **B**yte String; **SCA**n **W**ord String: The byte or word at address (DI) is subtracted from AL or AX. The result is lost; however, flags are set. See **MOVS** for segment use, (SI) and (DI) modification, and alternative forms.
LODS src- str **LODSB**; **LODSW**	**LO**ad String: **LO**aD **B**yte String: **LO**aD **W**ord String: The byte or word at address (SI) is transferred to AL or AX. See **MOVS** for segment use, (SI) and (DI) modification, and alternative forms.
STOS dest-src **STOSB**; **STOSW**	**STO**re String: **STO**re **B**yte String; **STO**re **W**ord String: The byte or word in AL or AX is transferred to the address at (DI). See **MOVS** for segment use, (SI) and (DI) modification, and alternative forms.
REP **REPE/REPZ** **REPNE/ REPNZ**	**REP**eat string operation: **REP**eat string operation while **E**qual/**Z**ero; **REP**eat string operation while **N**ot **E**qual/**N**ot **Z**ero: These instructions are used as a prefix to a string instruction (above). While (CX) is not equal to 0, the succeeding string operation is repeatedly executed. For all instruction forms, after each execution (CX) ← (CX) − 1. When (CX) = 0, repetition ceases and sequential instruction processing resumes (i.e., exits from the loop). For string operations where no flags are set (e.g., move) **REP** is used. String compare and scan set flags and may use **REPE/REPZ** or **REPNE/REPNZ** to provide additional termination conditions. For **REPNE/REPNZ**, repetition continues while ZF = 0.

There are five items which must be specified to perform such a move operation:

1. The location of the source string (**ASTRING** or **ASTRING + 100**) in a manner which permits indexing through string values.
2. The location of the destination string (**BSTRING** or **BSTRING + 100**) in a manner which permits indexing through string values.
3. Whether the string is a byte of word string.
4. The number of elements in the string (100).
5. The direction of element transfer. That is, does transfer start at low-memory-address elements (**ASTRING** and **BSTRING**) and proceed to higher addresses, or at high-memory-address elements (**ASTRING + 100** and **BSTRING + 100**) and proceed to lower addresses.

To show how these five items may be specified, consider the program fragment of Figure 6-3*a*, which performs the string move operation indicated above without the use of string instructions. The first two items above are accomplished by designating SI and DI to contain the offset of the source (**ASTRING**) and destination (**BSTRING**) strings, respectively. To access successive string values these registers are incremented in the body of the loop. Item 3 is determined by the assembler after examining the operands of the **MOV** instructions and recognizing that they are byte operands. Item 4 is specified by using the CX register as the count register and loading it with 100. CX is decremented automatically and tested for zero with the **LOOP** instruction. Notice if there were some possibility of CX being equal to zero, then they would have to be preceded with a **JCXZ** instruction. Item 5 is implicit in the program organization. That is, both SI and DI have been loaded and are incremented within the loop so that transfer proceeds from low-order memory addresses to high-order memory addresses.

The string instructions permit the same string move task to be performed more efficiently: Consider first the instruction **MOVSB** (**MOV**e **B**yte String). With this instruction, the offset of the source byte operand located at [SI] is moved to the destination byte operand whose offset is located at [DI]. The segment address for the source operand is found in the data segment register, while the segment address for the destination operand is found in the extra segment register. Use of the extra segment register here facilitates the transfer of strings between segments. Once the byte transfer has been completed, the **MOVSB** instruction then increments or decrements SI and DI by 1. In the above example these registers are incremented; however, if transfer proceeded from high-order memory addresses to low-order memory addresses, the registers would need to be decremented. The DF flag (see Section 3.4) determines whether SI and DI are incremented or decremented. With DF = 0, incrementing occurs, and with DF = 1 decrementing occurs. The **CLD** (**CL**ear **D**irection flag) and **STD** (**S**e**T** **D**irection flag) instructions can be used to clear and set DF. Using **MOVSB**, the program of Figure 6-3*a* can be modified to that of 6-3*b* with a clear increase in efficiency.

Notice that the transfer address of the **LOOP** instruction in Figure 6-3*b* is the address of the preceding string instruction. Since this is often the case, one can envision a **LOOP**-type instruction where this address need not be specified. The **REP** (**REP**eat string instruction) instruction is a 1-byte instruction used as a prefix to string instructions to perform loop-style operations (see Figure 6-3*c*). Used as a prefix to **MOVSB**, the **REP** instruction causes **MOVSB** to be executed repeatedly. After each execution

```
; ASTRING and BSTRING have been defined earlier with
; data directives as byte arrays of length 100. Both are
; located in the same segment.
          LEA    SI,ASTRING      ; (SI) <--- offset of ASTRING
          LEA    DI,BSTRING      ; (DI) <--- offset of BSTRING
          MOV    CX,100          ; (CX) <--- string length
NEXT:     MOV    AL,[SI]
          INC    SI
          MOV    [DI],AL
          INC    DI
          LOOP   NEXT
```

(*a*) String move without a string instruction.

```
; ASTRING and BSTRING have been defined as above.
          MOV    AX,DS           ;ASTRING and BSTRING are in
          MOV    ES,AX           ; the same segment.
          LEA    SI,ASTRING
          LEA    DI,BSTRING
          MOV    CX,100
          CLD                    ;Clear DF for incrementing
NEXT:     MOVSB
          LOOP   NEXT
```

(*b*) String move with **MOVSB**.

```
; ASTRING and BSTRING have been defined as above.
          MOV    AX,DS
          MOV    ES,AX
          LEA    SI,ASTRING
          LEA    DI,BSTRING
          MOV    CX,100
          CLD
REP       MOVSB                  ;As a coding convention the
                                 ; REPeat prefix is often placed
                                 ; on the same line with MOVSB
```

(*c*) String move with **REP   MOVSB**.

Figure 6-3   String move operations.

(CX) is decremented automatically and tested for the condition (CX) = 0. If the condition is true, the program continues at the next sequential execution; if it is false, the process repeats. If (CX) is zero initially, then **MOVSB** is not executed at all and execution proceeds to the next instruction in sequence. Finally, since moving long strings can take a relatively long time, it is important not to delay any interrupts which occur during a repeated string operation (e.g., time-critical data arriving from an input device might be lost). Normally, an interrupt must wait until the currently executing instruction has completed before it is serviced. Repeated string instructions, however, can be interrupted before the entire string operation has been finished. (In the case of **MOVSB** the interrupt is serviced after the current byte has been moved.) The operation will resume properly where it left off on returning from the interrupt (assuming that the contents of SI, DI, CX, DS, and ES have not been disturbed).

The discussion above concerned moving strings of bytes. Moving strings of words follows in the same manner except that the instruction **MOVSW** (**MOV**e **W**ord **S**tring) is employed. Actually, **MOVSB** and **MOVSW** have the same encoding except that the low-order w (word/byte) bit is 0 for **MOVSB**, and 1 for **MOVSW**. During execution, SI and DI are incremented (or decremented) by 2 for **MOVSW** rather than 1 as is the case with **MOVSB**. The repeat operation still decrements (CX) by 1, however; hence for **MOVSW**, CX should be initially loaded with the number of words in the string.

It is sometimes preferable to let the assembler determine whether a byte or word string operation is to be performed. The assembler permits one to designate a string move operation as:

    MOVS dest-string,src-string

Specification of the source and destination strings in this case allows the assembler to determine whether a **MOVSB** or **MOVSW** encoding is required, and to perform certain error checking (e.g., designating a byte string for one operand and word string for the other would cause an error). The source and destination offsets needed in SI and DI must still be explicitly loaded with separate instructions.

6.3.2 String Compare and Scan

The string compare instructions **CMPSB** (**C**o**MP**are **B**yte **S**tring), **CMPSW** (**C**o**MP**are **W**ord **S**tring), and **CMPS** (**C**o**MP**are **S**tring) subtract a byte or word destination operand from a source operand, set the resulting flags, and modify the two operand addresses. The result of the subtraction is lost. As with the string move operations, the offsets of the destination and source are found in DI and SI, and their segment addresses are found in the ES and DS registers. On execution of a string compare DI and SI are incremented or decremented, depending on DF (increment for DF = 0, Decrement for DF = 1), by either 1 or 2, depending on whether a byte or word operation is required. For a byte string compare **CMPSB** is used while for a word string compare **CMPSW** is used (they only differ in the low-order w bit). If it is desired that the assembler decide which string compare to employ, **CMPS** may be used with the operand strings specified. From the string definition statements, the assembler will determine whether a byte or word string operation is needed.

The real power of the string compare comes into play when it is immediately preceded by a **REP**eat prefix. Two types of repeat prefixes are used with string compares, **REPE/REPZ** (**REP**eat string operation while **E**qual/**Z**ero) and **REPNE/REPNZ** (**REP**eat string operation while **N**ot **E**qual/**N**ot **Z**ero). For both types,

1. The string-compare operation is repeated as long as (CX) is not zero and ZF = Q (for **REPE/REPZ**, Q = 1; for **REPNE/REPNZ**, Q = 0).

2. (CX) is decremented and ZF tested on each execution of the string compare instruction.

3. When either (CX) = 0 or ZF = NOT Q, repetition is terminated.

Notice that two conditions now govern termination of the string operation, one on (CX), and one on ZF. It is this additional test on the zero flag that permits one to use the repeat-move string combination to determine the equality of two strings (see Problem 6-9).

The string scan instructions, **SCASB** (**SCA**n **B**yte String), **SCASW** (**SCA**n **W**ord String), and **SCAS** (**SCA**n String) are analogous to the string-compare instructions above, the only difference being that the source field is a constant byte or word located in AL or AX. Thus, SI does not come into play. As with the string compare, the instruction is typically used in conjunction with the **REPE/REPZ** or **REPNE/REPNZ** prefix to form a complete string operation. The repeat-scan instruction can be used for instance to determine if a particular character is found in a ASCII string. The example below shows how it is used to implement a simplified version of the "find and replace" text editing function.

EXAMPLE 6-2 The procedure **CSWAP** is used to search a string for occurrences of a character, and replace each occurrence with another specified character. Thus, a string could be searched for the character A, with each A being replaced with the character B. The character to be replaced is passed to **CSWAP** in AL, and the replacement character is passed in AH. The string address (a single-word offset) and its length (a single word) are pushed on stack (in that order) immediately prior to calling **CSWAP**. Assume that the calling program has set up DS, SS, and ES.

```
;****                        CSWAP PROCEDURE                    ****
;
CSEG      SEGMENT
CSWAP     PROC     FAR              ;calling program
          ASSUME   CS:CSEG          ; has set up DS,SS,ES
          PUSH     BP               ;save caller's BP
          MOV      BP,SP
          MOV      DI,[BP + 6]      ;(DI <--- addr. of dest. string
          MOV      CX,[BP + 8]      ;(CX) <--- string length
          CLD                       ;clear DF for autoincrement
RSCAN:    REPNE    SCASB            ;scan string for occurrence of (AL)
          CMP      CX,0             ;check for end of string
          JE       EXIT             ;if end of string EXIT
          MOV      [DI - 1],AH      ;perform replacement
          JMP      SHORT RSCAN      ;continue search and replace
EXIT:     POP      BP               ;restore BP
          RET      4                ;return and discard 4 bytes
CSWAP     ENDP
CSEG
```

6.3.3 Store, Load, and Complex String Operations

The string store instructions **STOSB** (**STO**re **B**yte String), **STOSW** (**STO**re **W**ord String), and **STOS** (**STO**re **S**tring) provide for the contents of AL or AX to be transferred to a destination address. The destination address is determined by the contents of DI and ES, and the modification of DI follows that of prior string instructions. Since no flags are modified with this instruction, a repeat-store operation terminates when (CX) = 0. Such an instruction can be used to load a string with a single constant value. As will be shown, however, the principal use of the string store is in building up more complex string functions.

The string load instructions **LODSB** (**LO**a**D** **B**yte String), **LODSW** (**LO**a**D** **W**ord String), and **LODS** (**LO**a**D** **S**tring) provide for a byte or word operand to be transferred to AL or AX. The source address is determined by the contents of SI and DS, and the modification of SI follows that of string instructions already discussed. Although the string load instructions could be used in conjunction with a repeat prefix, this doesn't make any sense since the result would be a repeated loading of AL or AX with values which would be immediately overlaid when the next source value was transferred. As with the string store instructions, the string load instructions are also principally used in building up more complex string functions.

Complex string functions refer to string operations other than those implementable with the simple repeat-string instruction pairs discussed above. For instance, say that it is desired to create a new string (the destination string) from a given string (the source string). Each element in the new string is created by multiplying each corresponding element in the original string by 4, and then adding 1. One way of doing this is to use the string load instruction to access each source element, perform the desired transformations, use the string-store instruction to store the transformed value, and imbed this group of instructions within a **LOOP** structure. This is shown in Figure 6-4 where **SSTRING** and **DSTRING** are the source and destination strings, respectively. Both are 160 bytes in length and reside in the same segment. This is typical of the way the string-load and string-store instructions can be used to enhance the efficiency of imple-

```
        MOV    AX,DS           ;SSTRING and DSTRING are in the
        MOV    ES,AX           ; same segment.
        LEA    SI,SSTRING      ;Load SI with SSTRING offset.
        LEA    DI,DSTRING      ;Load DI with DSTRING offset.
        MOV    CX,160          ;Load CX with string length.
        CLD                    ;Clear DF for incrementing.
AGAIN:  LODSB                  ; (AL) <--- Source String Value
                               ;  (SI) <--- (SI) + 1
        SHL    AL,1            ;Multiply by 2.
        SHL    AL,1            ;Multiply by 2 again.
        INC    AL             ;Add 1.
        STOSB                  ;Destination String <--- (AL)
                               ;  (DI) <--- (DI) + 1
        LOOP   AGAIN
```

Figure 6-4 A complex string operation.

menting string operations. Notice that string operations can be terminated on the occurrence or nonoccurrence of a zero result by looping with the **LOOPE/LOOPZ** or **LOOPNE/LOOPNZ** instructions (Figure 6.4).

6.4 PROCESSOR CONTROL INSTRUCTIONS

Processor control instructions are divided into flag instructions and synchronization instructions. The flag instructions permit various flag bits to be set and cleared explicitly under program control. The synchronization instructions permit the Intel 8088 to share resources and synchronize operations with other attached processors (e.g., floating-point processor) and peripheral devices. One final miscellaneous instruction, the **NOP**, is also presented in this section. A listing and brief description of these instructions are given in Tables 6-6 and 6-7.

6.4.1 Flag Instructions

The carry, direction, and interrupt flags can be manipulated by directly using set (**STC**, **STD**, **STI**) and clear (**CLC**, **CLD**, **CLI**) instructions. The carry flag can also be complemented using the **CMC** (CoMplement Carry) instruction. Use of these flags has been considered in Sections 2.2.4, 3.4, 6.2.2, and 6.3. The interrupt flag is discussed further in Chapter 9.

6.4.2 Synchronization and NOP Instructions

The **HaLT** and **WAIT** instructions both facilitate process synchronization by suspending the normal execution of instructions until an external event occurs. In the case of the **HALT** instruction, that event is an enabled interrupt, while in the case of the **WAIT** instruction, it is the assertion of a particular signal (**TEST**) or the arrival of an enabled interrupt. In this latter case, returning from the interrupt routine will again place the processor in the wait state. An attached processor, for instance, could assert the **TEST** signal to indicate completion of an operation.

The **ESC**ape (**ESC**) instruction, on the other hand, can be used to initiate action by an attached processor. The processor, of course, would have to be set up so that it could monitor and respond to Intel 8088 bus signals. The escape instruction can be used to convey to the attached processor that a particular action (an attached processor instruction) is desired by specifying a 6-bit field (i.e, an external op code) within the escape instruction. This 6-bit field, along with the escape instruction operation code,

Table 6-6   Flag Instructions

STC	SeT Carry flag: (CF) = 1	**CLC**	CLear Carry flag: (CF) = 0
STD	SeT Direction flag: (DF) = 1	**CLD**	CLear Direction flag: (DF) = 0
STI	SeT Interrupt flag: (IF) = 1	**CLI**	CLear Interrupt flag: (IF) = 0
CMC	CoMplement Carry flag: If (CF) = 0 then (CF) = 1, else (CF) = 0		

Table 6-7   Synchronization and **NOP** Instructions

HLT	HaLT: The processor halts. It leaves the halt state on receipt of a nonmaskable interrupt or, if **IF** is set, a maskable interrupt.
WAIT	WAIT: The processor enters the wait state. It leaves this state and instruction execution resumes when the **TEST** input signal is asserted. It may also leave this state if an interrupt occurs. The wait state is reentered on returning from the interrupt routine.
ESC	external-opcode,source **ESCAPE**: No operation is performed in the Intel 8086/88. The 6-bit op code specified as part of the instruction is placed on the bus for examination by another processor. The source operand which may be either in memory or in a register is also placed on the bus when it is fetched and it too may be used by some attached processor.
LOCK	LOCK: The instruction acts as a prefix to another instruction. **LOCK** forces assertion of the **LOCK** signal during execution of the next instruction.
NOP	No OPeration: Causes no operation.

can be identified by the attached processor which is monitoring the bus. Recognizing this event, the attached processor can now watch for and capture an operand from the bus. This operand is specified as part of the escape instruction and can be located either in a register or in memory.

Notice that the **ESC**ape instruction can be used with the **WAIT** instruction to prevent an instruction from being sent to the attached processor until it is ready (**WAIT, ESC**), to prevent the Intel 8088 from continuing execution until the attached processor has completed an instruction that it has just been sent (**ESC, WAIT**), or both (**WAIT, ESC, WAIT**). In the context of the IBM PC, the **ESC** and **WAIT** instructions are most commonly used when an Intel 8087 Numeric Data Processor is present in the system. This more advanced topic is discussed in reference 12.

While the above instructions are useful in execution synchronization, the **LOCK** instruction is useful in resource synchronization, or in scheduling resource sharing. In particular, this comes into play when several independent processors share memory. An example of this would be a multiprocessor design (employing multiple 8088s) based on a shared memory approach to interprocessor communication. In such situations, it is important that while one processor is accessing a memory location and is operating on its contents, another processor not attempt to access the same location(s) and perhaps also alter its contents. The **LOCK** instruction, when used as a prefix to some main instruction, asserts the Intel 8088 **LOCK** signal during execution of the main instruction. Another processor, examining this signal, now knows that it should not access memory during this instruction execution period. The **LOCK** instruction can be used in conjunction with the eXCHanGe (**XCHG**) to establish a "test and set" resource synchronization mechanism (12).

Finally the Intel 8088 provides a 1-byte **NOP** instruction which, though fetched as a normal instruction, causes **No OP**eration to take place. **NOP** is sometimes used as a filler instruction to take up time (e.g., in a time-critical loop where some extra delay is needed) or space (e.g., during debugging, when one wants to reserve a few bytes for later replacement by an instruction).

6.5 SUMMARY

Data transfer instructions may be divided into four subgroups. The first contains general-purpose transfer instructions (**MOV**, **PUSH**, **POP**, **XCHG**, and **XLAT**) which perform a variety of move, stack-move, and translate operations. The second contains address object instructions (**LEA**, **LDS**, and **LES**) which are oriented toward transferring offset or segment register information. The third contains flag transfer instructions (**LAHF**, **SAHF**, **PUSHF**, and **POPF**) which are used to save, restore, and move the contents of the flag register. The final subgroup contains input/output instructions (**IN** and **OUT**) which are used to move data from or to an input/output port.

Bit-manipulation instructions allow one to perform logic operations (**AND**, **TEST**, **OR**, **XOR**, and **NOT**) at the bit level, and permit-bit level shifting (**SAL**, **SHR**, and **SAR**) and rotating (**ROL**, **ROR**, **RCL**, and **RCR**) of bytes and words.

String instructions permit efficient operation on sequential groups of bytes or words. When prefaced by a repeat instruction (**REP**, **REPE**, and **REPNE**), these instructions permit an entire string of bytes or words to be moved (**MOVS/MOVSB/ MOVSW**), two strings to be compared (**CMPS/CMPSB/CMPSW**), and a string to be scanned for a particular value (**SCAS/SCASB/SCASW**). Two other string instructions (**LODS/LODSB/LODSW** and **STOS/STOSB/STOSW**) may be used to build up more complex string programs.

Processor control instructions constitute the final instruction group. These instructions may be partitioned into two subgroups. The first contains instructions to set and clear the carry (**STC** and **CLC**), the direction (**STD** and **CLD**), and the interrupt (**STI** and **CLI**) flags. An instruction to complement the carry flag (**CMC**) is also in this subgroup. The second subgroup contains instructions which facilitate synchronization (**HLT**, **WAIT**, and **ESC**) and controlled resource sharing (**LOCK**) of the Intel 8088 with externally attached processors and peripheral devices. The final instruction considered is the **No OP**eration (**NOP**) instruction which, though fetched as a normal instruction, results in no operation being performed.

EXERCISES

6.1 AX, BX, and CX contain FF00H, 0F0FH, and 00FFH, respectively. Show how the contents of the stack changes as execution of each of the following instruction sequences proceeds. Indicate the contents of AX, BX, and CX after completion of each instruction sequence.

a		b		c	
PUSH	AX	PUSH	BX	PUSH	CX
PUSH	AX	POP	AX	PUSH	BX

POP	BX	PUSH	AX	PUSH	AX
PUSH	CX	POP	CX	POP	CX
POP	BX			POP	BX
				POP	AX

6.2 Write a program fragment using the **XLAT** instruction to translate from Excess-3 code (see Example 6-1) to CODE X given below.

DECIMAL	CODE X	DECIMAL	CODE X
0	0100	5	1100
1	0010	6	0001
2	0111	7	1000
3	1110	8	1101
4	1100	9	1011

6.3 A set of 10 arrays each 100 words in length are scattered throughout memory. The logical addresses of these arrays are themselves located in a 20-word array labeled **ARADD**. Each pair of words (i.e., each double word) in **ARADD** consists of an array offset and segment base address. The offset is stored in the lower addressed word and the segment base address in the higher addressed word. Write a program to increment each word in each of the 10 arrays.

6.4 A 128-byte array contains 8-bit ASCII characters. Write a program to convert this array to one containing a string of equivalent packed decimal digits.

6.5 An array of 20 bytes labeled **RARRAY** is viewed as being a binary string of length 240. Write a procedure to determine the location of the first and last bits in the string which are set to 1. Place their bit string locations in AL and AH, respectively. Clearly indicate how the array address is passed to the procedure.

6.6 Assume that an array **RARRAY** is present as in Problem 6.5. Write a procedure to determine how many times the bit pattern 11011 occurs in the bit string and place this value in AL.

6.7 Consider the two cases below of dividing a negative integer by a power of two.
a Dividend $= -12$, Divisor $= 2$
b Dividend $= -11$, Divisor $= 2$
Division can be performed either by shifting or by use of the **IDIV** instruction. Explain any differences which may occur in the results of each division method.

6.8 **ASTRING** and **BSTRING** are defined as byte arrays of length 100 which reside in the same segment. Write a procedure, to be called **INVERSE**, which takes the 1st element of **ASTRING** and places it in the 100th element of **BSTRING**, takes the 2nd element of **ASTRING** and places it in the 99th element of **BSTRING**, etc. Indicate how the **ASTRING** and **BSTRING** addresses are passed to the procedure.

6.9 **ASTRING** and **BSTRING** are defined as byte strings of length 100 which reside in the same segment. Write a procedure which determines if the two strings are equal. If they are equal, place FFH in AL. If they are unequal, determine the first two string positions where they differ. Place the first in AL and the second in AH. If they differ in only a single byte, place its position in AL and FFH in AH.

6.10 **AASCII** is an 80-byte ASCII character string (one character per byte). Write a procedure to determine whether the ASCII carriage return (CR) character is present in the string. Place FFH in AL if it is not present, and its position in AL if it is present.

6.11 **BCDSTR** is an 80-byte string containing unpacked decimal digits. Write a procedure utilizing string instructions to translate the string into one containing equivalent Gray code digits (see Table 6-2).

6.12 Write a program utilizing the shift, rotate, and logical instructions to translate a byte string of length 10 containing unpacked BCD digits (starting at address **UBCD**) into a byte string of length 5 (starting at address **PBCD**) containing the equivalent digits in packed BCD form.

6.13 Write a program to perform the reverse operation of Problem 6.12. That is, the program should take a packed BCD string of length 5 (starting at address **PBCD**) and translate it into the equivalent unpacked BCD string (starting at address **UBCD**).

6.14 **AASCII** is an ASCII character string (one character per byte) which contains text material. The string is terminated with carriage return and line feed characters. Included in the string are blank characters which separate text words. Sometimes multiple blank characters are present. Write a procedure which compacts the string by removing extra blank characters which may appear between words. After executing the procedure only a single blank character should remain between words.

7

Assembly Language

In previous chapters we introduced many of the *macro* assembler features needed to effectively write assembly language programs. This chapter completes these earlier discussions and places the full range of assembler features within a more general framework. (Chapter 8 considers other assembler features of a more advanced nature.) Additional assembler capabilities are presented including assembler expressions, operators, and a number of pseudo-ops. Some features, handy but not essential to most programming tasks, are not discussed here but may be found in reference 23. As before, the assembler assumed to be used is the IBM Macro Assembler, referred to as MASM (23). (Other discussions of the assembler can be found in references 24, 25 and 26.)

7.1 AN OVERVIEW

It will be useful to review Figure 1-8, which indicates just how the assembler fits into the program development process. The figure describes steps along the way to creation of a program module which can be loaded and executed directly by the operating

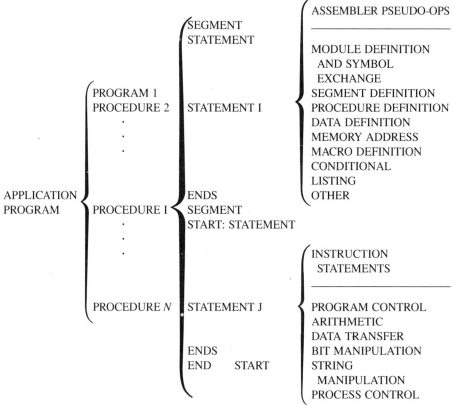

Figure 7-1 Program structure.

system. Figure 7-1 presents another view of this process, this time in terms of the components which make up various objects in the process.

The final application program may be made up of one or more programs and procedures which are linked together by the linker utility. Each one of the programs and procedures, in turn, consists of sequences of statements grouped in segments defined by **SEGMENT-ENDS** pairs, with the entire program or procedure terminated by an **END** statement. This **END** statement indicates to MASM that it has encountered the last source code statement to be assembled as part of this program module. It also identifies the first instruction statement to be executed. The statements themselves are one of two types: *assembler pseudo-operation* or *instruction statements*.

Instruction statements have already been used throughout the text. A typical sequence of instruction statements is shown below.

The central purpose of the assembler is to translate such mnemonic representations (assembly language) into their binary equivalents (machine language). The binary machine language sequences can then be directly interpreted and executed by the computer's central processor. The instruction **MOV   SI,0**, for instance, is translated by MASM into BE0000 (in hexadecimal), where BE is the opcode for an immediate move

ASSEMBLY LANGUAGE SEQUENCE	MACHINE LANGUAGE SEQUENCE

```
        MOV   SI, 0               BE 0000
        MOV   CX, COUNT           8B 0E 000A R
NEXT:   CMP   NUMSET[SI], 0       80 BC 0000 R 00
        JL    NXTNUM              7C 04
        ADD   AL, NUMSET[SI]      02 84 0000 R
NXTNUM: INC   SI                  46
```

Figure 7-2 A program fragment.

to SI, and 0000 is the immediate data. The next **MOV** instruction involves a memory location, **COUNT**, and a register, CX. In this case the assembler determines that the opcode for a memory to CX register transfer is 8B0E. The assembler must also associate a memory address with **COUNT**. If it has been defined elsewhere in the program, MASM can determine its memory address (000A) relative to the beginning of some defined segment. The final value for **COUNT**, however, won't be known until the actual memory locations into which the program is loaded are specified. Since this is generally determined at load time, the address, as specified after assembly, is followed by an R, which indicates that the address is "relocatable." Notice also that MASM must determine addresses and offsets associated with **NUMSET** and **NXTNUM**. **NUMSET** refers to a relocatable address, while the evaluation of **NXTNUM** has resulted in an absolute address offset difference being generated. That is, **NXTNUM** represents a position relative to the **JL** instruction, which is independent of where the program is loaded in memory.

Of course, these tasks could be performed manually with the user determining the area of memory to be used, performing the translation to binary, and then entering the result into the computer's memory. This indeed was done in the early 1950s, before assemblers. Clearly, performing such tasks and dealing with this binary level of detail is time-consuming and error-prone, and likely to drive one at least mildly insane. MASM, LINK, and the loader together remove at least these burdens from the already difficult set of programming tasks.

The tasks described above principally involve translation and address relocation, and result in actual executable instructions. That is why the associated MASM statements are referred to as "instruction statements." *Assembler pseudo-operations* (*pseudo-ops*), on the other hand, are not directly associated with executable instructions; instead they direct MASM to perform certain tasks, set up the overall context within which proper assembly can proceed, or facilitate coding by providing the user with various aids. The **END** statement in Figure 7-1 is one such pseudo-op, as are the various data definition pseudo-ops such as **DB** (**D**efine **B**yte) encountered earlier. Table 7-1 presents the principal assembler pseudo-ops available in MASM. *Macro* and *conditional* pseudo-ops are considered in Chapter 8 and are not included in the table. *Listing* directives which permit the user to control the contents and format of the listing (**.LST**) file created by MASM are not considered since these are conveniences, but are not central to the programming task. The same holds true for those starred (*) pseudo-ops in Table

Table 7-1   Assembler Pseudo-Operations I

Type	Pseudo-op	Purpose
MODULE DEFINITION AND SYMBOL EXCHANGE	**NAME** module-name	Used to give a program module a **NAME**.
	END [expr.]	Specifies the **END** of the source code. The optional expression defines the starting address of the program.
	EXTRN name:type [,...]	Indicates that a symbol used in the current program module is defined **EXTeRN**ally in some other module.
	PUBLIC identifier [,...]	Requests that certain symbols defined in the current module be made available to other modules (i.e., be made **PUBLIC**).
SEGMENT DEFINITION	seg-name **SEGMENT** [align- type][combine-type][class] seg-name **ENDS**	**SEGMENT** and **ENDS** are used to specify a group of statements to be placed within the same memory segment.
	ASSUME seg-reg:seg-name[,...]	**ASSUME** tells MASM what assumptions to make about seg-reg contents.
	GROUP*	**GROUP** collects segments together so that they reside within a single 64K segment.
PROCEDURE DEFINITION	proc-name **PROC** [**NEAR**] or proc-name **PROC** **FAR** proc-name **ENDP**	**PROC** and **ENDP** specify a block of code to be treated by MASM as a procedure.
DATA DEFINITION	identifier **DB** expr.	**DB** (**D**efine **B**yte) permits the allocation and initialization of byte-type variables.
	DW, DD, DQ, DT	**DW, DD, DQ**, and **DT** perform the same function for word, double word, quadword and tenword type data variables.
	RECORD* **STRUCTURE***	**RECORD** may be used to define bit records (0–16 bits). **STRUCTURE** is used to define more complex data structures.

SYMBOL DEFINITION	identifier **EQU** expr. = *	**EQU** and = permit names and labels to be set **EQU**al to expressions.
	identifier **LABEL** type	**LABEL** is used to change the attributes associated with a name or label.
LOCATION COUNTER SPEC	**ORG** expression	**ORG** (**ORiG**in) is used to specify the starting address for instruction or data statements that follow.
	EVEN	**EVEN** directs the next instruction or defined data to begin on a word boundary (i.e., an **EVEN** memory address).
OTHER	**.RADIX** expression	**.RADIX** permits the default radix (normally decimal) to be changed.
	COMMENT del. text del.	**COMMENT** permits the user to enter comments within the program text. The first user-selected character after **COMMENT** acts as a delimiter for the text.
	INCLUDE filespec	**INCLUDE** permits assembler statements found in another file to be entered into the current assembly process.

7-1. Discussions of these may be found in reference 23. Details related to pseudo-op usage are considered later in the chapter.

Before considering particular instructions and assembler pseudo-ops, it is necessary to examine their components. A statement has the following general syntax:

```
NAME/LABEL    MNEMONIC/PSEUDO-OP    argument, . . . ,argument    ;comment
```

NAMES and **LABELS** are composed of characters as indicated in Table 7-2. Various reserved words are used for instruction *mnemonics* (see Chapters 4, 5, and 6, and Appendices B and C) and *pseudo-ops*. Statement arguments will vary from one statement type to another. In some cases the argument may be a general type of expression, while in another it may have a very limited syntax. Table 7-2 defines some of the basic components found in statements, while the next section considers some of the next-level components which make up statement names, labels, and arguments.

Table 7-2 Fundamental Statement Components

Item	Purpose and Constraints	Examples
IDENTIFIERS (SYMBOLS)	User-developed names for identifying constants, variables, or address labels. Can be up to 31 characters in length, including alphabetic (A thru Z), numeric digits (0 thru 9), or characters ?, @, and $. First character cannot be a digit. See reference 23 for special constraints on the use of ".".	**NXTNUM** **Z** **Z23_ABS** **PORT1_VAL** **LOOP1_LOC**
RESERVED WORDS	To provide instruction/control information to the assembler. Reserved words include standard instruction mnemonics, register abbreviations, assembler pseudo-ops, and other assembler operators. Use of these words as names for constants, variables, or address labels will lead to MASM confusion.	**ADD, CALL, AX, AH, AL, END, PUBLIC, OFFSET, NEAR, DUP, SIZE**
SPECIAL CHARACTERS	Blanks and horizontal tabs are used as separators between identifiers, reserved words, etc. Carriage return (CR) and CR/line feed are used as separators between successive statements.	
,	Used as an argument separator.	**MOV SI,[BP + 6]**
?	Used in data definition pseudo-ops to specify indeterminate data initialization.	**X DB ?**
;	Characters following ; on the same line are treated as a user comment.	**X DB ? ;comment**
+ − * /	Used as operators in expressions.	**Y EQU X1 + X2/4**
( )	Used to specify operator precedence in expressions, and repeat blocks in data pseudo-ops.	**Y EQU (X1 + X2)/4**
'	Delimiter for defining ASCII strings.	**TWOCHAR DB 'AB'**
:	Used in specifying **NEAR** labels and segment-override conditions	**MOV AX,ES:[SI]**

Table 7-2   continued

Item	Purpose and Constraints	Examples
[ ]	Used in defining various addressing modes.	
< >	Used in record and structure definitions.	
.	Used in structure definitions.	
=	A pseudo-op used to associate a value with a name.	
− , ! , % , ; ;	Special symbols used with the macro facility.	

7.2 CONSTANTS, VARIABLES, LABELS AND THEIR ATTRIBUTES

The use of mnemonic reserved words for op codes and pseudo-ops, coupled with the ability to create identifiers for constants, variables, and address labels, greatly eases the assembly language programming task. We now examine the properties and attributes of user-defined constants, variables, and address labels and, in the course of this discussion, introduce certain of the pseudo-ops.

7.2.1 Constants

A constant is a data item whose only attribute is its fixed value. Constants are used for immediate data values in instruction statements and are also used in various pseudo-ops wherever an expression is permitted. Expressions, also considered later, are groups of operators and operands which are evaluated during assembly to produce a value. There are three type of constants: integer, character string, and real number.

Integer constants may be represented in binary, decimal, hexadecimal, or octal number systems by attaching B, D, H, or Q, respectively, to the integer value. In the following statements the 16-bit constants moved into AX all are equal.

```
MOV    AX,1111010101111010B
MOV    AX,62842D
MOV    AX,0F57AH
MOV    AX,172572Q
```

Note that hexadecimal constants must start with an integer (0 to 9) so that it can be distinguished from variable names or labels. If the default radix is decimal (the normal case), then the D can be omitted and the above instruction can be written as **MOV   AX,62842**. The default radix can be changed by using the **.RADIX** pseudo-op. For instance,

```
.RADIX 16        ;make default radix hexadecimal.
       .
       .
MOV  AX,0F57A    ;H is omitted. Default base is 16.
```

The **.RADIX** command has no effect on the **DD**, **DQ**, or **DT** pseudo-ops, which assume a decimal default unless specifically overridden with some other data suffix. Note also that **.RADIX** is a command to the assembler which tells it how to interpret various numbers and does not result in the generation of any machine instructions.

Since some constants are used frequently within a program, it often is convenient to define them symbolically at the beginning of the program using the **EQU**al pseudo-op. This also may help clarify the program's intent. For instance, say that the ASCII character for carriage return (13D) is periodically used within a text processing program. The **EQU**al pseudo-op could be used as follows.

```
CR    EQU    13D    ;define CR as carriage return
             .
             .
             .
      MOV    AL, CR
```

In this situation the assembler will replace CR by its ASCII binary equivalent whenever it appears in the program. Remember **EQU**, like **.RADIX**, is also a pseudo-op and thus does not produce any instructions. It merely tells the assembler to replace the symbol on the left with the value on the right whenever the former is encountered during the assembly process.

Alphanumeric characters and character string constants are defined by enclosing the characters in single quotes (e.g., **'D'**, **'ABLE'**). The constants thus produced are the ASCII representation of the characters within the quotes. Two examples using character constants as immediate operands are given below.

```
MOV   AL, 'A'
MOV   BX, 'AB'
```

The first instruction moves the ASCII value for A (01000001B) into AL, while in the second statement the ASCII values for AB are copied into BX. Longer character string constants are often defined with the **DB** (**D**efine **B**yte) pseudo-op. For instance,

```
CR          EQU   13D    ;define ASCII carriage return
LF          EQU   10D    ;define ASCII line feed
                   .
                   .
STARTMES1   DB    'HELLO', CR, LF
STARTMES2   DB    'ENTER PASSWORD', CR, LF
                   .
                   .
```

HELLO and **ENTER PASSWORD** are character string constants. In each case, the assembler will translate the characters enclosed in the quotes into their ASCII equivalents and then perform operations associated with the **DB** pseudo-op. In this case, the strings are followed by carriage return and line feed characters.

In a similar fashion, real number constants using either base 10 or base 16 may be defined. Real decimal numbers require either a decimal point or explicit exponent specification using the E notation (e.g., 2.56, 596.34E-2). Hexadecimal real numbers must be followed with the letter R (e.g., FF29A3R, A39CFR). Such constants may be used, for instance, in data pseudo-ops. Consider, for example, the following defined short real numbers (see Section 2.2.4 for a review of real number representations) which are equivalent:

```
SHORTREAL1   DD   2482.0    ;decimal short real
SHORTREAL2   DD   .2482E4   ;decimal short real
SHORTREAL3   DD   9A02R     ;hexadecimal short real
```

7.2.2 Variables

A variable is an actual area of memory where values are stored. Variables are named (note that constants need not be named) and typically are defined with a data definition pseudo-op. Thus **STARTMES1**, **SHORTREAL1**, and the identifiers associated with data pseudo-ops found in the data segment of our various sample programs all are variables. Variables have three attributes: *segment*, *offset*, and *type*. Values for these attributes are developed and maintained by the assembler during the assembly process and can be accessed during assembly to aid in the programming process.

Consider first the two attributes *segment* and *offset*. Each variable is initially defined within a program segment. The segment attribute is the paragraph address (i.e., paragraph addresses are all those 20-bit addresses which have their lower-order 4 bits equal to zero) associated with the variable's segment. The offset attribute is the address offset of the variable within its segment. In Figure 7-3 two segments are used to initialize data variables. The variables **ABYTE**, **AWORD** and **XTABLE** all have as their segment attribute the address given by the assembler to the **ZDATA** segment, while the variables **BBYTE** and **SECOND10** have the segment address of **XDATA** as their segment attribute. **ABYTE** and **BBYTE** have an offset of 0000 since they are the first defined data elements in the segment. **AWORD** and **SECOND10** have an offset of 0001, while **XTABLE** has an offset of 0003.

Why does the assembler maintain these attributes? The reason relates to how the assembler determines offset addresses and segment registers to associate with variables encountered during the instruction encoding process. Consider the **MOV** instruction labeled **AMOVE** in Figure 7-3. Since the offset address and segment have been stored as **ABYTE** attributes (done when the **ABYTE** data pseudo-op was encountered), this information is now available when the **MOV** instruction is encoded. While the offset can be used directly in the instruction encoding, a question arises regarding the segment.

The default segment register used for the memory operand in a **MOV** instruction is DS. But how does the assembler know that the contents of DS corresponds to the segment associated with **ABYTE**? The answer to this relates to the **ASSUME** pseudo-op. Basically the **ASSUME** pseudo-op tells the assembler what to assume about the contents of the various segment registers. In the case of **ABYTE**, since its segment attribute is the same as the segment associated with DS in the **ASSUME** statement, the instruction can be encoded directly.

Consider next the **MOV** instruction labeled **BMOVE**. In this case the memory operand **BBYTE** is not in the DS segment as specified by the **ASSUME** statement. This is known to the assembler by comparing the **BBYTE** segment attribute with the assumed DS contents. The **BBYTE** segment attribute, however, does correspond to the assumed ES contents. The assembler in this case generates an ES override prefix

```
ZDATA       SEGMENT
ABYTE       DB          10
AWORD       DW          ?
XTABLE      DB          0FFH, 0FFH, 0FFH, 00H, 01H, 03H, 02H
            DB          06H, 07H, 0AH, 0BH, 09H, 08H
ZDATA       ENDS
;
XDATA       SEGMENT
BBYTE       DB          20
SECOND10    DB          'KLMNOPQRST'
XDATA       ENDS
;
CODE        SEGMENT
ASSUME      CS: CODE, DS: ZDATA, ES: XDATA, SS: NOTHING
BEGIN:      MOV         AX, ZDATA
            MOV         DS, AX          ; set up Data Segment
            MOV         AX, XDATA
            MOV         ES, AX          ; set up Extra Segment
                        .

AMOVE:      MOV         AL, ABYTE
BMOVE:      MOV         AH, BBYTE       ; don't need ES: BBYTE since
                                    ;  assembler automatically generates
                                    ;  segment override
            INC         ABYTE
MISMOV:     MOV         AL, AWORD       ; type mismatch
                        .
                        .
            MOV         AL, ABYTE       ; ABYTE contains character to
                                        ; be translated
OFFMOV:     MOV         BX, OFFSET XTABLE
            XLAT        XTABLE
                                ; AL now contains translated value
                        .
                        .
TYPVAL:     MOV         AL, TYPE AWORD  ; (AL) <--- 2 since AWORD
                                        ;  has been defined as a word
                        .
SRCALL:     MOV         AX, SEG AWORD  ; push segment address
            PUSH        AX                  ;  for AWORD on the stack
            MOV         AX, OFFSET AWORD ; push offset address
            PUSH        AX                  ;  for AWORD on the stack
            CALL        ALPHA
                        .
            ENDS
```

Figure 7-3 A sample program.

for the instruction. Generation of the **BBYTE** address during program execution will then use ES to obtain the segment address.

Note that it is the programmer's responsibility to ensure that assumptions regarding DS, ES, and SS segment register contents are correct. This is typically done by beginning each program with a series of **MOV** instructions as shown in Figure 7-3.

Type is the final variable attribute. Using the data pseudo-op, the assembler determines the variable *type*. That is, is it a byte, word, double word, quadword, tenbyte, structure, or record? The latter two advanced types are not considered in this text. This type information is used in instruction encoding and operand type matching. Consider, for example, the **INC**rement instruction in Figure 7-3. The mnemonic **INC** does not in itself specify whether a byte or word is to be incremented and, as you may recall, the w bit in the encoded **INC** instruction must reflect whether a byte (w = 0) or word (w = 1) increment is to be performed. The assembler determines how to set this bit by examining the *type* attribute of the operand. In this case since **ABYTE** is of type *byte*, the **INC** opcode is encoded with w = 0. Notice that this is very convenient since this allows us to have a single instruction mnemonic for byte and word instructions.

The *type* attribute is also used by the assembler to determine whether there is a type mismatch. This is illustrated in Figure 7-3 with the **MOV** instruction labeled **MISMOV**. In this case, **AWORD** has type *word* (it has been defined with a **DW** statement) and an attempt is being made to move it into a byte-sized register. The assembler will flag this as an error.

Clearly the assembler needs to access these attributes to perform its instruction encoding tasks properly. During the assembly process it is sometimes also helpful to make these attributes available to the programmer. This is permitted through use of a set of *assembler operators*. Consider, for instance, the situation where it is necessary to load the offset address of a translation table into BX prior to execution of the translate instruction (**XLAT**), as illustrated by the **MOV** instruction labeled **OFFMOV** in Figure 7-3. Here the reserved word **OFFSET** acts as an assembler operator. It tells the assembler to access the offset attribute of **XTABLE**. This value is then used as an immediate operand in the **MOV** instruction.

In a similar manner **SEG** (for **SEG**ment) and **TYPE** are reserved words which act as assembler operators. **SEG** and **OFFSET** are sometimes useful when it is necessary to place both the offset and segment of a parameter on the stack prior to calling a subroutine. This is shown in Figure 7-3 with the instructions starting with label **SRCALL**. When using the **TYPE** operator, the assembler produces a value for each variable type (byte = 1, word = 2, double word = 4, quadword = 8, ten bytes = 10). Figure 7-3, the **MOV** instruction labeled **TYPVAL** moves **TYPE AWORD** into AL. Since **AWORD** has been defined with a **DW** statement, the assembler replaces **TYPE AWORD** with the immediate operand 2.

7.2.3 Labels

A label is an identifier referring to the memory address of a labeled instruction or a procedure. It represents a location which can be used as a destination in a **JMP** or **CALL** instruction. Labels, like variables, have three attributes: *segment*, *offset*, and *type. Segment* and *offset* correspond directly to the variable attributes discussed in the previous section. They represent the segment and offset location where the label was defined. For instance, the label **BEGIN** in Figure 7-3 has the paragraph address of **CODE** for its segment and 0000 for its offset. Also, as in the case of variables, the **SEG** and **OFFSET** operators can be used to access these attributes during the assembly process.

The *type* attribute, in the case of labels, refers to whether the label is **NEAR** or **FAR**. **NEAR** labels are accessible by jump or call instructions within the same physical segment. In this case, only offset address information is needed, and the assembler can encode an intrasegment transfer. **FAR** labels are accessible by jump or call intructions in different segments. Here both offset and segment information must be encoded for the proper transfer within a segment. A colon (:) after a label identifies it as being **NEAR**; otherwise it is **FAR**. Labels associated with procedure definitions are defined to be **NEAR** or **FAR** by having the words **NEAR** or **FAR** present in the **PROC** pseudo-op statement. Thus, the procedure **TRIG** is defined to be **NEAR** with the statement

```
TRIG    PROC    NEAR
```

The procedure is defined to be **FAR** with

```
TRIG    PROC    FAR
```

The **TYPE** operator, when used with labels, returns -1 if the label is **NEAR** and -2 if it is **FAR**.

7.3 ASSEMBLER EXPRESSIONS AND OPERATORS

MASM expressions consist of operators which act on operands to produce a value at assembly time. Expressions may appear in certain assembler pseudo-ops. For instance, one place where they are useful is in the initialization of data.

```
XADDR    DW    OFFSET ABYTE + 10
```

The expression in this case is **OFFSET ABYTE + 10**. Here the operator **OFFSET** acts on the operand **ABYTE** (a variable or label) to obtain its offset address. This offset is then added to 10 with the result being the initial value to be placed in location **XADRR**. In general, the use of a variable or label name within an expression refers to the offset of the variable or name within its defined segment. Thus, the above expression is equivalent to **ABYTE + 10**.

Expressions may also be used within instructions. For example, consider the shift right assembly operator, **SHR**, in the following instruction:

```
MOV    AX, 0FB36H SHR 4      ; (AX) <--- 0FB3H
```

The expression **0FB36H SHR 4** directs the assembler to shift the number FB36H right four bit positions. The result is 0FB3H, which is now used as an immediate operand in encoding the **MOV** instruction.

MASM provides a variety of operators, and the ability to create fairly complex expressions. Their use represents a more advanced programming technique and thus the remainder of this section may be omitted by those desiring to gain an overview of MASM without initially going into many of its details.

To form expressions we must first know the set of available operators and their permissible operands. Two types of operands are considered—numbers and identifiers (variables or labels). While operations on numbers follow generally accepted arithmetic rules, operations on identifiers are more complex and the complete set of rules governing them is beyond the scope of this book (see reference 24). In general, an identifier operation is acceptable if its results make physical sense. Thus, multiplying **ABYTE** and **AWORD** of Figure 7-3 (**ABYTE * AWORD**) is not permitted since the meaning of multiplying two offsets is not clear (e.g., in what segment would the resultant address reside?). In a similar fashion, subtracting **AWORD** from **SECOND10** (**AWORD − SECOND10**) has questionable meaning since the two variables are defined in different segments. Table 7-3 presents MASM operators along with a brief explanation of their purpose.

Note that an operand designated as "number" means an individual number value known at assembly time (e.g., **2436H**, **128D**, etc.). A numeric expression is an expression involving numbers which can be evaluated to a number at assembly time (e.g, **2436H**, **2436H * 2**, **(2 + 128)*5**, etc.).

We have already encountered expressions involving addresses and the simple arithmetic operators **+** and **−**. MASM permits such expressions as **NUMBER + 4** and **[BX + 2]** to be written as **NUMBER[4]** and **[BX][2]**. This alternative form is illustrated below.

```
ADD    AX, NUMBER [4]        ; ADD AX, NUMBER + 4
ADD    AX, [BX] [2]          ; ADD AX, [BX + 2]
ADD    AX, [SI] [2]          ; ADD AX, [SI + 2]
ADD    AX, [BX] [SI]         ; ADD AX, [BX + SI]
ADD    AX, [BX] [SI] [2]     ; ADD AX, [BX + SI + 2]
```

Many of the operators shown in Table 7-3 are useful in conjunction with conditional pseudo-ops, which are treated in the next chapter. As a preliminary example, however, consider the situation where a variable (**DQWORD**) may be either a double word or a quadword. Assume that **DQWORD** is defined with a data pseudo-op early in the program. Say that for a particular operation of interest, a different code has been developed for each possible **DQWORD** type. At assembly time it is desired to include in the program the code that is appropriate for the **DQWORD** type defined. Figure 7-4 below illustrates how this might be done.

The assembler, on encountering the **IF** conditional pseudo-op statement, evaluates the expression to its right—in this case, **TYPE DQWORD EQ 4**. **TYPE DQWORD** is evaluated first and is equal to 4 if **DQWORD** is of type double word, or 8 if **DQWORD** is of type quadword. If **DQWORD** is a double word, then the relational operator **EQ** returns all 1s (*true* condition) and the double-word code (from **IF** to **ELSE**) is assembled and included in the program. If **DQWORD** is a quadword, then the relational operator returns all 0s (*false* condition) and the quadword code (from **ELSE** to **ENDIF**) is assembled and included in the program. In this way, the program is specialized at assembly time to include only that code needed for the particular

Table 7-3 Assembler Operators

Category	Operator	Explanation
ARITHMETIC	**HIGH,LOW**	**HIGH** and **LOW** act to produce the **HIGH** or **LOW** byte of the operand (numeric expression, label, variable): **MOV AL,HIGH(1B4FH) ;(AL) <--- 1B**
	+ , −	Normal addition and subtraction of two operands (expression, labels/variables) in the same segment: **MOV AL,ABYTE + 2**
	*, /, MOD	Normal multiplication, division, modulo operations on two operands (numbers): **CMP AX,3445/5**
	SHR,SHL	**SH**ift **R**ight (**SHR**) or **L**eft (**SHL**) the operand (numeric expression) by the number of bits specified (number): **CMP AL,0F117H SHL 2**
LOGICAL	**OR,XOR,** **AND,NOT**	Normal logical operations of two operands (numbers): **MOV AH,6CH OR 16H ;(AH) <--- 7EH** **MOV AH,6CH AND 16H ;(AH) <--- 04H**
RELATIONAL	**EQ, NE** **LT, LE** **GT, GE**	Normal relational operations of **EQ**ual, **N**ot **E**qual, **L**ess **T**han, **L**ess than or **E**qual, **G**reater **T**han, and **G**reater than or **E**qual. Operations are performed on two operands (both numbers, or both variables or labels, defined in same module and segment). All 1s (true), or all 0s (false) are returned: **MOV AL,42 GE 32 ;(AL) <--- FFH**
RETURN ATTRIBUTE VALUE	**SEG, OFFSET,** **TYPE,** **LENGTH,** **SIZE**	**SEG**ment, **OFFSET**, and **TYPE** operate on either a variable or a label and return the designated attribute (see Section 7.2). **LENGTH** and **SIZE** operate on variables and return the number of data items and number of bytes (**SIZE = LENGTH*TYPE**) defined for the variable: **ARRAY1 DB 0,1,2,4,8,16,32,64** **;LENGTH =SIZE=8** **ARRAY2 DW 10 DUP (0)** **;LENGTH=10, SIZE=20** **MOV AL,LENGTH ARRAY1 ;(AL) <--- 8** **MOV AH,SIZE ARRAY2 ;(AH) <--- 20**

Table 7-3   continued

Category	Operator	Explanation

SET/ OVERRIDE ATTRIBUTE VALUE	**SEG.OVR.**	**SEG**ment **OVeR**ide operators specify the segment to be associated with a variable or label. One form uses the segment mnemonics CS,DS,ES, and SS:
		**MOV AL,ES:ABYTE ;Use ES for
		                          ;ABYTE segment**
		Another form uses the segment name (Figure 7-3):
		**MOV AL,XDATA:BBYTE ;Use XDATA
		                              ;segment**

	SHORT	**SHORT** requests encoding of a **SHORT** jump instruction (Section 4.3): **JMP SHORT LABEL ;LABEL must be ;NEAR.**

	PTR	**PTR** (format: **TYPE PTR VARIABLE** or **LABEL**) permits a variable, label, or expression to have its *type* set or overriden. For example,
		**QWORD DW F124H ;QWORD is type
		                          ;WORD**
		**MOV AL,BYTE PTR QWORD
		                      ;override QWORD's type**

	THIS	**THIS** (format: **THIS TYPE**) specifies a new variable or label of a given type. No memory is allocated for the variable or label so specified. For example,
		**AWORD EQU THIS WORD ;Contents of
		ABYTE1 DB ? ;ABYTE1 and
		ABYTE2 DB ? ;ABYTE2 can be
		                       ;referenced with AWORD
		                       ;whose type is WORD.**

existing conditions; hence the term "conditional assembly expansion." Logical, relational, and return attribute operators are widely used in such conditional assemblies.

As already indicated, the return value operators **SEG** and **OFFSET** are useful when segment or offset address values of a variable or label are needed in the program. In a similar fashion, the **LENGTH** and **SIZE** operators are useful when developing vector or array programs where the length or size of the vector is needed in the program (e.g., to initialize a counter). For example, consider moving the contents of the byte array **ASTRING** to the byte array **BSTRING** where both arrays are of equal length and are in the same segment. A program to do this was presented in Figure 6-3. This program could also be written as follows:

```
      DQWORD               ;data pseudo-op for DQWORD
             .             ;program statements
             .
             .

      IF   (TYPE DQWORD EQ 4)   ;pseudo-op beginning IF/ENDIF pair
             .             ;beginning of code for TRUE condition
             .             ;double-word code
             .

      ELSE         ;pseudo-op defining end of code for TRUE condition
             .             ;beginning of code for FALSE condition
             .             ;quadword code

      ENDIF                ;pseudo-op defining end of IF/ENDIF pair
             .             ;other program statments
             .
             .

      END  START       ;final statement in module
```

Figure 7-4   Expressions with conditional code Expansions.

```
      MOV    AX, DS
      MOV    ES, AX                 ;set up ES for string operation
      MOV    SI, OFFSET ASTRING     ;set up ASTRING offset in SI
      MOV    DI, OFFSET BSTRING     ;set up BSTRING offset in DI
      MOV    CX, LENGTH ASTRING     ;set up string length in CX
      CLD                           ;set up direction of move
      REP       MOVSB               ;perform string move
```

The **PTR** and **THIS** operators require a bit more discussion. The **PTR** operator can be used to override the previously defined type definition of a variable with a new type. Thus

```
      AWORD    DW    0F124H        ;AWORD is type WORD
               .
               .
               .

             MOV  AL, BYTE PTR AWORD    ;override AWORD's type
```

In this case, the **PTR** operator directs MASM to assemble a byte **MOV** even though **AWORD** was defined as a word. Another way of doing this would be to define a new variable, **ABYTE1**, as the first byte of **AWORD**, as shown below.

```
      AWORD    DW    0F124H        ;AWORD is type WORD
      ABYTE1   EQU   BYTE PTR AWORD
               .
               .
               .

             MOV  AL, ABYTE1  ; (AL) <--- low byte of AWORD
```

The second byte of **AWORD** could be accessed as **ABYTE2** using the statement **ABYTE2 EQU BYTE PTR (AWORD + 1)**.

Another place **PTR** is used is in those situations where a label has been defined as being of a particular type (say **NEAR**); however, at some other point in the program it is necessary to reference the label as having the opposite type (say **FAR**). This is illustrated in the following code segment where MASM assembles **NPLACE** as a label of type **NEAR** and **FPLACE** as a label of type **FAR**.

```
NPLACE:  MOV    AL,02        ;The : makes NPLACE a NEAR label
            .
            .
         JMP    NPLACE       ;NEAR JMP
            .
            .
FPLACE   EQU    FAR PTR NPLACE
         JMP    FPLACE       ;FAR JMP
```

Finally, there is a situation where it is necessary that the **PTR** operator be used in order to ensure correct assembler operation. Consider the following statement.

```
MOV    [BX],10
```

How does MASM know whether to encode a byte or a word **MOV** instruction? It doesn't, and in this case it is necessary to use the **PTR** operator to guide the assembler. If a byte **MOV** is desired, then **PTR** is used as follows:

```
MOV    BYTE PTR [BX],10
```

While if a word **MOV** is needed,

```
MOV    WORD PTR [BX],10
```

In certain cases the assembler issues a warning error message if it cannot determine whether a word or byte operation is desired. However, this does not always occur and care should be taken to explicity provide this information where needed.

The final operator to discuss is the **THIS** operator. **THIS** is similar to **PTR** in that it establishes an attribute to be associated with a variable or label. The offset and segment address of the variable or label defined with **THIS** is the address associated with the next memory address to be allocated. **THIS** often is used with the **EQU** pseudo-op (as shown below), where it performs the equivalent function as **PTR** in the **ABYTE1** example considered earlier.

```
ABYTE1   EQU    THIS BYTE    ;ABYTE1 is a BYTE variable at location
AWORD    DW     F124H        ;AWORD. AWORD is type WORD
```

ABYTE1 is given the segment and offset address of **AWORD**, and can be used to access the first byte of **AWORD**.

THIS also can be used to define alternate labels for the same address, one being **NEAR**, and one **FAR**.

```
FPLACE   EQU    THIS FAR     ;FPLACE has the address of NPLACE
                             ;however, has the attribute FAR
NPLACE:  MOV    AL,02        ;The : makes NPLACE a NEAR label
```

Given the group of MASM operators, various complex expressions can be developed. To evaluate these expressions properly, however, it is necessary to know the order in which the operator actions will occur (i.e., their precedence). This is given in Table 7-4.

7.4 PSEUDO-OPERATION STATEMENTS

Instruction mnemonics, pseudo-ops, constants, variables, labels, expressions, operators, and special characters all are used to make up MASM statements. Instruction statements (i.e., statements which translate directly into machine instructions) have been considered extensively during discussions of each individual instruction and are not dealt with further in this chapter. We now concentrate on the pseudo-op statement groups summarized in Table 7-1.

7.4.1 Module Definition and Symbol Exchange

Each block of source code which is assembled as a unit is referred to as a *source module*, with the result of assembly being an *object module*. Now, when the *linker* is called on to bring together all the object modules required for an application program to form a single executable module, object module names must be given to the *linker*. Often object module names will, by default, be the names associated with the source module file, with the file name extension being changed to **.OBJ**.

If one wants to name the object module explicitly with a source statement, though, the **NAME** pseudo-op may be used. Thus **NAME APROG** is an assembler pseudo-op which gives the name **APROG** to the module being assembled. When linking, the name **APROG** must now be used (note that the listing pseudo-op **TITLE** can also be used to specify an object module name).

In addition to the module names, the linker also must know the location of the first instruction to be executed. This information is passed to the linker with the object

Table 7-4   Assembler Operator Precedence (high to low goes from top to bottom)

(expression), [expression]
LENGTH, **SIZE**
Segment Override (e.g., ES:)
PTR, **OFFSET**, **SEG**, **TYPE**, **THIS**
HIGH, **LOW**
*, /, **MOD**, **SHL**, **SHR**
+, −
EQ, **NE**, **LT**, **LE**, **GT**, **GE**
NOT
AND
OR, **XOR**
SHORT

module produced by the assembler. The assembler, in turn, obtains this information from the **END** pseudo-op statement. **END** has a dual purpose: First, as the last statement in the source module, it indicates to the assembler that all statements in the current module have been read and that assembly should begin. Second, it may include an expression (i.e., **END** [expression]) which specifies the first instruction to be executed. Thus, the statement **END START** tells the assembler that program execution is to begin at the instruction labeled **START**. Of course, when several object modules are linked together, it would be confusing if each module's **END** statement included a first-instruction expression, especially if they were all different. To avoid errors only one module should contain such a first-instruction expression.

When dealing with multiple modules which are to be linked together, it often is necessary within one module to reference variables and labels which are defined in another module. Consider the situation where there are two object modules, **APROG**, which contains the main program, and **BPROG**, which contains a called procedure (Figure 7-5). **APROG** contains a variable, **AWORD**, which is referenced by **BPROG**, and **BPROG** contains a label, **BPLACE**, which is referenced by **APROG**. In order to alert the assembler that these undefined names are to be passed to, or found in, other modules at link time, the pseudo-ops **EXTRN** and **PUBLIC** must be employed.

As seen in Figure 7-5, the **APROG** module contains a data segment, **DSEG**, and a program segment, **CSEG**. **AWORD** is a variable defined within **DSEG**; however, it is referenced from the **BPROG** module. The pseudo-op **PUBLIC AWORD** alerts the

```
NAME    APROG                      NAME    BPROG
DSEG    SEGMENT PUBLIC             DSEG    SEGMENT PUBLIC
AWORD   DW   ?                             EXTRN   AWORD:WORD
        PUBLIC AWORD               BWORD   DW   ?
DSEG    ENDS                       DSEG    ENDS

        .                          PSEG    SEGMENT
CSEG    SEGMENT                    BPLACE  PROC FAR
        ASSUME CS:CSEG                     PUBLIC BPLACE
        ASSUME DS:DSEG                     ASSUME CS:PSEG
        EXTRN   BPLACE:FAR                 ASSUME ES:DSEG
BEGIN:  PUSH BP
        .                                  MOV AX,AWORD
        .                                  .

        CALL BPLACE                BPLACE  ENDP
        .                          PSEG    ENDS
        .                          END
CSEG    ENDS
        END BEGIN
```

Figure 7-5 Passing names between modules.

assembler that **AWORD** will be needed by another module at link time. In a similar fashion, **PUBLIC BPLACE** is used in the **BPROG** module. The pseudo-op **EXTRN** tells the assembler that an undefined variable or label will be found in the current assembly and that this variable or label (found in another module) will be defined at link time. In the **APROG** module, **EXTRN BPLACE** indicates that the label **BPLACE**, needed in the **CALL** statement, is defined elsewhere. Thus, the module requiring the variable or label must declare it to be **EXTeRN**al, while the module in which the variable or label is defined must declare it to be **PUBLIC**.

One final point requires some clarification. Consider the case of the variable **AWORD**. How does the assembler, when assembling **BPROG**, know what segment register to associate with references to **AWORD**? This knowledge is needed to encode instructions which reference **AWORD**. One way of providing this information is to redefine the segment **DSEG** within **BPROG**, and place the **EXTRN** statement within **DSEG**. That is, the segment associated with the **EXTRN** statement is the segment within which it resides. In this case the variable **BWORD** is also defined in the **DSEG** segment within **BPROG**. The fact that the same segment has been defined twice is fine in this situation since the word **PUBLIC** in the **SEGMENT** statement indicates that the two segments with the same name are to be concatenated (see Section 7.4.2). Note that in this case the **ASSUME ES:DSEG** will lead the assembler to produce the **ES:** override whenever a reference to **AWORD** (and **BWORD**) occurs.

Another approach to solving this problem is to place the **EXTRN** statement outside of all defined segments. In this case one would explicitly load, say ES, with the segment address of the variable defined in the **EXTRN** statement (e.g., **MOV   AX,SEG AWORD** / **MOV   ES,AX**). A user-supplied segment override could now be used when referencing **AWORD** (e.g., **MOV   AX,ES:AWORD**).

Note that these problems don't occur when referencing **BPLACE** since it is a **FAR** label and thus generating a segment override byte does not occur. That is, assembler encoding of the **CALL** statement is not dependent on the segment in which the **EXTRN BPLACE** statement was placed (the segment and offset addresses are necessary in forming the final **CALL** instruction and are obtained at link time).

7.4.2 Segment Definition

We already have discussed the segment organization of the IBM PC. To take advantage of this organization, the assembler must be told which segment register to associate with each variable and label in the program. The **SEGMENT**, **ENDS**, and **ASSUME** pseudo-op statements provide this information to the assembler. There are three main components necessary for proper utilization of the computer's segment organization.

First, pseudo-ops and instruction statements must generally be placed within named **SEGMENT–ENDS** pairs, thus associating variable and label identifiers with segment names (see Figures 7-1 and 7-5). Second, the **ASSUME** statement must be used to tell the assembler what addresses it should assume will be present in the segment registers when the instructions are later executed. Third, with the exception of the CS register (and the SS register, if a run time stack has been defined), **MOV** instructions must be provided to ensure that the assumptions given in the **ASSUME** statement are indeed fulfilled. These have all been illustrated in various programs throughout the book.

The format of the **SEGMENT** statement is:

    segname   SEGMENT   [align-type] [combine-type] ['class']

For many situations, the use of the **SEGMENT** pseudo-op without the optional parameters is sufficient. If needed, however, these parameters provide more programmer control over where and how the defined segment is later placed in memory by the linker. The align-type parameter determines the address boundary where the defined segment begins. The default value is **PARA**, which indicates that the segment will begin on a **PARA**graph address boundary (i.e., lower-order 4 bits are 0). **BYTE**, **WORD**, and **PAGE** also are permissible align-type parameters, indicating that the segment may begin on a byte, word, or page (i.e., lower-order 8 bits are 0). Thus, if it is desired to permit the segment **DSEG** to begin at any address, the following **SEGMENT** statement would be used:

    DSEG   SEGMENT   BYTE

The combine-type parameter directs the linker to map logical segments into physical segments in a prescribed manner. If unspecified, the linker will not attempt to place the segments in memory in any user-prescribed manner. If the combine-type parameter is **PUBLIC**, then the linker will attempt to concatenate all segments of the same name into a single physical segment. Its length will equal the sum of the lengths of the segments being combined. Thus, in Figure 7-5 the **DSEG** segment is defined in two separate modules. In one of the modules **AWORD** is defined in **DSEG** while in the other **BWORD** is defined in **DSEG**. After linking, the final **DSEG** segment will contain the two words **AWORD** and **BWORD**.

If the combine-type parameter is **COMMON**, then the linker will take all other segments of the same name and have them begin at the same address. These segments will thus overlap each other and the length of the resulting physical segment will be the length of the longest segment being combined. Other combine-type parameters are **STACK** (specifies that the segment is to be part of the run time stack), **MEMORY** (specifies that the segment is to be placed at a memory address above that of all other segments being linked together), and **AT** expression (expression evaluates to a 16-bit number which represents a paragraph address where the segment will be loaded; segments can therefore be placed in memory at a specified absolute address). See Section 9.2.3.4 for an example of **AT** usage.

As an example of **STACK** usage, say that it is desired to have a 64-byte stack within the program which can be accessed by the various stack instructions (e.g., **PUSH, POP**, etc.). The following segment might be defined:

```
SSEG      SEGMENT    STACK        ; define
MYSTACK   DB         64 DUP (?)   ;  a stack
SSEG      ENDS                    ;      segment
```

Note that the statement **ASSUME SS:SSEG** would have to be present to inform the assembler of the presence of the stack segment.

The **ASSUME** statement has already been discussed. One final form which uses the keyword **NOTHING** should, however, be mentioned. For example,

```
ASSUME CS:CSEG, DS:DSEG, SS:SSEG, ES:NOTHING
```

Using **NOTHING** tells the assembler to assume nothing about the contents of ES during the assembly process. Thus, the assembler will not generate any instruction memory addresses using this segment register.

The final **SEGMENT** parameter is 'class'. Suppose that it is desired to place a number of segments into a contiguous area of memory (perhaps in a ROM). At the same time each segment is to retain its own segment name and segment addressing characteristics. That is, we do not want to combine segments into a single addressable segment as occurs with the combine-type parameter **PUBLIC**. All segments with the same user-selected 'class' name will be placed into a contiguous memory area. Thus the two segments **ADATA** and **BDATA** below will reside adjacent to each other in memory. Their ordering in memory is determined by the order with which they are presented to the linker.

```
ADATA    SEGMENT BYTE 'PROM'
INT10    DB      0,1,2,3,4,5,6,7,8,9
ADATA    ENDS

BDATA    SEGMENT BYTE 'PROM'
LET10    DB      'ABCDEFGHIJ'
BDATA    ENDS
```

7.4.3 Procedure Definition

Procedures have been discussed in Section 4.2. A procedure is defined by enclosing a group of statements within a **PROC-ENDP** pseudo-op pair (see Example 4-1 and Figure 7-5). In Figure 7-5, for instance, **BPLACE** is the unique user-selected name for the defined procedure. This name must appear in both the **PROC** and **ENDP** statements.

Procedures must be defined as being **NEAR** or **FAR** so that the assembler, when encountering procedure **CALL** and **RET**urn instructions, can assemble the correct intrasegment or intersegment instruction forms. This may be specified by including the word **NEAR** or **FAR** in the **PROC**edure statement (e.g., **BPLACE PROC FAR**) with the default taken as being **NEAR**.

7.4.4 Data Definition

Table 7-5 shows some common applications of data definition pseudo-ops. (You may wish to review the data definition pseudo-ops by referring to Chapter 2.)

7.4.5 Symbol Definition

The **EQU** pseudo-op provides a mechanism for associating a user-defined identifier with a broad variety of expression types. In its simplest form, a value or expression that evaluates to a value can be defined.

Table 7-5 Data-Pseudo-Op Examples

Use			Examples
Single constant numbers	TWO	DB	10B
	PI	DQ	3.14159
Multiple constant numbers	INT10	DB	0,1,2,3,4,5,6,7,8,9
	COMPLEX	DQ	1.3593,3.8572
Single ASCII character	AASCII	DB	'A'
(**DB** only)	BLET	DB	'B'
ASCII character string	HELLO	DB	'HELLO'
(**DB** only)	LOGIN	DB	'LOG ON'
Mixed definitions	BYE	DB	'GOOD BYE',13,10
(**DB** only)	INTLET	DB	0,'A',1,'B',2,'C'
Undefined initializations	HOLD	DW	?
Repeated initiatializations	FIVE	DB	10 DUP (5);10 bytes each
			;holding the integer 5
	TEN	DW	20 DUP (?) ;20 words of
			;undefined initialization
	BYTWOS	DW	100 DUP (2,4,8)
			;100 repeated initializations
			;of a 3 word sequence, each
			;sequence containing 2, 4, 8
Address expressions	TOFFSET	DW	TEN ;initialize TOFFSET
(**DW** and **DD** only)			;with OFFSET TEN
	TADDR	DD	TEN ;initial TADDR with
			;OFFSET TEN and then SEG TEN
	ADDRSEQ	DW	TEN,TEN+1, TEN+2
General expressions	AVALUE	DQ	2*3.1415
	BCONST	DQ	10*N + 2

```
ACONS   EQU   OFFSET ABYTE + 8  ;ABYTE was defined earlier in a
                                ;data pseudo-op. The value of
                            ;the expression will replace ACONS
                            ;everywhere it appears in the program
```

In addition the user can set up his or her own mnemonics for instructions, operands, and address expressions as shown below.

```
REGMOV    EQU   MOV        ;user defined instruction mnemonic
          REGMOV CX,100     ;assembles as MOV  CX,100

          .

INITC     EQU   CX,100     ;user defined operand string mnemonic
          REGMOV INITC      ;assembles as MOV CX,100

          .

          ADDR   EQU ES:[BP+6] ;user defined addressing
                              ;mode mnemonic
```

```
        MOV    SI,ADDR    ;assembles as MOV SI,ES:[BP+6]
```

In the first case above, wherever **REGMOV** (**REG**ister **MOV**e) is used, it is replaced with **MOV**. In the second case, **INITC** (**INIT**ialize **CX**) will be replaced with **CX,100**. In the last case, **ADDR** will be replaced by **ES:[BP + 6]**.

The pseudo-op **LABEL** and the operator **THIS** have essentially the same function and operation. **LABEL** defines the attributes of a variable or label at the current segment and offset address location. Thus **ABYTE1** can be used to access the first byte of **AWORD** as shown below.

```
ABYTE1   LABEL   BYTE     ;ABYTE1 is a BYTE variable at location
                          ;AWORD, i.e., the first byte of AWORD
AWORD    DW      0F124H   ;AWORD is TYPE WORD
```

Similarly **LABEL** can be used to define address labels referencing the same location, but having different attributes.

```
FPLACE   LABEL   FAR      ;FPLACE has the address of NPLACE
                          ;however, has the attribute FAR
NPLACE:  MOV     AL,02    ;The : makes NPLACE a NEAR label
```

7.4.6 Location Counter Specification

As the assembler operates on data pseudo-op and instruction statements, it keeps track of their offset addresses by maintaining an address counter referred to as the *location counter*. This information is needed by the assembler principally to perform its address encoding function properly. The contents of the location counter can be accessed and manipulated through various assembler pseudo-ops during the assembly process. The current counter value is symbolically referenced by use of the $ character. The character $ can be considered a label whose segment and offset are the current segment and offset, and whose type is **NEAR**.

For example, consider the sequence of instructions below. The comment after each instruction indicates the value of $ on encountering the instruction on that line. Notice how $ can be used with an **EQU** pseudo-op to obtain the offset of **STEST**. It is also used in the **JL** instruction to indicate a jump address without having to explicitly specify a label.

```
     ;****  say location counter EQUals 8 at this point  ****
          NLABEL  EQU     $           ;NLABEL=OFFSET STEST=8
     STEST:  CMP     NARRAY[SI] ,0     ;$=8
             JL      $ + 6             ;$=D, JMP addr. is INC SI
             ADD     AL,NXTNUM[SI]     ;$=F
             INC     SI                ;$=14
             .
             .
```

While the $ operator allows one to access the location counter, the **ORG** pseudo-op (format: **ORG** [expression]) allows one to modify its contents. The expression term must evaluate to a 2-byte number. **ORG** is useful in reserving areas of memory within a program or data segment. Say it is desired to skip 100 bytes in the midst of a program.

```
              JMP      CONTINUE      ; the MOV instruction
              ORG      $ + 100       ; is 100 bytes beyond
CONTINUE:     MOV      AX,1234       ; the JMP instruction
```

ORG is also often used in conjunction with the **SEGMENT AT** expression statement to access specific memory addresses. In the program segment below the label **CTRLVEC** is associated with the physical address **1BH*4**. A program can now access this absolute memory address by referencing **CTRLVEC**.

```
DSEGB     SEGMENT AT 0000       ; this segment begins at 0000
          ORG 1BH*4             ; the offset address of the
CTRLVEC   LABEL WORD            ; word labeled CTRLVEC is 1BH*4
DSEGB     ENDS
```

The final pseudo-op in this group is **EVEN**. If the location counter is currently odd, then **EVEN** directs the assembler to increment the counter by 1, making it even. If already at an even address boundary, no action is taken.

7.4.7 Other Pseudo-Ops

The final group of three psuedo-ops do not naturally fit into any of the groups discussed above. The first to be considered is **.RADIX** (format: **.RADIX** [expression]), which is used to change the default radix (decimal) to any radix between 2 and 16. The expression term which follows **.RADIX** assumes the decimal radix. For instance, if one is entering much data in hexadecimal, it may be convenient to change the radix to hexadecimal as shown below.

```
DATA      SEGMENT
.RADIX    16    ; change default radix to hexadecimal
HELLO     DB    48,45,4C,4C,4F
LOGIN     DB    4C,4F,47,10,4F,4E
DATA      ENDS
```

The second pseudo-op is **COMMENT** (format: **COMMENT** [delimiter text delimiter]). We have already noted that comments can be entered into the source file by using the semicolon. Long comments explaining overall program algorithms in some detail often are placed at the beginning of the program source file. While these can be entered using the semicolon, some consider it a bit more esthetic to use the **COMMENT** pseudo-op. The delimiter is the first nonblank character encountered after **COMMENT**. Thus using * as the delimiter, the following comment might be entered into the source file.

```
COMMENT *PROCEDURE ATSM
        PURPOSE
            NDIM POINTS OF A GIVEN TABLE WITH MONOTONIC
            ARGUMENTS ARE SELECTED AND ORDERED SUCH THAT:
            ABS(ARG(I0-X).GE.ABS(ARG(J)-X) IF I.GT.J
```

USAGE

.
.
.

*

Say that a commonly used subprogram containing a number of assembly language statements has been placed in a separate file. It is now desired to **INCLUDE** this subprogram at a particular point in a new assembly language program being developed. One would like to **INCLUDE** the subprogram without having to manually reenter all of its statements. This is easily done using the **INCLUDE** (format: **INCLUDE** [file-spec]) pseudo-op.

For example, suppose that it often is necessary to obtain the absolute value of a number found in AX, and add it to the number found in BX with the result being in AX. The following code performs this operation.

```
       CMP    AX, 0
       JG     HOP
       NEG    AX
HOP:   ADD    AX, BX
```

Say that these four statements are contained in a file named **AXBX.SRC**. In the program fragment shown below, the four statements are automatically placed between the two **MOV** instructions during the assembly process and are assembled in the program at that point.

```
MOV     AX, VAR
INCLUDE    AXBX. SRC
MOV     VAR, AX
```

7.5 SUMMARY

The macro assembly language provides the user with a host of aids and language constructs to simplify the task of assembly language programming. The primary purpose of the language is to permit the user to represent instructions and memory addresses with convenient mnemonics and user-selected labels. During the assembly process these mnemonics and labels are translated by the assembler into the machine's binary instruction representations.

An application can be thought of as composed of subprograms and procedures with each subprogram and procedure itself composed of segments defined by starting and ending statements containing unique key words (**SEGMENT** and **ENDS**). Because of their special **CALL** and **RET**urn capabilities, defining procedures require additional start and end statements (**PROC** and **ENDP**). In addition, the final statement (**END**) in an entire source file must be identified to the assembler so that the assembly process can begin. The **END** statement may also specify the label of the first instruction to be executed.

These special statements (**SEGMENT**, **ENDS**, etc.) are referred to as assembler pseudo-operation statements. They direct the assembler to perform some function or service. Instruction statements (e.g., **INC   CX**), on the other hand, when translated by the assembler, directly result in machine instructions. Statements themselves are composed of elements arranged in a general format given below.

NAME/LABEL MNEMONIC/PSEUDO-OP   argument, . . . ,argument ;comment

Statements are made up of identifiers (i.e., user-selected names for variables and labels), reserved words (i.e., op codes, register names, operators, pseudo-op names), and special characters (i.e., delimiters such as blank and carriage return, and operator and pseudo-op characters such as $+$, $-$, and **?**).

Operators are used within statements as parts of expressions. Various traditional operators are available such as the arithmetic operators $+$, $-$, $*$, $/$, and **MOD** (e.g., **MOV   AX,COUNT + 10**); the logical operators **OR, XOR, AND**, and **NOT** (e.g., **MOV   AH,6CH OR 16H**); and the relational operators **EQ, NE, LT, LE, GT** and **GE** (e.g., **MOV   AL,42 GE 32**). In addition, a variety of operators are present to access and change the attributes associated with variables and labels.

The assembler associates the attributes segment, offset, length, and size with variables, and segment, offset and type with labels. As an example, say that it is desired to load the number of bytes in an array (**ARRAY1**, defined earlier as a 20-long-word array) in the register AL. This can be done using the **SIZE** operator as follows: **MOV   AH,SIZE ARRAY1**.

The IBM Macro Assembler Language (MASM) provides a wide variety of pseudo-ops to also aid in the assembly language programming task. Broadly, these are divided into 10 groups. The first 7 groups are considered in this chapter. Conditional and macro pseudo-ops are covered in Chapter 8. Listing pseudo-ops, an advanced convenience feature, is not covered in this book. A summary of pseudo-ops is given in Table 7-1.

EXERCISES

7.1   When assembling a program, certain addresses are labeled as relocatable. Why is this so? What happens when a label is identified as **EXTRN**? What is the function of the **PUBLIC** pseudo-op?

7.2   Consider the following code fragment:

```
DATA      SEGMENT
ABYTE     DB
EVEN
AWORD     DW
DWORD     DW
DDBYTE    DB        FFH, 00H, 01H
NEXTWORD  DW        2 DUP (0, 1)
LAST      DB
DATA      ENDS
```

What are the offsets of each of the labels within this data segment?

7.3   What is the purpose of having segment definitions and associated processor mechanisms? Are there any reasons for separating data and code? Why define a separate stack segment?

7.4 Why must the assembler keep track of the three attributes of a variable (offset, segment, and type)?

7.5 Write a code fragment which will jump to a location called **XPLACE**. The label **XPLACE** may be either **NEAR** or **FAR** so that attribute will have to be checked. If the label is **FAR**, you will need its segment and offset. If the label is **NEAR**, you will need only its offset.

7.6 A program fragment in Section 7.3 copies a string from one location to another. Say that you want to reverse the string so that the first letter is copied into the last position, the second letter into the second-to-last position, and so on. Modify the given program fragment to perform this task. Use the **LENGTH** and **OFFSET** pseudo-ops.

7.7 Both the **PTR** and **THIS** pseudo-ops can be used when trying to access a variable or label with a *type* different from its original definition. Discuss the differences in usage between these two pseudo-ops. How could **THIS** be used when trying to reference a global variable?

7.8 Consider the example of Figure 7-5. These two modules are to be modified to call a procedure **CPLACE** and access a word called **CWORD**. Make the necessary changes to the existing routines, and then give an outline of the new module **CPLACE**.

7.9 Experimentally determine how the assembler encodes the following statements. Are word or byte operations encoded? Discuss your results and indicate how to explicitly force the assembler to encode either a word or byte operation.

a
```
DEC   [DI]
```
b
```
MUL   [SI]
```
c
```
ADD   [SI],10
```

7.10 Consider the following program fragment:
```
MOV   DS,AX
INC   AX
ORG   ($ - 4)
DEC   BX
PUSH  AX
```

What is the result of assembling these instructions? Does permitting this sort of **ORG** statement present any difficulties and, if so, could the assembler be modified to prevent these difficulties?

Part

II

Advanced Topics

8

Advanced Assembly Language Features

This chapter considers two advanced assembly language features. The first is the *macro* feature, which permits the user to specify and name statement groups which later, when named during the assembly process, are automatically inserted into the assembly language program and assembled in place. This is very convenient in situations where there are frequently used statement groups. The second is the *conditional assembly* feature, which permits statement groups to be included or excluded from the program at assembly time depending on the conditions of specified assembly time parameters.

This feature permits programs to be tailored at assembly time to anticipated run time situations (e.g., the peripherals on the system). Together, these two features are of enormous help to the assembly language programmer who must develop large systems that must operate under a variety of conditions.

8.1 AN INTRODUCTION TO ASSEMBLER MACROS

Consider the development of a large application program where it is often necessary to perform the following sequence of operations:

1. Obtain the absolute value of a signed word integer found in AX
2. Add this absolute value to the contents of BX
3. Place the result in some other labeled memory location (say **OUT_VAL**)

The following program segment performs the indicated tasks.

```
        CMP    AX, 0         ;sign flag set if AX < 0
        JNS    PLUS          ;jump if AX positive
        NEG    AX            ;AX is neg., take 2's comp.
PLUS:   ADD    BX, AX        ;BX <--- AX + BX
        MOV    OUT_VAL, BX   ;move result to OUT_VAL
```

If this code is used a number of times, it could be incorporated into the assembly language source by the programmer each place it is needed. A different label might be substituted for **OUT_VAL** depending on where the result is to be stored. Also the destination label in the **JNS** instruction would have to be unique for each instruction group. After a few times this no doubt would become tiresome.

One way of overcoming this difficulty is to create a procedure which performs the indicated operations and then provide a procedure **CALL** each time the set of instructions is needed. While this certainly is possible (see Problem 8.1), for short instruction sequences there is a time overhead associated with this solution which may not be reasonable. That is, when a procedure is invoked with a **CALL** and terminated with a **RET**urn, various stack operations are required. In addition, the contents of several registers typically are saved and restored. These operations can take times comparable to the desired instruction operations themselves. Thus, having a procedure for each small repeated code segment is generally not time efficient.

The IBM PC assembler *macro* facility permits the programmer to name a group of statements and then have them placed within the assembly code automatically whenever the name is invoked. Say that the group of absolute-value add statements shown above is given the name **ABSAX_ADDBX**. Written as a *macro* it would be entered into your assembly language source program as follows. **DUM_VAL** is a dummy identifier indicating the destination location of the result.

```
ABSAX_ADDBX   MACRO    DUM_VAL       ;DUM_VAL is a dummy
              LOCAL    PLUS          ; symbol name.
              CMP      AX, 0         ;sign flag set if AX < 0
              JNS      PLUS          ;jump if AX positive
              NEG      AX            ;AX <0, take 2's comp.
PLUS:         ADD      BX, AX        ;BX <--- AX + BX
              MOV      DUM_VAL, BX   ;move result to DUM_VAL
              ENDM
```

The general form of a macro definition is

```
    name MACRO    dummylist

        .
                        macro
        .
                        body
    ENDM
```

The **MACRO** pseudo-op denotes the beginning of a macro definition. It also specifies the name of the macro (**ABSAX_ADDBX** in this case) and provides a list of dummy arguments (**DUM_VAL** in our example). These dummy arguments are replaced by user-selected arguments when the macro is invoked. The **ENDM** indicates the end of the macro definition (the **LOCAL** pseudo-op will be considered later). Once defined at the beginning of an assembly program, the macro then can be invoked whenever the programmer desires to include this code in the program. Invoking a macro causes a replacement operation to occur at the spot where the macro is named. This is referred to as *macro expansion* and is shown below, in Figure 8-1.

In Figure 8-1 **ABSAX_ADDBX** is expanded twice. The label **OUT_VAL** is substituted for the dummy label **DUM_VAL** in the first expansion and the label **AN_ANSWER** is used in the second expansion.

One difference you may have noted between the macro definition and the expansions is that the **PLUS** label associated with the **JNS** instruction has been changed in the first expansion to **??0000** and in the second expansion to **??0001**. Clearly, using the **PLUS** label in both expansions would confuse the assembler. To distinguish between the target locations of the **JNS** instruction in the two expansions, the assembler creates unique labels for each expansion (first **??0001** and then **??0002**). The assembler is directed to do this with the **LOCAL** pseudo-op, which identifies those labels in the macro definition requiring assembler-generated labels.

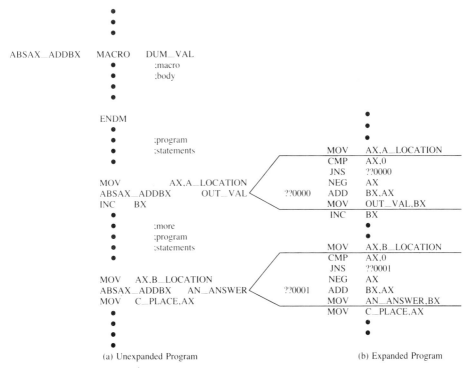

Figure 8-1 Macro expansion.

Table 8-1 Macro Pseudo-Ops

Type	Pseudo-Op	Purpose
MACRO DEFINITION	name **MACRO** dummylist	Used to begin and name a macro. Dummylist is a set of arguments to be replaced by user parameters each time the macro is invoked.
	ENDM	**ENDM** terminates the macro.
REPEATED MACRO	**REPT** expression	Statements in an **REPT-ENDM** block are repeated the number of times determined by the expression.
	IRP dummy,<arg1, arg2, . . . ,argN>	Statements in an **IRP-ENDM** block are repeated a number of times equal to the number of arguments. On each repetition the next argument in the list is substituted for every occurrence of dummy in the block.
	IRPC dummy,string	Statements in an **IRPC-ENDM** block are repeated once for each character in the string with each repetition substituting the next string character for every occurrence of dummy in the block.
OTHER PSEUDO-OPS	**LOCAL** dummylist	The assembler creates a unique identifier for each element in the dummy list and substitutes this identifier everywhere the dummy appears in the macro.
	PURGE macro-name 1, macro-name2, . . . ,macro-name*N*	**PURGE** removes the definition of the named macros from the assembler.
	EXITM	Used within a macro definition in conjunction with conditional pseudo-ops to terminate macro expansion based on some condition.

Table 8-1   continued

Type	Pseudo-Op	Purpose
SPECIAL SYMBOLS	text&text	Indicates the two text pieces to be concatenated.
	%expression	Indicates the expression is to be evaluated to a number.
	!character (not discussed)	Indicates the character is entered literally as an argument.
	;;text (not discussed)	Comments following ;; do not appear in the macro expansion.

Finally, note that the descriptive name **ABSAX_ADDBX** was used for the above macro. The use of descriptive names in this manner can enhance source code documentation and permit other people to get the gist of the program's operation without going into the details. The details, of course, are available after assembly in an expanded assembly language listing.

8.2 MACRO PSEUDO-OPS

In addition to **MACRO, ENDM,** and **LOCAL,** there are other pseudo-ops associated with the assembler's macro facility. These are summarized in Table 8-1 and discussed below.

8.2.1 Macro Definition and Expansion

As indicated earlier, macros are defined by enclosing a named group of statements within a **MACRO-ENDM** pseudo-op pair. The macro is invoked and expanded by using the macro name within the source program. Macro expansion can be viewed as a string replacement process which occurs before the translation and encoding assembly tasks take place. A special feature of this replacement process is the ability to establish dummy parameters within the macro definition which are later replaced by program parameters given when the macro is invoked. In the example of Figure 8-1, the dummy parameter **DUM_VAL** was replaced first by **OUT_VAL** and then by **AN_ANSWER** in the two successive macro expansions. When more than one dummy parameter is present in a macro definition, they must be separated by commas, as shown below in the macro MOV_AND_SUB.

```
MOV_AND_SUB      MACRO    INPAR1, INPAR2, OUTPAR1
                 MOV      AX, INPAR1
                 SUB      AX, INPAR2
                 MOV      OUTPAR1, AX
                 ENDM
```

This macro, when invoked with

```
MOV_AND_SUB      SOURCE1, INPUT1, RESULT
```

results in

```
        MOV     AX, SOURCE1
        SUB     AX, INPUT1
        MOV     RESULT, AX
```

In this situation dummy parameters represent variable names. They could represent registers, instructions, op codes, strings, or values. For instance, consider the macro **INI_SEG** where one of the dummy parameters represents a segment register:

```
INT_SEG    MACRO    SEG_DEF, SEG_REG
           MOV      AX, SEG_DEF
           MOV      SEG_REG, AX
           ENDM
```

This might be invoked at the beginning of a program to initialize the data segment register as follows:

```
        INI_SEG   DATA_SEG, DS
```

and would result in:

```
        MOV     AX, DATA_SEG
        MOV     DS, AX
```

A dummy parameter may be an instruction as shown below with the macro **REG_OPR**.

```
REG_OPR    MACRO    OPR, REG
           OPR      REG
           ENDM
```

Say this is invoked first to save a register contents and then to increment another register.

```
REG_OPR    PUSH, BP
REG_OPR    INC, AX
```

When expanded this results in

```
        PUSH       BP
        INC        AX
```

It is also possible to pass values to a macro by using the special percent (%) symbol. This is particularly helpful when used with the = assembler operator. The = operator works like the **EQU** operator except that the value of the identifier on the left of the = sign can be redefined as many times as required.

For instance, suppose we want to define a set of words which initially contain increasing powers of 2 and which can be individually addressed as **TWO1** (containing 2), **TWO2** (containing 4), etc. Define the macro **P_2** as follows:

```
P_2          MACRO    DCTR, DEXPON
TWO&DCTR     DW       DEXPON
             ENDM
```

The special macro symbol **&** indicates that string **TWO** is to be concatenated with **DCTR**. Next define the initial values for the variables **CTR** and **EXPON** as follows:

```
CTR  =  0
EXPON  =  1
```

Form the next values of **CTR** and **EXPON**, and then invoke **P_2**.

```
CTR  =  CTR  +  1
EXPON  =  2*EXPON
P_2      %CTR, %EXPON
```

The **%** symbol indicates that **CTR** and **EXPON** are expressions which are evaluated to a number. These numbers are to be substituted for the dummy variables **DCTR** and **DEXPON**. When expanded for the first time, this results in

```
TWO1   DW   2
```

Other powers could be defined by repeatedly invoking the **P_2** macro in the same manner. Thus, a second invocation with

```
CTR  =  CTR  +  1
EXPON  =  2*EXPON
P_2      %CTR, %EXPON
```

when expanded results in the data definition statement

```
TWO2   DW   4
```

Repeating the two = statements could be avoided if they could themselves be included within a macro. This is possible by creating another macro, **POWER_2**, which invokes **P_2** as shown below.

```
POWER_2    MACRO
           CTR  =  CTR  +  1
           EXPON  =  2*EXPON
           P_2    %CTR, %EXPON
           ENDM
```

Now each time **POWER_2** is invoked, another word containing the next power of 2 is defined. Macros can invoke other macros as long as the invoked macros already have been defined.

8.2.2 Repeated Macros

In the previous example a series of words were initialized to contain powers of 2 by repeatedly invoking a macro (**POWER_2**). Is it possible to have these repeated invocations done automatically? As you might expect, the answer is yes. The assembler provides three pseudo-ops designed specifically for the task of repeating blocks of statements (which may or may not be macros). The simplest of these is the **REPT** pseudo-op whose general form is

```
REPT     expression
```

The block to be repeated is enclosed within a **REPT-ENDM** pseudo-op pair. Say that the first 10 powers of 2 (starting with 2^1) are to be defined and that the macro **P_2** of the previous section is present. **POWER_2** can be redefined as follows:

```
APOWER_2    MACRO
                    REPT    10
                    CTR = CTR + 1
                    EXPON = 2*EXPON
                    P_2   %CTR, %EXPON
                    ENDM    ; end of repeat block
            ENDM            ; end of macro block
```

The **REPT** pseudo-op directs the assembler to repeat the statements between the **REPT-ENDM** pair 10 times. If **APOWER_2** is preceded by initialization statements for **CTR** and **EXPON**, and by the **P_2** definition, then it can now be invoked and expanded to yield the following set of statements:

```
TWO1        DW    2
TWO2        DW    4
TWO3        DW    8
              .
              .
              .
TWO10       DW    1024
```

Say that the labels associated with the powers of 2 in the above example are to have the form **TWO_2** (containing 2^1), **TWO_4** (containing 2^2), **TWO_8** (containing 2^3), etc., and that the powers of 2 are already known and needn't be calculated. The **IRP** pseudo-op, whose format is

```
IRP     dummy, <arg1, arg2, . . ., argN>
```

can be used in this situation to develop the set of word initialization statements. This is illustrated below for the first five powers of 2.

```
                    IRP     PTWO, <2, 4, 8, 16, 32>
TWO_&PTWO    DW     PTWO
                    ENDM
```

Expansion by the assembler yields

```
TWO_2         DW     2
TWO_4         DW     4
TWO_8         DW     8
TWO_16        DW     16
TWO_32        DW     32
```

PTWO is a dummy argument. The **IRP-ENDM** pseudo-op pair directs the assembler to repeat the statements within the **IRP-ENDM** block a number of times equal to the number of arguments within the angle brackets (the argument list). Beginning with the leftmost argument, on each repetition the assembler replaces the dummy argument with an argument from the argument list. Note that the arguments in this case are numbers. However, the assembler views each argument as a character string and performs the appropriate replacement as directed (see Problem 8.3).

The **IRPC** pseudo-op

    IRPC   dummy,string

is a variation of the **IRP** pseudo-op where the argument list is replaced by a character string. In this case the statements within an **IRPC-ENDM** block are repeated a number of times equal to the number of characters in the string. Starting with the leftmost character, on each repetition a character from the string replaces every occurrence of the dummy in the block. For example, say that it is desired to initialize a sequence of 6 bytes with the first six entries of a series called **SUM**. The series **SUM** is obtained by successively adding each integer in the sequence 1,2,3,4, . . . to a variable which initially is 0. Thus, the first element of the series is 1, the second, 3, the third, 6, etc. This can be done with the following **IRPC-ENDM** block, which works up to the integer 9.

    Y = 0
    IRPC   SUM, 12345
    Y = Y + SUM
    DB   Y
    ENDM

The assembler would expand this to produce

    DB   1
    DB   3
    DB   6
    DB   10
    DB   15

8.2.3 The LOCAL, PURGE, and EXITM Macro Pseudo-Ops

The **LOCAL** pseudo-op

    LOCAL   dummylist

is used when there is a need for the assembler to create unique identifiers during macro expansion as is the case when there is a labeled statement within the macro. Placing the label in the **LOCAL** pseudo-op dummylist directs the assembler to replace the dummy label with a unique assembler-generated label on each expansion. This was illustrated in the example of Section 8-1.

Once a macro has been defined, it can be redefined by reusing the name in a new macro definition. Subsequent references to the macro will use its most recently defined version. The **PURGE** pseudo-op, whose format is

```
PURGE      macro-name1, macro-name 2, . . .
```

deletes the macro definition entirely. Subsequent references to the macro will cause an error.

Conditional pseudo-ops, discussed in Section 8.4, permit statements and macros to be included or excluded from the assembly process depending on the condition of some defined assembler variables. It is therefore possible to have situations where macro expansion is terminated prior to encountering the **ENDM** statement. The **EXITM** pseudo-op

```
EXITM
```

acts in a similar manner to **ENDM**, except that it is placed within the body of the macro to indicate a possible macro expansion termination point other than **ENDM**. This is illustrated later when conditional assembly is considered.

8.3 MACRO LIBRARIES

Consider now the general use of macros in the development of application programs. As the program at hand is being analyzed, it sometimes becomes apparent that a certain group of macros and procedures would be helpful, not only for yourself, but perhaps also for other programmers working on the same project. One approach here is to set up a separate file (a macro library, **MACRO.LIB**) which contains these macros, procedures, and their documentation, and agree upon those steps necessary for entering new items into the file. Using the **INCLUDE** pseudo-op (e.g., **INCLUDE   MAC-RO.LIB**) at the beginning of your assembly language program now allows you to include these macros and procedures in your assembly language source, and then invoke (call) them as needed. For example, say that **MACRO.LIB** contains the previously defined macros

```
ABSAX_ADDBX
INI_SEG
P_2
APOWER_2
```

These may be included and invoked with the assembly program of Figure 8-2. The reader may expand this when solving Problem 8.13.

8.4 AN INTRODUCTION TO CONDITIONAL ASSEMBLY

While the assembly language has been viewed principally as a language for expressing and encoding IBM PC machine instructions, it also provides commands (pseudo-ops) for performing more general types of language functions. The ability to define and process variables and constants using the **EQU** and = pseudo-ops, the ability to express and evaluate complex expressions, and the ability to perform repeated operations are a few of the broader assembly language capabilities already considered. Completing this group are the assembler's conditional operations. These operations permit user-supplied parameters to direct just which instructions are to be included in the assembly process. Assembly programs can thus be customized to specific operating conditions.

```
                INCLUDE  MACRO.LIB
                CTR = 0
                EXPON = 1
      DSEG      SEGMENT
                APOWER_2
      RESULT    DW    ?
      DSEG      ENDS
      SSEG      SEGMENT    STACK
                DB     128 DUP (?)
      SSEG      ENDS
      CSEG      SEGMENT
                ASSUME  CS: CSEG, DS: DSEG, SS: SSEG
                INI_SEG    DSEG, DS
                INI_SEG    SSEG, SS
                MOV   AX, TWO1
                MOV   BX, TWO2
                ABSAX_ADDBX    RESULT
                END
```

Figure 8-2   Invoking a macro library.

As an example, consider a scientific application program in which a good deal of floating-point arithmetic takes place. The program must operate in two different equipment environments. In the first, a standard IBM PC is present and floating-point operations are encoded as software procedures. In the second, an IBM PC equipped with the Intel 8087 Numeric Data Processor (floating point) chip is present and floating point operations are performed directly by executing floating point machine instructions. It has been decided to distribute two separate versions of the application program, one for each equipment environment. The approach taken is to create a single assembly source program which can be customized, using conditional assembly techniques, to reflect the presence or absence of the numeric data processor.

As a general strategy, assume that software procedures have been developed to perform operations associated with each Intel 8087 instruction. Further, since our concern here is with illustrating conditional assembly techniques and not solving this particular problem in the most elegant fashion, assume that a separate procedure is present for each of the possible Intel 8087 instruction formats. Note that since the Intel 8087 has a built-in hardware stack (and other hardware features), any software attempt at replicating Intel 8087 actions (called *emulation*) must provide memory-based data structures comparable to this stack. We shall refer to this software stack that mimics the 8087's hardware stack as **FSTACK**.

Consider, for example, the floating add instruction, **FADD**, whose format is

```
      FADD      label
```

In this situation one of the operands is found at the memory location designated by label while the other is the top element of the stack. The resulting sum replaces the top of stack operand. We shall assume that the assembler will recognize and properly encode such a floating-point instruction. [Note that this is not typically true, and provision may be required to ensure correct assembly of such 8087 floating-point instructions (see Problem 8.7).]

```
        INTEL_8087      EQU     1                       ;1 ---> 8087 present,
                                                        ;0 ---> 8087 not present.
        ;
        MP3_FADD        MACRO   SRC_OPR                 ;2nd operand is on top
                                                        ;of 8087 stack
                        IF      INTEL_8087              ;check for presence of 8087
                        FADD    SRC_OPR                 ;perform addition on 8087
                        ELSE
                        MOV     AX,OFFSET SRC_OPR
                        PUSH    AX                      ;push offset of operand
                        CALL    P3_FADD                 ;8087 not present CALL
                                                        ;floating add procedure

                        ENDIF
                        ENDM
```

Figure 8-3   **IF-ELSE-ENDIF** conditional assembly.

Say that the procedure that performs this equivalent operation is called **P3_FADD**. **P3_FADD** assumes that the offset address of label is found at the top of the system stack. Our objective is to avoid having to create separate application programs, one using the Intel 8087 **FADD** instruction and the other using the software procedure **P3_FADD**. Of course, this objective would apply to all of the roughly 70 instructions present on the Intel 8087 even though here we deal only with certain cases of floating addition. One approach to solving this problem is to create a macro and call it **MP3_FADD**, which contains conditional assembly statements to direct selection of the proper floating addition instructions. This is shown in Figure 8-3, where the assembler variable **INTEL_8087** is used to indicate the presence or absence of the Intel 8087 chip.

The **IF** statement first checks the value of the expression (in this case the simple variable **INTEL_8087**). If it is not 0, then the statements in the **IF-ELSE** block are included in the assembly. If it is 0, then the statements in the **ELSE-ENDIF** block are included in the assembly. Defining **INTEL_8087** once at the beginning of the assembly source directs expansion to the correct floating addition statements. With the macro defined, the programmer can code floating-point additions using a format similar to that of the corresponding Intel 8087 instruction, without being concerned about the presence of an Intel 8087. For example, if no 8087 is present (**INTEL_8087 EQU   0**) and the macro is invoked with

```
    MP3_FADD    A_OPERAND
```

then the macro will be expanded to produce

```
    MOV     AX,OFFSET A_OPERAND
    PUSH    AX
    CALL    P3_FADD
```

The 8087 **FADD** instruction has several possible formats. For instance, the format **FADD** (no operands specified) indicates that the top two elements on the 8087 stack are popped and added with the result being pushed back onto the stack. This can be

```
MP13_FADD          MACRO      SRC_OPR
                   IFNB       <SRC_OPR>    ;chk. argument
                                          ;not blank
; argument Not Blank
                   IF         INTEL_8087
                   FADD       SRC_OPR      ;8087 present
                   ELSE
                   MOV        AX,OFFSET SRC_OPR
                   PUSH       AX           ;8087 not
                   CALL       P3_FADD      ;present
                   ENDIF
; argument Blank                          ;end IFBN-ELSE block
                   ELSE
                   IF         INTEL_8087
                   FADD                    ;8087 present
                   ELSE
                   CALL       P1_FADD      ;8087 not present
                   ENDIF
;
                   ENDIF                   ;IFNB-ENDIF block
                   ENDM
```

Figure 8-4 Nested conditional assembly.

handled by using the macro **MP13_FADD** shown in Figure 8-4. **P1_FADD** is a procedure which operates on **FSTACK** to perform the same operation as **FADD**.

The **MP13_FADD** macro illustrates a second type of conditional statement, **IFNB**, with the format

    IFNB   <argument>

The **NB** stands for **N**ot **B**lank. The **IFNB** statement checks whether the dummy argument, in this case **SRC_OPR**, is present in the macro call (i.e., it is not blank). If **SRC_OPR** is present (i.e., stack/memory reference addition), the statements in the **IFNB-ELSE** block are included in the assembly process. If the argument is not present (i.e., pure stack addition), then the statements in the **ELSE-ENDIF** block are included. In this situation, the **IFNB** statement allows us to differentiate between the pure stack and stack/memory formats of the floating addition instruction. This example also demonstrates how conditional statements can be nested. Once again note that for this approach to work, the **FADD** instruction must be recognized and encoded. Either the assembler performs this operation or else other provisions must be made (see Problem 8.7).

8.5 CONDITIONAL PSEUDO-OPS

Other conditional pseudo-ops are available in addition to **IF**, **IFNB**, **ELSE**, and **ENDIF**. Table 8-2 summarizes the complete set of conditional pseudo-ops available with the

```
IFxx    argument                    IFxx    argument
            .                           .
            ;include
            ;   on                                  ;include
            ;      TRUE                              ;   on
ELSE                                                 ;      TRUE
            .
            ;include                        .
            ;   on
            ;      FALSE           ENDIF
            .
                                            .       ;skip to
ENDIF                                       .       ;   here on
                                            .       ;      FALSE
            (a)                                 (b)
```

Figure 8-5   General Format of Conditional Blocks

IBM PC macro assembler, with further discussion following the table. The general format for conditional statements and blocks is shown in Figure 8-5.

The conditional IF statement is said to be TRUE or FALSE depending on its type and arguments. For instance, in the case of a simple conditional statement IF expression, the statement is TRUE if the expression evaluates to a number not equal to 0, and is FALSE otherwise.

Notice that the ELSE statement is optional. When ELSE is present (Figure 8-5a) and the conditional statement is TRUE then the statements in the IFxx-ELSE block are included in the assembly and those statements in the ELSE-ENDIF block are excluded. The reverse happens when the conditional statement is FALSE. When ELSE is not present, a TRUE statement results in the statements in the IF-ENDIF block being included and a FALSE condition causes the entire IFxx-ENDIF block to be skipped over and assembly continues following the block.

The previous section discussed the operation of the simple conditional **IF** expression statement. The expression part of the statement can be a single variable, as in the case of **INTEL_8087**, or a complex expression of the sort discussed in Chapter 7. For instance, say that both the variable **INTEL_8087** must be equal to 1, and another variable, **NDP_X**, must be greater than zero to indicate the presence of the 8087. The **IF** statement of Figure 8-3 could be modified to:

```
IF   INTEL_8087 AND  (NDP_X GT 0)
```

IFE operates similarly to **IF** except that the *true* condition occurs when the expression evaluates to 0.

The **IFDEF**, with the format

```
IFDEF     symbol
```

and **IFNDEF**, with the format

```
IFNDEF    symbol
```

pseudo-ops check to see whether or not a symbol has been defined. For **IFDEF**, the statement is *true* if the symbol has been defined or has been declared external. For

Table 8-2 Conditional Pseudo- Ops (angle bracket < and > are required where indicated)

	Pseudo-Op	Explanation
IF	expression	True if expression evaluates to a nonzero number.
IFE	Pseudo-Op expression	True if expression evaluates to zero.
IFDEF	symbol	True if symbol is: (*a*) defined and (*b*) declared external via **EXTRN** pseudo-op.
IFNDEF	symbol	True if symbol is: (*a*) not defined and (*b*) not declared external via **EXTRN**.
IFB	<argument>	True if argument is blank.
IFNB	<argument>	True if argument is not blank.
IFIDN	<arg-1>,<arg-2>	True if string argument 1 is identical to string argument 2.
IFDIF	<arg-1>,<arg-2>	True if string argument 1 is different from string argument 2.
IF1		True if encountered on assembly pass 1 (not considered here).
IF2		True if encountered on assembly pass 2 (not considered here).
ENDIF		Each **IF**xx statement must have a matching **ENDIF** statement to correctly form a conditional block.
ELSE		Optional pseudo-op to permit including other code on the **FALSE IF** condition.

IFNDEF, the statement is *true* if the symbol has not been defined or has not been declared external. Thus, in the floating-point arithmetic example, another approach to specifying the presence or absence of an 8087 would be to include or exclude a statement defining the variable symbol **INTEL_8087** (e.g., the **EQU** statement) and then check for its presence with an **IFDEF** or **IFNDEF** statement. In macro **MP3_FADD** of Figure 8-3 this could be done by replacing the **IF INTEL_8087** statement with an **IFDEF INTEL 8087** statement.

The **IFB** <argument> and **IFNB** <argument> pseudo-ops are used to determine whether or not a dummy argument is present. This is useful when a macro has a number of arguments; however, on calling the macro, not all arguments are always used. Thus, one can conditionally expand a macro depending on the arguments present. In the floating addition example **IFNB** was used to determine whether a pure stack or stack/ memory addition format was to be used. In the example below the **IFB** pseudo-op is used to determine the number of parameters to **PUSH** onto the stack prior to a procedure call.

Consider a situation where an application consists of a variety of procedures, each one requiring a different number of parameters (say up to a maximum of eight). Each parameter is one word long and is passed by being pushed onto the stack. We would like to develop a macro (to be called **PCALL**) which will generate the necessary sequence of **PUSH** instructions and appropriate procedure call. Consider the macro definition below.

```
PCALL       MACRO       PNAME, P1, P2, P3, P4, P5, P6, P7, P8
            IRP         NXT_PARA, <P8, P7, P6, P5, P4, P3, P2, P1>
; ***
            IFB         <NXT_PARA>   ;do nothing if blank
            ELSE
                PUSH        NXT_PARA      ;PUSH if not blank
            ENDIF
; ***
            ENDM
            CALL        PNAME
            ENDM
```

PNAME is the name of the procedure to be called, and the dummy list **P1,P2, . . . ,P8** defines the parameters to be pushed onto the stack prior to issuing the procedure call. **P8** is pushed first, **P7** second, etc. The **IRP-ENDM** block provides for repetition of the set of statements between the starred (;***) comment lines. On each repetition the next parameter is removed from the parameter list and replaces the dummy parameter **NXT_PARA.** The **IFB** conditional statement tests whether the symbol **NXT PARA** is not defined (i.e., blank). If it is not defined, a repeat occurs and the next parameter is considered. If the parameter is defined, then it is **PUSH**ed onto the stack (after the **ELSE** statement), and a repeat occurs once again. After all eight parameters have been examined, the final procedure **CALL** statement is included and macro expansion terminates with **ENDM**. Say that the macro is invoked with the statement

```
            PCALL       A_PROCEDURE, SI, DI, AX, BX
```

When expanded, the result is

```
            PUSH        BX
            PUSH        AX
            PUSH        DI
            PUSH        SI
            CALL        A_PROCEDURE
```

Notice that the **PNAME** macro could also have been written utilizing the **IFNB** conditional pseudo-op in lieu of the **IFB** (see Problem 8.6).

IFIDN and **IFDIF** pseudo-ops have the formats

```
IFIDN   <arg-1>,<arg-2>
IFDIF   <arg-1>,<arg-2>
```

and permit conditional assembly based on the comparison of two string arguments. For example, say that there is an Intel 8087 floating addition instruction format

```
FADD    ST,ST(0)
```

that permits the top element of the 8087 stack to be doubled. The result of the doubling replaces the top of stack element.

If the 8087 is not present, assume an equivalent software procedure is available called **P20_FADD**. Macro **MP2_FADD** given in Figure 8-6 is a modification of macro **MP13_FADD** (Figure 8-4), which provides for pure stack, stack/memory, and doubling floating addition formats and illustrates the use of the **IFIDN** pseudo-op (see Problems 8.8 and 8.9). The **IFDIF** pseudo-op operates in a similar manner.

8.6 RECURSIVE MACRO CALLS

As discussed in Section 4.4, recursion is the ability of a program, procedure, or macro to call itself. Recall from that section the problem of calculating the factorial of an integer ($N!$). The factorial of a number is defined as

$$N! = N \cdot (N - 1) \cdot (N - 2) \cdots \cdots 1$$

or may be defined recursively as

$$N! = N \cdot (N - 1)! \qquad \text{where } 0! = 1$$

In Section 4.4 a recursive procedure was developed to evaluate factorials.

Macros can also be called recursively and the *factorial* macro below demonstrates a recursive macro solution to this same problem. Notice that the **IF** pseudo-op is used to detect the presence of 0! and terminate the recursion process. Assume that prior to calling the macro, N has been moved into AX. The factorial result resides in AX.

```
FACTORIAL       MACRO       N
                IF          N - 1 ;chk. N not 0.
                MOV         BX,N - 1
                MUL         BX
                FACTORIAL N-1
                ENDIF
                ENDM
```

Say that the macro is called as follows to obtain 4!:

```
X       EQU     4
        MOV             AX,X
        FACTORIAL %X
```

```
MP2_FADD      MACRO       SRC1_OPR, SRC2_OPR
              IFNB        <SRC1_OPR>    ;chk. argument
                                       ;not blank
; argument not blank            chk. for doubling format
          . IFIDN        <SRC1_OPR>,<ST>
            IFIDN        <SRC2_OPR>,<ST(0)>
                                       ;doubling format
    ;         IF         INTEL_8087
                FADD     ST,ST(0)      ;8087 present
              ELSE
                CALL     P20_FADD      ;8087 not present
              ENDIF
              EXITM
    ;
              ENDIF
              ENDIF
; argument not blank            stack/memory format
              IF         INTEL_8087
                FADD     SRC1_OPR      ;8087 present
              ELSE
                MOV      AX,OFFSET SRC1_OPR
                PUSH     AX            ;8087 not present
                CALL     P3_FADD
              ENDIF
; argument blank                pure stack format
              ELSE                    ;end IFNB-ELSE block
              IF         INTEL_8087
                FADD                   ;8087 present
              ELSE
                CALL     P1_FADD       ;8087 not present
              ENDIF
    ;
              ENDIF                   ;IFNB-ENDIF block
              ENDM
```

Figure 8-6   Multiple and nested conditional pseudo-ops.

The results after each recursive expansion are shown below with the fourth expansion being the final assembled factorial routine.

```
          MOV       BX, 3      1st expansion
          MUL       BX
          FACTORIAL 3


          MOV       BX, 3      2nd expansion
          MUL       BX
          MOV       BX, 2
          MUL       BX
          FACTORIAL 2
```

```
        MOV         BX, 3        3rd expansion
        MUL         BX
        MOV         BX, 2
        MUL         BX
        MOV         BX, 1
        MUL         BX
        FACTORIAL   1

        MOV         BX, 3        4th expansion
        MUL         BX
        MOV         BX, 2
        MUL         BX
        MOV         BX, 1
        MUL         BX
```

8.7 SUMMARY

The IBM PC Macro Assembler has two additional features and associated sets of pseudo-operations designed to ease the programming task when large and complex programs are being developed. The first, the *macro* feature, permits the user to specify and name statement groups which automatically will be inserted into the assembly language program and assembled in place. The second, the *conditional assembly* feature, permits statements groups to be included or excluded from the program at assembly time depending on conditions of specified assembly time parameters.

Macros have a specified format. Each macro begins with a **MACRO** statement which indicates the beginning of the macro, its name, and any associated dummy parameters. A **MACRO** ends with an **ENDM** statement which tells the assembler that the macro has terminated. The body of the macro contains statements which may be included in the assembly process in response to a macro call. A macro is called, or invoked, by using its name and substituting actual parameters for the dummy parameters in the macro definition. In response to a macro call, the assembler inserts the statements in the macro body into the assembly language program at the spot where the macro call is located. References to the dummy parameters are replaced with references to the parameters provided in the macro call statement. Macros can be called any number of times and each time the assembler will place the set of statements in the assembly program at the designated position. Thus, commonly used statement groups need only be defined once in a macro definition to be placed within a program numerous times.

The conditional assembly language feature allows conditional operations to be performed on statement groups (which may or may not be macros). A conditional block begins with an **IF**xx statement and ends with an **ENDIF** statement. The block may include an **ELSE** statement. The **IF**xx statement specifies a condition which, when evaluated by the assembler at assembly time, may be *true* or *false*. If *true*, then the statements between the **IF**xx statement and the **ELSE** statement are included in the assembly process for that version of the program. If *false*, then the statements between the **ELSE** statement and the **ENDIF** statement are included instead.

EXERCISES

8.1   Consider the **ABSAX_ADDBX** macro presented in Section 8.1. Write a procedure which performs the same functions as this macro. Say that it is necessary to perform these functions 10 times during the execution of a given program. Contrast the use of a macro with the use of a procedure in this situation in terms of memory requirements and execution time.

8.2   *N* factorial (or *N*!) is defined as

$$N! = N(N-1)(N-2)(N-3) \cdots \quad (1)$$

Using the **REPT** pseudo-op, show how a macro can be developed to perform the factorial operation for a given *N*. Call the macro **N_FACTORIAL**. It should be invoked with the statement **N_FACTORIAL   %N**.

8.3   At the start of a procedure it is often necessary to save a group of registers on the stack. This is typically done with a series of **PUSH** instructions. Say that the registers to be saved are BP, AX, BX, DI, SI, and CX. Show how a repeat pseudo-op can be used with a single **PUSH** instruction to generate all the other necessary **PUSH** instructions.

8.4   Using the **REPT** pseudo-op show how to generate a sequence of reserved bytes containing the integers 1,2, . . ., 20.

8.5   A manufacturing company produces 200 different items. Associated with each item is a part identification code which is 2 bytes in length. The first hundred items have codes which range from A00 to A99, and the second hundred items have codes which range from B00 to B99. Associated with each item are 28 bytes of information. Use one of the repeat pseudo-ops to initialize memory with a sequence of **200*30** reserved memory locations each beginning with an items code.

8.6   Consider the macro **PCALL** of Section 8.5 which uses the **IFB** conditional pseudo-op. Rewrite this macro using the **IFBN** pseudo-op.

8.7   Section 8.4 and Figure 8-3 considered the problem of conditionally expanding a floating-point addition macro so that the presence or absence of the Intel 8087 Numeric Data Processor is taken into account. If the 8087 is present, there is still the problem of encoding the **FADD** instruction. Say that the assembler does not recognize and encode the **FADD   ST,ST(0)** instruction. Present a method for encoding this instruction as part of the application source program [For instance, **FADD   ST,ST(0)** itself could be made a macro]. Say that the **FADD ST,ST(0)** instruction is to be encoded as D8C0H.

8.8   Consider the macro of Figure 8-6. On encountering the **EXITM** statement, macro expansion is terminated. What would be the result of not having the **EXITM** statement in the macro?

8.9   Say that macro **MP2_FADD** of Figure 8-6 is called with the statement: **MP2_FADD   ST(0),ST(0)**. What would be the result?

8.10   In Section 4.4 a recursive procedure was presented for calculating *N*!. Compare this procedure with the code produced by the recursive macro **FACTORIAL** (Section 8.6) in terms of memory requirements and execution time. Note that this may be dependent on the number of factorial calculations that are needed in a given program, and the particular factorials required.

8.11 The **SUM** series of Section 8.2.2 is a series created by summing successive integers 1,2,3,4,5,. . . . The first five elements of **SUM** are thus 1,3,6,10, and 15. Develop a recursive macro to produce a series of *N* memory words initialized to the first *N* integers in **SUM**.

8.12 Under what conditions will assembling and calling the macro **MP2_FADD** result in the assembler message

```
Open Conditionals: 3
```

Should this message be of concern?

8.13 Using the macro definitions of Sections 8.1 and 8.2, show the result of assembling the program of Figure 8-2. What is the contents of the location **RESULT** after program execution?

9

Interrupts, Traps, and DOS

This chapter considers the *interrupt* and *trap* capabilities of the IBM PC. The interrupt feature provides a powerful mechanism to alter sequential instruction flow and cause automatic transfer to a target location where another program, the *interrupt service routine*, can commence execution. Once the interrupt routine is completed, the original program can be resumed. Unlike jumps and procedure calls, transfer to the target interrupt routine can be initiated not only under software control (called *software interrupt*) but also in response to both internal and external hardware (called *internal hardware interrupt* and *external hardware interrupt*) conditions which require attention. Thus hardware interrupts are used by peripheral devices to alert the IBM PC that they require attention (e.g., "I have data to send you.") and are used by the execution unit when special conditions internal to the processor occur (e.g., division by zero).

The term *trap* generally connotes the idea of altering program flow when a special condition occurs. Thus interrupting on an overflow condition may be referred to as a "trap on overflow." In the context of the IBM PC, the trap facility is specifically associated with the use of the flag register's *trap bit*. This facility causes an interrupt to take place after each instruction has been executed and is used in debugging and program tracing modes.

Software interrupts are used extensively by the operating system to access various system software and hardware resources. These interrupts may be used to perform I/O functions, such as reading from the keyboard or printing a character string, or for more general system support such as obtaining the time of day or listing the file directory. A good part of this chapter is devoted to categorizing and summarizing the operation of these interrupt-accessed routines.

9.1 INTERRUPT INSTRUCTIONS AND TYPES

9.1.1 Software Interrupts

Software interrupts occur in response to executing an **INT**errupt instruction whose assembly language format is

    INT   interrupt-type

Interrupt-type is an integer which specifies 1 of 256 memory addresses. This address is found by multiplying interrupt-type by 4. Thus, a type 0 interrupt refers to address 0, a type 1 interrupt to address 4, a type 2 interrupt to address 8, etc. Each one of these memory addresses identifies a 4-byte vector (called the *interrupt vector*) which contains a complete logical address (2 bytes for an offset address and 2 bytes for a segment address). The address specified by the interrupt vector is the address of the *interrupt service routine* associated with that interrupt-type.

Figure 9-1 shows low-order memory where the interrupt vectors are stored. The first five reserved vectors are common to all Intel 8088 systems and are used (with the exception of **INT   2**) with internal hardware interrupts. As will be discussed later, other vectors are reserved for specific IBM PC external hardware and internal software interrupts. The reserved software interrupts correspond to software facilities provided by the Disk Operating System (DOS interrupts) and the Basic Input/Output System (BIOS interrupts). Other vector addresses are unreserved and are available for user-defined software purposes. Of course, users can also change reserved interrupt vectors to refer to user-developed interrupt routines. Care should be taken, however, to make sure that various operating system functions needed for proper system operation are not disturbed. Figure 9-2, on page 207, shows the interrupt-types, with most of these being considered in detail later in this chapter.

Table 9-1 contains a list of all reserved interrupt vectors and indicates their general function, as well as the location of the associated interrupt service routine. DOS, for instance, means that the interrupt is normally serviced by the operating system. The notation (**IRET**) is used to denote that when this interrupt occurs, the system interrupt routine will consist of the single instruction **IRET**. In these situations the system does

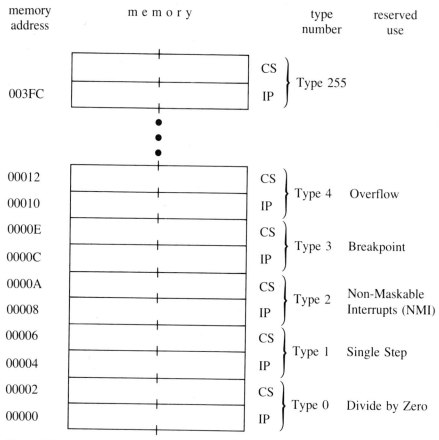

Figure 9-1   Intel 8088 interrupt vectors.

not know what action the user desires to take when the associated interrupt occurs, and thus does nothing. The user must change the interrupt vector and supply his or her own interrupt routine if particular actions are required.

On executing the **INT** instruction the processor saves the flag register, and the offset and segment addresses of the interrupted program on the stack, clears the trap and interrupt-enable flags, calculates the interrupt vector address, and loads the CS and IP registers with the address of the interrupt routine. Effectively, current program addresses and flag register contents are saved, and the CS and IP registers are reset so that the interrupt routine can begin executing.

The program transfer part of this process is similar to performing a **FAR CALL** to the interrupt routine. Note, however, that with a **CALL** instruction the starting address of the called procedure must be known, while in the case of an **INT** instruction only the interrupt-type number is necessary. Thus if the memory location of an interrupt routine changes (perhaps with a new version of the operating system), it is necessary

Table 9-1 Interrupt Vectors

| Interrupt | | | | |
Type	Vector Address	Category	Function	Interrupt Routine Location
0	0–3	8088	Divide by zero	DOS
1	4–7	Interrupts	Single step	DOS (**IRET**)
2	8–B		Nonmaskable Inter. (NMI)	BIOS
3	C–F		Breakpoint	DOS (**IRET**)
4	10–13		Overflow	DOS (**IRET**)
5	14–17		Print screen	BIOS
6,7	18–1B		Reserved	
8	20–23	8259	Timer	BIOS (**IRET**)
9	24–27	Hardware	Keyboard	BIOS
A,B,C,D	28–37	Interrupts	Reserved	
E	38–3B		Diskette	BIOS
F	3C–3F		Reserved	
10	40–43	Software	Video I/O)	BIOS
11	44–47	Interrupts	Equipment check	BIOS
12	48–4B	to BIOS	Memory size check	BIOS
13	4C–4F		Diskette I/O	BIOS
14	50–53		Communication I/O	BIOS
15	54–57		Cassette I/O	BIOS
16	58–5B		Keyboard input	BIOS
17	5C–5F		Printer I/O)	BIOS
18	60–63	Misc.	ROM Basic	ROM BASIC
19	64–67	Software	Bootstrap from disk	BIOS
1A	68–6B	interrupts	Time of day	BIOS
1B	6C–6F		Keyboard break	BIOS
1C	70–73		Timer tick	BIOS
1D	74–77	Table pointers	Video table pointer	
1E	78–7B		Diskette table pointer	
1F	7C–7F		Graphics character table ptr.	
20	80–83	Software	Program terminate	DOS
21	84–87	Interrupts	Function call (see Table 9.4)	DOS
22	88–8B	to DOS	Terminate address	DOS
23	8C–8F		CTRL-BRK exit address	DOS
24	90–93		Fatal error	DOS
25	94–97		Absolute disk read	DOS
26	98–9B		Absolute disk write	DOS
27	9C–9F		End program, remain resident	DOS
28–3F	A0–FF		Reserved/used internally DOS	DOS
40–7F	100–1FF	User	Reserved for user use	User
80–FO	200–3C3	BASIC	Reserved for BASIC use	BASIC

to change only the interrupt vector. This could be done on initializing the system (e.g., when the system is booted and the operating system performs initialization tasks). The key point here is that none of the programs which use the interrupt routine have to be changed since the interrupt vector address (i.e., interrupt-type) has not changed. If, on the other hand, transfer to an interrupt routine were performed with a **CALL** instruction, the address associated with each **CALL** instruction referencing that routine would have to be modified to reflect any change in memory placement. This feature is an important reason behind the extensive use of software interrupts in accessing operating system and BIOS service routines.

For instance, consider the BIOS routine which provides keyboard support. This routine is accessed with **INT 16H**. Since the routine performs several functions, the particular function desired is specified by loading the AH register with a value prior to issuing the **INT 16H** instruction. With AH equal to 0, the **INT 16H** BIOS routine waits for a key to be struck and then places the ASCII value of the struck key in AL (the special case of AL = 0 is considered in Section 10.1). The instruction sequence below receives this character and checks whether the received character is a carriage return (CR, ASCII code = 0DH).

```
CHKCR    MOV    AH, 0      ; set up AH for BIOS INT 16H
                          ; keyboard read routine.
         INT    16H        ; transfer to BIOS keyboard routine.
                          ; the next key struck will be read
                          ; and placed in AL.
         CMP    AL, 0DH    ; check for CR character
         JE     YESCR      ; if CR present jump to YESCR
                .          ; if CR not present, continue
                .
                .
```

Table 9-2   Actions on Interrupting

(SP) <— (SP) − 2	Decrement (SP) by 2.
((SP) + 1:(SP)) <— FLAG REG	Push flag register on stack.
(IF) <— 0 : (TF) <— 0	Clear interrupt-enable and trap flags.
(SP) <— (SP) − 2	Decrement (SP) by 2.
((SP) + 1:(SP)) <— (CS)	Push (CS) of ongoing program on stack.
(CS) <— (TYPE*4 + 2)	Load CS with interrupt service routine's segment address.
(SP) <— (SP) − 2	Decrement (SP) by 2.
((SP) + 1:(SP)) <— (IP)	Push (IP) of ongoing program on stack.
(IP) <— (TYPE*4)	Load IP with interrupt service routine's offset address.

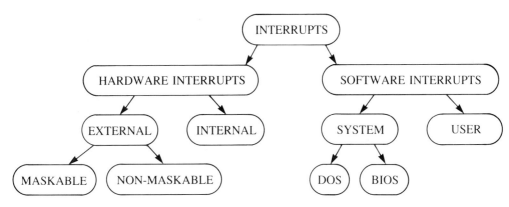

Figure 9-2   Interrupt types.

The sequence of actions which occurs on executing the **INT** instruction (or on receiving any internal or external hardware interrupt) is specified in Table 9-2 and illustrated in Figure 9-3.

Note that in the case of a software-generated interrupt, the flag register could have been saved by issuing a **PUSHF** instruction prior to the **INT** instruction. This could not be done for hardware interrupts since the program in general can't anticipate when such interrupts will occur. Thus the **PUSHF** instruction is effectively made part of the interrupt mechanism for all types of interrupts. Note also that clearing the trap and interrupt-enable flags prevents the interrupt routine itself from being interrupted. This will be considered further in the next sections.

The **INT** instruction may be encoded as a single-byte or double-byte instruction. The single-byte encoding (CCH) is reserved for interrupts of type 3, which correspond to the breakpoint interrupt. This will be discussed in Section 9.2.1.4. All other software interrupt-types are encoded in 2 bytes, the first containing the op code (CDH) and the second the type number.

Figure 9-3 (*a*) and (*b*) illustrate the stack just prior to and just after executing the **INT** instruction. On completion of the interrupt routine, the **IRET** (Interrupt **RET**urn) instruction is normally executed to return to the interrupted routine (i.e., the one that contained the **INT** instruction). Just as the **INT** instruction is comparable to the **CALL** instruction, **IRET** is comparable to the **RET** instruction. The difference is that in addition to popping the offset and segment addresses from the stack and loading them into the IP and CS registers, **IRET** also obtains the flag bits from the stack and loads the flag register with its former contents. Execution of the interrupted routine now resumes as indicated in Figure 9-3 (*c*).

The **INTO** (**INT**errupt on **O**verflow) is the only other interrupt instruction available on the Intel 8088. **INTO** is a conditional interrupt instruction in that it causes an **INT   4** instruction to be executed if the overflow flag is set. Thus **INTO** is typically

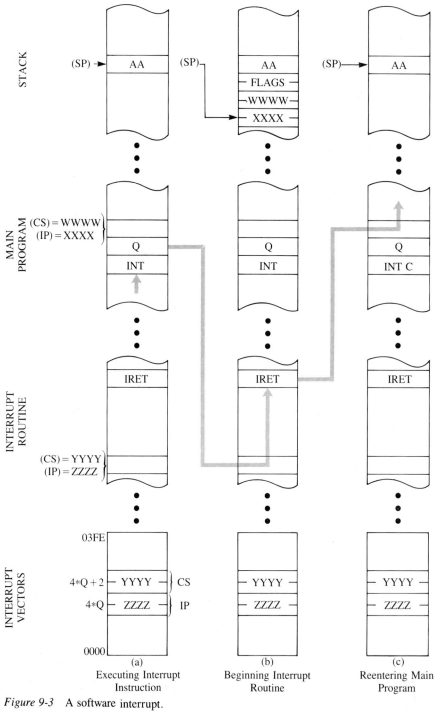

STACK

MAIN PROGRAM

INTERRUPT ROUTINE

INTERRUPT VECTORS

Figure 9-3   A software interrupt.

used after a sequence of arithmetic instructions to test and branch to an overflow error routine when overflow occurs. The interrupt process is the same as described earlier (Table 9-2). If overflow has not occurred, then execution continues with the instruction following **INTO**.

9.1.2 Hardware Interrupts

While software interrupts are a handy programming tool, the principal reason for having interrupts is to provide an efficient way for external devices to get the attention of the main processor. For instance, say a key is struck on the keyboard. How does the processor know that this event has occurred? One approach is to provide the keyboard with a status bit which indicates when a key is struck or released. If this bit could be interrogated by the processor, then by repeatedly testing its status, the processor could determine when keyboard action has occurred. The code corresponding to the key and action could now be read in and keystroke processing ensue. The program flowchart appears in Figure 9-4.

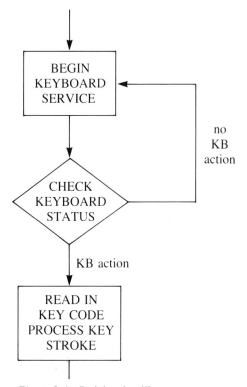

Figure 9-4   Peripheral polling.

Notice with this approach that even when the keyboard (or other peripheral device) does not require attention, the computer is still completely occupied with the task of repeatedly checking (sometimes called "polling") device status. This time might be better spent performing other useful processing tasks if only there were some way to alert the computer of external actions needing attention. The external interrupt facility performs such a function and is used in the IBM PC to alert the processor that a peripheral device requires attention.

In the case of the IBM PC keyboard, striking or releasing a key on the keyboard causes an external interrupt of type 9 to occur. This is equivalent to issuing the instruction **INT   9**; however, in this case, it is the peripheral device which is issuing the instruction. The result is the same, and all the actions indicated in Table 9-2 take place. Thus, a main program can run without concerning itself with when the keyboard needs attention. When it does need attention, an interrupt is automatically generated by the action of the keyboard in conjunction with the Intel 8259 interrupt controller, and transfer to the keyboard interrupt service routine is effected.

Note that earlier in this chapter an internal interrupt, **INT   16H**, was used to read a character from the keyboard. One might wonder what the relationship is between this internal interrupt and the external interrupt, **INT   9**. **INT   9** is produced by the hardware and is the attention-getting interrupt for keyboard action. **INT   16H** is a software-generated interrupt which accesses the BIOS (Chapter 10) keyboard routine. Within this BIOS keyboard routine is the interrupt service routine normally accessed by **INT   9**. The BIOS keyboard routine provides basic user keyboard services and shields the user from a host of detailed tasks which must be performed in dealing with the keyboard (e.g., distinguishing between key striking and releasing, checking for buffer overflow, handling combination keystrokes). It represents a higher-level program interface to the keyboard than using **INT   9** and directly reading the keyboard port. At a still higher level DOS (Section 9.3.2) has facilities for reading a character string from the keyboard directly into a buffer, where reading, for instance, continues until a carriage return character is encountered. DOS also provides for echoing each character read on the display. Finally, at the "highest" level, interactions with the keyboard can take place from within a higher-level language such as BASIC or PASCAL. In total, this represents a hierarchy of keyboard functions where the user, depending on his or her application, chooses the appropriate level of interaction. Normally one would interact with the keyboard at one of these higher levels. However, in special situations dealing more directly with the keyboard may be advantageous.

Interrupts of the INT 9 sort are referred to as *maskable* interrupts. Such interrupts use the **INTR** (**INT**errupt **R**equest) signal line on the Intel 8088 and are masked (disabled) if the **IF** (**I**nterrupt **F**lag) bit in the flag register is clear. Thus, in order to permit interrupts to arrive, the IF flag must be set. This may be done with the **STI** (**S**e**T I**nterrupt) instruction. On the other hand, if it is desired to execute an instruction sequence without being interrupted, the IF flag should be cleared. This is done automatically when an interrupt is serviced (see Table 9-2) to prevent the interrupt service routine from itself being interrupted. At other times the **CLI** (**CL**ear **I**nterrupt) instruction may be used. Note that since such interrupts occur asynchronously with the executing program, it is important that the interrupt routine save and restore any register information which it may modify. Note also that in general an interrupt occurring during the execution of an instruction waits until the instruction is completed before taking effect. One exception relates to prefix instructions such as repeat, lock, segment override, and the **MOV** to a segment register and **POP** from a segment register instructions. In these cases, another instruction is executed before the interrupt is processed. Another exception concerns **WAIT** and repeated string instructions. Since these instructions can take a relatively long time, interrupting may take place after completion of instruction's "minor" cycle (e.g., after moving 1 byte in a string of bytes).

Nonmaskable interrupts use the NMI signal line on the Intel 8088. These interrupts cannot be disabled and are typically used when very speedy time critical events occur which require processor attention. In the IBM PC the type 2 interrupt is nonmaskable and is used to signal the processor when a parity error occurs.

9.2 8088 AND 8259 HARDWARE INTERRUPTS

We now consider certain of the hardware interrupts (types 0 to F) in more detail. Many of the hardware interrupts are associated with servicing various peripheral devices. While a brief review of device operation will be presented where necessary, the reader is directed to the IBM technical reference manual (22) for detailed hardware information. This manual also contains program listings for BIOS.

9.2.1 8088 Interrupts (Types 0 to 7)

With the exception of the type 5 (print screen) interrupt, these interrupts are common to all Intel 8088 systems.

9.2.1.1 Divide-by-Zero Error—A Type 0 Interrupt   This interrupt occurs when the hardware detects an attempt to divide by zero. The interrupt vector is set by DOS, and the system interrupt routine displays "Divide overflow" and then returns to the instruction following the offending divide instruction.

9.2.1.2 Single-Stepping—A Type 1 Interrupt   This interrupt is used when it is desired to execute a program one instruction at a time (single-stepping). After setting the trap flag, a type 1 interrupt will occur on completion of the **NEXT** instruction. When the interrupt occurs, all of the actions of Table 9-2 ensue. Of particular note here is the fact that after the flag register is pushed onto the stack, the IF and trap flag are set to zero. Thus, the instructions which are part of the interrupt service routine are not themselves interrupted. These instructions can now be used to inform the user of the status of various registers, and of the next instruction to be executed in the main program. On returning from the interrupt routine, popping the flag register from the stack once again sets TF. One more instruction in the main program is now executed, and then another type 1 interrupt occurs. The interrupt service routine is again executed. In a typical debugging situation this might continue for some time until the user has obtained the information he or she needs and commands the interrupt routine to terminate the single-stepping process. The interrupt routine now clears the TF stored on the stack as part of the main routine's flag register. Returning to the main program this time will not cause an interrupt since, when the flag register is restored, TF is zero and the main program resumes execution in a normal manner.

Since a single-step capability is provided by the DOS **DEBUG** facility through use of the **TRACE** command, the type 1 interrupt is seldom used in application programs and its associated vector is set by DOS to point to an **IRET** instruction.

9.2.1.3 The nonmaskable interrupt—A Type 2 Interrupt
This interrupt cannot be masked out by clearing the interrupt flag in the flag register. In the IBM PC, it is used to alert the processor when a memory or I/O parity error has occurred. The interrupt vector is initialized by BIOS and the interrupt routine is a BIOS routine. Its starting address can be found by using **DEBUG** to examine the interrupt vector at address 8. Memory and I/O parity errors result in the display of messages PARITY CHECK 1 and PARITY CHECK 2, respectively.

9.2.1.4 The Breakpoint Feature—A Type 3 Interrupt
This interrupt may be generated with the single-byte form of the interrupt instruction (op code CCH). It is used in conjunction with program debugging when it is desired to execute a program until an instruction at a particular address (the breakpoint address) is encountered. In most situations, use of **DEBUG**'s breakpoint facility is adequate; therefore, DOS initializes the type 3 vector to point to an **IRET** instruction.

In implementing a breakpoint capability, the first byte of the instruction at the breakpoint address is replaced with the single-byte type 3 interrupt instruction. This causes an interrupt to occur when attempting to execute the instruction at that location. The interrupt routine can now display status information to the user and await further user commands. Typically, the debugging routine will save the instruction byte which the type 3 interrupt has replaced so that it can be restored and executed when the user issues a command to continue.

Of course, the type 3 interrupt also can be generated with a 2-byte interrupt instruction. The single-byte interrupt instruction, however, is necessary for the breakpoint operation to avoid the following error possibility: Consider the situation where there is a single-byte instruction (e.g., **CL**ear Carry) followed by a multiple-byte instruction (e.g., **MOV**) and it is desired to place a breakpoint at the **CLC** location. Substituting a 2-byte type 3 interrupt instruction at the **CLC** location would result in the second byte of the interrupt instruction overlapping the succeeding **MOV** instruction. This would cause a problem if there happened to be a jump to the **MOV** instruction from elsewhere in the program. The jump would encounter the second byte of the 2-byte **INT** instruction, causing an error. Using a single-byte **INT** instruction avoids this difficulty.

9.2.1.5 Overflow Errors—A Type 4 Interrupt
This interrupt is generally associated with the conditional interrupt instruction **INTO** (**INT**errupt on **O**verflow). The interrupt occurs when **INTO** has been issued, and the overflow flag in the flag register is set. The user must provide his or her own interrupt routine and vector initialization if special actions are to be taken on such a condition since DOS initializes the type 4

vector to point to an **IRET** instruction. Naturally, this interrupt also can be invoked directly with the **INT   4** instruction.

9.2.1.6 Printing the Screen—A Type 5 Interrupt   Though grouped with the Intel 8088 interrupt vectors, this interrupt really relates to an IBM PC function. It is often necessary to send output to both the screen display and also to an attached printer. The IBM PC provides this capability by having a key on the keyboard labeled PrtSc (Print-Screen), which, when pressed at the same time as the Shift key, causes the screen contents to be printed. The printing action continues until Shift-PrtSc is again depressed. This feature is implemented by having the Shift-PrtSc key depression cause a type 5 interrupt.

The type 5 interrupt vector is initialized by BIOS and points to a BIOS routine (**PRINT_SCREEN**). Output to the display can now also be easily routed to the printer by placing the instruction **INT   5** in your assembly language program. Since the print screen routine executes with interrupts enabled, care must be taken to prevent a new print screen operation from taking place while a prior operation is in progress. To prevent this, and also to have a place to record any errors which might occur during the print operation, BIOS maintains a status byte (located at 0050:0000 on the IBM PC) . A 0 in this byte indicates that a print screen operation is not in progress, or has been completed successfully. A 1 indicates that a print screen operation is in progress, and an 0FFH means that an error has occurred during the print operation. The print screen routine tests and sets this status byte to prevent a print screen operation from occurring while one is already in progress. Note that higher-level routines can also use this facility by calling a small assembly language routine (**INT   5** and **IRET**). This is discussed in Chapter 11.

Type 6 and 7 interrupts are reserved by IBM for future use.

9.2.2 8259 Interrupts (Types 8 to FH)

The Intel 8259 Interrupt Controller Chip within the IBM PC accepts interrupts from other devices and, in turn, controls and passes these interrupts over the **INTR** interrupt signal line to the Intel 8088. Up to eight devices may be attached to the 8259. Interrupts from these devices may be disabled as a group by clearing the 8088 interrupt flag bit in the flag register. It is also possible to disable interrupts associated with individual devices by altering bits within the *interrupt mask register* in the 8259. This register is accessed through port 21H and bits (the rightmost corresponds to device 0, the leftmost to device 7) can be set and cleared using the **OUT** instruction. A 0 in a bit position indicates that the corresponding device interrupt is enabled and a 1 indicates that it is disabled (i.e., masked).

Although up to eight devices may be attached to the 8259, an unexpanded IBM PC provides services for three devices, an interval timer (device 0), the keyboard (device 1), and the diskette controller (device 6). Since these devices might attempt to execute their interrupts "simultaneously," one of the 8259's tasks is to establish priority ordering among the interrupts. The priority established gives device 0, the timer, highest priority, and device 7, if one is present, lowest priority.

When an interrupt arrives while another is being serviced, the 8259 holds the second (and third, etc.) interrupt until completion of service for the current interrupt. The 8088 signals the 8259 that the interrupt routine has been completed by placing an *end of interrupt* (EOI) character (20H) in the 8259's *interrupt command register*. This register may be accessed through port 20H and the EOI command issued with the instructions **MOV   AL,20H** and **OUT   20H,AL** (it is just coincidence that 20H is both the port number and the EOI character). These instructions should complete any interrupt service routine for 8259-generated interrupts. After receiving the EOI signal, the 8259 generates the next interrupt, if any is pending.

9.2.2.1 The System Timer—A Type 8 Interrupt

The IBM PC contains a timer chip, the Intel 8253, which causes (through the 8259) a type 8 interrupt to occur 18.2 times per second (i.e., about every 0.0549 seconds). BIOS initializes the associated interrupt vector to point to a BIOS routine (BIOS label **TIMER_INT**). This routine maintains a count of these timer interrupts or clock ticks in a double word whose low order-byte is at 0000:006C (BIOS labels **TIMER_LOW** and **TIMER_HIGH**). The routine also executes a type 1C interrupt each time it is called, and it is this interrupt (which naturally also occurs at 18.2 times per second) that is typically used when an application routine is developed which requires individual clock ticks (see Problem 9.6).

Another function of the **TIMER_INT** routine is to turn off the diskette motor if it is not used for a given time period. Finally, if your program just wants to read or set the **TIMER_LOW/TIMER_HIGH** counter, then the BIOS routine **TIME_OF_DAY** (Section 9.2.3.3) invoked with a type 1A interrupt is an easy way to perform these tasks. At a somewhat higher level, DOS provides facilities for setting and obtaining both the date and time through use of interrupt 21H, functions 2A, 2B, 2C, and 2D (Section 9.3).

9.2.2.2 Keyboard Action—A Type 9 Interrupt

As indicated earlier, a host of actions result from a key being struck or released on the IBM PC keyboard. These actions can be viewed in terms of a hierarchy extending from low-level keyboard servicing to high-level character and message buffering. This hierarchy is illustrated in Figure 9-5.

At the lowest level within the keyboard is a dedicated processor, the Intel 8048, which handles basic keyboard interactions. For instance, when a key is depressed, the contact often bounces about for a short period of time appearing to be depressed, then released, then depressed, and so on. Eventually it settles down. However, this bouncing action must be distinguished from the single user action of key depression or release. A debouncing routine in the 8048 performs this function. Another example concerns determining which of the keys is being depressed or released. The 8048 scans the keyboard looking for key contact connections or breaks, and identifying the key where activity has been detected. After having detected keyboard action, determined the key involved, and performed the debouncing function, the 8048 communicates this information over a serial line to the 8259, which in turn interrupts the IBM PC's 8088 processor with a type 9 interrupt. In addition to these services, the 8048 also provides a character buffering function and a power-on keyboard test.

Receipt of keyboard characters using higher-level-language commands

DOS Keyboard Functions : INT 21H
A user-invoked software interrupt (DOS Functions 1,6, 7,8,A,B, and C) to perform a variety of functions, including character input with or without display echoing and Ctrl-Break testing. Also buffered keyboard input, and input buffer clearing.

BIOS Keyboard Functions (KEYBOARD IO): INT 16H
A user software interrupt to enable reading keyboard characters, determining if a character is available, or returning keyboard status.

8259 Keyboard Interrupt : INT 9
The 8259 interrupts the 8088 when a key is depressed or released. INT 9 is normally serviced by BIOS routine KB INT, which buffers characters and detects key combinations requiring special handling.

8048 Keyboard Servicing
The Intel 8048 resides in the keyboard and scans the keyboard for activity, determines the key on which activity has been detected, does key debouncing, and communicates activity to the 8259. Power-on keyboard test functions are also performed.

Figure 9-5   The keyboard servicing hierarchy.

The type 9 interrupt occurs whenever a key is depressed or released. The scan code of the key depressed or released can now be obtained from port 60H (BIOS label **KB_DATA**). Keyboard control bits are found in port 61H (BIOS label **KB_CTL**). Scan codes are discussed in Section 10.1. Use and interpretation of the port 61H is discussed in the IBM PC hardware reference manual (22).

The BIOS routine **KB_INT** typically services the type 9 interrupt: It accepts keyboard characters, buffers them, keeps track of key depression and release, and tests for special character combinations such as shift key combinations. Unless special circumstances arise, it is generally best to let this routine perform type 9 interrupt processing and use higher-level BIOS (Section 10.1) or DOS (Section 9.3.2) facilities when interacting with the keyboard.

9.2.2.3 The Diskette Drive Needs Attention—A Type E Interrupt The diskette drives and their associated control unit comprise a fairly complex IBM PC subsystem. The physical drive unit holds and spins the floppy disks, moves the read/write heads, and generally provides the electrical interface to run the motors and transfer information between the read/write heads and the floppy disk. This unit is interfaced with a micro-processor-based control unit (the Diskette Adapter Unit) whose job it is to control both the mechanical and information transfer aspects of drive operation. The adapter unit, in turn, interfaces with the main IBM PC system board and interrupts the processor through use of the 8259 interrupt controller. The result is a type E interrupt which is normally serviced by BIOS through its **DISK_INT** service routine. This routine obtains status information and provides the most basic disk control operations. The diskette drives, adapter unit, and associated BIOS routines are documented in the IBM PC technical reference manual (22). Because of the complexity of this subsystem, substi-tuting user-created routines for **DISK_INT** is not advised. Higher-level disk services are provided through BIOS (Section 10.5) interrupt 13H, and DOS interrupts 25 and 26 (Section 9.3). A group of disk-related file services are available under DOS using interrupt 21.

9.2.3 Miscellaneous Software Interrupts (Types 18H to 1CH)

9.2.3.1 Calling Cassette (ROM) Basic—A Type 18H Interrupt Several versions of the BASIC language interpreter are available with the IBM PC. The lowest level in terms of general capabilities is *Cassette*, or *ROM*, BASIC, which is contained in 32K of read-only memory. This version of BASIC has no inherent minimum memory con-straints; however, it has certain functional limitations, the most important being that it can only save information on a cassette tape recorder (i.e., disks are not supported). The interpreter may be invoked by issuing an interrupt of type 18H. For instance, with the standard IBM PC, on power-up BIOS tests for the presence of a properly loaded diskette drive and, if no drives are present or the diskette drives present are empty, issues an **INT 18H** instruction which begins execution of Cassette BASIC.

9.2.3.2 Booting the System—A Type 19H Interrupt When the IBM PC is powered up, or when a system reset command has been given (e.g., holding down the Ctrl, Alt, and Del keys together), BIOS is called upon to perform two key functions. First, BIOS tests the system components to determine if they are operating correctly. Second, BIOS determines if a properly loaded diskette drive is present. If present, then DOS is loaded into memory from the diskette and begins execution. If a properly loaded diskette is not present, then an **INT 18H** is executed as indicated earlier and Cassette BASIC begins. The process of loading in the DOS routines is referred to as *booting* the system and the BIOS routine which performs this task is called the *bootstrap loader*. This routine can be invoked by issuing a type 19H interrupt. Problem 9.7 examines the question of determining what disk sector is being booted, and where in memory it is placed. Note for PC XTs and systems with XT compatible hard disks, the system will boot from the hard disk if no properly loaded floppy is present.

Table 9-3   Using the System Time Counter

READING THE CLOCK COUNTER:

  1. Register setup   (AH)◄——————— 0

  2. Issue the interrupt   **INT   1AH**

  3. Information return   (CX) = High 16 bits of count
                                          (DX) = Low 16 bits of count
                                          (AL) = 0 means less than 24 hours has passed
                                                   since counter was last read.
                                          (AL) <> 0 means greater than 24 hours has
                                                     passed since counter was last read.

SETTING THE CLOCK COUNTER

  1. Register setup   (AH)◄——————— 1
                                          (CX)◄———————High 16 bits of count
                                          (DX)◄———————Low 16 bits of count

  2. Issue the interrupt   **INT   1AH**

  3. Information returned   None

9.2.3.3 *Reading and Setting the Clock Counter—A Type 1AH Interrupt*   As indicated earlier, a type 8 interrupt occurs 18.2 times per second and acts as a clock tick to the system. These ticks are used by a BIOS routine **TIMER_INT** to increment a double-word clock counter (BIOS labels **TIMER_LOW** and **TIMER_HIGH**). The type 1A interrupt invokes a related BIOS routine **TIME_OF_DAY**, which provides counter reading and setting services. For many applications there is thus no need to maintain a separate counter for clock ticks. Table 9-3 indicates how various registers are set to use this BIOS facility.

    As an example of clock counter and **INT   1AH** use, consider the problem of timing program or device operations. For instance, say that it is of interest (for system performance evaluation) to gather statistics on the time it takes to perform diskette read operations. Assume that there is a procedure **DISK_READ** which reads a randomly selected disk sector. Figure 9-6 presents a code segment to determine the number of clock ticks it takes to perform each read operation. The routine **DISK_STAT** aggregates the individual read times to obtain the necessary statistics over 100 read operations. The number of clock ticks is passed to **DISK_STAT** by **PUSH**ing CX and DX onto the stack. Note that sequencing disk reads in this manner will produce a certain bias in the results since the disk motor (with its associated delay) need not be turned on for each read operation. BX is used as a loop counter and should not be disturbed by the **DISK_READ** and **DISK_STAT** procedures. Problems 9.8 and 9.9 illustrate other uses of the clock timer.

```
          MOV     BX,100    ;BX <--- loop count
;*** SET CLOCK COUNTER TO ZERO ***
PLOOP:    XOR     CX,CX     ;clear tick counter
          XOR     DX,DX
          MOV     AH,1      ;AH <--- 1 to set counter
          INT     1AH       ;call BIOS routine
;*** PERFORM RANDOM DISK READ ***
          CALL    DISK_READ
;*** DETERMINE READ TIME ***
          MOV     AH,0      ;AH <--- 0 to read counter
          INT     1AH       ;call BIOS routine
;*** GATHER STATISTICS ***
          PUSH    CX        ;load stack with
          PUSH    DX        ;   count values
          CALL    DISK_STAT
          DEC     BX
          BLE     PLOOP     ;loop back if < 100 reads
```

Figure 9-6   Using the clock counter.

9.2.3.4 Keyboard Break—A Type 1BH Interrupt

Depressing the Ctrl-Break keys on the keyboard allows one to halt an executing program and return control to the operating system. The Ctrl-Break action first causes a keyboard hardware interrupt of type 9 to occur, which normally invokes the BIOS keyboard service routine **KB_INT**. This routine in turn, having detected the Ctrl-Break key combination, executes a type 1B software interrupt (initially set up to point to an **IRET**).

By changing the type 1B vector and supplying an appropriate routine, the action which is initiated on Ctrl-Break can be determined by the user. That is, let BIOS perform all the keyboard servicing; however, after it has detected Ctrl-Break, the **INT   1B** instruction calls the user supplied routine. This is shown below in Example 9-1.

EXAMPLE 9-1   The routine shown in Figure 9-7 modifies the Ctrl-Break interrupt vector so that it points to a user-developed interrupt routine labeled **IROUT**. **IROUT**, invoked when the Ctrl-Break keys are depressed, merely prints out the message CTRL-BRK and then returns to the executing program.

The **DSEGA** data segment is used to associate a label (**INTBRK**) with the physical address for the control break interrupt vector. The **DSEGB** data segment contains the message to be displayed when the Ctrl-Brk keys are depressed. The first part of the code segment is used to load the interrupt vector with the address of the interrupt routine. A DOS software interrupt, **INT   27H**, is now used to return to the operating system while leaving the **CSEGB** and **DSEGB** code and data segments (including the **IROUT** interrupt routine which has not yet been executed) resident in memory. Other programs which are to be executed will now be loaded into memory above these segments. **IROUT**, though loaded, will not be executed until the Ctrl-Brk keys are depressed. Within **IROUT**, the CTRL-BRK message is displayed using the **INT   10H** BIOS facility (see Section 10.3.1.3). Control is then returned to the interrupted program.

```
;        *** PROGRAM FOR CONTROL BREAK KEY ACTION ***
DSEGA    SEGMENT AT 0          ;define segment that starts
                               ; at physical address 0000
         ORG    1BH*4          ;offset address for keyboard
                               ;break interrupt vector
INTBRK   LABEL  WORD           ;the interrupt vector can now
                               ;be accessed with label INTBRK
DSEGA    ENDS
DSEGB    SEGMENT
CMESS    DB     'CTRL-BRK',13,10 ;13=CR, 10=LF
DSEGB    ENDS
;
CSEGB    SEGMENT               ;define code segment
         ASSUME  CS:CSEGB,DS:DSEGB
;*** PROGRAM TO SET UP INTERRUPT VECTOR ***
START:   XOR    AX,AX          ; (AX) <--- 0
         MOV    ES,AX          ; (ES) <--- 0
         MOV    ES:INTBRK,OFFSET IROUT  ;load interrupt routine
         MOV    ES:INTBRK+2,SEG IROUT   ; offset and segment addr.
;*** RETURN TO OPERATING SYSTEM BUT REMAIN RESIDENT ***
         MOV    DX,$+50H        ;load DX with an address beyond the
                                ;interrupt routine instructions and
         INT    27H             ;data. Return to DOS but remain
                                ;resident. Programs will now be loaded
                                ;above the value in DX.
;*** INTERRUPT ROUTINE ***
IROUT:   PUSH AX                ;save caller's registers
         PUSH DS
         PUSH BX
         PUSH CX
         PUSH SI
         MOV  AX,DSEGB          ;set up DS
         MOV  DS,AX
;*** DISPLAY CONTROL BREAK MESSAGE ***
         MOV  CX,10             ;set up character counter
         XOR  SI,SI             ; (SI) <--- 0
ZLOOP:   MOV  AL,[SI+CMESS]     ; (DL) <--- character to display
         MOV  AH,14             ;set AH for INT 10H BIOS Teletype
         XOR  BX,BX             ; like display function
         INT  10H               ;select BIOS function
         INC  SI                ;pick next character
         LOOP ZLOOP
;
         POP  SI                ;restore caller's registers
         POP  CX
         POP  BX
         POP  DS
         POP  AX
         IRET                   ;return from interrupt routine
CSEGB    ENDS
         END  START
```

Figure 9-7   A control break interrupt routine.

9.2.3.5 A User Clock Tick—A Type 1CH Interrupt The system clock tick was discussed earlier in connection with the hardware interrupt of type 8. As indicated, BIOS routine **TIMER_INT** normally services this interrupt. One of its services is to issue a type 1C interrupt. BIOS initially sets the 1C interrupt vector to point to an **IRET** instruction. However, the user may modify this vector so that it points to his or her own routine. The objective here is to provide the user with his or her own clock tick interrupt, thereby discouraging use of the type 8 interrupt by user programs.

9.3 DOS INTERRUPTS (TYPES 20H to 3FH)

The disk operating system provides a large and powerful set of system services which are accessible by issuing various software interrupts. While some of these overlap with those services available through BIOS, many are at a somewhat higher level. The details of these DOS interrupts may be found in the Appendices of the IBM disk operating system manual (27) and are not pursued here. Several tables, however, are presented to indicate the type of services available with DOS. Table 9-4 presents a number of the fundamental DOS interrupt types.

One item which requires some further discussion concerns normal program termination using DOS **INT   20H**. To ensure proper termination, the CS register must contain the segment address of the program's Program Segment Prefix (PSP) just prior to executing **INT   20H**. The PSP is a 100H-byte long segment created by the operating system to hold data related to the program to be executed. It is placed just before the program when the program is loaded into memory. The first byte of the PSP contains the normal termination instruction **INT   20H**. The question is, just how can one ensure the proper contents of CS just prior to executing **INT   20H**?

One approach is to use the fact that just after an executable (**.EXE**) program receives control from the operating system and begins execution, DS (and ES) contains the segment address of the program's PSP. Say that a program is declared to be a **FAR** procedure and begins with the instructions

```
PUSH    DS      ;stack gets segment address of PSP
XOR     AX,AX   ;clear AX
PUSH    AX      ;stack gets 0 return offset address
```

Being a procedure, the program ends with the instruction

```
RET             ;FAR procedure return
```

The beginning instructions ensure that the stack contains the CS:IP address for the start of the PSP. The **RET** instruction loads CS:IP from the stack and jumps to the start of the PSP. However, the first location of the PSP contains the instruction **INT   20H**. Hence, the program is terminated properly. This termination approach has been used in numerous examples throughout this book.

Table 9-4 DOS Interrupts

INT Num.	Name	Function
20H	PROGRAM TERMINATE	Used for normal program termination. DOS performs various cleanup functions and then awaits the next user DOS command. The CS register must contain the segment address of the PSP, Program Segment Prefix, for the program being terminated prior to issuing the interrupt.
21H	FUNCTION CALL	A host of services is provided with this interrupt. The particular service may be selected by setting AH to the service number and then issuing **INT 21H**. The services available are outlined in Tables 9-5 to 9-8.
22H	TERMINATE ADDRESS	DOS activates this interrupt when a program ends. Control transfers to a termination address. The associated interrupt vector may be modified (e.g., using **INT 21H**, function 25H) to invoke user cleanup and termination routines.
23H	CTRL-BRK EXIT ADDR	DOS activates this interrupt when the Ctrl-Break key is depressed. The type 23H interrupt vector may be modified (e.g., using **INT 21H** function 25H) to invoke a user routine to provide Ctrl-Break service (also see Example 9-1).
24H	FATAL ERROR	DOS activates this interrupt when it runs into a critical error such as a disk error. Information is passed by DOS indicating the type of error. If desired, type 24H interrupt vector can be modified to point to a user error handling routine.
25H	ABSOLUTE DISK READ	By providing the appropriate information in AL, CX, DX, DS, and BX, selected disk sector(s) can be read into a designated area of memory. This service is also provided by BIOS interrupt 13H but with somewhat less error checking.
26H	ABSOLUTE DISK WRITE	Same as 25H above except the information is written onto the disk sector(s).
27H	TERMINATE, BUT REMAIN RESIDENT	This service allows a program to end execution but remain resident in memory. DOS adjusts its memory map so that later, when other programs are loaded, the program which has executed **INT 27H** initially is not overwritten (see Example 9-1). **INT 21H** function 31H provides a similar service but also includes the ability to return a completion code to DOS.
28H–3FH		Reserved or used internally by DOS.

Table 9-5 DOS **INT** **21H** Functions For Character-Oriented Input/Output
(Keyboard, Display, Printer, and Communications Adapter)

(AH)	Name	Purpose and Operation
1	KEYBOARD INPUT/ DISPLAY	Waits for a keyboard character and then echoes the received character on the display and places it in AL. Ctrl-Break results in **INT** **23H**. See BIOS **INT** **16H** for related services.
2	DISPLAY CHARACTER	The character in DL is displayed.
3	ASYNC. INPUT	Waits for an input character on the asynchronous communications adapter and places received character in AL. BIOS **INT** **14H** provides similar services.
4	ASYNC. OUTPUT	The character in DL is sent out to the asynchronous communications adapter. BIOS **INT** **14H** provides similar services.
5	PRINT CHARACTER	The character in DL is printed. BIOS **INT** **17H** provides similar services.
6	KEYBOARD INPUT/ CHARACTER DISPLAY	There are two operation modes with this interrupt. The user sets the contents of DL to select the mode. **a** (DL) = FFH : If a keyboard character is ready, ZF is cleared and the character is placed in AL. If no character is available, ZF is set. No waiting takes place and no Ctrl-Brk services are provided. **b** (DL) not FFH : The character in DL is displayed.
7	KEYBOARD INPUT/ NO DISPLAY	Waits for an input character from the keyboard and, when it arrives, places it in AL. Ctrl-Brk and display echo services are not provided.
8	KEYBOARD INPUT/ NO DISPLAY	Same as function 7 except Ctrl-Brk services are provided.
9	DISPLAY STRING	The character string starting at the address found in DS:DX and ending with a $ character (24H) is displayed.
A	KEYBOARD STRING	A character string is read from the keyboard into a buffer beginning at the user-supplied address given in DS:DX. The first byte of the buffer, set by the user, defines its length. Characters are read in beginning with the third byte and continuing until either the ENTER key is read or the buffer is filled to one less than its maximum length. When the ENTER key is read, the interrupt routine returns with the second byte of the buffer containing the number of characters read (excluding CR). The last byte of the buffer will contain the CR character. Extra charac-

Table 9-5   continued
(Keyboard, Display, Printer, and Communications Adapter)

(AH)	Name	Purpose and Operation
		ters are ignored and the bell is rung if an overflow condition is about to occur.
B	KEYBOARD STATUS	If a character is available from the keyboard, AL is returned containing FFH; otherwise, AL is returned with 00. A check for Ctrl-Brk is made.
C	KEYBOARD BUFFER CLEAR	The keyboard buffer within the keyboard is cleared, and the **INT 21H** function (only 1,6,7,8, and A are allowed) specified in AL is performed.

The type 21H interrupt is of particular importance and provides numerous DOS services (functions). Individual functions may be invoked by setting AH equal to the code of the desired function prior to executing the **INT   21H** instruction. The functions available with **INT   21H** are outlined in Tables 9-5 to 9-8. Table 9-5 focuses on functions which provide input/output services to character-oriented devices such as the keyboard, display, printer, and asynchronous communications adapter. These functions are available with all versions of DOS. Table 9-6 concerns disk maintenance, disk I/O, and general file manipulation functions; and Table 9-7 summarizes functions related to general system control and access. Functions numbered 2F and greater are only available with DOS versions 2.0 and later. Those newer DOS functions not presented in Tables 9-5 to 9-7 are listed in Table 9-8. Note that a number of these newer functions overlap with functions present in earlier DOS versions. The later functions are typically more general and powerful. See IBM DOS manual Appendix D for details.

The remainder of this section presents three short but typical programs which utilize these services.

9.3.1 Displaying Messages with DOS

As a first example, consider the common problem of sending messages to the user of a program in a simple convenient manner. Say that there are four messages which are to be sent to the display and a common message display procedure (call it **DISPLAY**) is required. For this example, the messages are error messages and have an associated error number. The error message for error 3, say, is

```
ERR 3: SECURITY VIOLATION
```

The calling procedure for the message routine is to be a near procedure call with AL loaded with the error message number prior to issuing the procedure call. Thus to display error message 3 would only require the instructions

```
MOV    AL, 3        ; load AL to display error 3
CALL   DISPLAY      ; DISPLAY is the display routine
```

Table 9-6 DOS **INT** **21H** Functions for Disk and File Manipulation

(AH)	Name	Purpose and Operation
D	DISK RESET	Resets the diskette system.
E	DEFAULT DISK SELECT	The default disk drive is selected by setting DL ($0 \rightarrow$ A, $1 \rightarrow$ B, etc.). The number of drives in the system is returned in AL. Also see BIOS **INT** **11H**.
F	OPEN FILE	Files in DOS are defined with a FCB (File Control Block). Each diskette has a directory of the files it contains. Opening a file establishes the logical connection between the file's FCB and its entry in the diskette directory. Prior to invoking the function, DS:DX points to the file's FCB. On return, AL contains 00 if the file was found, FFH if it was not found.
10	CLOSE FILE	After writing a file, it should be closed to update directory information. DS:DX points to the file's FCB prior to invoking the function. On return AL is interpreted as in function F.
11	FILENAME SEARCH	DS:DX holds the address of unopened file FCB prior to invoking the function. The directory of the currently defined disk is searched for the filename and on return AL indicates as in function F whether the file was found.
12	NEXT FILENAME SEARCH	Function 11 above can be used to search for an ambiguous filename. For example **A:DRAW.*** refers to all files on drive **A** whose prefix is **DRAW**, but whose suffix is undefined. This may include several files. Function 11 will find the first occurrence of **DRAW**, while function 12 will find the next. (AL) is interpreted as above.
13	DELETE FILE	As in function 11, except that all files found with matching filenames are deleted.
14	SEQUENTIAL READ	DS:DX holds the address of an opened FCB. The record specified in the FCB is read, and then the record address incremented. On return, if (AL) = 0, the record was read successfully; if (AL) = 1, no data was present; if (AL) = 2, insufficient space was available; and if (AL) = 3, only a partial record was read.
15	SEQUENTIAL WRITE	As in 14, except that a disk write is performed. On return, if (AL) = 0, the record was written successfully; if (AL) = 1, the diskette was full; if (AL) = 2, not enough space was available.

Table 9-6 continued

(AH)	Name	Purpose and Operation
16	CREATE FILE	DS:DX holds the address of an unopened FCB. Attempts to create a file entry in the disk directory. On return, if (AL) = 0, file entry was created and file was opened; and if (AL) = FF, no entry is available.
17	RENAME FILE	DS:DX holds the address of a modified FCB, which has both old and new filenames. Searches for old filenames and renames them with new filenames. On return, if (AL) = 0, renaming was successful; and if (AL) = FF, no match was found.
19	GET CURRENT DISK	Used to determine the current default disk drive. On return, (AL) has current default drive number (0 = A, 1 = B, etc.).
1A	SET TRANSFER ADDRESS	DS:DX is set to contain the disk transfer address desired and then the interrupt is invoked.
1B	GET FAT	Used to obtain information about the File Allocation Table (FAT) for the default drive.
1C	GET FAT	As in 1B with disk drive being specified (DOS > 2.0).
21	RANDOM READ	As in function 14, except that the current block and record fields are set to reflect the random record fields prior to reading and no record address incrementing is performed.
22	RANDOM WRITE	As in function 21, except that a write is performed.
23	RANDOM FILE SIZE	DS:DX is set to point to an unopened FCB. Invoking the interrupt causes the diskette directory to be searched for a matching entry. If found, the random record field is set to hold the number of records in the file and (AL) = 0; otherwise, (AL) = FF.
24	SET RANDOM RECORD FIELD	DS:DX is set to point to an unopened FCB. Invoking the interrupt sets the random record field to the file address found in the current block and record fields.
27	RANDOM BLOCK READ	As in function 21, except that CX must be set to contain a record count prior to invoking the interrupt. If possible, the number of records specified in CX are read. On return CX contains the actual number of records read. (AL) is interrupted as in function 14.

Table 9-6   continued

(AH)	Name	Purpose and Operation
28	RANDOM BLOCK WRITE	As in function 27, except that a block write is performed. Also (AL) = 01 on return if there is insufficient disk space.
29	PARSE FILENAME	Used to parse a filename (typically entered by a user from the keyboard) and create an unopened FCB from that name. See DOS manual for details.
2E	SET DISK VERIFY SWITCH	Used to direct DOS to perform a verify operation on every disk write. Set (DL) = 0 and (AL) = 1 to turn on verify; (DL) = 0 and (AL) = 0 to turn off verify prior to invoking interrupt.
2F	GET DTA	On return ES:BX ← current DTA (Disk Transfer Address) (DOS > 2.0)
36	GET DISK FREE SPACE	Used to determine the amount of free space left on the disk. See DOS manual for details (DOS > 2.0).
54	GET VERIFY STATE	Used to determine disk verify switch setting (see 2E above). On return, (AL) = 00 if OFF: (AL) = 01 if ON (DOS > 2.0).

Figure 9-8 contains both a **DISPLAY** procedure and a procedure **TEST** which tests the **DISPLAY** procedure. The **TEST** procedure calls **DISPLAY** four times, each time displaying a different message.

The **DISPLAY** procedure makes use of a fixed-length message format (see Problem 9.14) to establish a character display loop which is the same for all messages. AL, the message number passed by the calling routine, is multiplied by the message length to establish an offset from the beginning of the first message. This offset establishes the starting address of the message to be displayed. The register SI is used to pick out each character in the message and is incremented after each character is displayed. The character is moved into DL, AH is set to select the display function, and the DOS character display routine is called with **INT   21H**. The procedure then loops through all the characters in the message, exiting when CX is decremented to zero. **TEST** calls **DISPLAY** four times, displaying each message in turn.

If one has DOS version 2.0 or later, the **DISPLAY** routine can be simplified using the more advanced general-purpose I/O capabilites of **INT   21H** function 40H (write to file or device). The **DISPLAY** routine using this function is shown in Figure 9-9.

Function 40H of **INT   21H** provides a more powerful and general method of writing files. Prior to executing **INT   21H**, DS:DX must contain the address, and CX the length (e.g., number of bytes) of the data to be written. BX must contain the file "handle," where 0000 and 0001 are the handles for the standard input and output devices, respectively. Handles are a concept introduced with DOS version 2.0 and basically constitute a file or device identifier which is needed by the interrupt service

Table 9-7 DOS **INT** **21H** Functions for General Control

(AH)	Name	Purpose and Operation
0	PROGRAM TERMINATE	Normal program termination (same as **INT** **20H**). The only non-I/O-oriented interrupt in this group.
25	SET INTERRUPT VECTOR	DS:DX and AL are set to contain a vector address and interrupt-type number, respectively. Invoking the interrupt sets the interrupt vector for the type in AL to (DS:DX).
26	CREATE NEW PROGRAM SEGMENT	Used to create a new program segment. The newer version, function 4B, should be used where possible.
2A	GET DATE	Returns date as (CX) = YEAR (1980–2099 in binary), (DH) = month (1 = Jan., 2 = Feb., etc.), and (DL) = Day.
2B	SET DATE	Use the format of function 2A to set the date. Returns (AL) = 00 if operation successful; (AL) = FF otherwise.
2C	GET TIME	Returns time as (CH) = hours (0–23); (CL) = minutes (0–59); (DL) = seconds (0–59); and (DL) = 1/100 of seconds (0–99).
2D	SET TIME	Use the format of function 2C to set the time. Returns (AL) = 00 if operation successful; (AL) = FF otherwise.
30	GET DOS VERSION	Returns the DOS version number as (AL) = major version number, (AH) = minor version number. If (AL) = 0, it is version 1.0 or 1.1.
31	TERMINATE BUT STAY RESIDENT	Similary to type 20H DOS interrupt. This newer version permits return of an exit code to process that has initiated termination. See DOS 2.0 manual for details.
33	CHECK/SET CTRL-BRK	Checks or sets the DOS BREAK switch. If BREAK is ON, then DOS checks for Ctrl-Break whenever any DOS function is requested. If BREAK is OFF, then checking is only done during screen, keyboard, printer, or asynchronous operations. To set BREAK ON (AL) = 01, (DL) = 01; to set OFF (AL) = 01 and (DL) = 00. To check setting (AL) = 00, and on return DL contains state as above.
35	GET INTERRUPT VECTOR	Does the opposite of function 25. Set (AL) = interrupt type number (hex). On return ES:BX contains interrupt vector (CS:IP).

Table 9-8   Some Functions with DOS Version 2.0 and Later

38:	GET COUNTRY INFORMATION	46:	FORCED DUPLICATE OF A
39:	CREATE A SUB-DIRECTORY		HANDLE
3A:	REMOVE DIRECTORY ENTRY	47:	GET CURRENT DIRECTORY
3B:	CHANGE CURRENT DIRECTORY	48:	ALLOCATE MEMORY
3C:	CREATE A FILE	49:	FREE ALLOCATED MEMORY
3D:	OPEN A FILE	4A:	SETBLOCK
3E:	CLOSE A FILE HANDLE	4B:	LOAD OR EXECUTE A PROGRAM
3F:	READ FROM A FILE OR DEVICE	4C:	TERMINATE A PROCESS (EXIT)
40:	WRITE TO A FILE OR DEVICE	4D:	GET SUB-PROCESS RETURN
41:	DELETE A FILE		CODE
42:	MOVE FILE READ/WRITE POINTER	4E:	FIND FIRST MATCHING FILE
43:	CHANGE FILE MODE	4F:	FIND NEXT MATCHING FILE
44:	I/O CONTROL FOR DEVICES	56:	RENAME A FILE
45:	DUPLICATE A FILE HANDLE	57:	GET/SET FILE DATE/TIME

routine to perform its function. When a file is opened with function 3DH, a file handle is returned as a 16-bit integer in AX. This handle can now be used with a number of advanced functions (see the DOS manual, Appendix D).

For certain standard devices, there is no need to perform an open operation. In the example above, the predefined handle for the standard output device is loaded into BX prior to executing **INT   21H**. Contrasting the **DISPLAY** program of Figure 9-9 with that of Figure 9-8, the principal difference is that the user no longer must perform the loop operation necessary to display each character individually. In other words, the user now deals with messages and communicates the message length, position, and output device to the interrupt service routine.

9.3.2 Reading the Keyboard with DOS

Another common problem encountered is that of reading the keyboard. The functions 1,6,7,8,A,B, and C of **INT   21H** provide basic keyboard input facilities. Differences between the functions include whether the interrupt routine should wait for a character, whether the received character should be displayed, and whether a check should be made for the Ctrl-Break key sequence. More advanced keyboard functions are provided with DOS version 2.0. As an example, consider the problem of reading lines from the keyboard (a line is a series of key strokes terminated with depression of the ENTER key) and displaying them on the standard display device. Say that hitting the dollar sign ($) key should cause the program to return control to the operating system. Figure 9-10 illustrates a procedure called **ENTRY** which performs these functions using function 3F of **INT   21H**.

The **ENTRY** procedure sets DS:DX to hold the address of the buffer into which the characters are read and BX to hold the "handle" for the standard input device (0000). CX is set to hold the maximum number of characters to be read (the reader should note that our experience with DOS Version 2.0 indicates that there is currently

```
; *** DATA AND STACK SEGMENTS ***
DSEG          SEGMENT                    ;define data segment
CR            EQU 13D                    ;define carriage return
LF            EQU 10D                    ;define line feed
ERROR         DB    'ERR 0: ILLEGAL OPERATION ',CR,LF
              DB    'ERR 1: DISK FULL         ',CR,LF
              DB    'ERR 2: DISK READ ERROR   ',CR,LF
              DB    'ERR 3: SECURITY VIOLATION',CR,LF
MESLENGTH     DW    27D                  ;length of all messages
DSEG          ENDS
SSEG          SEGMENT      STACK         ;define stack segment
              DB    256 DUP (?)
SSEG          ENDS
; *** DISPLAY TEST PROCEDURE ***
CSEG          SEGMENT                    ;define code segment
TEST          PROC           FAR
              ASSUME         CS:CSEG, DS:DSEG, SS:SSEG
START:        PUSH DS                    ;stack <--- return seg. addr.
              XOR   AX,AX                ;clear AX
              PUSH AX                    ;stack <--- 0 return address
              MOV   AX,DSEG              ;set up data segment register
              MOV   DS,AX
              MOV   AL,0                 ;initialize message selection
              MOV   CX,4                 ;of messages to be displayed
DISPTEST:     CALL DISPLAY               ;call DISPLAY procedure
              INC   AL                   ;select next message
              LOOP DISPTEST
              RET                        ;return to DOS
TEST          ENDP
; *** DISPLAY PROCEDURE ***
DISPLAY       PROC NEAR
              PUSH CX                    ;save CX and AX registers
              PUSH AX
              XOR   SI,SI                ;clear SI, character pointer
              MOV   CX,MESLENGTH         ;CX <--- message length
              MUL   BYTE PTR MESLENGTH   ;AH,AL <---AL*MESLENGTH
              MOV   BX,AX                ;BX <--- displacement from ERROR
DISPLOOP:     MOV   DL,[BX+SI+ERROR]     ;DL <--- display char.
              MOV   AH,2                 ;select INT 21H function
              INT   21H                  ;display (DL)
              INC   SI                   ;pick next character
              LOOP DISPLOOP              ;display entire message
              POP   AX                   ;restore registers
              POP   CX
              RET
DISPLAY       ENDP
CSEG          ENDS
              END    START
```

Figure 9-8 Displaying messages with DOS.

```
DISPLAY   PROC    NEAR
          PUSH    CX
          PUSH    AX
          MOV     CX, MESLENGTH        ; CX <--- message length
          MUL     BYTE PTR MESLENGTH ; AH, AL <--- AL*MESLENGTH
          ADD     AX, OFFSET ERROR   ; AX <--- offset mes. addr.
          MOV     DX, AX  ; DS: DX start address for message
          MOV     BX, 0001 ; load BX with file ''handle''
          MOV     AH, 40H  ; select write option with function 40H
          INT     21H      ; display message
          POP     AX
          POP     CX
          RET
DISPLAY   ENDP
```

Figure 9-9   Advanced message display with DOS.

```
; *** DATA AND STACK SEGMENTS ***
DSEG      SEGMENT
BUFFER    DB        80 DUP (?)
DSEG      ENDS
SSEG      SEGMENT STACK
          DB        128 DUP (?)
SSEG      ENDS
; *** KEYBOARD ENTRY AND DISPLAY ROUTINE ***
CSEG      SEGMENT
ENTRY     PROC      FAR
          ASSUME    CS: CSEG, DS: DSEG, SS: SEG, ES: DSEG
BEGIN:    PUSH      DS          ; stack gets PSP return segment
          XOR       AX, AX      ; address. clear AX
          PUSH      AX          ; stack gets 0 return offset addr.
          MOV       AX, DSEG    ; set up DS and ES registers
          MOV       DS, AX
          MOV       ES, AX
          MOV       DX, OFFSET BUFFER ; DS: DX has addr. of buffer
INLOOP:   MOV       CX, 80      ; CX has maximum num. of characters
          MOV       BX, 0000 ; BX gets standard input device handle
          MOV       AH, 3FH     ; AH gets function number
          INT       21H         ; read a line from the keyboard
          MOV       CX, AX      ; on return AX has num. char. read
          MOV       AL, '$'     ; put $ character into AL
          MOV       DI, OFFSET BUFFER  ; set up DI for String Scan
          REPNE     SCASB       ; scan for $ character
          JNE       INLOOP      ; jump if $ has not been found
          RET                   ; return to DOS if $ has been found
ENTRY     ENDP
CSEG      ENDS
END       BEGIN
```

Figure 9-10   Keyboard input and display with DOS.

a bug here in that the value of CX appears to have no effect on the operation of the function when used with a 0000 handle). The function 3FH (read from a file or device) is then placed in AH and **INT   21H** executed. The interrupt routine will now read the keyboard characters and place them in the designated buffer until the ENTER key is depressed. Note that an internal buffer of about 125 characters apparently exists, and any characters received beyond that limit are lost. If no characters are received, the interrupt service routine waits. As part of the interrupt routine DOS also provides for the characters to be echoed on the display. After receiving a line from the keyboard, the **ENTER** routine checks for the presence on a dollar sign character ($) using the **SC**a**N** String **B**yte instruction. If present, control is returned to DOS; if not, then the routine calls function 3FH again and awaits the next line.

9.3.3 Printing with DOS

There are several ways to print individual characters or character strings using DOS functions. Function 5 may be used to print a character which has been loaded into DL. Thus, for instance, the **DISPLAY** routine may be modified to both print error messages and display them by inserting the following instructions after the **DISPLOOP**-labeled **MOV** instruction.

```
MOV     AH, 5    ; select print character function
INT     21H      ; print character in DL
```

Finally, the more advanced function 40H (write to a file or device) may be used. In this situation, BX must be loaded with the standard handle for the printer (0004), CX with the number of characters to be printed, and DS:DX with the starting address of the print buffer. For example, the **ENTRY** program of Figure 9-10 can be modified to print entries from the keyboard on a line-by-line basis by inserting the following instructions after the **INT   21H**.

```
MOV     CX, AX   ; on return AX has num. of characters read
MOV     BX, 0004 ; BX gets standard printer device handle
MOV     AH, 40H  ; AH gets function number
INT     21H      ; print line of characters
```

Note that in this situation there was no need to set up DS:DX since this was already done in preparation for the earlier function 3FH interrupt call.

9.4 SUMMARY

Interrupts provide a mechanism for transferring control from a main program to an *interrupt service routine*. When such a transfer is initiated by the hardware in response to special internal or external conditions, a *hardware interrupt* is said to have occurred. *External hardware interrupts* are generated by peripheral devices and are the main mechanism used by these devices to get the attention of the processor. As an example, an external hardware interrupt is generated when a key on the keyboard is depressed.

Certain external hardware interrupts are *maskable* in that they may be disabled by clearing the IF (Interrupt Flag) bit in the flag register.

Internal hardware interrupts are hardware interrupts which are generated internally to the processor, generally on the occurrence of an error condition. For example, such an interrupt occurs when a divide-by-zero operation is attempted. Internal hardware interrupts are sometimes referred to as *traps* since they "trap" a condition.

Software interrupts occur when an **INT**errupt instruction is executed. The general form of this instruction is **INT** <integer>, where <integer> specifies an *interrupt-type*. Interrupt-type is an integer which specifies 1 of 256 memory addresses obtained by multiplying the interrupt-type by 4. Thus, for example, interrupt-type 2 refers to address 8. At the memory address specified by the interrupt-type are 4 bytes of address information (the *interrupt vector*) which are interpreted as two 16-bit addresses.

The idea of interrupt-type is associated both with hardware and software interrupts. With software interrupts, the type is generally specified as part of the interrupt instruction. With hardware interrupts, the type is supplied by the interrupting hardware. In both cases, when an interrupt occurs, the addresses specified in the interrupt vector are used to set the CS and IP registers with the starting address of the associated interrupt service routine. It is this routine which performs whatever functions necessary in servicing the interrupt.

Other actions also taken when an interrupt occurs include saving the return address of the interrupted program and the contents of the flag register on the stack, and clearing the trap and interrupt flags. After completing execution of the interrupt routine, an **I**nterrupt **RET**urn (**IRET**) instruction is typically executed. This instruction restores the CS and IP and flag registers with their former values which had been saved on the stack. Thus the control is easily returned to the interrupted program.

Note that IF and TF are cleared when an interrupt occurs to avoid having another interrupt take place immediately on entering the interrupt service routine. IF can be set as needed to allow maskable interrupts to occur. TF is used for debugging purposes and when set will cause an interrupt to occur after each instruction execution.

There are 256 possible interrupt types available on the IBM PC with certain of these reserved for various system purposes, and certain available for user-developed interrupt routines. The first 16 interrupt-types are reserved for Intel 8088 and 8259 hardware interrupts. The 8088 interrupts are common to all Intel 8088 systems and include such interrupts as divide by zero and interrupt on overflow. The 8259 is an interrupt controller present on the IBM PC and is used in generating maskable interrupts from the keyboard, clock timer, and diskette. Interrupt-types 10H to 17H are software interrupts associated with accessing ROM BIOS (Basic Input/Output System) routines. These are discussed in the next chapter. Interrupt-types 18H to 1CH are software interrupts associated with a variety of general functions, such as bootstrapping programs from the disk and obtaining a system timer tick.

The main body of software interrupts supported by DOS (Disk Operating System) encompasses interrupt-types 20H to 27H. These provide a host of I/O device, file, and general operating system support. Writing to a disk file, reading the keyboard, obtaining the time of day, terminating programs, writing to the display or printer, obtaining file directories, and opening and closing files are just some of the tasks which these powerful interrupt routines perform. Interrupt-types 40H to 7FH are reserved for user purposes. Use of interrupt types 80H to F0H is reserved for BASIC use.

EXERCISES

9.1 Use **DEBUG** to display the interrupt vectors for interrupts from type 0 to type 27. Use the print-screen keyboard command to print the **DEBUG** display. From this printed output, make up a neat table of the interrupt-types and the addresses found in their associated vectors.

9.2 Using **DEBUG**, determine if Table 9-1 is correct with respect to the presence of **IRET** instructions where indicated.

9.3 Using **DEBUG**, examine vector 0 and determine the location of the divide-by-zero interrupt service routine. Insert the instruction **INT   0** into some unused interrupt vector area and use **DEBUG** to execute this instruction. Trace through a few instructions, and use the **GO** command to see if the "Divide by zero" message appears.

9.4 Write your own divide-by-zero interrupt service routine. If a divide-by-zero occurs, query the user whether he or she wants to proceed with program execution ("Divide by zero error. Proceed with program execution? Type Y for Yes, N for No."). If the answer is "Yes," return to executing the program. If the answer is "No," return to the operating system. Use appropriate DOS function calls (**INT   21H**) for display and keyboard interrogation.

9.5 Using **DEBUG**, determine where the BIOS routine **PRINT_ SCREEN** begins (called with an interrupt of type 5). Using **DEBUG**, unassemble the first 13 instructions in the routine. Explain the purpose of the 5 instructions beginning with the first **MOV** instruction encountered.

9.6 Write a routine to send the message "One Minute Has Elapsed" to the display with the passage of each minute. Use the type 1C interrupt to obtain "clock ticks." Use the DOS function 25 to initialize the type 1C interrupt vector appropriately. The first minute begins when your routine first responds to the type 1C interrupt. Use the DOS function 9 to display your message.

9.7 Using **DEBUG**, determine where the bootstrap loader routine begins. Examine the instructions in this routine using **DEBUG**'s U command. **INT   13H** invokes a BIOS diskette service routine. It is first invoked to check for any diskette errors, and then invoked a second time to read information from the diskette. Prior to issuing the second **INT   13H**, various registers are set. (DL),(DH),(CH), and (CL) are set to contain the drive, head, track, and sector numbers, (AL) to contain the number of sectors, and (ES:BX) to contain the memory address where the information is to be placed. Determine where the boot record is located on the disk, and where it is written into memory.

9.8 Say it is desired to experimentally determine the speed of a register-to-register **MOV** instruction. Design and execute such an experiment. Use the BIOS type

1AH interrupt to aid in measuring time. Document your experiment, the program(s) used, and your results.

9.9   Since the clock counter used by BIOS (**TIMER_LOW** and **TIMER_HIGH**) is incremented 18.2 times per second, from the viewpoint of most programs of reasonable length the low-order bits appear to be random. Using this idea, write a procedure which uses the clock counter to obtain a random number over the range 0 to 127.

9.10   Write a program which, after a suitable delay, calls the random number generator of 9.9, displays the random number obtained, and then modifies its delay based on the random number value. Use an appropriate DOS service routine to perform the display task. Make a table of the random numbers produced and do a rough check on their randomness.

9.11   How can the procedure of Problem 9.9 be modified to obtain random numbers over the range 0 to 99?

9.12   Consider the statistics procedure needed in the example of Figure 9-6. Write the procedure **DISKSTAT** so that the final statistic of interest that is obtained is the average time (in milliseconds) to perform a disk read. For test purposes, supply a dummy routine for **DISKREAD** which provides delay of a couple of hundred milliseconds. Use the appropriate DOS software interrupt to display the average time obtained. Debug and run your program.

9.13   It is desired to modify the Ctrl-Break operation so that when the user hits Ctrl-Break a message appears on the display which says

```
DO YOU WANT TO TERMINATE PROGRAM ?  (Y OR N)
```

If the user answers **Y**, or **YES**, then the program should be terminated and control returned to the operating system. If the user answers **N**, or **NO**, then the executing program should be resumed. Write an interrupt routine which modifies the type 1B interrupt vector and performs the operations specified. Debug and execute your program. Write a dummy program to test the operation of your interrupt routine.

9.14   The program presented in Figure 9-8 wastes memory by fixing the error message length. Modify the program so that variable length messages may be defined in the data segment definition. Write, debug, and run a test program that displays all the messages.

9.15   Rewrite the **ENTRY** program of Figure 9-10 so that striking the dollar sign ($) character causes the routine to immediately return to the operating system without waiting for the entry of the carriage return character. Use one of the other console read and echo functions in performing this task.

10

Input/Output Programming with BIOS

This chapter considers program control of input/output devices using the facilities provided by IBM PC with its *Basic Input/Output System* (BIOS). BIOS consists of a group of software routines which are stored in read-only memory. They constitute a powerful utility for controlling peripheral devices and as such are frequently used by the operating system. Individual routines can be accessed by the user by issuing the appropriate software interrupt (see Table 9-1). BIOS assembly language listings may be found in the IBM technical reference manual (22), which is the principal source of technical information for this system.

Our discussion is divided into two broad sections. The first deals with BIOS's use in support of the five major peripheral devices found on most systems, i.e., the keyboard, printer, video display, asynchronous communications controller, and diskette. The second focuses on other BIOS routines relating to memory size and equipment determination, and on the problem of generating tones through the speaker. Note that a few BIOS services (such as printing the screen, and obtaining timer tick information) were covered in the previous chapter.

10.1 THE KEYBOARD (A TYPE 16H INTERRUPT)

The type 9 keyboard interrupt and its associated BIOS service routines perform basic keyboard functions such as determining which key has been struck or released, buffering characters, and identifying special key combinations such as CTRL-BREAK (see Section 9.2.2.2). Keys are identified by means of a *scan code* which is communicated to the 8088 by the keyboard processor each time a keyboard action occurs. The codes range from 1 to 83D (53H) for key depression and have a one-to-one correspondence to the physical keys on the keyboard. Adding 128D to the key depression code yields the scan code sent to the 8088 when a key is released. For instance, striking the A key results in a scan code of 30D, and releasing the key results in the scan code 158D.

Just how these scan codes are interpreted is normally determined by the type 9 BIOS keyboard service routine. In many cases, the codes are translated into a standard ASCII character code (see Table 2-8). However, since the number of keys and acceptable key combinations exceeds the number of ASCII codes, IBM has established an *extended code* to handle various special keys (e.g., the function keys) and key combinations (e.g., ALT-A). Finally some key combinations represent a call for a particular processor action (e.g., print screen). On recognizing these key combinations, BIOS performs the designated tasks. These special key combinations are listed in Table 10-1.

Table 10-2 lists the scan codes and the BIOS return codes for most of the keyboard. The key entries indicate how the key is labeled on the keyboard. The base case corresponds to depressing the single designated key without holding down any other keys. The Code here is the ASCII code returned by BIOS when it is interrogated (just how this is done is discussed later in this section). Upper Case, Ctrl, and ALT correspond to the action of striking the designated key while at the same time holding down the shift, Ctrl, or ALT key. Most of the codes returned by BIOS when holding down the

Table 10-1   Special Key Actions

Key Combination	Name	Action
Ctrl-NumLock	PAUSE	Suspends current processor operations until a key (other than NumLock) is struck.
Ctrl-Alt-Del	REBOOT	Restarts the system in the same manner as turning on the power (i.e., causes a type 19H interrupt; see Section 9.2.3.2).
Ctrl-Break	BREAK	The current executing program is halted and control is returned to the operating system (i.e., causes a type 1B interrupt; see Section 9.2.3.4).
Shift-PrtSc	PRINT SCREEN	The contents of the screen are printed (i.e., causes a type 5 interrupt; see Section 9.2.1.6).

Table 10-2 Keyboard Scan, ASCII, and Extended (*) Codes

Key	Scan Code	Base Case Char.	Code	Upper Case Char.	Code	Ctrl Char.	Code	ALT Code
ESC	1	ESC	1E	ESC	1E	ESC	1E	--
1 !	2	1	31	!	21	---	---	78*
2 @	3	2	32	@	40	NULL	3*	79*
3 #	4	3	33		23	---	---	7A*
4 $	5	4	34	$	24	---	---	7B*
5 %	6	5	35	%	25	---	---	7C*
6 ∧	7	6	36	∧	5E	---	---	7D*
7 &	8	7	37	–	26	---	---	7E*
8 *	9	8	38	*	2A	---	---	7F*
9 (	A	9	39	(	28	---	---	80*
0)	B	0	30	)	29	---	---	81*
- _	C	–	2D	_	5F	US	1F	82*
=+	D	=	3D	+	2B	---	---	83*
BS	E	BS	80	BS	80	DEL	7F	--
→|	F	→|	09	|←	F*	---	---	--
Q	10	q	71	Q	51	DC1	11	10*
W	11	w	77	W	57	ETB	17	11*
E	12	e	65	E	45	ENQ	05	12*
R	13	r	72	R	52	DC2	12	13*
T	14	t	74	T	54	DC4	14	14*
Y	15	y	79	Y	59	EM	19	15*
U	16	u	75	U	55	NAK	15	16*
I	17	i	69	I	49	HT	09	17*
O	18	o	6F	O	4F	SI	0F	18*
P	19	p	70	P	50	DLE	10	19*
[{	1A	[	5B	{	7B	ESC	1B	--
] }	1B	]	5D	}	7D	GS	1D	--
CR	1C	CR	0D	CR	0D	LF	0A	--
Ctrl	1D	--	--	--	--	---	---	--
A	1E	a	61	A	41	SOH	01	1E*
S	1F	s	73	S	53	DC3	13	1F*
D	20	d	64	D	44	EOT	04	20*
F	21	f	66	F	46	ACK	06	21*
G	22	g	67	G	47	BEL	07	22*
H	23	h	68	H	48	BS	08	23*
J	24	j	6A	J	4A	LF	0A	24*
K	25	k	6B	K	4B	VT	0B	25*
L	26	l	6C	L	4C	FF	0C	26*
; :	27	;	3B	:	3A	---	---	--
' "	28	'	27	"	22	---	---	--
' ~	29	'	60	~	7E	---	---	--

Table 10-2 continued

Key	Scan Code	Base Case Char.	Code	Upper Case Char.	Code	Ctrl Char.	Code	ALT Code
L.Shift	2A	--	--	--	--	---	---	--
\\ |	2B	\\	5C	|	7C	FS	1C	--
Z	2C	z	7A	Z	5A	SUB	1A	2C*
X	2D	x	78	X	58	CAN	18	2D*
C	2E	c	63	C	43	ETX	03	2E*
V	2F	v	76	V	56	SYN	16	2F*
B	30	b	62	B	42	STX	02	30*
N	31	n	6E	N	4E	SO	0E	31*
M	32	m	6D	M	4D	CR	0D	32*
, <	33	,	2C	<	3C	---	---	--
. >	34	.	2E	>	3E	---	---	--
/ ?	35	/	2F	?	3F	---	---	--
R.Shift	36	--	--	--	--	---	---	--
* PrtSc	37	*	2A	Table 10-1		---	72*	--
Alt	38	--	--	--	--	---	---	--
Space Bar	39	SP	20	SP	20	SP	20	20
Caps Lock	3A	--	--	--	--	--	--	--
F1	3B	--	3B*	--	54*	--	5E*	68*
F2	3C	--	3C*	--	55*	--	5F*	69*
F3	3D	--	3D*	--	56*	--	60*	6A*
F4	3E	--	3E*	--	57*	--	61*	6B*
F5	3F	--	3F*	--	58*	--	62*	6C*
F6	40	--	40*	--	59*	--	63*	6D*
F7	41	--	41*	--	5A*	--	64*	6E*
F8	42	--	42*	--	5B*	--	65*	6F*
F9	43	--	43*	--	5C*	--	66*	70*
F10	44	--	44*	--	5D*	--	67*	71*
Num Lock	45	--	--	--	--	Table 10-1		--
Scroll Lock	46	--	--	--	--	Table 10-1		--

shift and Ctrl keys are also ASCII codes, with a few being part of the extended code group. These extended codes are noted in Table 10-2 by a * next to the code entry. Dashes in the table represent unavailable or undefined codes. Almost all of the codes returned when using the ALT key are part of the extended code group, with the extended codes themselves often being identical to the scan codes of the base key being depressed. The Char. (CHARacter) table entries are the keyboard or ASCII symbols or mnemonics for the given code.

Table 10-3 deals with those keys on the right side of the keyboard which are part of the numeric keypad. Codes for these keys are dependent on the use of the NumLock key. Depressing NumLock places these keys in the Num Lock state wherein the keys act as a standard numeric keypad. In this state, BIOS returns normal ASCII characters associated with the numbers struck. The keys can be removed from this state and placed in the base state by depressing NumLock once again. In the base state, the keys function as cursor, screen, and edit controls when using BASIC, and BIOS returns codes from the extended code set. Keys in this area, when used with the Ctrl key, also invoke BASIC edit commands and have associated extended codes. Using the shift key with this same group acts to shift from the Num Lock to Base (or Base to NumLock) states for as long as the shift key is depressed.

As keys are struck, the scan codes sent by the keyboard are interpreted by BIOS, and the resultant character codes are placed in a BIOS buffer. The type 16 interrupt is used to call one of three BIOS keyboard facilities (see Table 10-4). The particular facility is called by loading AH with the proper value prior to executing the **INT 16H** instruction. Information is returned in AH, AL, and ZF.

With the first facility, (AH) = 0, the keyboard routine checks the BIOS keyboard buffer to see if a key has been struck. If a key has been struck, the resulting code is read from the buffer and delivered to the calling program. If the buffer is empty, the routine waits for keyboard action. This is useful with interactive programs involving user response. An example was given in Section 9.1.1.

With the second facility, (AH) = 1, the keyboard routine indicates to the calling program whether or not a key has been struck and its code entered into the BIOS buffer.

Table 10-3 Codes for Numeric Keypad

Key	Scan Code	Num Lock Char.	Num Lock Code	Base Case Char.	Base Case Code	Ctrl Char.	Ctrl Code	ALT Code
7 Home	47	7	37	Home	47*	Clear	77*	--
8	48	8	38		48*	--	--	--
9 PgUp	49	9	39	Page Up	49*	Top of text (home)	84*	--
-	4A	-	2D	-	2D	--	--	--
4 ←	4B	4	34	←	4B*	Reverse word	73*	--
5	4C	5	35	---	---	--	--	--
6	4D	6	36	→	4D*	Adv word	74*	--
+	4E	+	2B	+	2B	--	--	--
1 End	4F	1	31	End	4F*	Erase to EOL	75*	--
2	50	2	32		50*	--	--	--
3 PgDn	51	3	33	Page Dn	51*	Erase to EOS	76*	--
0 Ins	52	0	30	INS	52*	--	--	--
Del	53	.	2E	Del	53*	--	--	--

Table 10-4   BIOS Keyboard Facilities: A Type 16H Interrupt

READ THE NEXT KEY FROM THE KEYBOARD:
  1. Register setup   (AH) ← 0
  2. Information return   **IF** (AL) .NE. 0, **THEN** (AL) = ASCII code of key;
                                                    (AH) = SCAN code of key;
                              IF (AL) = 0,   **THEN** (AH) = IBM extended code of key;
                              Remove codes from BIOS keyboard buffer.

DETERMINE IF A KEY HAS BEEN STRUCK:
  1. Register setup   (AH) ← 1
  2. Information return   **IF** (ZF) = 1, **THEN** no code in BIOS keyboard buffer.
                              IF (ZF) = 0, **THEN** key has been struck and character is
                              available in buffer. The ASCII and scan codes are placed in
                              AL and AH as above; however, the codes are not removed
                              from the BIOS keyboard buffer.

RETURN CURRENT KEYBOARD STATUS:
  1. Register setup   (AH) ← 2
  2. Information return   (AL) = (KBFLAG); see Figure 10-1.

Unlike the first facility, the routine does not wait for a key to be struck. This is useful in situations where processing must continue whether or not a key action has been struck.

The third facility, (AH) = 2, returns the keyboard status to the calling program. This status consists of 8 bits of information maintained in the BIOS KBFLAG byte (see Figure 10-1). The key depression bits indicate whether the designated key is currently being held down. The state bits are set and reset by depressing and releasing the corresponding key on the keyboard. These bits reflect the toggle action associated with these keys. (NumLock was discussed earlier.) When in the Caps Lock state, BIOS interprets scan codes as if a Shift key were depressed. Scroll Lock and Insert states are available for application usage (e.g., insert mode in an editor).

10.2 THE PRINTER (A TYPE 17H INTERRUPT)

Printers may be interfaced to the IBM PC in two ways: The first uses a *parallel printer adapter* and the second uses a *serial* (asynchronous) *communications adapter*. With the former, information is transferred between the processor and the printer in parallel, over a group of lines, while with the serial adapter only a single line is used for information transfer. These two approaches are discussed later in this chapter.

Consider now the case of printers connected to the IBM PC via the parallel printer adapter. Up to three such printers (numbered 0, 1, and 2) may be serviced through the BIOS facilities. Using a type 17H interrupt, BIOS provides for three basic printer communications operations (see Table 10-5). All operations begin by loading DX with the number of the printer to be accessed. In most situations where there is a single

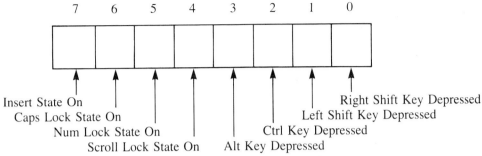

Figure 10-1 Keyboard status (a 1 indicates presence of the condition).

printer, DX ← 0. The first operation, (AH) = 0, is printing an ASCII character (see Problem 10.5). AL is loaded with the character to be printed, AH is set to 0, and the **INT   17H** instruction is executed. Since it may not be possible for the printer to perform this task (e.g., it has run out of paper), status information is returned to the processor and, through BIOS, to the calling program. The status information is placed in AH and may be interpreted as shown in Table 10-5. A TIME OUT error occurs if the printer has been busy for too long a time. (*Note*: On early versions of BIOS this error indication was sometimes itself in error.) A printer is SELECTed if it has been placed on line. The ACKNOWLEDGE signal is sent by the printer to indicate the receipt of data. The printer is BUSY when it is printing, or an error condition exists.

Table 10-5   BIOS Printer Facilities: A Type 17H Interrupt

PRINT THE CHARACTER IN AL:
1. Register setup	(AH) ← 0; (DX) ← printer number;
	(AL) ← character to be printed
2. Information return	(AH) = printer status (see below)

INITIALIZE PRINTER AND OBTAIN STATUS:
1. Register setup	(AH) ← 1; (DX) ← printer number;
2. Information return	(AH) = printer status (see below)

OBTAIN PRINTER STATUS:
1. Register setup	(AH) ← 2; (DX) ← printer number
2. Information return	(AH) = printer status (a 1 indicates presence of condition)

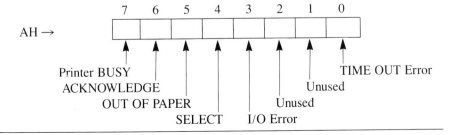

The second BIOS printer service, AH = 1, initializes the printer and returns its status in AH. The final service, AH = 2, merely returns the printer status without performing any initialization.

Let us turn now to the situation where the printer is connected to the processor via a serial communication port. Information sent using the BIOS Type 17 interrupt (AH = 0) will be routed to the printer properly if DOS has been properly alerted. This may be done using the DOS **MODE** command, which is discussed in the DOS manual (28). Since there are no parallel status lines between the printer and asynchronous adapter in this situation, status information will not be correctly returned when using the type 17 BIOS calls. Generally, devices connected through the asynchronous adapter are best serviced using the BIOS routines written specifically for that unit (see Section 10.4).

10.3 THE DISPLAY (A TYPE 10H INTERRUPT)

The IBM PC provides for two types of displays and associated adapters. The *mono-chrome* adapter is used to display black and white (or green) alphanumeric characters. These may be numbers, letters, symbols, or special block graphic characters. Up to 2000 characters may be placed on the screen using an 80 column by 25 line character grid.

The *color/graphics* adapter may operate in two modes; alphanumeric or graphic. In the alphanumeric mode, 80 column by 25 line, or 40 column by 25 line, color character displays can be generated. In the graphics mode, the screen may be viewed as consisting of a rectangular grid pattern consisting of either 320 by 200 (medium-resolution mode), 640 by 200 (high-resolution mode), or 160 by 100 (low-resolution mode) dots. Graphic patterns are produced by selecting dot groups to intensify with color graphics being limited to the medium- and low-resolution modes. Use of the 40 by 25 alphanumeric and low-resolution graphic modes permits the adapter to operate with television-type displays. BIOS, however, doesn't support the low-resolution graphics mode and it is not considered here.

In both the monochrome and color graphics cases, the displayed characters or patterns reflect characters and patterns contained in memory. The memory used, referred to as *display memory*, is physically located on the adapter boards. However, it is still part of the Intel 8088 address space and, as such, may be manipulated using normal 8088 instructions. Thus, one way of controlling what is displayed on the screen is to operate directly on display memory.

BIOS video routines also can be used to control the screen (Table 10-8). This represents a display interface standard and, as such, is unlikely to change with new IBM PC models. On the other hand, working directly with display memory is generally more efficient and appears to be the preferred approach when commercial display packages are being developed.

As indicated earlier, the color/graphics adapter can operate in a number of different modes. For this adapter to operate in the proper mode, a mode-setting command must be sent to it by the 8088. BIOS provides a convenient mode-setting facility associated with the type 10H software interrupt [see Table 10-8(a)]. The instructions below indicate how to set the adapter for 80 by 25 black/white display.

```
MOV     AL,2      ;set mode to 80×25 B/W
MOV     AH,0      ;set AH for set mode service
INT     10H       ;all BIOS
```

10.3.1 The Monochrome Display

10.3.1.1 Alphanumeric Displays and Display Memory Screen positions associated with the monochrome adapter (and with the color/graphics adapter operating in 80 by 25 alphanumeric mode) are identified either by specifying column and row numbers, or by using a corresponding integer. This is shown in Figure 10-2, where identifying integers range from 0 to 1999.

The symbol to be displayed at each position is specified by a 2-byte character/attribute pair. Thus, a total of 4000 bytes are needed to specify the entire screen display. Using the full 8 bits in the character byte, there are 256 possible characters available (Table 10-6). These include the standard ASCII characters and symbols, plus extra symbols which are handy in developing pseudo graphic displays. This will be shown later in Example 10-1.

The attribute byte specifies various character display possibilities such as blinking, underlining, and high intensity available. As will be seen in the next section, the color/graphics adapter adds color to this attribute set. Figure 10-3 and Table 10-7 indicates how the attribute byte is encoded.

With the monochrome adapter, the 4000 bytes needed to specify the character/attribute pairs for an entire 80 by 25 screen are stored in memory, beginning at location B0000H. Even-numbered memory locations hold the character code and the next higher

COLUMNS

	0	1	2				78	79
0	0,0 (0)	0,1 (1)	0,2 (2)	•	•	•	0,78 (78)	0,79 (79)
1	1,0 (80)	1,1 (81)	1,2 (82)	•	•	•	1,78 (158)	1,79 (159)
2	2,0 (160)	2,1 (161)	2,2 (162)	•	•	•	2,78 (238)	2,79 (239)
	• • •	• • •	• • •				• • •	• • •
23	23,0 (1840)	23,1 (1841)	23,2 (1842)	•	•	•	23,78 (1918)	23,79 (1919)
24	24,0 (1920)	24,1 (1921)	24,2 (1922)	•	•	•	24,78 (1998)	24,79 (1999)

ROWS

Figure 10-2 The 80 by 25 alphanumeric screen.

Table 10-6 Alphanumeric Display Symbols
(Taken from the IBM PC technical manual, Appendix C. Reprinted by permission of the IBM Corporation.)

High Order Bits

DECIMAL VALUE ➡		0	16	32	48	64	80	96	112	128	144	160	176	192	208	224	240
⬇	HEXA DECIMAL VALUE	0	1	2	3	4	5	6	7	8	9	A	B	C	D	E	F
0	0	BLANK (NULL)	►	BLANK (SPACE)	0	@	P	`	p	Ç	É	á	▒	└	╨	∝	≡
1	1	☺	◄	!	1	A	Q	a	q	ü	æ	í	▓	┴	╤	β	±
2	2	☻	↕	"	2	B	R	b	r	é	Æ	ó	▓	├	╥	Γ	≥
3	3	♥	‼	#	3	C	S	c	s	â	ô	ú	│	├	┴	π	≤
4	4	♦	¶	$	4	D	T	d	t	ä	ö	ñ	┤	─	╚	Σ	∫
5	5	♣	§	%	5	E	U	e	u	à	ò	Ñ	╡	┼	╞	σ	∫
6	6	♠	▬	&	6	F	V	f	v	å	û	ª	╢	┌	╓	µ	÷
7	7	•	↨	'	7	G	W	g	w	ç	ù	º	╖	╟	τ	≈
8	8	◘	↑	(	8	H	X	h	x	ê	ÿ	¿	╕	╚	Φ	°
9	9	○	↓	)	9	I	Y	i	y	ë	Ö	⌐	╣	╔	Θ	•
10	A	◎	→	*	:	J	Z	j	z	è	Ü	¬	║	╩	Ω	·
11	B	♂	←	+	;	K	[	k	{	ï	¢	½	╗	δ	√
12	C	♀	∟	,	<	L	\	l			î	£	¼	╝	∞	ⁿ
13	D	♪	↔	—	=	M	]	m	}	ì	¥	¡	╜	φ	²
14	E	♫	▲	.	>	N	^	n	~	Ä	₧	«	╛	∈	■
15	F	☼	▼	/	?	O	_	o	△	Å	ƒ	»	∩	BLANK FF

odd locations hold the character attribute (see Figure 10-4). The memory itself is physically located on the adapter board and is DUAL PORTed. That is, it is accessible both by the adapter for use in establishing and refreshing the monitor display, and by the standard 8088 instructions for changing character codes and their attributes. Accessing the memory is sufficiently fast so that for most purposes there is negligible interference between 8088 and adapter memory accesses. Display programs can thus be viewed as memory manipulation routines. Note that for the IBM *PCjr* a single ported memory arrangement is used, resulting in slower operation.

One approach to addressing display memory is first to load the ES register with B000H. Specific character/attribute pairs can now be accessed through ES by supplying the appropriate offset. Assuming an 80 by 25 display, the offset for a row-column pair

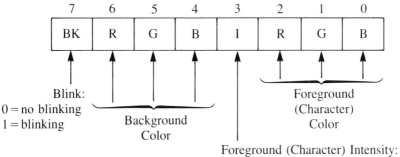

Figure 10-3   The monochrome display attribute byte.

Table 10-7   Monochrome Display Attribute Encoding

BACKGROUND R G B	FOREGROUND R G B	DISPLAY CHARACTERISTICS
0 0 0	0 0 0	Nondisplay (Black on black).
0 0 0	0 0 1	Underline normal character display.
0 0 0	1 1 1	Normal display off-white foreground character on black background.
1 1 1	0 0 0	Reverse video display of black character on white background.
1 1 1	1 1 1	Display a white box at character position.

(R-C) is easily calculated as R·160 + C·2. The **MOVSB** (**MOV**e String **B**yte) instruction is useful here in loading display memory since it automatically uses ES in developing the destination address for the string.

EXAMPLE 10-1   A monochrome display, or color/graphics display, is to be used in developing a computer card game. As part of this game a rectangular card shape must be displayed on the screen. The procedure below displays a set card shape 13 columns wide and 10 rows long. The location of the upper left hand corner of the card is passed to the procedure in AL (which contains the row position) and AH (which contains the column position). A 25 row by 80 column display is assumed.

We first set up a template for the card outline within the data segment. The card figure is constructed out of block graphics characters in the alphanumeric symbol set. The **REPT** operator is used to generate the eight middle rows of a ten-row-long card. Given this data definition, the procedure now has two main tasks. The first is to use the passed parameters for the row and column position to establish the address in display memory where the template of the card is to be placed. The second is to actually move

memory contents		memory address	description
8	7	B0005	attribute: blinking, normal video
4	3	B0004	character C displayed at (0,2)
7	0	B0003	atrribute: reverse video
4	2	B0002	character B displayed at (0,1)
0	7	B0001	attribute: reverse video
4	1	B0000	character A displayed at (0,0)

Figure 10-4 Monochrome adapter display memory example.

the template. The **SAL**, **MUL** and **ADD** instructions perform the operation (row number) $\cdot$ 160 + 2 $\cdot$ (column number). This yields the offset into the display memory where the top row of characters in the template is to be placed. The instructions beginning at **MOV   SI,OFFSET TLINE** set up the SI, DI, and CX registers for a byte string move of a template row into the display memory. AX and related instructions form a loop to move successive rows. Finally, the AH and AL setup followed by **INT   10H** instruction call a BIOS routine which establishes the **MODE** of monitor and adapter operation (i.e., 80 by 25, 40 by 25, etc.). This is considered later in this section. This procedure can now be used in the development of a card game (see Problem 10-10).

10.3.1.2 Controlling the Cursor with BIOS The discussion thus far has considered how alphanumeric characters may be placed on the monochrome display screen by modifying display memory. Another display feature requiring control is the *cursor*. The cursor is a blinking rectangle one character wide and up to one character high. It is typically used as a screen pointer indicating to the user where his or her next keyboard action is to have effect. Both the monochrome and color/graphics adapters have provision for setting and reading the screen position of the cursor in addition to determining its length.

For the monochrome adapter, characters are 14 scan lines long with the top and bottom scan lines labeled 0 and 13, respectively. For the color/graphics adapter only eight scan lines are present; thus the bottom scan line is number 7. Cursor length is set by specifying a range of scan lines. On power-up, for example, the IBM PC sets the cursor for lines 12 and 13 on the monochrome display, and line 7 on the color/graphics display. This presents a blinking underline style cursor.

While cursor position and length can be controlled by directly accessing registers in the *6845 CRT controller* (used with both types of adapters), the approach taken here is to use the BIOS services designed for this purpose. The entire set of BIOS services available for video control is presented in Table 10-8(*a*). For example, placing a cursor

```
; *** DATA AND STACK SEGMENTS ***
DATAS    SEGMENT
         .RADIX 16   ;card template
TLINE    DB    0DA,07,0C4,07,0C4,07,0C4,07,0C4,07 ;top row
         DB    0C4,07,0C4,07,0C4,07,0C4,07,0C4,07
         DB    0C4,07,0C4,07,0BF,07
         REPT 8                ;middle 8 rows
         DB    0B3,07,0FF,07,0FF,07,0FF,07,0FF,07
         DB    0FF,07,0FF,07,0FF,07,0FF,07,0FF,07
         DB    0FF,07,0FF,07,0B3,07
         ENDM
         DB    0C0,07,0C4,07,0C4,07,0C4,07,0C4,07; bottom row
         DB    0C4,07,0C4,07 0C4,07,0C4,07,0C4,07
         DB    0C4,07,0C4,07,0D9,07
         .RADIX 10
ONE60    DB    160
DATAS    ENDS
STAKS    SEGMENT STACK
         DB    128 DUP (?)
STAKS    ENDS
; *** CODE SEGMENT ***
CODES    SEGMENT                        ;define code segment
CARD     PROC     FAR
         ASSUME   CS:CODES,DS:DATAS,SS:STAKS,ES:NOTHING
START:   MOV      DX,DATAS          ;set up segment registers
         MOV      DS,DX             ;no registers saved
         MOV      DX,0B000H         ;set up ES for display
         MOV      ES,DX             ;         memory address
         XOR      DH,DH             ;clear DH
         MOV      DL,AH             ;DL <--- column number
         SAL      DL,1              ;DL <--- (column number)*2
         MUL      ONE60             ;AX <--- (row number)*160
         ADD      DX,AX        ;DX <--- offset addr. in disp.mem.
         MOV      AL,2         ;set to 80×25 B/W (color adapter use)
         MOV      AH,0              ;set for screen mode service
         INT      10H               ;call BIOS
         MOV      SI,OFFSET TLINE ;SI <--- source addr. for MOVSB
         MOV      DI,DX             ;DI <--- disp. mem. offset addr.
         MOV      AX,10             ;set up row counter
DISP:    MOV      CX,26             ;set up MOVSB byte counter
REP      MOVSB                      ;move string to display memory
         ADD      DX,160            ;inc. display mem. offset addr.
         MOV      DI,DX             ;set up new destination addr.
         DEC      AX                ;decrement row count
         JG       DISP              ;loop through 10 rows
         RET                        ;return to calling routine
CARD     ENDP
CODES    ENDS
END      START
```

Figure 10-5 Monochrome display example.

covering the top half of a character at column 20, row 10 can be achieved with the following code segment:

```
MOV     CH, 0      ; set cursor start scan line
MOV     CL, 6      ; set cursor end scan line
MOV     AH, 1      ; set AH for set cursor type service
INT     10H        ; call BIOS
MOV     DH, 10     ; set cursor row position
MOV     DL, 20     ; set cursor column position
MOV     AH, 2      ; set AH for set cursor position service
INT     10H        ; call BIOS
```

10.3.1.3 Alphanumeric displays with BIOS

Thus far we have discussed how alphanumeric displays can be created by directly manipulating display memory, and how BIOS service routines may be used to control cursor size and position. Having positioned the cursor at a particular column-row location, BIOS also provides services for reading and writing characters and their attributes at that location. These services apply to both the monochrome and color/graphics adapter boards and are outlined in Table 10-8(*b*).

Say, for example, that in a text editor there is a command to erase the characters from the cursor position to the end of the line. The BIOS AH = 9 and AH = 10 services provide for repeated writing of the same character on the screen at successive screen locations. The number of times the character is repeated is passed to the BIOS routine in CX. With AH = 9, both the character and attribute are supplied, while with AH = 10, only the character is supplied and the existing attributes in display memory are used. The code segment below shows how an "erase to end of line" operation might be done when operating in 80 by 25 mode.

```
MOV     AL, 2      ; set mode to 80 by 25 B/W
MOV     AH, 0      ; set AH for mode service
INT     10H        ; call BIOS
MOV     AH, 3      ; set AH for cursor position service
INT     10H        ; call BIOS
                   ; (DL) <--- cursor column position
SUB     DL, 80     ; (DL) <--- num. col. left in row
XOR     CH, CH     ; clear CH
MOV     CL, DL     ; (CX) <--- column count
MOV     AL, 20H    ; (AL) <--- blank character
MOV     AH, 10     ; set AH for character write service
INT     10H        ; call BIOS
```

While these BIOS services provide for close control of the display, they are often more than is needed. For instance, let's say that one just wants to list a text file on the screen without any bells and whistles. For this situation, characters are to be displayed in the normal fashion without any underlining or fancy attributes. The cursor position is to be automatically incremented and the standard carriage return and line feed characters are to be recognized and acted upon in the usual manner.

Table 10-8(a) BIOS Screen Mode, Cursor, and Light Pen Facilities: A Type 10H Interrupt

SETTING THE DISPLAY MODE
1. Register setup: (AH) ← 0

(AL)	Mode (alphanumeric)	Adapter	(AL)	Mode (graphics)	Adapter
0	40 × 25 B/W	C/G	4	320 × 200 Color	C/G
1	40 × 25 Color	C/G	5	320 × 200 B/W	C/G
2	80 × 25 B/W	C/G	6	640 × 200 B/W	C/G
3	80 × 25 Color	C/G	7	80 × 25 B/W	MONO.

2. Information return: None

READING THE DISPLAY MODE
1. Register setup: (AH) ← 15
2. Information return: (AL) = Current mode (as above)
   (AH) = Number of character columns on screen
   (BH) = Current active display page

SETTING THE CURSOR TYPE
1. Register setup: (AH) ← 1
   (CH bits 4 – 0) ← Start scan line; (CL bits 4 – 0) ← End scan line
2. Information return: None

SETTING THE CURSOR POSITION
1. Register setup: (AH) ← 2
   (DH,DL) ← Row, Column Number; (BH) ← Page number
2. Information return: None

READING THE CURSOR POSITION
1. Register setup: (AH) ← 3; (BH) ← Page number (0 – 4)
2. Information return: (DH,DL) = Cursor row, column position
   (CH,CL) = Cursor type (see setting cursor type)

READING THE LIGHT PEN
1. Register setup: (AH) ← 4
2. Information return: **IF** (AH) = 0, **THEN** light pen is not triggered.
   IF (AH) = 1, **THEN** light pen is triggered and
   (DH,DL) = Row, column position of light pen,
   (CH) = Raster line (0 – 199), and
   (BX) = Pixel column line (0 – 319,639).

Realizing that this is a common problem, IBM has provided a simple BIOS service for performing this task. This is referred to as the "ASCII TELETYPE ROUTINE FOR OUTPUT" since it mimics the old-fashioned teletype machines. With this routine, the ASCII carriage return, line feed, bell, and backspace characters are interpreted as commands rather than as displayable characters. Other characters are displayed in their normal fashion with the cursor position being incremented after each character is displayed.

Table 10-8(b)   BIOS Video Character Facilities: A Type 10H Interrupt

SETTING THE ACTIVE PAGE (Alphanumeric Modes)
   1. Register setup: (AH) ← 5; (AL) ← New page value (0–7 for graphic modes 1 and 2 and 0–3 for graphic modes 2 and 3; only 1 page is present with monochrome adapter)
   2. Information return: None

SCROLL ACTIVE PAGE UP
   1. Register setup: (AH) ← 6; (BH) ← attribute for blank lines; (AL) ← Number of lines to scroll; (AL) ← 0, Blank window; (CH,CL) ← Row, column of upper left corner of scroll window; (DH,DL) ← Row, column of lower right corner of scroll window
   2. Information Return: None

SCROLL ACTIVE PAGE DOWN
   1. Register setup: (AH) ← 7; (as in SCROLL ACTIVE PAGE UP)
   2. Information return: None

WRITING CHARACTER/ATTRIBUTE PAIR AT CURSOR POSITION
   1. Register setup: (AH) ← 9; (BH) ← Display page (alpha modes); (AL) ← Character to write; (BL) ← Char. Attr. (alpha modes)/color (graphics modes); (CX) ← Number of characters to write
   2. Information return: None

WRITING CHARACTER AT CURSOR POSITION
   1. Register setup: (AH) ← 10; (BH) ← Display page (alpha modes); (AL) ← Character to write; (CX) ← Number of characters to write
   2. Information return: None

READING CHARACTER/ATTRIBUTE AT CURSOR POSITION
   1. Register setup: (AH) ← 8; (BH) ← Display page (alpha modes)
   2. Information return: (AL,AH) = Character, attribute (alpha modes) read

ASCII TELETYPE LIKE CHARACTER WRITE
   1. Register setup: (AH) ← 14; (BH) ← Display page (alpha modes); (AL) ← Character to write; (BL) ← Foreground color (graphics modes)
   2. Information return: None

10.3.2 The Color/Graphics Display

10.3.2.1 Alphanumeric Displays, Display Memory Pages, and Scrolling   Alphanumeric displays can be achieved with the color/graphics adapter by using display modes 0 to 3 [Table 10-8(*a*)]. These modes provide for monochrome or color, and 80 by 25 or 40 by 25 displays. As with the monochrome adapter, character/attribute pairs are associated with each column, row position and are stored in adapter display memory in the sequential manner indicated in Figures 10-2 and 10-4. There are three principal differences between alphanumeric display modes using the monochrome and color/graphics adapters. The first is the availability of the extra 40 × 25 mode. The second

Table 10-8(c)   BIOS Video Graphics Facilities: A Type 10H Interrupt

SET COLOR PALETTE
1. Register setup: (AH) ← 11;
   IF (BH) ← 0, THEN BL selects background/border color
      (BL low 4 bits) ← background/border color
   IF (BH) ← 1, THEN BL selects pallette (320 by 200 mode)
      (BL low order bit) ← 0 for green, red, yellow colors
      (BL low order bit) ← 1 for blue, cyan, magenta colors
2. Information return: None

WRITE DOT
1. Register setup: (AH) ← 12; (DX) ← Row num.; (CX) ← Column num.; (AL) ← Color value: IF (AL bit 7) = 1 Color value is exclusive or'd with current dot contents
2. Information return: None

READ DOT
1. Register setup: (AH) ← 13; (DX) ← Row num.; (CX) ← Colum num.
2. Information return: (AL) ← Dot color value

---

relates to the larger display memory supplied with the color/graphics adapter. The third concerns the availability of color as an attribute for both the alphanumeric characters and screen borders.

The color/graphics adapter has 16K of on-board memory compared to 4K available with the monochrome adapter. Although this larger memory is present primarily to support graphics facilities (to be discussed in the next section), it is also available to aid in alphanumeric display processes. One implication of having more memory is that several screens worth of alphanumeric information can be stored concurrently. Since 80 column by 25 row displays require 4K for a full screen of character/attribute byte pairs, the color/graphics display memory can hold up to four screens of information. With 40 column by 25 row displays, up to eight screens of information can be held.

A screen's worth of information is referred to as a *page*, and pages are placed sequentially in memory starting at the lowest color/graphics display memory location, which is B8000H. Thus, for an 80 by 25 display, page 0 starts at B8000H and extends 4K to B8FFFH, page 1 starts at B9000H and extends 4K to B9FFFH, and so on. For a 40 by 25 display, page 0 starts at B8000H and extends 2K to B87FFH, page 1 starts at B8800H and extends 2K to B8FFFH, and so on (see Problem 10.13). As with the monochrome display, these memory locations can be modified with standard 8088 instructions to determine both the character to be displayed (Table 10-6) and its associated attributes. The adapter must, however, know which page is to be displayed at a given point in time (i.e., which page is "active") and BIOS provides a facility for issuing just such a command to the adapter [Table 10-8(b)].

The availability of multiple pages provides a powerful application tool. For instance, consider a computer system which interactively takes an individual's preliminary medical history for subsequent printout and review. The questionnaire might be laid out as a tree structure where a page's worth of questions is conceptually located at each node.

The pages to be displayed might depend in part on answers given to questions on previously displayed pages. Thus, the individual would traverse different parts of the tree, requiring different pages of information. By having the ability to store several pages of information at once, one could design a program to anticipate the pages which might be required, prefetch these pages from mass storage, and load them into the nonactive display memory pages in parallel with the question answering process. When a page is required, a simple change in the active page specification now displays the page with no delay.

As indicated above, display information is stored in the form of character/attribute byte pairs where the displayed character is defined in Table 10-6. There are four alphanumeric modes available with the color/graphics adapter. The 80 by 25 black and white mode corresponds directly to the monochrome adapter mode described earlier. In this situation, attribute encoding, as shown in Figure 10-3 and Table 10-7, is the same except that the underline attribute is unavailable. The additional 40 by 25 black and white mode operates in the same manner except that the number of columns available is reduced.

For the two alphanumeric color modes, bits 0 to 3 (B,G,R,I) of the attribute byte are used to encode the foreground color, and bits 4 to 6 (B,G,R) are used to encode the background color. Bit 7 is still used for the blinking attribute. This color encoding is shown in Table 10-9.

The red, green, and blue bits are used in specifying both foreground and background colors with other colors being obtained as combinations of these three primary colors. The I bit is used only for the foreground color. With many color monitors this bit is not recognized and only the first eight colors are available in foreground. Note also that the Intensity bit, when recognized by the monitor, provides extra brightness

Table 10-9 Alphanumeric Color Attributes

Intensity	Red	Green	Blue	COLOR
0	0	0	0	Black
0	0	0	1	Blue
0	0	1	0	Green
0	0	1	1	Cyan
0	1	0	0	Red
0	1	0	1	Magenta
0	1	1	0	Brown
0	1	1	1	Light grey (white)
1	0	0	0	Dark grey (black)
1	0	0	1	Light blue
1	0	1	0	Light green
1	0	1	1	Light cyan
1	1	0	0	Light red
1	1	0	1	Light magenta
1	1	1	0	Yellow
1	1	1	1	White

to the base color. Though somewhat counterintuitive, this extra brightness causes the base color to appear lighter.

In addition to choosing the colors of each individual character, the color of the screen border can also be specified. This may be done using the BIOS color palette service (AH ← 11), as indicated in Table 10-8(*c*).

The final alphanumeric service provided by BIOS is *scrolling*. The term *scrolling* refers to the ability to move the screen contents up or down a number of rows. In scrolling up, as the top rows leave the screen, blank rows enter from the bottom. In scrolling down, as the bottom row leaves the screen, blank rows enter from the top. The BIOS service (AH = 6 for scroll active page up, AH = 7 for scroll active page down) permits one to define a rectangular window within the active page, within which scrolling takes place. Thus, for fancy interactive displays, a portion of the screen can be kept constant while another portion is scrolled out or blanked. In addition, the attribute associated with the blank lines that are scrolled in can be specified. This is handy in certain text editing applications where, say, a scrolled-in line is displayed in reverse video to emphasize that the next user entries or corrections are to appear on that line.

10.3.2.2 Graphics Both black and white and color graphics screen modes are supported by the color/graphics adapter. In these graphics modes, the screen can be viewed as a rectangular grid of points (as opposed to characters) whose attributes can be individually modified. The high-resolution black and white mode consists of a 640 column by 200 row grid of points whose locations are identified as shown in Figure 10-6. Pictures are placed on the screen by modifying attributes of the appropriate groups of points which are in fact stored in display memory.

Each addressable point is referred to as a *pixel*, or picture element. In the high-resolution mode a total of 640·200, or 128,000, pixels are present. For black and white graphics display, since each point requires only a single bit of information (to specify On or Off), a full screen would require 128,000 bits or 16,000 bytes of storage. This

			COLUMNS					
	0	1	2				638	639
0	0,0	0,1	0,2	•	•	•	0,638	0,639
1	1,0	1,1	1,2	•	•	•	1,638	1,639
2	2,0	2,1	2,2	•	•	•	2,638	2,639
ROWS	•	•	•				•	•
	•	•	•				•	•
	•	•	•				•	•
198	198,0	198,1	198,2	•	•	•	198,638	198,639
199	199,0	199,1	199,2	•	•	•	199,638	199,639

Figure 10-6 The 640 by 200 Graphics Mode Screen

corresponds exactly to the amount of display storage on board with the color/graphics monitor. Thus, the color/graphics adapter has enough display memory for just one high resolution black and white image.

In medium resolution the screen grid is 320 columns by 200 rows and thus contains 64,000 pixels. With 128,000 bits of display memory present, 2 bits may be allocated to each pixel. These bits are used to specify one of four colors for each of the 64,000 pixels.

Consider next how pixels are stored in display memory. The CRT controller (Motorola 6845) on the color/graphics adapter requires that information contained in the even-numbered rows on the screen and information contained in the odd-numbered rows on the screen be kept in separate memory areas. For this reason, in graphics modes, display memory is divided into two parts separated by a small memory gap. The lower-order part (starting at B8000H) contains information for the even rows, and the upper part (starting at BA000H) information for the odd rows.

Notice that for high-resolution black and white graphics, a row consists of 640 pixels. With 1 bit needed per pixel, 80 bytes are needed per row. For medium-resolution color graphics, a row consists of 320 pixels. However, each pixel requires 2 bits; hence once again 80 bytes are needed. For both medium and high resolution, pixels are oriented within each byte so that the first pixel displayed in that byte is in the leftmost byte position. This is illustrated below in Figure 10-7 for the case of high-resolution graphics.

For the high-resolution mode, since each displayable point corresponds to a bit in memory, screen images can be directly altered by changing the appropriate memory bits. Of course, care must be taken to identify correctly the bit being manipulated within each byte, and to operate on the correct area of display memory (i.e., even-row or odd-row area). This requires some address and bit juggling. For many applications

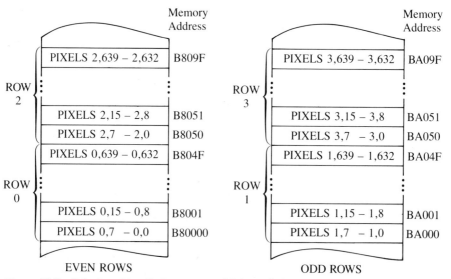

Figure 10-7   Color/graphics display memory (high-resolution mode).

where display speed is not at a premium, the BIOS routines available for dot display are adequate. They also relieve the programmer of many of these address- and bit-processing chores. Table 10-8(c) describes the BIOS calls available for writing or reading a dot at a given coordinate location. Section 11.1.3 of the next chapter presents an algorithm and program to draw lines on the screen in high-resolution graphics mode using the BIOS write dot facility.

In the medium-resolution color mode, 2 bits are present for each grid position. Even and odd rows are positioned in display memory in the same manner described above, with each row requiring 80 bytes. Each byte position now, however, holds information for four pixels. This is shown in Figure 10-8 for the first four pixels of row 0.

The color for each pixel is determined by the value of its C1,C0 bit combination. While 2 bits can only specify four colors, and thus only four colors will be displayed at a particular time, two color sets or palettes are available from which these four colors may be drawn. Set one contains the colors cyan, magenta, and white, while set two contains the colors green, red, and yellow. Each of these sets, however, only contains three colors. The fourth color is the color which has been selected for the background. This background color can be one of the sixteen colors specified in Table 10-9. Of course, pixels displayed in the background color merge with the background and are not seen.

Table 10-10 summarizes the material on medium-resolution pixel color selection. Once again, while one may change pixel color by performing direct memory operations on corresponding pixel bit pairs, BIOS routines are available to write and read pixel elements using screen coordinates. This tends to be a good deal easier and more natural than performing these operations directly on pixel bit pairs.

One final point should be mentioned with regard to character displays while in graphics modes. Consider the situation where the color/graphics adapter has been put in high-resolution mode, and then the BIOS character write facility has been used to write a character. In this situation, BIOS looks up the selected character in a display table, determines the appropriate pixel settings, and accesses display memory to set these pixels. Each character is defined in the display table by an 8 by 8 dot matrix which is encoded as an 8-byte sequence. The bytes are ordered, with the first byte corresponding to the top row of pixels in the character.

With BIOS **INT   10H**, (AH) = 9 a character may be written at a designated screen position by loading AL prior to issuing the BIOS call. Although 256 character possibilites are available, only the first 128 which correspond to the normal ASCII

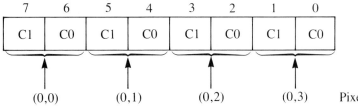

Figure 10-8 Byte format for medium-resolution color graphics.

Table 10-10   Pixel Color Selection in Medium Resolution

C1	C0	Pixel Code Pixel Color
0	0	Pixel <--- background color (Table 10-9) Background color selected with BIOS **INT 10H,** (AH) = 11, (BH) = 0, (BL low 4 bits) = Background and color.

		PALLETTE SET ONE	PALLETTE SET TWO
0	1	Pixel ← Cyan	Pixel ← Green
1	0	Pixel ← Magenta	Pixel ← Red
1	1	Pixel ← White	Pixel ← Yellow

Pallette set is selected with BIOS **INT   10H**, (AH) = 11, (BH) = 1. (BL low bit) = 0 for set 2, 1 for set 2.

codes have been implemented in the BIOS ROM display table. IBM has left the other 128 codes available to the user to establish his or her own set of characters. When a code is submitted outside of the normal ASCII range, BIOS uses the pointer vector located at 7CH to access a user-established display table. The vector contains the offset and segment addresses for the table in the same form as ordinary interrupt vectors. The display table should contain 8 bytes (in a top-to-bottom display order) for each character to be defined. For instance, if the display table address found at 7CH were AAAA:BBBB, then the 8 bytes starting at AAAA:BBBB should contain the character which the user desires to associate with ASCII code 128D. Similarly, the 8 bytes starting at AAAA:(BBBB + 8) should contain the character to be associated with the ASCII code 129D, and so on. In this way additional characters, symbols or designs can be added to the basic character set. Once established in a display table, they can be used by making simple BIOS calls.

10.4 THE ASYNCHRONOUS COMMUNICATIONS ADAPTER (A TYPE 14H INTERRUPT)

With a parallel interface, eight data lines (wires) and a number of control lines connect the printer to the computer. Such a data transmission method is fast since an entire byte is transmitted or received with each data transaction. However, it is costly from the point of view of wire usage. While this may not be a problem when devices are physically near the computer, it can be burdensome if all these wires must be strung to a computer resource in another room or building. In addition, the main existing communications network, the telephone network, uses a single data line. Finally, even though the transmission and reception of data on a single data line in a *serial* fashion are slower than in parallel, the process is still sufficiently fast so that it is perfectly acceptable for many applications.

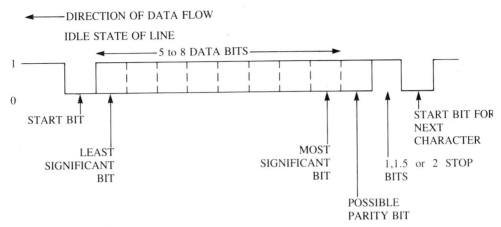

Figure 10-9 Asynchronous communication format.

Since the opportunities for data sharing, remote computer access, and other "computer networking" applications are enormous and rapidly growing, it was essential that the IBM PC provide a serial communications ability. The *asynchronous communication adapter* offers this capability and BIOS provides facilities for controlling the adapter and exchanging information with the serial asynchronous communications world.

Before discussing BIOS facilites, consider first the data and protocol associated with serial asynchronous communications. Figure 10-9 illustrates how a single character is transmitted in such a system.

When no data are being sent, the data line is said to be in the 1, *idle*, or *marking* state. To initiate transmission of a character, the sender drops the line to the 0, or *spacing*, state for a 1-bit time. This leading bit, called the *start* bit, is followed by 5 to 8 bits of information which represent the character to be sent. While this number may vary, depending on the transmitter and receiver characteristics, for any given transmitter/receiver pair the number of bits in the character is generally fixed, and must be known by both parties to the data transmission. Since the ASCII code has 7-bit characters, this is a commonly used length. When sending the character, the low-order, or least significant, bit is sent first.

After the data bits are sent, an optional parity bit may be present. If it is, either odd or even parity must be selected. The character is then terminated with a minimum of 1, 1.5, or 2 *stop bits*. These stop bits raise the line back to the 1 state for a period of time prior to the start bit for the next character. Again both the sender and receiver must agree on both parity selection and the number of stop bits to be used for proper data transmission. For example, a receiver expecting characters using even parity, and receiving characters using odd parity, would believe these characters to be in error.

Finally, for proper reception, both sender and receiver must agree on the bit transmission rate. This is typically stated in terms of bits per second, or *baud*. For unconditioned dial-up phone lines this is typically 300 or 1200 baud while for conditioned or dedicated lines (e.g., between a terminal and a computer) rates of up to 9600 Baud are common.

Note that each character is framed with a beginning start bit and ending stop bits. Knowing the various transmission parameters (i.e., number of data bits, transmission rate, etc.), having an internal clock of sufficiently high frequency, and possessing the appropriate hardware logic, the receiver can detect the start of character reception, read and count the individual bits in the character, and determine when the character has ended. Transmission in this situation is not dependent on both the receiver and transmitter having clocks which are synchronized (i.e., clock cycles start at the same time instant). For this reason the communications protocol described above is termed *asynchronous*. The price that is paid for this asynchronous capability is the extra start and stop bits which are used for character synchronization. This naturally cuts down on the amount of information that can be passed in a given period of time; however, it avoids the difficult problems associated with clock synchronization. This complex subject is discussed in more detail in reference 16.

As indicated above, for the asynchronous protocol to work correctly, both the transmitter and receiver must agree on certain transmission parameters. These are:

1. Number of data bits per character (i.e., word length)
2. Parity designation
3. Number of stop bits
4. Transmission rate (i.e., baud rate)

Since your IBM PC may be communicating with a variety of devices, provision was made in the asynchronous communication adapter to permit transmission parameter selection under program control. The BIOS type 14H interrupt with (AH) = 0 may be used for this purpose, with the AL register specifying the transmission parameters. After initialization, BIOS may now be used to send, (AH) = 1, or receive, (AH) = 2, data or obtain port status information, (AH) = 3. These BIOS services are outlined in Table 10-11.

To understand the meaning of the status bits, we shall consider the process of sending and receiving a character in more detail. Within the communications adapter, a dedicated device called a UART (Universal Asynchronous Receiver Transmitter) actually performs the transmission and reception of characters. On transmission, a character is first loaded into the *transmission holding register*. When the previous character has been sent, the contents of the holding register are transferred to a *transmission shift register*. Bits are then shifted out of this register with the UART adding in the correct parity and stop bits as necessary. Bits 5 and 6 of AH, when containing line status, indicate whether these two registers are empty. When BIOS is called on to transmit a character (AH = 1), it effectively waits until the holding register is empty before sending another character to the communications adapter.

On reception, the UART shifts the individually received bits into its *receiver shift register*, checks for parity and stop bits, and when a character has been assembled, places it in its *receiver data register*. Bit 0 of AH indicates when a character has been received. When BIOS is called on to receive a character (AH = 2), it waits until bit 0 is set and then moves the received character into its own buffer and into AL. The

Table 10-11   BIOS Asynchronous Communications Adapter Facilities: A Type 14 Interrupt

INITIALIZE ASYNCHRONOUS COMMUNICATIONS PORT
1. Register setup: (AH) ← 0; (AL) ← initialization parameters

AL → | 7 | 6 | 5 | 4 | 3 | 2 | 1 | 0 |

7 6 5	Baud rate	4 3	Parity	2	Stop bit	1 0	Word length
0 0 0	110	X 0	none	0	one	0 0	5 bits
0 0 1	150	0 1	odd	1	two	0 1	6 bits
0 1 0	300	1 1	even			1 0	7 bits
0 1 1	600					1 1	8 bits
1 0 0	1200						
1 0 1	2400						
1 1 0	4800						
1 1 1	9600						

2. Information return: Status as in status request AH = 3 below

TRANSMIT CHARACTER TO COMMUNICATIONS PORT
1. Register setup: (AH) ← 1; (AL) ← character to send
2. Information return: (AH bit 7) = 1 **IF** unable to send character; (AH bit 7) = 0 **IF** character sent. (AH bits 0–6) = Status as in status request AH = 3 below

WAIT TO RECEIVE A CHARACTER FROM COMMUNICATIONS PORT
1. Register setup: (AH) ← 2
2. Information Return: (AL) = character received; (AH) = 0 **IF** no error has occurred; (AH bits 5,6) = 0; (AH bits 7,4–1) = Status as in status request AH = 3 below

OBTAIN COMMUNICATIONS PORT STATUS
1. Register setup: (AH) ← 3
2. Information return: (AH) = Line control status as shown below; (AL) = Modem status as shown below; (A 1 indicates error or status condition)

AH LINE CONTROL STATUS BITS		AL MODEM STATUS BITS	
7-time out	3-framing error	7-data carrier	3-delta rec. line signal detect
6-transmitter shift register empty	2-parity error	6-ring indicator	2-delta ring indicator
5-transmitter holding register empty	1-overrun error	5-data set ready	1-delta data set ready
4-break detect	0-received data ready	4-clear to send	0-delta clear to send

UART also checks for correct parity and sets this bit if a parity error has occurred. It also checks for the correct placement and number of stop bits and signals a *framing error* if improper placement or number occur. Naturally, as characters arrive, they must be taken from the data register to make room for the next arriving character. If a character has not been removed from the data register in time and gets overwritten by the next arriving character, an *overrun error*, signaled in bit 1 of AH, occurs.

The *break-detect* and *time-out* line control status bits are normally associated with data transmission over a phone line. For telephone transmission, the asynchronous adapter is interfaced to the telephone through a device called a *modem*. The modem takes the voltage levels provided by the communications adapter and translates them into tones which can be passed over the telephone network. The four basic signals which the modem sends back to the adapter are *data carrier detect*, *ring indicator*, *data set ready*, and *clear to send*. These correspond to bits 7 through 4 of AL when status information is requested through BIOS (AH = 3). Data carrier detect indicates that a connection has been made to the modem on the other end of the line. Ring indicator indicates that the telephone connected to the modem is ringing. Data set ready indicates that the modem has power and is ready to be used. Clear to send indicates that the modem is ready to send data.

A time-out error can occur on transmission or reception. On transmission, prior to sending out the bits from the transmission shift register, the communications adapter signals the modem to determine if it is ready. In reply, data set ready and clear to send signals should be received by the adapter. If they are not received within a certain time period, then a time-out error has occurred. Similarly, on reception, if the data set ready signal is not received after a given time, a time-out error is set. The break-detect signal occurs when the UART has detected that the line has been held in the 0 or spacing state for more then one character's time. When this is detected, bit 4 in AH is set. The detection of the break signal usually means that the phone at the other end is about to be disconnected.

Finally, it should be noted that the adapter may be controlled directly by accessing its internal registers through their associated port addresses. In addition, various error and status conditions are often used to produce an adapter interrupt. Thus, for instance, the receive data ready condition can be used to activate an interrupt. Details related to these items may be found in the IBM PC technical reference manual (22).

10.5 THE DISKETTE ADAPTER (A TYPE 13H INTERRUPT)

The principal data and program storage devices for many IBM PCs are the floppy diskette drives and associated adapter. These are complex devices whose operation is closely linked to the operating system. For a more detailed view of diskette and related file organization issues see references 22, 27, and 28. In this section we discuss the BIOS facilities available for diskette control and file transfer. Higher-level disk and file interactions are available through use of various operating system calls (see Chapter 9) and higher-level language facilities. These typically shield the user from considerable detail and associated programming drudgery, and automatically provide for various error checking functions. In most situations they are the preferred method for interacting with the diskettes.

The media for storing information in a diskette drive is the *floppy disk*. The circular disk itself is made of flexible material coated with a magnetic oxide and residing within the familiar square jacket. Earlier IBM PC systems supported information recording on only a single side of the disk with eight sectors per track. To achieve higher information capacities per disk, double-sided disks were introduced with DOS 1.1 and nine sectors per track were introduced with DOS 2.0. The sides are labeled 0 and 1 with single-sided disks having only side 0. Information is stored on the diskette in concentric circular tracks, as shown in Figure 10-10. Each side has 40 tracks with the outermost track labeled track 0, and the innermost track labeled 39. With the standard format (as of DOS 2.0), tracks are divided into nine sectors labeled 1 through 9, with each sector holding 512 bytes of information.

Each diskette drive is equipped with *read/write head(s)* which may be positioned over a particular track. A sensor is also provided to indicate when sector 1 passes over a fixed location (that's the purpose of the small hole in the jacket off to the side of the larger center or hub hole). A command to transfer information to or from the disk

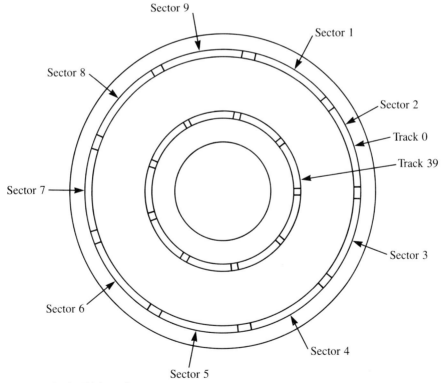

Figure 10-10   Diskette layout.

results in the head being moved to the correct track location and then, after the addressed sector appears beneath the head, transfer of information proceeds. In many file-oriented applications head movement is the most time consuming part of a file operation (29).

When operating on tracks in a sequential manner, the disk adapter assumes a standard ordering for sectors and tracks. For single-sided disks, sectors proceed from 1 to 9 and then move to the next higher track number and proceed again from 1 to 9. For double-sided disks, sectors proceed from 1 to 9 on side 0, from 1 to 9 on side 1 at the same track location, and then from 1 to 9 on side 0 of the next higher track location, and so on. Notice that in the double-sided case this ordering effectively has tracks on side 0 continue on side 1. This is done to reduce the amount of read/write head movement and, hence, time necessary when reading strings of sectors on the same track. Note also that the disk layout presented above is the standard one used with DOS 2.0 and later systems. Controls are available to modify this layout and in fact are used as part of a variety of diskette copy protection schemes (28).

Given this layout, DOS now organizes information placed on the diskette in a fixed manner. There are four types of records placed on the disk (see Table 10-12) with certain sectors on the disk reserved for certain usage. See Appendix C of the IBM PC DOS manual (27) for details on how these records are to be interpreted (also Problems 10.17 and 10.18).

Given this introduction to the diskette organization, we now can turn to the BIOS functions available for performing various disk operations. These are given in Table 10-13. All operations are invoked by initializing various registers and then executing **INT   13H**.

BIOS facility AH = 0 resets the diskette drives and is equivalent to DOS service invoked with **INT   DH**. A reset is automatically done on power-up. If an error is detected after a diskette operation is attempted, a reset operation should be performed prior to retrying the disk operation.

Table 10-12   Diskette Information Types

Information Category	Use	Single Sided		Double Sided		
		Track	Sector	Side	Track	Sector
Boot Record	The first sector read on power-up	0	1	0	0	1
FAT—File Allocation Table	Stores information on sector use linking together sector clusters which are part of the same file	0	2,3	0	0	2,3
Directory	Holds a list of disk file names, and associated information (e.g., date when created, size, link to starting cluster in FAT)	0	4,5, 6,7	0 1	0 0	4,5,6 7,8 9,1
Data	Stored file data	e l s e		w h e	r e	

Table 10-13   BIOS Diskette Facilities: A Type 13H Interrupt

RESET THE DISKETTE
   1. Register setup: AH ← 0
   2. Information returned: AH = Disk status (see below)

OBTAIN THE DISKETTE STATUS
   1. Register setup: AH ← 1
   2. Information returned: AH = 0 **IF** no error; *otherwise*, see below.

AH	Error	AH	Error
1	Bad command issued to disk	9	DMA transfer across 64K boundary
2	Address mark not found	10H	Read data error
3	Write attempt to protected disk	20H	Disk controller has failed
4	Requested sector not found	40H	Seek error, failure to find track
8	DMA overrun	80H	Time out error

READ SECTORS INTO MEMORY
   1. Register setup: AH ← 2; DL ← Drive (0–3); DH ← Side (0 or 1); CL ← Sector (1–9); CH ← Track (0–39); AL ← Number of sectors (1–9); ES:BX ← memory address for transfer
   2. Information return: AH = Disk status as above; AL = Number of sectors actually read; CF = 0 **IF** no error; CF = 1 **IF** error

WRITE SECTORS FROM MEMORY
   1. Register setup: AH ← 3; DL,DH,CL,CH,AL and ES:BX as in **READ**
   2. Information return: As in **READ**.

VERIFY SELECTED SECTORS (i.e., compare disk contents with memory contents)
   1. Register setup: AH ← 4; DL,DH,CL,CH,AL and ES:BX as in **READ**
   2. Information return: As in **READ**

FORMAT A TRACK
   1. Register setup: AH ← 5; ES:BX ← address of sector information fields. One 4 byte field for each sector with: byte 1 ← track number (0–39); byte 2 ← side number (0,1) byte 3 ← sector number (1–X); byte 4 ← number bytes/sector (0 = 128 bytes, 1 = 256 bytes, 2 = 512 bytes, 3 = 1024 bytes)
   2. Information return: AH ← Disk status as above

The second BIOS diskette facility, obtaining the disk status, is invoked with AH = 1. This status refers to the status set after the last disk operation (e.g., the last read). The status is returned in AH and is interpreted as shown in Table 10-13. Most of these are the result of hardware errors. When such an error occurs, the program should retry the disk operation several times before giving up and reporting with an error message. This is particularly true on timeout errors which often occur after issuing a read operation. In this situation, the disk motor often needs some time to get up to speed before the read operation can proceed. An attempt to read during this time will result in a read error; thus, reads should be reattempted at least three times when a timeout error is encountered. Note also that the status is returned after each of the BIOS disk operation so that obtaining the status with a separate BIOS call is typically unnecessary.

Sector read and write operations are performed through BIOS with AH = 2 and AH = 3. In both cases, the drive number, side number (which must be zero for single-sided disks), track number, and starting sector number must be specified. Up to nine sectors on the specified track may be transferred in a single operation by setting AL appropriately (1 to 9). This is a speedy way of getting a lot of information into memory since all nine sectors are obtained in a single disk revolution time. The area of memory accessed on disk reads and writes is specified in ES:BX. Note that unless the segment containing this memory buffer changes, the extra segment need only be specified once for the duration of the disk operations. Note also that the contents of DS, BX, DX,CH, and CL are left undisturbed as a result of these and the verify BIOS calls.

The BIOS verify operation (AH = 4) compares the contents of memory starting at ES:BX with the contents of the specified disk sector(s) and reports any differences. This is the same facility that is used with the DOS **VERIFY** command.

The final BIOS facility (AH = 5) is used in *formatting* the disk. The IBM PC uses what are referred to as *soft sectored* disks. With such disks, sectors on each track are defined under program control and may be different sizes. Thus, the first thing typically done prior to using a disk is to run the **DOS FORMAT** program, which sets up the sectors in accordance with the DOS standard (i.e., eight 512 byte sectors per track). The **DOS FORMAT** program also loads the bootstrap program, and initializes the file allocation table and file directory. The BIOS format facility may be used to format a disk on a track-by-track basis and is used by **DOS FORMAT** in performing the overall disk formatting task. With BIOS, the format of the track is specified in terms of a sequence of four byte fields which are pointed to by ES:BX. These fields hold the track number, side number, sector number and sector size, (i.e., number of bytes). Thus disks may be formatted with nonstandard sector sizes. This is useful in writing disks which cannot be copied (i.e., are copy protected) using the standard **DOS COPY** commands. For a discussion of how to read such nonstandard disks see reference 28.

10.6 GENERATING SOUNDS

Every IBM PC is equipped with a small speaker which can be controlled by the user. At the BASIC programming level, the frequency and duration of a sound can be conveniently set with the **SOUND** command. Unfortunately, BIOS does not contain any comparable user facilities for generating sounds. However, there are several ways of directly controlling the speaker at the assembly level. The approach taken here uses the 8253 *Timer Chip* to generate a square wave at a given frequency and the 8255 *Programmable Peripheral Interface* to control passage of this square wave to the speaker. Interactions between these devices at the functional level are shown in Figure 10-11.

The low-order 2 bits of the 8255 output register (port 61H) are used to control the timer chip and the speaker. If bit -0 is a 1, then the output of channel 2 of the 8253

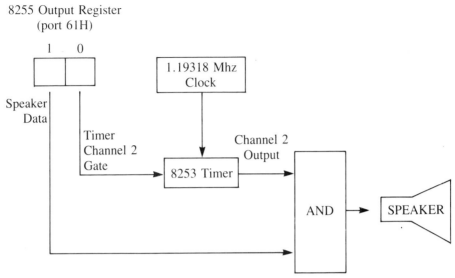

8255 Output Register
(port 61H)

1   0

Speaker
Data

1.19318 Mhz
Clock

Timer
Channel 2
Gate

Channel 2
Output

8253 Timer

AND

SPEAKER

Figure 10-11   Using the speaker.

Timer will be enabled; otherwise, it is disabled. Bit 1 of the 8255 output register effectively goes to an **AND** gate which also has Timer channel 2 as an input. The approach we will take to generating sounds will be to set both bits 0 and 1 to 1, thus enabling Timer channel 2 and also gating its output to the speaker.

The 8253 Timer contains three "channels," each of which can operate in six modes. Mode 3, the one of concern here, generates a square wave on the channel's output based on the input clock signal and the setting on a 2-byte internal counter register. The channel 2 output is connected to the speaker through the **AND** gate shown, and is enabled by bit 0 of the 8255. A *timer command register* (port 43H) must be loaded with the proper value to place each channel into the desired mode and to specify how transfers are to be made into the channel's counter register. Loading the command register with B6H places Timer channel 2 in mode 3 while at the same time permitting the counter register (port 42H) to be loaded in two successive byte transfers using a standard **OUT** instruction.

When in mode 3, a given timer operation begins with the contents of the counter register being saved in another internal 8253 register. The counter is then decremented at the input clock frequency until zero is reached. The counter is now reloaded with its saved value, and the decrementing process is restarted. In mode 3, the output of the channel is held high until the counter has decremented to half its initial value, and then it is held low until it has decremented to zero. As this process is repeated, a square wave is generated at the channel output, and in the case of channel 2 this output is fed (with the proper setting of the 8255) into the speaker, thus generating a tone. This cycle continues and the tone remains until a change of mode or a change in the 8255 control bits. Once this is started, no further program interaction is necessary (e.g., background music).

Table 10-14 Note Frequencies

Note	Frequency	Note	Frequency
C	130.8	middle C	261.6
$C^\sharp/D^\flat$	138.6	$C^\sharp/D^\flat$	277.2
D	146.8	D	293.7
$D^\sharp/E^\flat$	155.6	$D^\sharp/E^\flat$	311.1
E	164.8	E	329.6
F	174.6	F	349.2
$F^\sharp/G^\flat$	185.0	$F^\sharp/G^\flat$	370.0
G	196.0	G	392.0
$G^\sharp/A^\flat$	207.7	$G^\sharp/A^\flat$	415.3
A	220.0	A	440.0
$A^\sharp/B^\flat$	233.1	$A^\sharp/B^\flat$	466.2
B	246.9	B	493.9

Since the input clock to the timer chip is 1.19318 MHz (1,193,180 cycles per second), the counter value required to generate a frequency of X can be computed as 1,193,180 divided by X. For instance, the musical note middle C corresponds to the frequency 261.6 Hz. Thus the value loaded into the counter to generate this tone would be 4561. For convenience the frequencies associated with notes in two middle octaves of the piano are given in Table 10-14. Example 10-2 below illustrates how the various registers discussed above are loaded in controlling the speaker to produce a musical scale.

EXAMPLE 10-2 The **SOUND** procedure below plays the 12 notes of the octave starting at middle C. Note that the Timer channel 2 internal count register (port 42H) is loaded in two successive **OUT** operations with the lower byte being loaded first. For this to work properly, the Timer command register has to be loaded first with B6H. CX is used as a note counter with the frequency effectively being incremented by a half tone and the corresponding count being loaded into the count register on each iteration.

10.7 DETERMINING EQUIPMENT CONFIGURATION (TYPES 11H AND 12H INTERRUPTS)

It often is important for an application program to know what optional equipment is present on the system on which it is executing. Based on this knowledge, the program can tailor itself to take advantage of the available equipment. An example is an editing program which may be able to execute more quickly the more memory it has available. Another example relates to the self-test sequence which the IBM PC performs on power-up. To do this test properly, the self-test program must know the equipment configuration to test.

The IBM PC has two switches on the system board which are manually set to indicate the equipment configuration. Other switches are also present on additional

```
DSEG      SEGMENT    ;note of the scale starting with middle C
NOTES     DW    262,277,294,311,330,349,370,392,415,440,466,494
DSEG      ENDS
SSEG      SEGMENT STACK
          DB         128 DUP(?)
SSEG      ENDS
CSEG      SEGMENT
SOUND     PROC       FAR
          ASSUME  CS:CSEG,DS:DSEG,SS:SSEG
START:    PUSH       DS              ;stack <--- return seg. addr.
          XOR        AX,AX           ;clear AX
          PUSH       AX              ;stack <--- 0 return address
          MOV        AX,DSEG         ;set up DS register
          MOV        DS,AX
          XOR        SI,SI           ;SI used as note pointer
          MOV        BX,12           ;BX <--- note count
;*** SET UP TIMER COMMAND REGISTER AND COUNTER REGISTER ***
          MOV        AL,0B6H         ;set 8253 command register
          OUT        43H,AL          ; for channel 2, Mode 3, etc.
NLOOP:    MOV        AX,34DCH        ;AX <--- low part of clk. freq.
          MOV        DX,12H          ;DX <--- high part of clk. freq.
          DIV        [NOTES + SI]    ;AX <---  clk. freq./note freq.
          OUT        42H,AL          ;8253 ctr.<---least significant byte
          MOV        AL,AH           ;AL <--- most significant byte
          OUT        42H,AL          ;8253 ctr.<--- most significant byte
;*** TURN ON LOW BITS IN 8255 OUTPUT PORT ***
          IN         AL,61H          ;read in current value of 8255 port
          OR         AL,3            ;set low bits
          OUT        61H,AL          ;send out new port value
;*** LOOP WHILE NOTE IS SOUNDING ***
          PUSH       CX              ;save current CX value
          MOV        CX,28000
RPTA:     LOOP       RPTA            ;about 1/10 second delay
;*** TURN OFF SPEAKER, CHECK NOTE COUNT, SET UP NEXT NOTE ***
          XOR        AL,3            ;turn off speaker bit and timer gate
          OUT        61H,AL          ;send out new 8255 port value
          MOV        CX,2800
RPTB:     LOOP       RPTB            ;about 1/100 second delay
          INC        SI              ;increment note pointer
          INC        SI
          DEC        BX              ;decrement note counter
          JNZ        NLOOP           ;loop until BX = 0
          RET
SOUND     ENDP
CSEG      ENDS
          END        START
```

Figure 10-12 A scale-playing program.

Table 10-15 BIOS Equipment Determination Facilities: Types 11H and 12H Interrupts

MEMORY SIZE DETERMINATION (A Type 12H Interrupt)

Register setup: None

Information output: (AX) = Total number of contiguous 1K blocks in low memory (both system board and any extra memory boards, but not including ROM or display memory)

EQUIPMENT DETERMINATION (A Type 11H Interrupt)

Register setup: None

Information output: (AX) = Equipment configuration as given below (bits 13, 8, 1 unused).

AX   15 14 13 12 11 10 9 8 7 6 5 4 3 2 1 0

Number Printers 15 14	12	Number of Asynchronous Comm. Cards 11 10 9	Diskette Drives 7 6 0	Initial Video Setup 5 4	System Memory 3 2	Diskette Present 0
0 0 → 0	G	0 0 0 → 0	X X 0 → 0	0 0 → Unused	0 0 → 16K	0 → no
0 1 → 1	A	0 0 1 → 1	0 0 1 → 1	0 1 → 40 × 25 B/W — Color card	0 1 → 32K	1 → yes
1 0 → 2	M	0 1 0 → 2	0 1 1 → 2	1 0 → 80 × 25 B/W	1 0 → 48K	
1 1 → 3	E	. . . → .	1 0 1 → 3	1 1 → 80 × 25 B/W — B/W Card	1 1 → 64K	
		. . . → .	1 1 1 → 4			
	I/	. . . → .				
	O	1 1 1 → 7				

memory boards which may have been added to the system to increase its memory capacity. The contents of these switches are read by the BIOS types 11H and 12H services and equipment information is returned as indicated in Table 10-15.

The type 12H interrupt can be used to find out how much memory is available to the system. This call indicates the amount of memory in terms of contiguous 1K blocks in low memory and doesn't include ROM and display memory.

The type 11H interrupt is used to find out what optional equipment is on the system. Note that bit 0 indicates whether or not there is a diskette present. If bit 0 is a 1, then on power-up the bootstrap routine will be loaded from the diskette; otherwise ROM BASIC will be called. Note also that bits 2 and 3 are only useful for the early IBM PC systems, which were limited to a maximum of 64K on the system board. New versions allow up to 256K on the system board with minimum systems having at least 64K. For these systems bits 2 and 3 are 1, BIOS interrupt 12H should be used to determine the full memory available on the system. Bits 5 and 4 indicate the power-up video mode. A 01, for instance, means that on power-up, the color adapter is set for the 40*25 black/white alphanumeric mode.

10.8 SUMMARY

To aid in system and peripheral device control, the IBM PC is provided with a set of programs called BIOS (BASIC Input Output System). These programs are stored in read-only memory and provide the principal routines used by the operating system in interacting with peripheral devices. They represent a level of device interaction generally below that of the operating system, but above that of directly controlling the devices by accessing their internal registers and dealing directly with device-generated interrupts. In many situations device control can be adequately performed using either DOS or higher-level-language commands. Working at these higher levels is often preferable since many tedious details are avoided, and error checking is often provided as part of the device service. If high speed is required, or if special control is necessary, the use of BIOS or lower level approaches may be necessary.

BIOS routines may be called from assembly language programs by setting up the appropriate registers, and then issuing a software interrupt. The BIOS routine in turn attempts to perform the requested operations and, when necessary, uses selected registers to return information to the calling program. For example, to determine if a key has been struck on the keyboard, the assembly language program would load AH with 1 (**MOV   AH,1**) and then issue software interrupt 16H (**INT   16H**). In this case BIOS uses the zero flag to return information with (ZF) = 1 indicating that no key has been struck, and (ZF) = 0 that a key has been struck. For most BIOS-supported devices a table is provided indicating register setup requirements and information return interpretations.

For certain devices, information also is provided on direct device control. In the case of the video display screen, control via direct access to display memory often is more efficient than using BIOS. In the case of generating sound on the speaker, no BIOS routines are available, and direct control is necessary through use of the *8255 Programmable Peripheral Interface* and *8253 Timer*.

EXERCISES

10.1 Write a program that uses BIOS interrupt 16H to read the keyboard and then display the individual bits contained in AH and AL. Display the ASCII character associated with the bit pattern on the same line. Use this program to check various entries in Tables 10-2 and 10-3. Note when various extended codes occur.

10.2 In designing a new edit program it has been decided to include a shorthand feature for certain common words. Noting that separate codes and status bits are associated with the right and left shift keys, it has been decided to retain the right shift key for its normal function and use the left shift key for calling up these common words. Thus, for example the word "and" is called for when the keys L. Shift and "a" are depressed simultaneously. Write a program which will read keys from the keyboard and then display them. Include in the program the shorthand feature for displaying the words "and," "bit," "for," "when," and "then" using the L. Shift key in conjunction with the A, B, F, W, and T keys, respectively.

10.3 Numbers can be entered from the keyboard using either top row number keys or using the numeric keypad in its Num Lock state. Develop a flowchart or structured English specification for a procedure to distinguish between numbers entered from these two parts of the keyboard.

10.4 Write a procedure to read three digits entered from the keyboard and then, interpreting the digits as a positive integer, translate the integer into its binary equivalent. Integers are terminated by striking the ENTER key.

10.5 Use the BIOS printer services in writing a procedure to print two tables of 8-bit codes and their associated printed characters. The first table should cover the normal ASCII range of printed characters, 20H to 7FH. The second should cover the range A0H to DFH. Use several columns with each table. Each column entry should contain the bit representation of the character and then the printed character itself (e.g., 0100 0001   A).

10.6 Using your monochrome display, or color/graphics display in alphanumeric mode, write, debug, and execute a program to display all 256 characters in normal video, reverse video, normal with blinking, normal with underlining (not available with color/graphics adapter), and reverse video with blinking.

10.7 Using your monochrome display, or color/graphics display in alphanumeric mode, develop and debug a procedure which displays a graph axis on the screen. Use the block graphics characters found in Table 10-6. Indicate clearly how the locations of the end of the vertical (X1,Y1) and horizontal (X2,Y2) axes are passed to the procedure.

10.8 Using your monochrome display, or color/graphics display in alphanumeric mode, develop and debug a procedure to position a vertical darkened bar one character in width on the screen. Indicate clearly how the position of the bar is communicated to the procedure.

10.9 Using the procedures developed in Problems 10.7 and 10.8, develop and debug a program to display the bar chart shown below.

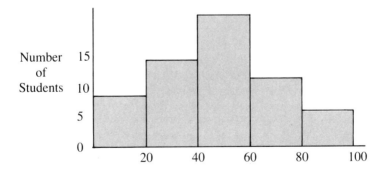

10.10 Using the card display procedure of Figure 10-6, develop a procedure which accepts four playing card designations (e.g., 1 of hearts, 5 of diamonds, etc.) as parameters, and displays the four cards across the screen. Each card should have in its upper lefthand, and lower righthand corners, its value and suit. Use the alphanumeric characters for hearts, spades, clubs, and diamonds.

10.11 Redo the error message display program of Figure 9-8 using BIOS rather than DOS facilities.

10.12 Assume the available display adapter is in alphanumeric mode. In a particular text processing program it is desired to be able to search text displayed on the screen for a designated character string. If the string is found, then the cursor is to be positioned over the first character in the string. If more then one match is possible, the search stops at the first match. If no match is possible, then the bell is to be rung. Develop a procedure to perform this task. For simplicity assume that the strings are a fixed three characters in length. The calling program passes the character string to the procedure using the stack.

10.13 Make a table showing the starting and ending addresses (in hexadecimal) of each alphanumeric mode display page for 80 by 25 and 40 by 25 screen displays.

10.14 Develop a program which displays two six-character-wide solid color bars across the screen. Divide each bar into eight equal parts. In the top bar each part should be one of the eight colors with $I = 0$. The bottom bar should hold the corresponding colors but with $I = 1$.

10.15 Redo Problem 10.6 for your color/graphics adapter and color monitor. In this situation use the color attributes to display all color combinations at least once. Note that the underlining attribute is unavailable.

10.16 This problem assumes that an asynchronous communications adapter is present in your system, and that a standard (RS232-compatible) alphanumeric terminal is available. Attach the available alphanumeric terminal to your communications adapter. Make sure that pins 2 and 3 are connected correctly. Set the terminal for 2400 baud, odd parity, 7-bit word length, and 1 stop bit. Write and debug a program which will transmit a simple ASCII message (no control codes) from the PC to the terminal.

10.17 As indicated in Table 10-12, the diskette file directory is stored on a fixed set of sectors. Each directory entry is 32 bytes in length. Bytes 0 to 7 contain the filename and bytes 8 to 10 the filename extension. An empty directory entry contains E5H in its first byte position. Write and debug a program which lists on the display the names of all files on a disk.

10.18 The date that a file was created or last updated is contained in the file's directory entry in bytes 24 and 25 with the following format.

←			BYTE 25				→	←			BYTE 24				→
7	6	5	4	3	2	1	0	7	6	5	4	3	2	1	0
Y	Y	Y	Y	Y	Y	Y	M	M	M	M	D	D	D	D	D

The month is 1-12, the day is 1-31, and the year is 0-119 (1980–2099). Write and debug a program to list on the display the names of all files on a disk and their associated creation/update dates.

10.19 Write a procedure to determine the amount of memory available on the system. Display the result.

10.20 Write a procedure to play "Mary Had A Little Lamb," or some other simple melody. Store the notes as a table and call them up as needed to set the timer counter.

10.21 You are to write a program which allows the keyboard to be played as a miniature piano. The Q key corresponds to the lower C note of Table 10-14. The major notes (C,D,E,F, . . .) continue across the Q key row (Q = C, W = D, E = E, R = F,. . .). The sharps and flats can be included as keys on the number row above the Q row. Every time a key is depressed, the corresponding note should be sounded until the next note key is depressed (which should sound that note) or until the space bar is depressed. Assume that only a single note is depressed at a time.

11

Higher-Level-Language Interfacing

It is generally acknowledged that using higher-level languages enhances programmer productivity and eases both the documentation and debugging tasks. One would therefore ordinarily prefer using such languages. In some situations, however, either the resulting programs are inordinately slow or certain special features of the computer, accessible only at the assembly language level, are needed. Careful assembly language coding of time-critical sections of an application often remedies these difficulties.

A technique which exploits the speed-up possibilities and special capabilities of assembly language programming, while retaining the advantages of higher-level-language programming, is discussed in this chapter. With this approach applications are coded principally in a higher-level language; however, subsections requiring either higher speed or special machine level control are coded in assembly language. These subsections are assembled separately, "linked" to the output of the higher-level program compiler or interpreter, and called by the higher-level program during execution.

There is, of course, a cost associated with interfacing assembly language routines with higher-level languages. It is mainly related to mastering the added complexity associated with calling and passing parameters between diverse language routines and with the difficulties of program debugging in a bilingual environment. This chapter discusses interfacing and debugging procedures for such circumstances. Three higher-level languages are considered: BASIC, FORTRAN, and PASCAL. The standard IBM DOS operating system, BASIC interpreter (1) and, FORTRAN (30) and PASCAL (31) compilers are assumed. Two detailed illustrative examples are provided.

11.1 TWO EXAMPLE APPLICATIONS

11.1.1 A Stock Market Simulation Problem

Simulation is a popular method for studying system behavior (32, 33, 34). The process begins by developing a model of the system of interest. Many types of models are possible. For instance, a road map is a kind of model, just as is a model airplane. In the context of computer-based simulation, the model is typically more formal and mathematical in nature. Unlike models which can be solved using analytical methods (e.g., a model requiring solution of a quadratic equation), computer simulation generally refers to formal models which cannot be solved analytically. (*Note:* Sometimes even if a problem can be solved analytically, simulation is used because it may be conceptually or operationally simpler to obtain an answer this way.) During computer simulation the action of the system model is "mimicked" by sequences of computer instructions, the computer model is executed many times with varying parameters or inputs, statistics are collected on each "simulation run," and the results are processed and displayed to the user.

The example simulation problem concerns predicting the future level of the stock market. The system in this case could be a stock exchange (e.g., New York Stock Exchange, American Stock Exchange, etc.). The "state" of the stock market level corresponds to the value of some stock market index (e.g., Standard and Poor's Index, Dow Jones Index, etc.). Changes in "state" (i.e., index value) are modeled as a simple one-step Markov chain. A Markov chain is a particular formal mathematical model possessing certain properties which, for our treatment here, need not be precisely defined. In terms of the market system of interest, assume that the system state moves up or down by a fixed amount (some average index price change) each day the stock market is open. Assume also that the direction of movement is random, with the up or down possibilites being equally likely. Thus the index value at the close of a given trading day is determined by the value at the close of the previous day, plus or minus some constant amount, with the direction of change being randomly determined. This corresponds to tossing a fair coin each day to determine whether the market goes up or down. If $AVG(k + 1)$ and $AVG(k)$ are the values of the index at the close of days k and $k+1$, respectively, and A is the constant value by which the index changes each day, our market model can be described in terms of the expression

$$AVG(k + 1) = AVG(k) + R \cdot A \tag{11-1}$$

where R is either $+ 1$ or $- 1$, with each R value having an equal probability of occurring. Figure 11-1 indicates two possible sequences of index values starting at the same initial

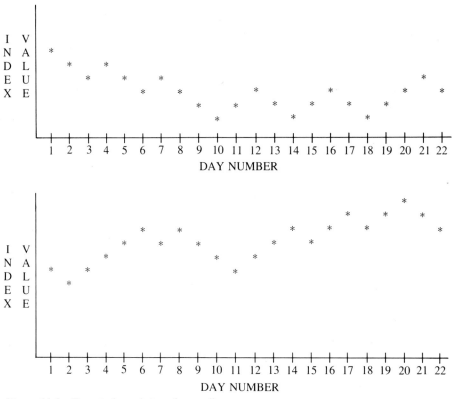

Figure 11-1 Two stock market random walks.

value and running for 22 market days. Note that the path (random walk) and final value of the index is different in both cases, indicating the probabilistic nature of the model. Clearly there is some question as to what constitutes a realistic market model and, as might be expected given the potential economic value of a "good" model, this question has been extensively studied. Some studies have even suggested that the model embodied in the above expression is realistic (35).

Given such a model, there are a number of questions which may be asked about the behavior of this system. For instance, say that the market index is at a given value X (i.e., $AVG(0) = X$) and one expects an average change per day of A. What is the probability that, after N trading days, the index is above $1.1 \cdot X$ (i.e., there has been more than a 10 percent increase in market value)? That is, what is the probability that $AVG(N-1) > 1.1 \cdot AVG(0)$? Such a question can be answered by developing a simulation program which implements Equation (11-1) with the appropriate parameters, performs many random walks (say M) over N trading days, notes after each walk whether the final index is above $1.1 \cdot X$ (i.e., a successful walk), and then divides the number of successful walks by the total number of walks M. As the number of walks becomes large, the final division yields the desired probability. In effect, M experiments have been performed on the computer model, and the averaging operation (the division)

```
PROGRAM MARKET
; Monte Carlo stock market simulation
; N = number of trading days; X = initial value of the index
; A = average value by which the index will change daily
; M = num. random walks
; P = probability of success; AVG = running value of index
N, X, A, M, AVG, Z are integers
P and Z are real numbers
B is a bit                ;random bit for index change direction
BEGIN
read in user supplied N, X, A and M values
Z := 0                                    ;num. of successful walks
FOR    I:= 1 to M
       BEGIN
       AVG := X
       FOR    J:= 1 to N
              BEGIN                       ;begin walk of N days
              develop random bit B
              IF    ( B := 0 )
              THEN  ( AVG := AVG - A)
              ELSE  ( AVG := AVG + A)
              END                         ;walk ends
       IF     ( AVG > 1.1*X )             ;success test
       THEN   ( Z := Z + 1)               ;inc. success counter
       ELSE (do nothing)
       END
P := Z/M;  display P                      ;probability calc.
END    MARKET
```
Figure 11-2   A Monte Carlo stock market simulation.

is performed over all experiments to determine the success probability. This is referred to as a *Monte Carlo simulation* because of the direct correspondence to gambling or gaming systems. An algorithm which represents this solution method is given in Figure 11-2. (Note that in this case the problem can be solved using other statistical methods, but that is not our concern here.)

Clearly this simulation is dominated by computations involving the N random walks. Therefore, to achieve high speed, it might be advantageous to program the inner **FOR** loop (i.e., **FOR J:= 1 to N**) in assembly language, leaving the initialization, user input, division, and display parts of the program to be done in the higher-level language.

11.1.2 Assembly Language Market Simulation Program

An assembly language subroutine that performs the inner loop of the **MARKET** algorithm is shown in Figure 11-3.

The procedure can be viewed as being divided into three parts. The first part, up to the beginning of the **WALK** loop, saves the calling programs registers and transfers

```
; ** Procedure To Generate Random Bits and Perform a Random Walk **
        PROG        SEGMENT
        RWALK       PROC    FAR
                    PUBLIC  RWALK
                    ASSUME  CS:PROG
                    PUSH    BP              ;save caller's registers
                    MOV     BP,SP
                    PUSH    BX
                    PUSH    CX
                    PUSH    SI
                    PUSH    DI
                    PUSH    DX              ;get parameters
                    MOV     SI,[BP+6]       ;SI <--- offset addr. seed
                    MOV     AX,[SI]         ;AX <--- seed
                    MOV     SI,[BP+8]       ;SI <--- offset addr. # days
                    MOV     CX,[SI]         ;CX <--- # trading days
                    MOV     SI,[BP+10]      ;SI <--- addr. daily change
                    MOV     DI,[BP+12]      ;DI <--- addr. ini. market avg.
                    MOV     DX,[DI]         ;DX <--- initial market avg.
        ; **** Walk Loop Begin ****
        RANDOM:     XOR     BX,BX           ;clear BX
                    TEXT    AX,02           ;is bit 1 = 1 ?
                    JZ      BIT1E0          ;if bit 1 = 0, (BL) <--- 0
                    MOV     BL,1            ;if bit 1 = 1, (BL) <--- 1
        BIT1E0:     TEST    AX,04           ;is bit 2 = 1 ?
                    JZ      BIT2E0          ;if bit 2 = 0, (BH) <--- 0
                    MOV     BH,1            ;if bit 2 = 1, (BH) <--- 1
        BIT2E0:     XOR     BL,BH           ;BL(BIT 0) <--- XOR of
                                            ;AX (bits 1 and 2)
                    SHR     BL,1            ;carry flag <--- BL (bit 0)
                    RCR     AX,1            ;rotate AX moving the carry
                                            ;flag into the high bit of AX
        ; ** test bit and adjust market avg **
        DONE:       TEST    AX,01H          ;IF low order bit = 1
                    JNZ     OVER1
                    ADD     DX,[SI]         ;DX <--- DX + daily change
                    JMP     OVER2
        OVER1:      SUB     DX,[SI]         ;DX <--- DX - daily change
        OVER2:      LOOP    RANDOM          ;do other days in random walk
        ; **** Walk Loop End ****
                    MOV     SI,[BP+6]       ;get offset of seed location
                    MOV     [SI],AX         ;save current seed
                    MOV     [DI],DX         ;return final market value
                    POP     DX              ;restore caller's registers
                    POP     DI
                    POP     SI
                    POP     CX
                    POP     BX
                    POP     BP
                    RET     8               ;discard 4 parameter addr.
        RWALK       ENDP
        PROG        ENDS
                    END
```

Figure 11-3 **RWALK**: Assembly language procedure for Monte Carlo simulation.

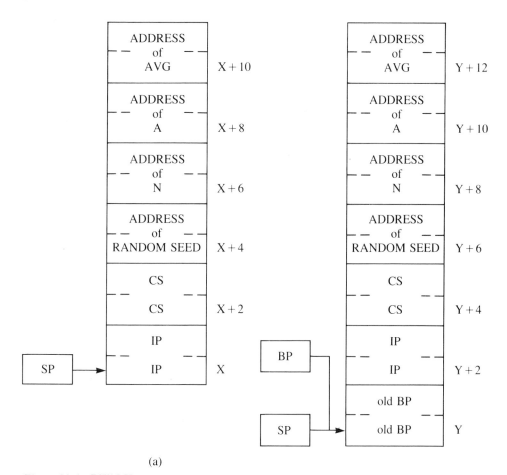

(a)

Figure 11-4 **RWALK** stack contents.

parameter addresses and values into procedure registers. The second part, the **WALK** loop itself, generates random bits and performs one market walk through the number of days specified. The third part, from the end of the **WALK** loop to the procedure end, transfers the final market value, restores calling program registers, and returns control to the calling program.

Four parameters are transferred to **RWALK** in the first program part; the initial market average value (moved into DX), the address of the average change in the market per day (moved into SI), the number of days in the simulation (moved into CX), and the random seed (moved to AX). It is assumed that the addresses of these parameters are pushed onto the stack when the procedure is called in the order given above. This is in fact what happens when the BASIC and PASCAL programs discussed later call **RWALK**. Thus, just after the higher-level program has called **RWALK**, the stack appears as shown in Figure 11-4*a*.

The first instruction saves the base pointer (BP) on the stack. Once saved, BP is now loaded with the contents of the current stack pointer (SP) so that the stack can be conveniently addressed through BP. Figure 11-4*b* shows the stack after BP is saved and then loaded. Various calling program registers (BX, CX, SI, DI, DX) are also saved. The parameter addresses are now accessed through BP and stored in SI. SI can then be used to obtain the parameters themselves by use of the indirect addressing mode, **[SI]**. AX is used to hold the random seed and acts as the shift register for a shift register random number generator. CX holds the number of times the program cycles through the **RANDOM** loop (i.e., the number of days in the simulation). DX holds the running value of the market, and SI holds the address of the average change in the market per day.

The first part of the **WALK** loop generates a random bit. This bit is produced using a shift register random number generator of the sort described earlier in Section 4.2.2. In this case, however, only a single random bit is needed since only two choices are required (i.e., an increase or decrease in the market value). After checking bits 1 and 2, AX is changed appropriately to produce a new random bit. The **TEST   AX,01H** instruction tests bit 0 (the designated random bit) to determine whether the market goes up or down on that day, and the average market change is then added to or subtracted from the current market value. The day counter, CX, is now automatically decremented with the **LOOP** instruction and, if not zero, the next day's market change is simulated. The process is repeated until an entire walk is completed.

The last part of the procedure begins by returning the latest random number (AX) and final market value (DX) to the calling program. Calling program registers are now restored, and the four parameter addresses discarded from the stack. Control is then returned to the calling program which determines whether more walks are needed and thus if **RWALK** is to be called again. This procedure will be used later in the chapter in conjunction with three higher-level languages to complete the stock market simulation.

11.1.3 A Graphics Problem

In the simulation problem above, the assembly language subroutine was used to speed up the calculation. Assembly language usage with the graphics problem considered next is motivated not by speed, but by the language's ability to exploit the computer's graphics hardware. With a few exceptions (e.g., IBM Advanced BASIC; see reference 1) most higher-level languages do not directly support graphics applications, and special-purpose graphics packages must be obtained for such purposes. Since the graphics capabilities of the computer are available at the assembly language level, the interested user can develop his or her own assembly language graphics procedures which are callable from a higher-level language.

Consider the following problem. Say that a software company desires to flash its logo on the screen for a moment each time one of its software products is used. Since the company's products are written in a variety of languages, it has been decided to produce a single assembly language subroutine, callable from any higher-level language, to draw the logo on the screen. The company has the fictitious name Tree Software Inc. and naturally its logo is a tree. *Tree* in this case refers to the tree data

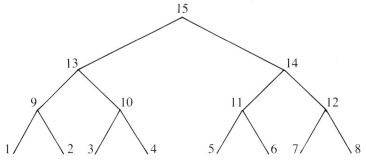

Figure 11-5   Logo for Tree Software Inc.

structure and in this case a *binary tree* structure has been selected (i.e., each node has a branching factor of two) as shown in Figure 11-5. The nodes are numbered for discussion purposes and are not part of the logo.

The binary tree figure is composed of straight lines; hence we begin by considering the fundamental graphics operation of drawing a line. Given the coordinates of two end points, the routine to be developed initially is to draw a line on a graphics display screen between the two defined points. Since any curve or figure can be constructed out of a series of appropriately positioned short lines, the line drawing routine is a basic component of many graphics systems.

We assume for this discussion that an IBM Color/Graphics Monitor Adapter with an attached video monitor is present (see Section 10.3.2) and operating in its *high-resolution mode*. As indicated in Section 10.3.2.2, in this mode the screen can be viewed as consisting of 640 horizontal and 200 vertical points which may be addressed by using the X,Y coordinate system indicated in Figure 11-6. BIOS may be used to select the screen mode by setting (AH) = 0, (AL) = mode number, and then issuing a type 10H interrupt. A general procedure to clear the screen and set its mode is given in Figure 11-7. The integer parameter named **I** designates the desired screen **MODE**. This will be used later in setting the screen to high-resolution mode prior to drawing the logo.   .

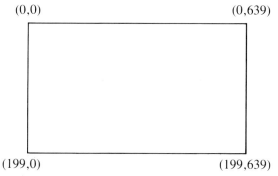

Figure 11-6   X,Y coordinates for high-resolution graphics.

```
PROCEDURE MODE (I)
; procedure to clear screen and set it to mode I
BEGIN
I is an integer
(AH) := 0            ;set up for mode selection
(AL) := I            ;select mode I
INT 10H              ;call BIOS video support facility
END MODE
```

Figure 11-7   **MODE**: A procedure to set screen mode.

Once a graphics mode is selected, particular screen pixels must be written. This is illustrated below using the BIOS **WRITE DOT** facility [see Table 10-8(c)] to display a point at location 100,200.

```
MOV     AH, 12       ;AH <--- 12,set WRITE DOT mode
MOV     AL, 0        ;AL <--- 0,no color selected
MOV     DX, 100      ;DX <--- 100,DX holds row number
MOV     CX, 200      ;CX <--- 200,CX holds column number
INT     10H          ;call BIOS video monitor facility
```

The **MODE** procedure and the above instruction sequence indicate how to set up the high-resolution graphics mode and display (write) a dot on the monitor at a given location. The problem to be considered next is that of drawing a line by means of writing sequences of dots. Drawing purely horizontal or vertical lines is straightforward given that line positions are specified in terms of the 640 × 200 coordinate system. That is, all points along any designated horizontal or vertical line will coincide with displayable pixels in the coordinate system. Since these picture elements are physically close together on a monitor of normal size, writing successive pixels will give the appearance of a smooth, continuous line. Consider, however, the case of drawing a line between the points 100,103 and 113,100. What dots should be written to construct this line? Two alternate approaches are shown below in Figure 11-8.

The line-drawing algorithm used will affect a line's quality in terms of its apparent straightness, density, and termination accuracy, in addition to the speed with which it can be drawn (36, 37). Given the line endpoints X1,Y1 and X2,Y2 in absolute screen coordinates, a simple algorithm which yields reasonable quality lines is presented in Figure 11-9 (36).

The algorithm first determines which dimension (X or Y) traversed by the line is longer. The greater of these two (stored in L) is used to determine an increment amount (**XINC** and **YINC**) for the running position indicator (X,Y). For the larger dimension this increment amount is always + or − 1, while for the smaller dimension the increment will be a fraction. Since fractional coordinate values cannot be displayed (e.g., X = 100.62, Y = 203), a decision must be made either to round or truncate the fractional coordinate. Rounding typically results in a more symmetrically drawn line and is used here. One way of performing the rounding operation is to add a factor of .5 to the variable in question, and then perform truncation. This is done when the initial X,Y position to be displayed is calculated from the coordinate pair (X1,Y1).

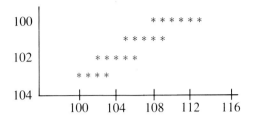

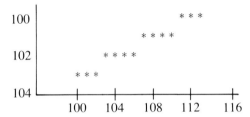

Figure 11-8 Line drawing.

Subsequent truncations occur in the inner loop where the successive dots that make up the line are drawn. In this loop, the (X,Y) position is incremented after each dot is placed on the screen, thereby determining the position of the next dot to be plotted. The sequence of truncating, plotting, and position incrementing continues until the longer dimension has been traversed.

Now we can call **LINE** to create a tree. One possible tree-drawing algorithm is given in Figure 11-10.

TREE begins at the lowest level of the tree (i.e., points 1 through 8 of Figure 11-5) and successively draws branch pairs (i.e., branches that meet at a common point)

```
PROCEDURE LINE (X1,Y1,X2,Y2)
; procedure to draw a line between X1,Y1, and X2,Y2
; abs = absolute value, trunc = truncated value
X1,Y1,X2,Y2 are integers
L, X, Y, XINC and YINC are reals
BEGIN
IF      (abs(Y2 - Y1) > abs(X2 - X1))
THEN    (L := abs(Y2 - Y1))
ELSE    (L := abs(X2 - X1))
XINC := (X2 - X1) / L, YINC := (Y2 - Y1) / L
X := X1 + .5,  Y := Y1 + .5
FOR I:= 1 to L
        BEGIN
        Plot Dot (trunc(X),trunc(Y))
        X := X + XINC, Y := Y + YINC
        END
END  LINE
```

Figure 11-9 **LINE**: A line-drawing algorithm.

```
PROGRAM TREE
; program to draw a 3 level binary tree on a
; 640 * 200 screen and display for about two seconds
I,J,K,X1,Y1,X2,Y2 and XDIF are integers
BEGIN
Clear screen and place in high resolution mode.
Y1 := 160                    ;Y position of lowest tree level
X1 := 96                     ;X position of left,lowest point
XDIF := 64                   ;X dif. btw. points on lowest level
FOR I := 1 to 3              ;loop for three tree levels
    BEGIN
    J := 2**(3 - I)      ;number of line pairs at level I
    Y2 := Y1 - 40        ;Y position of next level up
    FOR K := 1 to J      ;loop for line pairs within a level
        BEGIN
        X2 := X1 + XDIF/2      ;X of common pt. next level up
        LINE (X1,Y1,X2,Y2)     ;draw left branch of line pair
        X1 := X1 + XDIF        ;X of right branch of line pair
        LINE (X1,Y1,X2,Y2)     ;draw right branch of next line pr.
        X1 := X1 + XDIF        ;X of left branch of next line pr.
        END
    XDIF := 2*XDIF           ;X dif. btw. points at next level
    X1 := X2 - XDIF*(J-1) ;X pos. of left lowest pt. of next level
    Y1 := Y2                ;Y position of next level
    END
Loop delay for about two seconds.
Clear screen and return to original screen mode.
END TREE
```

Figure 11-10 **TREE**: A tree-drawing program.

moving from left to right across the tree. The first branch pair consists of the branches 1,9 and 2,9 with the left branch being 1,9 and the right being 2,9; the second branch pair consists of 3,10 and 4,10; etc. Since branch pairs have a common point at the next higher level, this point coordinate is calculated once per pair. Once all the branches at a given level are drawn (i.e., exit from the **K** loop), then coordinates and horizontal differences for the next higher level are calculated, and the branches at this next higher level are drawn. This continues (i.e., **I** loop iterations) until all the levels have been considered and all branches drawn. The program begins and ends by establishing the correct screen modes for graphic and alphanumeric operations.

11.1.4 Assembly Language Screen Mode and Line-Drawing Programs

All the operations associated with the **TREE** program can be programmed entirely at the assembly language level. However, to provide for flexibility, it is reasonable to associate assembly language subroutines only with screen mode establishment and line drawing, and to leave the formulation of the particular lines to be drawn to the higher-level-language program. With this approach, the assembly language routines could then also be used directly in other graphics applications. Thus, we shall code the **TREE** program above in a higher-level language, and it will call the assembly language procedures **MODE** and **LINE**. Parameter passing will differ slightly with each higher-level language used. In Figure 11-11 it is assumed that the address of the integer which designates the desired mode is pushed onto the stack immediately prior to calling the **MODE** procedure, and that both return values (IP and CS) are stored on the stack below this mode parameter address. The procedure directly follows the pseudocode specification given in Figure 11-7.

The assembly language procedure **LINE** is given in Figures 11-12 and 11-13. Figure 11-12 contains the data segment and program macros, while Figure 11-13 contains the code segment.

The assembly language program in Figure 11-13 directly follows the higher language representation given in Figure 11-9. To make the coding less obscure, four macros are used. The first, **SUBTRACT**, subtracts two variables, while the second, **ABSOLUTE**, takes the absolute value of a variable.

To explain the third and fourth macros, it first is necessary to discuss how fractional coordinate values are represented. Each coordinate (X and Y) is held in a 16-bit word which is broken up into an integer and fractional part as shown below.

b15,b14,b13,b12,b11,b10, b9, b8, b7, b6, b5, b4, b3, b2, b1, b0

INTEGER PART	FRACTIONAL PART

```
;  **** PROGRAM FILE:   MODE.ASM ****
MSEL        SEGMENT
MODE        PROC  FAR
;procedure to select screen mode and clear screen
            PUBLIC  MODE
            ASSUME  CS:MSEL
            PUSH  BP            ;save callers BP
            MOV   BP,SP         ; (BP) <--- (SP)
            PUSH  SI            ;save callers SI
;BEGIN PROCEDURE BODY
            MOV   SI,[BP+6]     ;parameter address moved to SI
            MOV   AX,[SI]       ;AX gets mode parameter (AH:AL=0:6)
            INT   10H           ;call BIOS graphics routine
;END PROCEDURE BODY
            POP   SI            ;restore SI
            POP   BP            ;restore BP
            RET   2             ;discard parameter and return
MODE        ENDP
MSEL        ENDS
            END
```

Figure 11-11 **MODE**: Assembly language program to set screen mode.

```
;  ****  PROGRAM FILE:  LINE.ASM ****
DATA      SEGMENT               ;data storage for LINE
X1        DW    ?               ;(X1,Y1) coordinate
Y1        DW    ?               ;  of 1st line endpoint
X2        DW    ?               ;(X2,Y2) coordinate
Y2        DW    ?               ;  of 2nd line endpoint
X2MX1     DW    ?               ;holds X2 - X1
Y2MY1     DW    ?               ;holds Y2 - Y1
ABSX      DW    ?               ;holds absolute value (X2 - X1)
ABSY      DW    ?               ;holds absolute value (Y2 - Y1)
XINCR     DW    ?               ;holds X increment
YINCR     DW    ?               ;holds Y increment
X         DW    ?               ;(X,Y) screen point to be written
Y         DW    ?
L         DW    ?               ;holds MAX[ABSX, ABSY]
DATA      ENDS
;***** some useful MACROS ** ** subtract macro **
SUBTRACT  MACRO  RESULT,X,Y      ;RESULT <--- X-Y
          MOV    AX,X
          SUB    AX,Y
          MOV    RESULT,AX
          ENDM
;  ** absolute value macro **
ABSOLUTE  MACRO  RESULT,VAR      ;RESULT <--- ABS. VALUE(VAR)
          LOCAL  HOP
          MOV    AX,VAR
          CMP    AX,0
          JG     HOP             ;if (var > 0) jump to HOP
          NEG    AX
HOP:      MOV    RESULT,AX
          ENDM
;  ** macro to determine increment to be used **
INCCALC   MACRO  ZINC,Z2MZ1,VINC,V2MV1,ABSZ
          XOR    DX,DX
          MOV    AX,V2MV1
          IMUL   BX              ;multiply by scale factor
          IDIV   ABSZ            ;AX <--- scaled V2MV1/ABSZ
          MOV    VINC,AX         ;VINC <--- inc.val.
          MOV    AX,Z2MZ1        ;  for one dimension
          IMUL   BX              ;multiply by scale factor
          IDIV   ABSZ            ;AX <--- scaled Z2MZ1/ABSZ
          MOV    ZINC,AX         ;ZINC <--- inc.val.
                                 ;  for other dimension
          MOV    ABSZ,AX         ;5 bits now hold frac. part
          ENDM
;  ** macro to determine initial value to be plotted **
```

Figure 11-12 Data segment and macros for **LINE** routine.

```
IVALUE    MACRO   Z1,Z          ;Z1 holds X or Y
          XOR     DX,DX         ;  starting line
          MOV     AX,Z1         ;endpoint provided by user
          IMUL    BX            ;scale initial point
          ADD     AX,16         ;add in .5
          MOV     Z,AX          ;Z <--- Z1 + .5
          ENDM
```

Figure 11-12   continued

Since the maximum coordinate value possible is 639D, it can be represented in the 11 bits corresponding to the integer part of the word. The remaining 5 bits are adequate for representing the fractional part.

The macro **INCCALC** calculates the increment associated with each dimension. It begins by scaling one of the dimensions **V2MV1 (IMUL   BX**). This corresponds to shifting left 5 bits. The result is then divided by the unscaled absolute value of the larger dimension. If **V2MV1** is the smaller dimension, the resulting increment will be a fraction using only the lower-order 5 bits of its word. The same process is then performed on the other dimension, **Z2MZ1**. If this corresponds to the larger dimension, the result will always be either + or − 1.

The macro **IVALUE** determines the initial point to be plotted. The starting endpoint is rounded to determine the actual initial point plotted. After moving the endpoint into AX, the **IMUL   BX** scales the coordinate to conform to the number representation discussed above. (Adding 16D effectively places a 1 in bit position 4 and this corresponds to adding in .5.)

Given these macros, the program can now be readily examined. The statements immediately after **BEGIN PROCEDURE LINE** act to set up BP and DS, and save several caller program registers. BP is used to access the stack to obtain the parameter addresses. As with the **RWALK** procedure, it is assumed that parameter addresses are pushed onto the stack when the higher-level-language program calls **LINE**. A slight complication arises here, however, since **LINE** has a data segment into which the parameters are placed, while with the **RWALK** example, parameters were just placed in registers and no data segment was necessary. The presence of a data segment requires that the DS be set up with the data segment address associated with **LINE**. Parameter addresses in the stack, however, represent offsets from the data segment associated with the calling program. One way of fulfilling the need for two data segments within the same code segment is to use the segment override feature (see Section 3.2.2.8). **LINE** begins by moving the calling programs DS into the extra segment ,ES. **LINE**'s own data segment address is then moved into DS. Subsequent instructions which move the parameters into **LINE**'s data area begin by placing the parameter address in SI, and then use the override feature (e.g., **MOV   X1,ES:[SI]**) to move the parameter itself into **LINE**'s data space. In this way parameters X1, Y1, X2, and Y2 are moved into the appropriate **LINE** data space.

```
PROG          SEGMENT
LINE          PROC    FAR
              PUBLIC  LINE
              ASSUME  CS: PROG,  DS: DATA
              PUSH    BP                  ; save callers BP
              MOV     BP, SP
              MOV     AX, DS
              MOV     ES, AX              ; ES <--- callers DS
              PUSH    SI                  ; save callers SI
              MOV     AX, DATA            ; set up
              MOV     DS, AX              ;        data segment address
              MOV     SI, [BP + 12]       ; SI <--- 1st X parameter addr.
              MOV     AX, ES: [SI]        ; XI <--- 1st X parameter
              MOV     X1, AX
              MOV     SI, [BP + 10]       ; SI <--- Y1 parameter address
              MOV     AX, ES: [SI]        ; Y1 <--- 1st Y parameter
              MOV     Y1, AX
              MOV     SI, [BP + 8]        ; SI <--- X2 parameter address
              MOV     AX, ES: [SI]        ; X2 <--- 2nd X parameter
              MOV     X2, AX
              MOV     SI, [BP + 6]        ; SI <--- Y2 parameter address
              MOV     AX, ES: [SI]        ; Y2 <--- 2nd Y parameter
              MOV,    Y2, AX
; BEGIN PROCEDURE BODY
; calculate length of maximum X or Y distance traversed
              MOV     BX, 32              ; BX <--- scale factor
              SUBTRACT X2MX1, X2, X1      ; X2MX1 <--- (X2-X1)
              ABSOLUTE ABSX, X2MX1        ; ABSX <--- ABS. VALUE (X2MX1)
              SUBTRACT Y2MY1, Y2, Y1      ; Y2MY1 <--- (Y2-Y1)
              ABSOLUTE ABSY, Y2MY1        ; ABSY <--- ABS. VAL. (Y2MY1)
; calculate X and Y increments
              MOV     AX, ABSX
              CMP     AX, ABSY            ; compare ABSX with ABSY
              JG      XHOP                ; jump if ABSX > ABSY
              INCCALC XINC, X2MX1, YINC, Y2MY1, ABSY      ; ABSY > ABSX
              MOV     AX, ABSY
              JMP     INIVAL
XHOP:         INCCALC XINC, X2MX1, YINC, Y2MY1, ASBX      ; ABSX > ABSY
              MOV     AX, ABSX
INIVAL:       MOV     L, AX       ; L holds max. length, used for c.
; calculate initial values
              IVALUE  X1, X               ; X <--- X1 + .5
              IVALUE  Y1, Y               ; Y <--- Y1 + .5
; plot line
LDRAW:        MOV     AX, X
              XOR     DX, DX
              IDIV    BX                  ; remove fractional part
              MOV     CX, AX              ; load X coordinate
```
Figure 11-13 **LINE**: Assembly language program to draw a line.

```
        MOV       AX, Y
        XOR       DX, DX
        IDIV      BX              ;remove fractional part
        MOV       DX, AX          ;load Y coordinate
        MOV       AL, 0           ;no color selected
        MOV       AH, 12          ;set write dot mode
        INT       10H             ;call graphics monitor routine
        MOV       AX, XINC
        ADD       X, AX           ;X <--- X + XINC
        MOV       AX, YINC
        ADD       Y, AX           ;Y <--- Y + YINC
        MOV       AX, L
        DEC       AX              ;dec. L for looping control
        MOV       L, AX
        JNZ       LDRAW
;  END  PROCEDURE  BODY
        MOV       AX, ES          ;restore callers DS
        MOV       DS, AX
        POP       SI
        POP       BP
        RET       8
LINE    ENDP
PROG    ENDS
        END
```

Figure 11-13   continued

The **PROCEDURE BODY** begins with successive **SUBTRACT** and **ABSOLUTE** macro substitutions. These create the variables **X2MX1** (i.e., **X2 − X1**), **ABSX** [i.e., **ABS(X2 − X1)**], **Y2MY1** (i.e., **Y2 − Y1**), and **ABSY** [i.e., **ABS(Y2 − Y1)**]. These are now used with the **INCCALC** macro to obtain the maximum length dimension (**L**), and the X and Y increments (**XINC** and **YINC**). The initial values of the starting endpoints are next calculated using the **INIVAL** macro. The succeeding instructions between the comment "plot line" and **END PROCEDURE BODY** are part of an instruction loop which plots the desired line. The first four instructions of the loop remove the fractional part of the X and Y variables by dividing by 32 and placing the resulting truncated coordinate values in CX and DX. The next three instructions load AH and AL with the proper values and then call BIOS (**INT   10H**) to plot the point found in (CX,DX). The X and Y values are now incremented and the maximum dimension length **L** is decremented. When **L** is zero, the entire line has been plotted. If it is greater then zero, more points must be plotted, and a jump is executed to **LDRAW**. The next section shows how the **LINE** and **MODE** routines are called by higher-level-language routines to form a tree display on the monitor.

11.2 INTERFACING WITH BASIC

This section considers the problem of interfacing assembly language procedures with interpreted BASIC programs. The IBM Advanced BASIC (1) is assumed to be used along with the IBM DOS operating system. We begin with procedure calling and parameter passing methods, consider the question of debugging in such a mixed-language environment, and then we discuss how to arrange for the BASIC program to load the assembly language routine automatically. These methods are illustrated with the stock simulation and graphics problems discussed earlier.

The general approach presented here utilizes the BASIC language instructions **DEF SEG**, **CALL**, **BSAVE**, and **BLOAD**, and the IBM DOS **DEBUG** facilities. Note that much of the complexity found below results from the fact that the assembly language routine is being interfaced with an interpreted as opposed to a compiled language. Thus, it is not possible to link the executable assembly program directly with an executable BASIC program using the linker. A more roundabout procedure must be adopted for first loading the BASIC program, and then having the BASIC program itself load in the assembly language program. As will be seen with FORTRAN and PASCAL, the compiled higher-level and assembly language programs can be linked together directly more simply.

11.2.1 Basic Instructions for Loading and Calling Assembly Language Procedures

To **CALL** an assembly language procedure, the memory segment and offset addresses of the procedure must be specified so that the main program can jump to the procedure. The BASIC instruction **DEF SEG** defines a memory segment address for subsequent use by the **CALL** instruction. The offset address is defined within the individual **CALL** instruction, as discussed below. Other commands such as **BSAVE**, which saves a block of memory as a named binary file on a storage device (e.g., disk), and **BLOAD**, which loads a named binary file into memory from a storage device, also require segment and offset address specifications. In these cases, the address specification is needed to define the starting memory location for the designated operation. The **DEF SEG** instruction also may be used here to define the memory segment address. The general format for **DEF SEG** is

    DEF SEG = address

For example,

    DEF SEG = H1FFA

The prefix H is a BASIC language notation which indicates that a hexadecimal number up to four digits in length follows.

The **CALL** instruction in BASIC resembles the **FAR** procedure **CALL** in assembly language and is used to pass control and parameters from a main BASIC program to a called assembly language procedure. In both BASIC and assembly language, the current address is saved on the stack, a jump is executed to some specified location, and program execution continues at this new memory location. In addition, with the BASIC

CALL, parameter addresses specified in the **CALL** instruction also are saved on the stack. The format for the BASIC **CALL** instruction is

> CALL   numvar (var1, var2, var3, . . . , var*I*, . . ., var*N*)

where numvar is a BASIC variable defining the offset address, and var1, var2, . . . , var*N* are the parameters whose addresses are pushed on the stack. For example,

> DEF SEG = H1FFA
> WALKLOC = 0
> CALL WALKLOC (AVG%,A%,N%,SEED%)

Here, the **DEF SEG** instruction and **WALKLOC** variable together indicate the code segment and offset address (CS:IP) of the procedure to be called (1FFA:0000). Later we shall discuss how to determine the address 1FFA:0000. The **CALL** statement effectively performs an assembly language **FAR CALL** to that location. Prior to this **FAR CALL**, however, the addresses associated with the integer parameters **AVG%,A%**, **N%**, and **SEED%** are pushed onto the stack, thus making them available to the called assembly language program. The parameter addresses are pushed on the stack from left to right. Figure 11-4*a* indicates how the stack appears just after executing the **CALL** above.

If the first two instructions in a called assembly language procedure are **PUSH   BP** and **MOV   BP,SP**, then the addressing mode **[BP + X]** can now be used to access the parameter addresses. To access the address of var*I*, for instance, requires $X = 2 \cdot (N - I) + 6$. Thus, in the four-parameter case above ($N = 4$), moving the address of parameter **A%** ($I = 2$) into SI uses the instruction **MOV   SI,[BP + 10]**. This is further illustrated in the **RWALK** program of Figure 11-3.

Naturally, the assembly language procedure must be loaded into memory prior to issuing the **CALL** instruction. The BASIC command **BLOAD** performs this task. The format is

> BLOAD   filespec,offset

Filespec is a BASIC string expression which contains a standard IBM DOS file specification name. Offset is an offset from the segment address last specified with a **DEF SEG** instruction. This defines where the file is to be loaded into memory. For instance, consider the example below.

> DEF SEG = H1FFA
> BLOAD "RWALK.MEM",0

The quotes indicate a string expression and **RWALK.MEM** is a file name stored in the IBM DOS file directory. In this case, the **RWALK.MEM** file might contain the memory image of the assembly language program **RWALK**. **BLOAD** causes the DOS file directory to be examined, and the **RWALK.MEM** file to be loaded into memory from disk (or tape) at location 1FFA:0000. Note that if the file to be loaded was created with a **BSAVE** instruction (discussed next), and is to be loaded into the same memory area from which it was originally saved, then the offset address may be omitted. In this case, the BASIC instruction **BLOAD "RWALK.MEM"** is adequate for loading **RWALK.MEM** into the proper memory location.

One way of initially creating the file used in **BLOAD** is to use the BASIC command **BSAVE**. Assume for the moment that the assembly language program of interest is resident in memory, and executes properly, and that its location and length (i.e., the number of bytes) are known. The **BSAVE** instruction has the following format:

        BSAVE   filespec,offset,length

Filespec is a string expression containing a standard IBM DOS file specification name. Offset is the offset from the current segment address as last defined in a **DEF SEG** instruction, and length is the length of the memory image to be saved. For example,

        DEF SEG = H1FFA
        BSAVE "RWALK.MEM",0, H58

In this case, the 58H bytes starting at memory address 1FFA:0000 are stored away on the current disk under the name **RWALK.MEM**. Note that the particular disk on which the file is to be stored can be specified in the normal DOS manner. Thus, if **RWALK.MEM** is to be placed on disk B, the instruction would appear as **BSAVE "B:RWALK.MEM",0, H58**.

11.2.2 Debugging Assembly Language Programs Interfaced to BASIC

The above discussion assumed that we were able initially to load the assembly program of interest (actually the executable form ,.**EXE**, of the program) into memory and find its starting address and length. This section considers just how this may be done, and how to proceed with the debugging task.

Say that we begin with a file named **FILE.ASM** that contains the assembly language program prior to being assembled. (In the stock market simulation case, this might be named **RWALK.ASM** .) **FILE.ASM** now is processed by the assembler (MASM) to produce the object file **FILE.OBJ**, and then **FILE.OBJ** is processed by the linker to produce the executable file **FILE.EXE** (use the /**HIGH** link command to create an .**EXE** file which will be loaded into high memory and not overwrite the BASIC interpreter). Executable files produced by IBM DOS have a certain format (discussed in the IBM DOS manual) which is required by the loader in order to load and run the program properly. This format differs from the actual memory image of the assembled program after it is loaded into memory. It is this latter memory image which is needed by the main BASIC program's **BLOAD** and **CALL** instructions to load and run the assembly language program correctly.

One way of loading the assembly language memory image along with the main calling BASIC program is to use certain features of the DEBUG utility program. Assume that the executable file **RWALK.EXE** exists and consider the sequence of IBM DOS, DEBUG, and BASIC commands given in Figures 11-14 and 11-15. Note that A>, −, and **Ok**, are, respectively, IBM DOS, DEBUG, and BASIC system prompts.

SYSTEM RESPONSE	USER COMMAND	EXPLANATION
A>	DEBUG	Load and run the DEBUG utility
-	N BASICA.COM	Name the file (BASICA.COM) to be loaded. This file contains the Basic interpreter.
-	L	Load the file named above.
-	R	Display register information.

```
AX=0000 BX=0000 CX=4180 DX=0000 SP=FFF0 BP=0000 SI=0000 DI=0000
DS=04B5 ES=04B5 SS=04B5 CS=04B5 IP=0100 NV IP DI PL NZ NA PO NC
04B5:0100 E9E43E        JMP     3FE7
```

		In response to the R command, the register contents, flag settings, and instruction at the current CS:IP location are displayed. For a full explanation see the IBM DOS manual. In this case, the Basica interpreter is loaded in at 04B5:0100. Note that BX:CX contains the length of the program which has been loaded.
-	N RWALK.EXE	Name RWALK.EXE file for loading. This file has RWALK in executable form.
-	L	Load the RWALK.EXE file.
-	R	Display register information.

```
AX=0000 BX=0000 CX=0058 DX=0000 SP=0000 BP=0000 SI=0000 SI=0000
DS=045B ES=045B SS=1FFA CS=1FFA IP=0000 NV UP DI PL NZ NA PO NC
1FFA:0000 55           PUSH    BP
```

EXE. files contain loading information such as starting addresses, file length, and register values. This display indicates that RWALK has been loaded at address 1FFA:0000, its first instruction is PUSH BP, and it is 58H bytes in length. At this point both the Basica interpreter and RWALK are resident in memory.

After executing the series of commands given in Figure 11-14, both the BASIC interpreter and the assembly language program are in memory. The length of the latter is known, as well as its location in memory. It is now possible to run the BASIC interpreter, load the main BASIC program, and execute it and the assembly language procedure under control of DEBUG. This is illustrated in Figure 11-15, which assumes that the commands of Figure 11-14 preceded it.

The technique described in Figures 11-14 and 11-15 is used during the debugging phase of program development. Once the debugging process is completed, it is time to save the final memory image of the assembly language procedure as a file so that it can be automatically loaded using **BLOAD**, thereby avoiding all of the above described complexity during production runs of the program.

11.2.3 Constructing Memory Image Files for Use with BLOAD

Let's assume that the debugging process has been completed. If not already present, use **DEBUG** to place the debugged assembly language procedure and BASIC interpreter in memory (i.e., perform the operations of Figure 11-14). Next correct the SS and SP registers as shown at the top of Figure 11-15. We can now run the BASIC interpreter and write a small BASIC program to save the assembly language memory image with **BSAVE**. This is shown in Figure 11-16.

The file RWALK.MEM now can be loaded with a BLOAD command. To complete the process the user need only include this command prior to the CALL instruction.

11.2.4 The Stock Market Simulation Problem with BASIC

Let us now apply the techniques of the preceding section to the stock market simulation program. To illustrate the differences between a pure BASIC solution to the simulation problem and one that uses the **RWALK** assembly language procedure, consider Figure 11-17.

The program directly follows that of Figure 11-2 and doesn't use **RWALK**. **RND** is a BASIC function call which returns a random real number between 0 and 1. By testing whether this is above or below .5, the program decides whether the market has gone up or down. **RND** begins with a "seed" number from which random numbers are generated. As written above, the system-supplied seed is used with each run; thus the same set of random numbers are used during each simulation. The BASIC command **RANDOMIZER** can be placed at the beginning of the program if the user wants to supply his or her own seed, thus changing this sequence with each run.

Given the straightforward nature of this program, only a considerable speed-up in execution time could really justify getting involved with an assembly language program to perform the inner loop. Experiments indicate that over an order-of-magnitude speed increase results when the inner loop of the stock market simulation program is implemented in assembly language. For a run involving 1000 walks (one would need about this number to obtain a reasonable estimate of the probability), execution times reduce from over 10 minutes to under a minute.

Figure 11-18 contains the **MARKET** program modified to include the assembly language subroutine **RWALK** (Figure 11-3) to perform the inner-loop calculations.

| SYSTEM | USER | EXPLANATION |
| RESPONSE | COMMAND | |

–	R SS	Display the contents of SS.
SS 1FFA		
:	045B	Restore the contents of SS for BASICA.COM.
		This is known from the initial R display.
–	R SP	Display the contents of SP.
SP 0000		
:	FFF0	Restore the contents of SP for BASICA.COM.
		This and the starting address of BASIC are
		known from the initial R display. The BASIC
		interpreter can now be run.

–	G=045B:0100	1FFA:0000 Go to the address specified
		(045B:0000) and begin executing the
		BASIC interpreter. Also set a breakpoint
		at location 1FFA:0000. This is the starting
		location of RWALK. When this address is
		encountered, control will return to DEBUG
		and an R command will be executed.

Direct statement in file
Ok   You are now in the BASIC interpreter.

	LOAD"AMARKET	Load the main BASIC program. This program
		will have the proper DEF SEG and CALL
		instructions but no BLOAD instruction (RWALK
		has already been loaded with DEBUG).
	RUN	Run the BASIC program AMARKET.

```
AX=5D39  BX=1239  CX=4152  DX=1356  SP=FFDA  BP=1365  SI=5DD7  DI=1239
DS=086E  ES=086E  SS=086E  CS=1FFA  IP=0000    NV UP EI PL ZR NA PE NC
1FFA:0000 55       PUSH     BP
```

The breakpoint setting in the former G
command has resulted in the program stopping
just before executing the first instruction
(PUSH BP) in RWALK. RWALK can now be run
under DEBUG control. For instance, the Trace
command T will execute the PUSH BP
instruction and then perform the R command
again. Single stepping through the program
can thus be accomplished.

Figure 11-15 Debugging with BASIC under DEBUG.

The program of Figure 11-18 differs from the pure BASIC program of Figure 11-17 in that **BLOAD** now reads in **RWALK** from disk, **DEF SEG** and **WALKLOC** define the address of **RWALK**, and the **CALL** instruction calls **RWALK** and implements the inner loop of the program. As noted earlier, the order of the parameters is important because this determines the ordering of their addresses on the stack and **RWALK** assumes a particular order in accessing these address parameters. Luckily,

```
SYSTEM          USER                        EXPLANATION
RESPONSE        COMMAND
```

```
-               G=045B:0100          Run the BASIC interpreter.
Direct statement in file
Ok                                   The BASIC interpreter is now running.
                                     Enter the program below.
                10 DEF SEG= H1FFA    Set up a segment address equal to the
                                     beginning address of the RWALK program.
                20 BSAVE "RWALK.MEM",0, H58
                                     Save the memory image as a file RWALK.MEM.
                                     The offset address of RWALK is 0 and its
                                     length is H58 bytes.
                30 END               End the BASIC program.

                RUN                  Run the above BASIC program.
Ok                                   The BASIC program has run to completion.
                                     The result is creation of a file RWALK.MEM
                                     on disk which contains the memory image of
                                     RWALK and can be accessed by BLOAD.
                SYSTEM               Return to DEBUG.
Program terminated normally
-               Q                    Quit (leave) DEBUG.
A>                                   IBM DOS can now accept commands.
```

Figure 11-16 Saving an assembly language memory image with **DEBUG**.

```
10      REM  **** PROGRAM FILE NAME: PMARKET.BAS ****
20      REM Monte Carlo stock market simulation
30      REM P=Prob[gain after N% days > 1.1*X%]=Prob[success]
40      REM input simulation parameters
50      PRINT "input initial index value":    INPUT X%
60      PRINT "input avg daily index change": INPUT A%
70      PRINT "input number of trading days": INPUT N%
80      PRINT "input number of random walks": INPUT M%
90      Z=0                              'Z=success count
100     FOR I% = 1 TO M%                 'loop for walks
110        AVG% = X%
120        FOR J% = 1 TO N%              'loop for days in walk
130           IF RND>.5 THEN AVG%=AVG%+A% ELSE AVG%=AVG%-A%
140           NEXT
150        IF AVG% > 1.1*X%  THEN  Z = Z + 1 'check for success
160        NEXT                          'loop for walks
170     P = Z / M%:  PRINT "PROB [greater then 10% gain] = "P
180     END
```

Figure 11-17 **MARKET** program in pure BASIC.

```
10      REM **** PROGRAM NAME: AMARKET.BAS ****
20      REM Monte Carlo stock market simulation
30      REM P=Prob[gain after N% days > 1.1*X%]=Prob[success]
50      REM input simulation parameters
60      PRINT "input initial index value":      INPUT X%
70      PRINT "input avg daily index change":   INPUT A%
80      PRINT "input number of trading days":   INPUT N%
90      PRINT "input number of random walks":   INPUT M%
100     DEF SEG= H1FFA          'define assm. procedure CS addr.
110     WALKLOC=0               'define assm. procedure IP addr.
120     BLOAD "RWALK.MEM"       'load assembly lang. procedure
130     Z=0: SEED%=2357         'Z=success cnt;SEED%=ini. rand.
140     FOR I% = 1 to M%        'loop for walks
150            AVG% = X%
160            CALL WALKLOC (AVG%,A%,N%,SEED%)
170            IF AVG% > 1.1*X%  THEN  Z=Z+1      'check for success
180            NEXT
190     P = Z/M%:  PRINT "PROB [greater then 10% gain] = "P
200     END
```

Figure 11-18 **MARKET** program in BASIC with assembler.

the order shown above in **MARKET** corresponds to the order assumed in the **RWALK** procedure of Figure 11-3. Note finally that **SEED%**, the random number seed, is set initially in the program to 2357. As this program stands, every simulation will use the same "random" numbers beginning with 2357. This could, of course, be made an input value supplied by the user.

11.2.5 The Graphics Problem with BASIC

A BASIC program implementing the **TREE** algorithm of Figure 11-10 is given in Figure 11-19.

The program follows directly from the original algorithm of Figure 11-10. Note that **SCREEN** and **SOUND** are Advanced BASIC instructions which, respectively, set the screen mode, and make a sound of a given frequency, for a specified duration. **SCREEN** is used at the beginning and end of the program to first establish the high-resolution mode and then to reestablish the normal alphanumeric black/white mode. **SOUND**   **32767,36** indicates that a sound of frequency 32767 hertz is to be played through the IBM PC speaker for a duration of 36 clock ticks. The particular frequency selected results in an inaudible sound. Since the IBM PC clock in this case ticks 18.2 times per second this amounts to about a 2-second period of silence. Normally, the instruction directly after **SOUND** would be executed while the sound is still being produced. Having another **SOUND** instruction ensures that the logo for our mythical Tree Software Company is kept on the screen for the entire 2 seconds before the screen is cleared and returned to text mode.

Interfacing the **LINE** assembly language procedure with the BASIC **TREE** program requires that a segment base and offset be present, that the memory image of the

```
10      REM **** PROGRAM FILE NAME: ATREE.BAS ****
20      REM program to draw a 3 level binary tree
30      Y1% = 160: X1% = 96: XDIF% = 64
40      DEF SEG = H1FEE; ATREELOC = H20
50      BLOAD   "LINE.MEM"
60      SCREEN 2
70      FOR  I% = 1 TO 3
80              J% = 2^(3-I%): Y2% = Y1% - 40
90              FOR K% = 1 to J%
100                 X2% = X1% + XDIF%/2
110                 CALL ATREELOC (X1%,Y1%,X2%,Y2%)
120                 X1% = X1% + XDIF%
130                 CALL ATREELOC (X1%,Y1%,X2%,Y2%)
140                 X1% = X1% + XDIF%
150                 NEXT
160             XDIF% = 2*XDIF%
170             X1% = X2% - XDIF%*(J%-1): Y1%=Y2%
180             NEXT
190     SOUND   32767,36: SOUND 32767,1
200     SCREEN 0
210     END
```

Figure 11-19 **TREE** program in BASIC with assembler.

LINE program be read in (in this case with **BLOAD**), and that procedure **CALL** instructions using the previously defined base and offset addresses be executed.

The value for the **DEF SEG** statement may be determined using the DEBUG procedure given in Section 11.2.1. Notice that the offset, specified in **ATREELOC = H20**, is not zero as in the case of **RWALK**. The reason is that the **LINE** procedure contains a data segment which begins at 1FEE:0000 (determined after loading in the **LINE.EXE** file under DEBUG) while the code segment begins as 1FEE:0020. One way to find the offset value is to use the DEBUG Unassemble (**U**) command with a starting address corresponding to the location where **LINE.EXE** is loaded. Following the contents of memory from the load address, the offset to the start of the code segment is easily identified and that value (in this case, stored in **ATREELOC**) now can be used in the **CALL** instruction.

A **BLOAD** instruction loads in the assembly language procedure memory image. This image may initially be created using the **BSAVE** instruction and procedures shown in Sections 11.2.2 and 11.2.3. The **CALL** instruction jumps to the **LINE** procedure and passes the appropriate parameters. **LINE** then performs the line-drawing operation. Notice that Advanced BASIC contains a **LINE** command having properties similar to the assembly language **LINE** procedure developed here. Naturally, unless speed was of some importance, using this BASIC graphics command would be a good deal more convenient than writing your own assembly language routine. In this case our primary motivation was to demonstrate BASIC/assembly language interfacing techniques. The assembly language routine developed, however, with minor modifications can also be used with PASCAL and FORTRAN as shown in the sections to follow.

11.3 INTERFACING WITH FORTRAN

This section considers interfacing assembly language procedures with FORTRAN programs. Use of the IBM PC FORTRAN Compiler (30) is assumed.

11.3.1 CALLing Assembly Language Procedures and Passing Parameters in FORTRAN

As with BASIC, FORTRAN provides a **CALL** instruction to pass control and parameters to a designated assembly language procedure. In this case, however, since FORTRAN is compiled rather than interpreted, there is no need to have the FORTRAN program read in a memory image of the assembly language procedure prior to issuing the **CALL**. The assembly language object module simply can be linked (using the linker) directly with the FORTRAN object module to create a single exectuable and loadable (**.EXE**) module. Figure 11-20 illustrates the general process.

Figure 11-20 illustrates the general process used when a single main FORTRAN program (**FMARKET**) is linked together with a single assembly language procedure (**FWALK**). Additional FORTRAN and assembly language subroutines and procedures can be linked together as needed. **FMARKET.EXE** is the final executable module which can be directly loaded and run. For a general discussion of the individual steps in Figure 11-20 see Section 1.3.5 and the IBM DOS manual.

Within the main FORTRAN program will be a **CALL** instruction to the assembly language routine. In the example of Figure 11-20 the **CALL** instruction will have the form

        CALL   FWALK   (var1, var2, var3, . . ., var*I*, . . . var*N*)

where var1, var2, . . . , var*N* are parameters defined within the calling FORTRAN program. **FWALK** is the name associated with the assembly language object module (**.OBJ**) which has been linked with the main FORTRAN program. The LINK utility provides the **FWALK** address to the **CALL** instruction during linking.

Just as with BASIC, executing the **CALL** instruction triggers a **FAR** jump to the address of **FWALK**. In addition, return program segment and offset addresses are stored on the stack as are the segment and offset addresses of the parameters. This differs from BASIC, where only the offsets for the parameters are pushed on the stack. For example, consider the **CALL** instruction shown below which is used in the stock market simulation program.

        CALL FWALK (AVG, A, N, SEED)

Just after the **CALL** instruction is executed, the stack appears as shown in Figure 11-21.

If the first two instructions in an assembly language procedure are **PUSH   BP** and **MOV   BP,SP**, then the addressing mode [**BP + X**] can now be used to access the parameter addresses. If all of the *N* parameters have the same segment address (usually the case), the parameters can be accessed as shown below.

1. Store the segment address in ES:
    MOV   ES,[BP + 8]

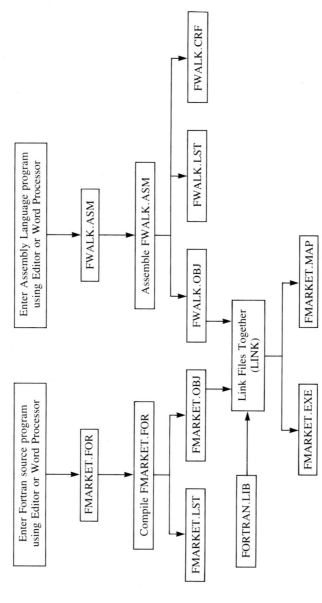

Figure 11-20 Linking FORTRAN and an assembly language routine.

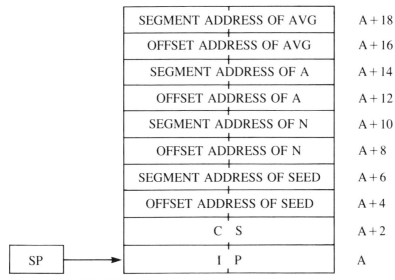

SEGMENT ADDRESS OF AVG	A + 18
OFFSET ADDRESS OF AVG	A + 16
SEGMENT ADDRESS OF A	A + 14
OFFSET ADDRESS OF A	A + 12
SEGMENT ADDRESS OF N	A + 10
OFFSET ADDRESS OF N	A + 8
SEGMENT ADDRESS OF SEED	A + 6
OFFSET ADDRESS OF SEED	A + 4
C S	A + 2
I P	A

Figure 11-21 **RWALK** stack contents with FORTRAN (just after execution of **CALL**).

2. For parameter I, let $X = 4 \cdot (N - I) + 6$
3. Move parameter I offset address into SI:
  MOV   SI,[BP + X]
4. Move parameter value into, say, AX.
  MOV   AX,ES:[SI]

Thus, for A, the second parameter ($I = 2$), $X = 4 \cdot (4 - 2) + 6 = 14$ and the offset address for A can be moved into SI with **MOV   SI,[BP + 14]**. (Another approach, not considered here, utilizes the **LES** instruction.)

11.3.2 Debugging Assembly Language Programs Interfaced to FORTRAN

For debugging purposes, the executable module also can be run under control of DEBUG by entering DEBUG, naming the executable program file (e.g., **−N FMAR-KET.EXE**), loading the program (**−L**), and then running the program with the desired breakpoints (**−G** = starting address breakpoint1 breakpoint2 · · ·). In order to perform the **G** command, both the starting address and the addresses of program breakpoints of interest must be known. This is the next question to be considered. First examine the .MAP file produced by the linker. An abbreviated version is shown in Figure 11-22 for the case where example programs **FMARKET.OBJ** and **FWALK.OBJ** were linked together.

The **MAP** listing indicates all program, stack, and data segments which **LINK** encounters during the linking process. The Start and Stop columns contain the starting and ending addresses (20-bit hexadecimal) of each segment relative to a common "zero" location. The Length and Name, respectively, contain the length and name associated with that segment. For our example, the name **PROG** corresponds to the code segment

```
Start   Stop    Length  Name                Class
00000H  00432H  0433H   MAINQQ              CODE
00434H  03C48H  3815H   FILVQQ  CODE        CODE
                        .
                        .
                        .
07670H  0776FH  0100H   STACK               STACK
07770H  07C9DH  052EH   DATA                DATA
                        .
                        .
                        .
083D0H  0842FH  0060H   PROG
```

Program entry point at 0510:0000

Figure 11-22   A **MAP** file listing.

of the **FWALK** assembly language routine. The relative address of the program entry point for the **FMARKET** is at 0510:0000 and that for **FWALK** is at 083D:0000.

The **DEBUG** routine is used to find the "zero" location from which absolute addresses can be calculated. First load the **.EXE** module under **DEBUG** control. The following command loads **DEBUG** and then loads **FMARKET.EXE**.

```
A> DEBUG FMARKET.EXE
```

Using the DEBUG register command ($-$**R**), note the value for CS:IP (e.g., 09D5:0000). This corresponds to the address of the first instruction to be executed (i.e., the first instruction in **FMARKET**). The "zero" location is calculated by subtracting the relative program starting address (e.g., 0510:0000) from the DEBUG CS:IP absolute value (e.g., 09D5:0000 $-$ 0510:0000 = 04C5:0000). This process effectively subtracts out the data portion of the program. That is, the "zero" location, 04C5:0000, is the beginning of the data portion of the program with the code portion following it at address 09D5:0000. Knowing the "zero" location, the starting absolute address for **FWALK** is obtained by adding its relative address to the "zero" address (e.g., 083D:0000 + 04C5:0000 = 0D02:0000). Executing the following DEBUG command will now cause a breakpoint to activate at the start of **FWALK** with further debugging proceeding from that point.

```
-g 0D02:0000
```

11.3.3 The Stock Market Simulation Problem with FORTRAN

The FORTRAN version of the stock market simulation program is given in Figure 11-23. It directly follows from the program given in Figure 11-2.

As indicated earlier, the FORTRAN **CALL** instruction results in both the segment and offset addresses of the **CALL** parameters being pushed onto the stack. Because of this, the assembly language program **RWALK** of Figure 11-3 must be modified since it assumes that only the offset addresses are pushed onto the stack. The modifications

```
c **** PROGRAM FILE NAME: FMARKET.FOR ****
c Monte Carlo stock market simulation
c P=Prob[gain after N days > 1.1*X]=Prob[success]
      PROGRAM  MARKET
      INTEGER  X, A, N, M, AVG, SEED, I, J
      REAL  P,Z
c input simulation parameters
      WRITE(*, 10)
10    FORMAT('0input initial index value: ')
      READ(*, 20) X
20    FORMAT(I6)
      WRITE(*, 30)
30    FORMAT('0input avg daily index change: ')
      READ(*, 20) A
      WRITE(*, 40)
40    FORMAT('0input number of trading days: ')
      READ(*, 20) N
      WRITE(*, 50)
50    FORMAT('0input number of random walks: ')
      READ(*, 20) M
      Z = 0
      SEED = 2357
      DO 200 J=1,M,1
          AVG = X
          CALL FWALK(AVG,A,N,SEED)
          IF (AVG .GT. 1.1*X) Z = Z + 1
200   CONTINUE
      P = Z / M
      WRITE(*, 300) P
300   FORMAT('0PROB [greater then 10% gain] = ',f6.2)
      STOP
      END1
```

Figure 11-23 **MARKET** program in FORTRAN with assembler.

occur at the beginning of the procedure when reading parameters from the stack, and at the end of the procedure when changing the stock index average, and when passing the final average and seed back to the calling program. The changed portions of the program are indicated in Figure 11-24.

11.3.4 The Graphics Problem with FORTRAN

The FORTRAN **TREE** program is given in Figure 11-25. It directly follows the version found in Figure 11-10 and the comments associated with that figure apply.

The **TREE** program follows directly from the original algorithm of Figure 11-10. As with the stock simulation example, minor modifications are necessary in the assem-

```
;  **** Procedure To Generate Random Bits and ****
;  ****            Perform a Random Walk         ****
                          .
                          .
;    ** get parameters **
           MOV    ES, [BP+8]     ; ES <--- para. seg. addr.
           MOV    SI, [BP+6]     ; SI <--- offset addr. seed
           MOV    AX, ES: [SI]   ; AX <--- seed
           MOV    SI, [BP+10]    ; SI <--- offset addr. # days
           MOV    CX, ES: [SI]   ; CX <--- # trading days
           MOV    SI, [BP+14]    ; SI <--- offset addr. daily
                                 ;   change
           MOV    DI, [BP+18]    ; DI <--- offset ini. value
           MOV    DX, ES: [DI]   ; DX <--- initial market avg.
RANDOM:    XOR    BX, BX         ; clear BX

                          .
                          .
           ADD    DX, ES: [SI]   ; DX <--- DX + daily change
           JMP    OVER2
OVER1:     SUB    DX, ES: [SI]   ; DX <--- DX - daily change
OVER2:     LOOP   RANDOM         ; do other days random walk
           MOV    SI, [BP+6]     ; get offset of seed location
           MOV    ES: [SI], AX   ; save current seed
           MOV    ES: [DI], DX   ; return final market value
                          .
                          .
```

Figure 11-24 **FWALK**: Assembly language procedure for Monte Carlo simulation.

bly language routines to account for the presence of parameter offset and segment addresses on the stack after issuing the FORTRAN **CALL** instruction. The modifications are straightforward and are left as an exercise (see Problems 11.8 and 11.9).

11.4 INTERFACING WITH PASCAL

This section considers interfacing assembly language procedures with PASCAL programs. The IBM PC PASCAL Compiler (reference 31) is assumed used.

11.4.1 PASCAL Interfacing Methods

The general procedure for obtaining an executable and loadable module consisting of both PASCAL and assembly language routines is shown in Figure 11-26 for the case of a single main PASCAL program and a single assembly language procedure.

The procedure for creating the executable module (**PMARKET.EXE**) is straightforward and was discussed previously in the context of the FORTRAN examples. Use of the **DEBUG** utility and the **.MAP** file for debugging in such a mixed-language environment is the same as with FORTRAN (Section 11.3.2).

Assembly language procedures to be called from PASCAL are first defined within the PASCAL program using the **PROCEDURE** statement. This statement provides the following information to the PASCAL compiler:

```
C **** PROGRAM FILE NAME: FTREE.FOR ****
C program to draw a 3 level binary tree
          PROGRAM  ATREE
          INTEGER I, J, K, X1, X2, Y1, Y2, XDIF
          Y1 = 160
          X1 = 96
          XDIF = 64
          CALL MODE(6)
          DO 200  I = 1,3
                  J = 2**(3-I)
                  Y2 = Y1 - 40
                  DO 100  K = 1,J
                          X2 = X1 + XDIF/2
                          CALL LINE(X1,Y1,X2,Y2)
                          X1 = X1 + XDIF
                          CALL LINE(X1,Y1,X2,Y2)
                          X1 = X1 + XDIF
100                CONTINUE
                   XDIF = 2*XDIF
                   X1 = X2 - XDIF*(J - 1)
                   Y1 = Y2
200       CONTINUE
C ** timer loop **
          DO 300  I = 1,15000
                  J = 10*10*10
300       CONTINUE
          CALL MODE(3)
          END
```

Figure 11-25 **TREE** program in FORTRAN with assembler.

1. The name of the procedure to be called.
2. Whether the procedure is internal or external.
3. Parameter names and their types (e.g., real, integer, string, etc.)
4. Whether parameter values or parameter addresses are to be passed.

The first three items are self-evident. The name in item 1 is the **PUBLIC** name declared in the assembly language procedure. Assembly language procedures are always external since they represent a call to some other code (i.e., code not compiled as part of the PASCAL program) loaded by the linker. The parameter names are those PASCAL names associated with the parameters to be passed. Their types are the standard PASCAL data types.

The fourth item refers to whether a "call by value" or "call by reference" is to be performed. In a call by value, the value of the specified parameters are pushed on the stack where they are then available to the called assembly language procedure. When the parameter types are simple ones having modest storage requirements (e.g., integers), then placing their values on and removing their values from the stack involves relatively little overhead. If the parameters are complex data structures or long strings,

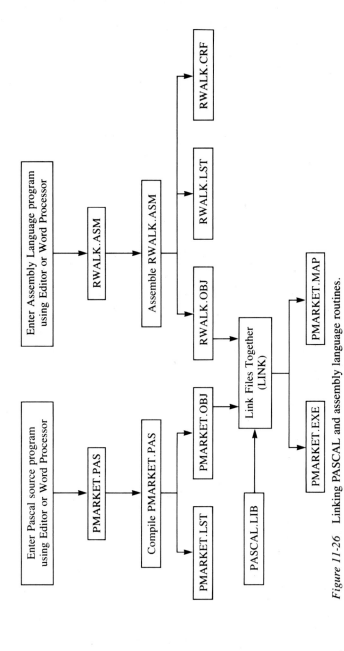

Figure 11-26 Linking PASCAL and assembly language routines.

however, it is much more efficient to pass the parameter addresses rather than their actual values. This is referred to as "call by reference" or "call by name." Call by reference is specified within a procedure statement by preceding the parameter names with the **VAR** prefix.

Another question which must be resolved in a call by reference is whether only the offset or both the offset and segment parts of the parameter addresses are to be pushed onto the stack. **VAR** indicates that only the offset is passed (the same as BASIC), while using **VARS** indicates that both offset and segment addresses are passed (the same as FORTRAN). The **PROCEDURE** statement used in the stock simulation program is shown below.

```
PROCEDURE RWALK (VAR AVG, A, N, SEED: INTEGER); EXTERNAL;
```

In this case, since **VAR** is used, the same assembly language procedure (**RWALK**) developed for the BASIC stock market program can be used. If **VARS** were used, then the assembly language procedure (**FWALK**) developed for the FORTRAN program could be used.

Once the assembly language procedure has been defined to the PASCAL program using the **PROCEDURE** statement, the procedure is actually called by just stating the procedure name and its parameters as shown below.

```
RWALK (AVG, A, N, SEED)
```

The PASCAL compiler, on encountering **RWALK**, knows that a procedure call is to take place since **RWALK** has earlier been defined with the **PROCEDURE** statement.

```
{ **** PROGRAM NAME: PMARKET.PAS ****
  Monte Carlo stock market simulation
  P=Prob[gain after N days > 1.1*X]}
PROGRAM PMARKET
VAR
     X, A, N, M, AVG, SEED, i: INTEGER;
     P, Z: REAL;
PROCEDURE RWALK (VAR AVG, A, N, SEED: INTEGER); EXTERNAL;
BEGIN
     WRITE(' input initial index value: '); READLN(X)
     WRITE(' input avg daily index change: ');READLN(A)
     WRITE(' input number of trading days: ');READLN(N)
     WRITE(' input number of random walks: ');READLN(M)
     Z := 0; SEED := 2357;
     FOR i := 1 TO M DO BEGIN
         AVG := X;
         RWALK (AVG, A, N, SEED);
         IF AVG > 1.1*X THEN Z := Z + 1
         END;
     P := Z/M;
     WRITELN(' PROB[greater then 10% gain] = ',p:6:2);
  END.
```

Figure 11-27 **MARKET** program in PASCAL with assembler.

```
PROGRAM TREE(input,output)
{ program to draw a 3 level binary tree on a
  640*200 screen and display it for about two seconds}
VAR
        i,j,k,X1,Y1,X2,Y2,XDIF,Z:integer;
        PROCEDURE LINE(VAR X1,Y1,X2,Y2:integer);external;
        PROCEDURE MODE(VAR mode:integer);external;
BEGIN
        Y1:=160;  X1:=96;  XDIF:=64;
        Z=6;  MODE(Z);
        FOR i = 1 TO 3 DO
                BEGIN
                j := TRUNC(EXP((3-i)*LN(2)));              {j=2**(3-i)}
                Y2 := Y1 - 40;
                FOR k := 1 TO j DO
                        BEGIN
                        X2 := X1 + XDIF div 2;
                        LINE(X1,Y1,X2,Y2);
                        X1 := X1 + XDIF;
                        LINE(X1,Y1,X2,Y2);
                        X1 := X1 + XDIF
                        END;
                XDIF:=2*XDIF;  X1:=X2-XDIF*(j-1);  Y1:= Y2
                END;
        FOR i:=1 TO 15000 DO j :=10*10;  {delay loop}
        Z=3;  MODE(Z)
END.
```
Figure 11-28 **TREE** program in PASCAL with assembler.

11.4.2 The Stock Market Simulation Problem with PASCAL

The PASCAL version of the stock market program follows directly from that of Figure 11-2 and is given in Figure 11-27. The assembly language program for **RWALK** is given in Figure 11-3.

11.4.3 The Graphics Problem with PASCAL

The PASCAL **TREE** program is given in Figure 11-28 and directly follows the version found in Figure 11-10 and the comments associated with that figure apply. The assembly language program **MODE** and **LINE** found in Figures 11-11, 11-12, and 11-13 apply directly to this program.

11.5 SUMMARY

The convenience of high-level programming languages may be accompanied by unacceptable penalties under certain conditions. Two common circumstances are those where execution times must be as rapid as possible and/or where the application must use system resources that are inaccessible via the high-level language. For such situations it is possible to construct high-level-language main programs that use (call) assembly language procedures. Facilities for organizing, preparing, and executing such programs are available through IBM PC DOS for the major languages (BASIC, FOR-TRAN, and PASCAL) supported by this system.

In general, the critical computations are prepared like an ordinary assembly language program. The assembly language program can be "incorporated" as part of a high-level-language program by equipping the (main) program with those statements/ commands needed to

1. Load the assembly language code and define its location
2. Prepare parameter values (or addresses) to be passed to the assembly language procedure
3. Call the procedure from the high-level-language main program

With interpreted BASIC, proper loading of the assembly language procedure is somewhat complicated because of the fact that the BASIC program itself must execute the appropriate load instructions to bring into memory an image of the procedure. One way of creating and loading this memory image is to

1. Load in both the BASIC interpreter and the executable assembly file under DEBUG.
2. Save the memory image of the debugged assembly procedure by writing a simple BASIC program which uses the **BSAVE** command.
3. Include the **BLOAD** command in the main BASIC program. This loads in the assembly language procedure during program execution.
4. Load and execute the resultant BASIC program.

With FORTRAN and PASCAL, both of which are compiled languages, this process is more straightforward.

1. Through the normal compilation and assembly processes obtain the object versions of both the higher-level and assembly programs.
2. Use the linker to link the object programs together to produce an executable load module.
3. Load and execute the final link-produced module.

Debugging in mixed-language environments tends to require somewhat more thought than debugging in a single-language environment. Points of confusion often revolve around determining the addresses of key points in the assembly language procedure. These addresses are needed so that breakpoints may be set when executing the program under DEBUG. Utilizing information obtained from DEBUG, and in the case of FOR-TRAN and PASCAL the appropriate **.MAP** file, procedure starting addresses may be obtained. Once obtained, breakpoints may be established using DEBUG, and debugging proceeds.

The ability to speed up critical code sections is one reason for employing assembly language subroutines. For numerically intensive applications similar to the stock market simulation example presented in this chapter, order-of-magnitude increases in execution speeds can often be obtained.

EXERCISES

11.1 Modify the stock market simulation program so that three events are possible each day:

1. The S and P index goes up by some average amount.
2. The S and P index goes down by some average amount.
3. There is no change in the index.

Show how the assembly language subroutine is changed. After interfacing the subroutine with a higher-level-language main program, determine the probability of having more than a 10 percent gain after 100 trading days given a starting index value of 1000 and an average daily change of 10. How does the addition of the no-change possibility affect the results?

11.2 Say that an upward trend has been detected in the stock market. This is reflected in the statement that on any given day the probability of the market going up is 9/16, and the probability of it going down is 7/16. Modify the stock market simulation assembly language subroutine to reflect this upward trend. Determine the probability of having a 10 percent gain after 100 trading days given a starting index value of 1000 and an average daily change of 10. How does this compare with the no-trend results?

11.3 In addition to plotting the raw data associated with some system of interest (e.g., the Standard and Poor's Index, daily rainfall and temperature, etc.), it is often interesting to display the moving average associated with this data. This gives a pictorial view of the longer time trends at work in the system. Consider a system where there are N data points [V(0) to V $(N-1)$) and it is desired to create an M point moving average. The moving average $A(i)$ at point i is computed as:

$$A(i) = \frac{V(i) + V(i-1) + V(i-2) + \cdots + V(i-M+1)}{M} \qquad \text{for } M \leqslant i \leqslant N$$

and

$$A(i) = \frac{V(i) + V(i-1) + V(i-2) + \cdots + V(0)}{i} \qquad \text{for } i < M$$

Define an N point integer array where the raw data is stored. Write an assembly language subroutine to compute a new N point integer array which corresponds to the trend line. Interface this with a higher-level-language main routine (say BASIC) which obtains the size of the array (N), and the value of M from the user.

11.4 Determine whether procedure **LINE** (Figure 11-9) was used in generating the points of upper or lower lines in Figure 11-8.

11.5 Consider the **LINE** program of Figures 11-12 and 11-13. Say it is desired to use the program to plot a point and the coordinate pair (X1,Y1),(X1,Y1) (i.e., a line of zero length beginning and ending at X1,Y1) is transferred to the program. What will happen? Modify the program to handle this situation, and plot a point at X1,Y1 when this occurs.

11.6 Modify the tree display programs of Figures 11-10, 11-11, 11-12, and 11-13 so that all left branches are displayed in red, and right branches in blue. Run the program and test its operation. Note that color is only available in low resolution (320 × 200).

11.7 Draw a diagram similar to that of Figure 11-4 indicating the contents of the stack after the **LINE** program has been called by the FORTRAN **TREE** routine.

11.8 Indicate what modifications are necessary for the **MODE** procedure of Figure 11-11 so that it may be called by the FORTRAN **TREE** program of Figure 11-25.

11.9 Indicate what modifications are necessary for the **LINE** procedure of Figures 11-12 and 11-13 so that it may be called by the FORTRAN **TREE** program of Figure 11-25.

11.10 Say that a main PASCAL program is to call an assembly language procedure and pass (back and forth) two 6-integer-long arrays worth of information. What are the advantages/disadvantages of using "call by value" as opposed to "call by reference" parameter passing methods.

11.11 Under what circumstances should the PASCAL call by reference procedure definition **VAR** versus **VARS** be used.

11.12 Write, debug, and run a BASIC, PASCAL, or FORTRAN program to display all symbols in the IBM PC character set. Next, develop an assembly language procedure to invoke the BIOS *print screen* routine (see Section 9.3) . Modify your original higher-level-language program so that it **CALL**s this procedure. Perform the necessary operations (e.g., *linking*) so that the two routines can be debugged and executed together. Run the modified program along with the procedure and obtain a printout of the screen. Submit your program listings and screen printout.

11.13 Write an assembly language procedure which duplicates the BASIC **SOUND** command and can be called from either FORTRAN or PASCAL. Test out this procedure by writing a FORTRAN or PASCAL program to play the scale for one octave starting at middle C by repeatedly calling the assembly language procedure.

11.14 Implement and debug the stock market simulation problem first entirely in a higher-level language, and then in that same language but employing an assembly language subroutine for the inner loop. Compare the results and corresponding execution times for runs of 1000 walks.

Appendix A

IBM PC
Memory Map

ADDRESS
(HEX)

00000	BIOS, DOS, BASIC, AND USER INTERRUPT VECTORS
00400	BIOS, DOS, AND BASIC DATA AREAS
00600	FREE USER MEMORY
A0000	RESERVED
B0000	MONOCHROME DISPLAY AREA
B4000	RESERVED
B8000	COLOR GRAPHICS DISPLAY AREA
BC000	RESERVED
C0000	ROM EXPANSION AREA
C8000	FIXED DISK CONTROL AREA
CC000	ROM EXPANSION AREA
F0000	RESERVED
F4000	CASSETTE BASIC AND BIOS ROM

Appendix B
8086/88 Instruction Encoding*

Key to Machine Instruction Encoding and Decoding

Identifier	Explanation
MOD	Mode field.
REG	Register field.
R/M	Register/Memory field.
SR	Segment register code: 00 = ES, 01 = CS, 10 = SS, 11 = DS.
W, S, D, V, Z	Single-bit instruction fields.
DATA-8	8-bit immediate constant.

Identifier	Explanation
DATA-SX	8- bit immediate value that is automatically sign-extended to 16-bits before use.
DATA-LO	Low-order byte of 16-bit immediate constant.
DATA-HI	High-order byte of 16-bit immediate constant.
(DISP-LO)	Low-order byte of optional 8- or 16-bit unsigned displacement; MOD indicates if present.
(DISP-HI)	High-order byte of optional 16-bit unsigned displacement; MOD indicates if present.
IP-LO	Low-order byte of new IP value.
IP-HI	High-order byte of new IP value.
CS-LO	Low-order byte of new CS value.
CS-HI	High-order byte of new CS value.
IP-INC8	8-bit signed increment to instruction pointer.
IP-INC-LO	Low-order byte of signed 16-bit instruction pointer increment.
IP-INC-HI	High-order byte of signed 16-bit instruction pointer increment.
ADDR-LO	Low-order byte of direct address (offset) of memory operand; EA not calculated.
ADDR-HI	High-order byte of direct address (offset) of memory operand; EA not calculated.
--	Bits may contain any value.
XXX	First 3 bits of ESC opcode.
YYY	Second 3 bits of ESC opcode.
REG8	8-bit general register operand.
REG16	16-bit general register operand.
MEM8	8-bit memory operand (any addressing mode).
MEM16	16-bit memory operand (any addressing mode).
IMMED8	8-bit immediate operand.
IMMED16	16-bit immediate operand.
SEGREG	Segment register operand.
DEST-STR8	Byte string addressed by DI.
SRC-STR8	Byte string addressed by SI.
DEST-STR16	Word string addressed by DI.

Identifier	Explanation
SRC-STR16	Word string addressed by SI.
SHORT-LABEL	Label within ± 127 bytes of instruction.
NEAR-PROC	Procedure in current code segment.
FAR-PROC	Procedure in another code segment.
NEAR-LABEL	Label in current code segment but farther than − 128 or + 127 bytes from instruction.
FAR-LABEL	Label in another code segment.
SOURCE-TABLE	XLAT translation table addressed by BX.
OPCODE	ESC opcode operand.
SOURCE	ESC register or memory operand.

8086/8088 Instruction Encoding

DATA TRANSFER

MOV = Move:

	7 6 5 4 3 2 1 0	7 6 5 4 3 2 1 0	7 6 5 4 3 2 1 0	7 6 5 4 3 2 1 0	7 6 5 4 3 2 1 0	7 6 5 4 3 2 1 0
Register/memory to/from register	1 0 0 0 1 0 d w	mod reg r/m	(DISP-LO)	(DISP-HI)		
Immediate to register/memory	1 1 0 0 0 1 1 w	mod 0 0 0 r/m	(DISP-LO)	(DISP-HI)	data	data if w = 1
Immediate to register	1 0 1 1 w reg	data	data if w = 1			
Memory to accumulator	1 0 1 0 0 0 0 w	addr-lo	addr-hi			
Accumulator to memory	1 0 1 0 0 0 1 w	addr-lo	addr-hi			
Register/memory to segment register	1 0 0 0 1 1 1 0	mod 0 SR r/m	(DISP-LO)	(DISP-HI)		
Segment register to register/memory	1 0 0 0 1 1 0 0	mod 0 SR r/m	(DISP-LO)	(DISP-HI)		

PUSH = Push:

Register/memory	1 1 1 1 1 1 1 1	mod 1 1 0 r/m	(DISP-LO)	(DISP-HI)
Register	0 1 0 1 0 reg			
Segment register	0 0 0 reg 1 1 0			

POP = Pop:

Register/memory	1 0 0 0 1 1 1 1	mod 0 0 0 r/m	(DISP-LO)	(DISP-HI)
Register	0 1 0 1 1 reg			
Segment register	0 0 0 reg 1 1 1			

DATA TRANSFER (Cont'd.)

	7 6 5 4 3 2 1 0	7 6 5 4 3 2 1 0	7 6 5 4 3 2 1 0	7 6 5 4 3 2 1 0	7 6 5 4 3 2 1 0	7 6 5 4 3 2 1 0
XCHG = Exchange:						
Register/memory with register	1 0 0 0 0 1 1 w	mod reg r/m	(DISP-LO)	(DISP-HI)		
Register with accumulator	1 0 0 1 0 reg					

IN = Input from:

Fixed port	1 1 1 0 0 1 0 w	DATA-8	
Variable port	1 1 1 0 0 1 1 0 w		

OUT = Output to:

Fixed port	1 1 1 0 0 1 1 w	DATA-8		
Variable port	1 1 1 0 0 1 1 1 w			
XLAT = Translate byte to AL	1 1 0 1 0 1 1 1			
LEA = Load EA to register	1 0 0 0 1 1 0 1	mod reg r/m	(DISP-LO)	(DISP-HI)
LDS = Load pointer to DS	1 1 0 0 0 1 0 1	mod reg r/m	(DISP-LO)	(DISP-HI)
LES = Load pointer to ES	1 1 0 0 0 1 0 0	mod reg r/m	(DISP-LO)	(DISP-HI)
LAHF = Load AH with flags	1 0 0 1 1 1 1 1			
SAHF = Store AH into flags	1 0 0 1 1 1 1 0			
PUSHF = Push flags	1 0 0 1 1 1 0 0			
POPF = Pop flags	1 0 0 1 1 1 0 1			

ARITHMETIC

ADD = Add:

Reg/memory with register to either	0 0 0 0 0 0 d w	mod reg r/m	(DISP-LO)	(DISP-HI)		
Immediate to register/memory	1 0 0 0 0 0 s w	mod 0 0 0 r/m	(DISP-LO)	(DISP-HI)	data	data if s: w=01
Immediate to accumulator	0 0 0 0 0 1 0 w	data	data if w=1			

ADC = Add with carry:

Reg/memory with register to either	0 0 0 1 0 0 d w	mod reg r/m	(DISP-LO)	(DISP-HI)		
Immediate to register/memory	1 0 0 0 0 0 s w	mod 0 1 0 r/m	(DISP-LO)	(DISP-HI)	data	data if s: w=01
Immediate to accumulator	0 0 0 1 0 1 0 w	data	data if w=1			

INC = Increment:

Register/memory	1 1 1 1 1 1 1 w	mod 0 0 0 r/m	(DISP-LO)	(DISP-HI)
Register	0 1 0 0 0 reg			
AAA = ASCII adjust for add	0 0 1 1 0 1 1 1			
DAA = Decimal adjust for add	0 0 1 0 0 1 1 1			

ARITHMETIC (Cont'd.)

SUB = Subtract:

	7 6 5 4 3 2 1 0	7 6 5 4 3 2 1 0	7 6 5 4 3 2 1 0	7 6 5 4 3 2 1 0	7 6 5 4 3 2 1 0	7 6 5 4 3 2 1 0
Reg/memory and register to either	0 0 1 0 1 0 d w	mod reg r/m	(DISP-LO)	(DISP-HI)		
Immediate from register/memory	1 0 0 0 0 0 s w	mod 1 0 1 r/m	(DISP-LO)	(DISP-HI)	data	data if s: w=01
Immediate from accumulator	0 0 1 0 1 1 0 w	data	data if w=1			

SBB = Subtract with borrow:

Reg/memory and register to either	0 0 0 1 1 0 d w	mod reg r/m	(DISP-LO)	(DISP-HI)		
Immediate from register/memory	1 0 0 0 0 0 s w	mod 0 1 1 r/m	(DISP-LO)	(DISP-HI)	data	data if s: w=01
Immediate from accumulator	0 0 0 1 1 1 0 w	data	data if w=1			

DEC Decrement:

Register/memory	1 1 1 1 1 1 1 w	mod 0 0 1 r/m	(DISP-LO)	(DISP-HI)
Register	0 1 0 0 1 reg			
NEG Change sign	1 1 1 1 0 1 1 w	mod 0 1 1 r/m	(DISP-LO)	(DISP-HI)

CMP = Compare:

Register/memory and register	0 0 1 1 1 0 d w	mod reg r/m	(DISP-LO)	(DISP-HI)		
Immediate with register/memory	1 0 0 0 0 0 s w	mod 1 1 1 r/m	(DISP-LO)	(DISP-HI)	data	data if s: w=1
Immediate with accumulator	0 0 1 1 1 1 0 w	data				
AAS ASCII adjust for subtract	0 0 1 1 1 1 1 1					
DAS Decimal adjust for subtract	0 0 1 0 1 1 1 1					
MUL Multiply (unsigned)	1 1 1 1 0 1 1 w	mod 1 0 0 r/m	(DISP-LO)	(DISP-HI)		
IMUL Integer multiply (signed)	1 1 1 1 0 1 1 w	mod 1 0 1 r/m	(DISP-LO)	(DISP-HI)		
AAM ASCII adjust for multiply	1 1 0 1 0 1 0 0	0 0 0 0 1 0 1 0	(DISP-LO)	(DISP-HI)		
DIV Divide (unsigned)	1 1 1 1 0 1 1 w	mod 1 1 0 r/m	(DISP-LO)	(DISP-HI)		
IDIV Integer divide (signed)	1 1 1 1 0 1 1 w	mod 1 1 1 r/m	(DISP-LO)	(DISP-HI)		
AAD ASCII adjust for divide	1 1 0 1 0 1 0 1	0 0 0 0 1 0 1 0	(DISP-LO)	(DISP-HI)		
CBW Convert byte to word	1 0 0 1 1 0 0 0					
CWD Convert word to double word	1 0 0 1 1 0 0 1					

LOGIC

NOT Invert	1 1 1 1 0 1 1 w	mod 0 1 0 r/m	(DISP-LO)	(DISP-HI)
SHL/SAL Shift logical/arithmetic left	1 1 0 1 0 0 v w	mod 1 0 0 r/m	(DISP-LO)	(DISP-HI)
SHR Shift logical right	1 1 0 1 0 0 v w	mod 1 0 1 r/m	(DISP-LO)	(DISP-HI)
SAR Shift arithmetic right	1 1 0 1 0 0 v w	mod 1 1 1 r/m	(DISP-LO)	(DISP-HI)
ROL Rotate left	1 1 0 1 0 0 v w	mod 0 0 0 r/m	(DISP-LO)	(DISP-HI)

Mnemonics Copyright © Intel Corporation 1981.

LOGIC (Cont'd.)

	7 6 5 4 3 2 1 0	7 6 5 4 3 2 1 0	7 6 5 4 3 2 1 0	7 6 5 4 3 2 1 0	7 6 5 4 3 2 1 0	7 6 5 4 3 2 1 0
ROR Rotate right	1 1 0 1 0 0 v w	mod 0 0 1 r/m	(DISP-LO)	(DISP-HI)		
RCL Rotate through carry flag left	1 1 0 1 0 0 v w	mod 0 1 0 r/m	(DISP-LO)	(DISP-HI)		
RCR Rotate through carry right	1 1 0 1 0 0 v w	mod 0 1 1 r/m	(DISP-LO)	(DISP-HI)		

AND = And:

Reg/memory with register to either	0 0 1 0 0 0 d w	mod reg r/m	(DISP-LO)	(DISP-HI)		
Immediate to register/memory	1 0 0 0 0 0 0 w	mod 1 0 0 r/m	(DISP-LO)	(DISP-HI)	data	data if w=1
Immediate to accumulator	0 0 1 0 0 1 0 w	data	data if w=1			

TEST = And function to flags no result:

Register/memory and register	0 0 0 1 0 0 d w	mod reg r/m	(DISP-LO)	(DISP-HI)		
Immediate data and register/memory	1 1 1 1 0 1 1 w	mod 0 0 0 r/m	(DISP-LO)	(DISP-HI)	data	data if w=1
Immediate data and accumulator	1 0 1 0 1 0 0 w	data				

OR = Or:

Reg/memory and register to either	0 0 0 0 1 0 d w	mod reg r/m	(DISP-LO)	(DISP-HI)		
Immediate to register/memory	1 0 0 0 0 0 0 w	mod 0 0 1 r/m	(DISP-LO)	(DISP-HI)	data	data if w=1
Immediate to accumulator	0 0 0 0 1 1 0 w	data	data if w=1			

XOR = Exclusive or:

Reg/memory and register to either	0 0 1 1 0 0 d w	mod reg r/m	(DISP-LO)	(DISP-HI)		
Immediate to register/memory	0 0 1 1 0 1 0 w	data	(DISP-LO)	(DISP-HI)	data	data if w=1
Immediate to accumulator	0 0 1 1 0 1 0 w	data	data if w=1			

STRING MANIPULATION

REP = Repeat	1 1 1 1 0 0 1 z
MOVS = Move byte/word	1 0 1 0 0 1 0 w
CMPS = Compare byte/word	1 0 1 0 0 1 1 w
SCAS = Scan byte/word	1 0 1 0 1 1 1 w
LODS = Load byte/wd to AL/AX	1 0 1 0 1 1 0 w
STDS = Stor byte/wd from AL/A	1 0 1 0 1 0 1 w

CONTROL TRANSFER

CALL = Call:

	7 6 5 4 3 2 1 0	7 6 5 4 3 2 1 0	7 6 5 4 3 2 1 0	7 6 5 4 3 2 1 0	7 6 5 4 3 2 1 0	7 6 5 4 3 2 1 0
Direct within segment	1 1 1 0 1 0 0 0	IP-INC-LO	IP-INC-HI			
Indirect within segment	1 1 1 1 1 1 1 1	mod 0 1 0 r/m	(DISP-LO)	(DISP-HI)		
Direct intersegment	1 0 0 1 1 0 1 0	IP-lo	IP-hi			
		CS-lo	CS-hi			
Indirect intersegment	1 1 1 1 1 1 1 1	mod 0 1 1 r/m	(DISP-LO)	(DISP-HI)		

JMP = Unconditional Jump:

Direct within segment	1 1 1 0 1 0 0 1	IP-INC-LO	IP-INC-HI	
Direct within segment-short	1 1 1 0 1 0 1 1	IP-INC8		
Indirect within segment	1 1 1 1 1 1 1 1	mod 1 0 0 r/m	(DISP-LO)	(DISP-HI)
Direct intersegment	1 1 1 0 1 0 1 0	IP-lo	IP-hi	
		CS-lo	CS-hi	
Indirect intersegment	1 1 1 1 1 1 1 1	mod 1 0 1 r/m	(DISP-LO)	(DISP-HI)

RET = Return from CALL:

Within segment	1 1 0 0 0 0 1 1		
Within seg adding immed to SP	1 1 0 0 0 0 1 0	data-lo	data-hi
Intersegment	1 1 0 0 1 0 1 1		
Intersegment adding immediate to SP	1 1 0 0 1 0 1 0	data-lo	data-hi
JE/JZ = Jump on equal/zero	0 1 1 1 0 1 0 0	IP-INC8	
JL/JNGE = Jump on less/not greater or equal	0 1 1 1 1 1 0 0	IP-INC8	
JLE/JNG = Jump on less or equal/not greater	0 1 1 1 1 1 1 0	IP-INC8	
JB/JNAE = Jump on below/not above or equal	0 1 1 1 0 0 1 0	IP-INC8	
JBE/JNA = Jump on below or equal/not above	0 1 1 1 0 1 1 0	IP-INC8	
JP/JPE = Jump on parity/parity even	0 1 1 1 1 0 1 0	IP-INC8	
JO = Jump on overflow	0 1 1 1 0 0 0 0	IP-INC8	
JS = Jump on sign	0 1 1 1 1 0 0 0	IP-INC8	
JNE/JNZ = Jump on not equal/not zer0	0 1 1 1 0 1 0 1	IP-INC8	
JNL/JGE = Jump on not less/greater or equal	0 1 1 1 1 1 0 1	IP-INC8	
JNLE/JG = Jump on not less or equal/greater	0 1 1 1 1 1 1 1	IP-INC8	
JNB/JAE = Jump on not below/above or equal	0 1 1 1 0 0 1 1	IP-INC8	
JNBE/JA = Jump on not below or equal/above	0 1 1 1 0 1 1 1	IP-INC8	
JNP/JPO = Jump on not par/par odd	0 1 1 1 1 0 1 1	IP-INC8	
JNO = Jump on not overflow	0 1 1 1 0 0 0 1	IP-INC8	

Mnemonics Copyright © Intel Corporation 1981.

CONTROL TRANSFER (Cont'd.)

RET = Return from CALL:

7 6 5 4 3 2 1 0 7 6 5 4 3 2 1 0 7 6 5 4 3 2 1 0 7 6 5 4 3 2 1 0 7 6 5 4 3 2 1 0 7 6 5 4 3 2 1 0

JNS = Jump on not sign	0 1 1 1 1 0 0 1	IP-INC8
LOOP = Loop CX times	1 1 1 0 0 0 1 0	IP-INC8
LOOPZ/LOOPE = Loop while zero/equal	1 1 1 0 0 0 0 1	IP-INC8
LOOPNZ/LOOPNE = Loop while not zero/equal	1 1 1 0 0 0 0 0	IP-INC8
JCXZ = Jump on CX zero	1 1 1 0 0 0 1 1	IP-INC8

INT = Interrupt:

Type specified	1 1 0 0 1 1 0 1	DATA-8
Type 3	1 1 0 0 1 1 0 0	
INTO = Interrupt on overflow	1 1 0 0 1 1 1 0	
IRET = Interrupt return	1 1 0 0 1 1 1 1	

PROCESSOR CONTROL

CLC = Clear carry	1 1 1 1 1 0 0 0			
CMC = Complement carry	1 1 1 1 0 1 0 1			
STC = Set carry	1 1 1 1 1 0 0 1			
CLD = Clear direction	1 1 1 1 1 1 0 0			
STD = Set direction	1 1 1 1 1 1 0 1			
CLI = Clear interrupt	1 1 1 1 1 0 1 0			
STI = Set interrupt	1 1 1 1 1 0 1 1			
HLT = Halt	1 1 1 1 0 1 0 0			
WAIT = Wait	1 0 0 1 1 0 1 1			
ESC = Escape (to external device)	1 1 0 1 1 x x x	m o d y y y r / m	(DISP-LO)	(DISP-HI)
LOCK = Bus lock prefix	1 1 1 1 0 0 0 0			
SEGMENT = Override prefix	0 0 1 reg 1 1 0			

Appendix C

Instruction Set Summary*

Flag Registers

AF = Auxiliary Carry
CF = Carry
DF = Direction
IF = Interrupt
OF = Overflow
PF = Parity
SF = Sign
TF = Trap
ZF = Zero

Legend for Flag Conditions

A = Altered to reflect results of operation
R = Replaced from storage
U = Undefined
0 = Unconditionally cleared to 0
1 = Unconditionally set to 1
None = No flags affected

AAA (no operands) — ASCII adjust for addition			
Operands	**Bytes**	**Example**	**Flags**
none	1	AAA	AF=A PF=U CF=A SF=U OF=U ZF=U

AAD (no operands) — ASCII adjust for division			
Operands	**Bytes**	**Example**	**Flags**
none	2	AAD	AF=U SF=A CF=U ZF=A OF=U PF=A

*Reprinted by Permission of the IBM Corporation.

AAM (no operands) — ASCII adjust for multiply			
Operands	Bytes	Example	Flags
none	1	AAM	AF=U PF=A CF=U SF=A OF=U ZF=A

AAS (no operands) — ASCII adjust for subtraction			
Operands	Bytes	Example	Flags
none	1	AAS	AF=A PF=U CF=A SF=U OF=U ZF=U

ADC destination, source — Add with carry			
Operands	Bytes	Example	Flags
register, register	2	ADC AX, SI	AF=A PF=A
register, memory	2-4	ADC DX, BETA [SI]	CF=A SF=A
memory, register	2-4	ADC ALPHA [BX] [SI] , DI	OF=A ZF=A
register, immediate	3-4	ADC BX, 256	
memory, immediate	3-6	ADC GAMMA, 30H	
accumulator, immediate	2-3	ADC AL, 5	

ADD destination, source — Addition			
Operands	Bytes	Example	Flags
register, register	2	ADD CX, DX	AF=A PF=A
register, memory	2-4	ADD DI, [BX] , ALPHA	CF=A SF=A
memory, register	2-4	ADD TEMP, CL	OF=A ZF=A
register, immediate	3-4	ADD CL, 2	
memory, immediate	3-6	ADD ALPHA, 2	
accumulator, immediate	2-3	ADD AX, 200	

AND destination source — Logical AND			
Operands	Bytes	Example	Flags
register, register	2	AND AL,BL	AF=U PF=A
register, memory	2-4	AND CX,FLAG WORD	CF=0 SF=A
memory, register	2-4	AND ASCII [DI] ,AL	OF=0 ZF=A
register, immediate	3-4	AND CX0,F0H	
memory, immediate	3-6	AND BETA, 01H	
accumulator, immediate	2-3	AND AX, 01010000B	

CALL target — Call a procedure

Operands	Bytes	Example	Flags
near-proc	3	CALL NEAR_PROC	none
far-proc	5	CALL FAR_PROC	
memptr 16	2-4	CALL PROC_TABLE [SI]	
regptr 16	2	CALL AX	
memptr 32	2-4	CALL [BX].TASK [SI]	

CBW (no operands) — Convert byte to word

Operands	Bytes	Example	Flags
none	1	CBW	none

CLC (no operands) — Clear carry flag

Operands	Bytes	Example	Flags
none	1	CLC	CF=0

CLD (no operands) — Clear direction flag

Operands	Bytes	Example	Flags
none	1	CLD	DF=0

CLI (no operands) — Clear interrupt flag

Operands	Bytes	Example	Flags
none	1	CLI	DF=0

CMC (no operands) — Complement carry flag

Operands	Bytes	Example	Flags
none	1	CMC	CF=A

CMP destination, source — Compare destination to source

Operands	Bytes	Example	Flags
register, register	2	CMP BX, CX	AF=A PF=A
register, memory	2-4	CMP DH. ALPHA	CF=A SF=A
memory, register	2-4	CMP [BP + 2] , SI	OF=A ZF=A
register, immediate	3-4	CMP BL, 02H	
memory, immediate	3-6	CMP [BX] RADAR [DI] , 3420H	
accumulator, immediate	2-3	CMP AL, 00010000B	

CMPS dest-string, source-string — Compare string			
Operands	**Bytes**	**Example**	**Flags**
dest-string, source-string (repeat) dest-string, source-string	1 1	CMPS BUFF1, BUFF2 REPE CMPS ID, KEY	AF=A PF=A CF=A SF=A OF=A ZF=A

CWD (no operand) — Convert word to doubleword			
Operands	**Bytes**	**Example**	**Flags**
none	1	CWD	none

DAA (no operand) — Decimal adjust for addition			
Operands	**Bytes**	**Example**	**Flags**
none	1	DAA	AF=A PF=A CF=A SF=A OF=A ZF=A

DAS (no operand) — Decimal adjust for subtraction			
Operands	**Bytes**	**Example**	**Flags**
none	1	DAS	AF=A PF=A CF=A SF=A OF=A ZF=A

DEC destination — Decrement by 1			
Operands	**Bytes**	**Example**	**Flags**
reg16 reg8 memory	1 2 2-4	DEC AX DEC AL DEC ARRAY [SI]	AF=A SF=A OF=A ZF=A PF=A

DIV source — Division, unsigned			
Operands	**Bytes**	**Example**	**Flags**
reg8 reg16 mem8 mem16	2 2 2-4 2-4	DIV CL DIV BX DIV ALPHA DIV TABLE [SI]	AF=U PF=U CF=U SF=U OF=U ZF=U

ESC external-op code, source — Escape			
Operands	Bytes	Example	Flags
immediate, memory	2-4	ESC 6,ARRAY [SI]	none
immediate, register	2	ESC 20,AL	

HLT (no operands) — Halt			
Operands	Bytes	Example	Flags
none	1	HLT	none

IDIV source — Integer division			
Operands	Bytes	Example	Flags
reg8	2	IDIV BL	AF=U PF=U
reg16	2	IDIV CX	CF=U SF=U
mem8	2-4	IDIV DIVISOR BYTE [SI]	OF=U ZF=U
mem16	2-4	IDIV [BX],DIVISOR_WORD	

IMUL source — Integer multiplication			
Operands	Bytes	Example	Flags
reg8	2	IMUL CL	AF=U PF=U
reg16	2	IMUL BX	CF=A SF=U
mem8	2-4	IMUL RATE_BYTE	OF=A ZF=U
mem16	2-4	IMUL RATE_WORD[BP] [DI]	

IN accumulator, port — Input byte or word			
Operands	Bytes	Example	Flags
accumulator, immed8	2	IN AL, 0FFEAH	none
accumulator, DX	1	IN AX, DX	

INC destination — Increment by 1			
Operands	Bytes	Example	Flags
reg16	1	INC CX	AF=A SF=A
reg8	2	INC BL	OF=A ZF=A
memory	2-4	INC ALPHA [DI] [BX]	PF=A

INT interrupt-type -- Interrupt

Operands	Bytes	Example	Flags
immed8(type = 3) immed8(type ≠ 3)	1 2	INT 3 INT 67	IF=0 TF=0

INTO (no operands) — Interrupt if overflow

Operands	Bytes	Example	Flags
none	1	INTO	IF=0 TF=0

IRET (no operands) — Interrupt return

Operands	Bytes	Example	Flags
none	1	IRET	AF=R PF=R CF=R SF=R DF=R TF=R IF=R ZF=R

JA/JNBE short-label — Jump if above/Jump if not below or equal

Operands	Bytes	Example	Flags
short-label	2	JA ABOVE	none

JAE/JNB short-label — Jump if above or equal/Jump if not below

Operands	Bytes	Example	Flags
short-label	2	JAE ABOVE_EQUAL	none

JB/JNAE short-label — Jump if below/Jump if not above nor equal

Operands	Bytes	Example	Flags
short-label	2	JB BELOW	none

JBE/JNA short-label — Jump if below or equal/Jump if not above

Operands	Bytes	Example	Flags
short-label	2	JNA NOT ABOVE	none

JC short-label — Jump if carry			
Operands	Bytes	Example	Flags
short-label	2	JC CARRY SET	none

JCXZ short-label — Jump if CX is zero			
Operands	Bytes	Example	Flags
short-label	2	JCXZ COUNT DONE	none

JE/JZ short-label — Jump if equal/Jump if zero			
Operands	Bytes	Example	Flags
short-label	2	JZ ZERO	none

JG/JNLE short-label — Jump if greater/Jump if not less nor equal			
Operands	Bytes	Example	Flags
short-label	2	JG GREATER	none

JGE/JNL short-label — Jump if greater or equal/Jump if not less			
Operands	Bytes	Example	Flags
short-label	2	JGE GREATER EQUAL	none

JL/JNGE short-label — Jump if less/Jump if not greater nor equal			
Operands	Bytes	Example	Flags
short-label	2	JL LESS	none

JLE/JNG short-label — Jump if less or equal/Jump if not greater			
Operands	Bytes	Example	Flags
short-label	2	JNG NOT GREATER	none

JMP target — Jump			
Operands	Bytes	Example	Flags
short-label	2	JMP SHORT	none
near-label	3	JMP WITHIN SEGMENT	
far-label	5	JMP FAR LABEL	
memptr16	2-4	JMP [BX], TARGET	
regptr16	2	JMP CX	
memptr32	2-4	JMP OTHER SEG [SI]	

JNC short-label — Jump if not carry			
Operands	Bytes	Example	Flags
short-label	2	JNC NOT CARRY	none

JNE/JNZ short-label — Jump if not equal/Jump if not zero			
Operands	Bytes	Example	Flags
short-label	2	JNE NOT EQUAL	none

JNO short-label — Jump if not overflow			
Operands	Bytes	Example	Flags
short-label	2	JNO NO OVERFLOW	none

JNP/JPO short-label — Jump if not parity/jump if parity ODD			
Operands	Bytes	Example	Flags
short-label	2	JPO ODD PARITY	none

JNS short-label — Jump if not sign			
Operands	Bytes	Example	Flags
short-label	2	JNS POSITIVE	none

JO short-label — Jump if overflow			
Operands	Bytes	Example	Flags
short-label	2	JO SIGNED_ OVRFLW	none

JP/JPE short-label — Jump if parity/Jump if parity even			
Operands	Bytes	Example	Flags
short-label	2	JPE EVEN_PARITY	none

JS short-label — Jump if sign			
Operands	Bytes	Example	Flags
short-label	2	JS NEGATIVE	none

LAHF (no operands) — Load AH from flags

Operands	Bytes	Example	Flags
none	1	LAHF	none

LDS destination, source — Load pointer using DS

Operands	Bytes	Example	Flags
reg16, mem32	2-4	LDS SI, DATA. SEG[DI]	none

LOCK (no operands) — Lock bus

Operands	Bytes	Example	Flags
none	1	LOCK XCHG FLAG.AL	none

LODS source-string — Load string

Operands	Bytes	Example	Flags
source-string	1	LODS CUSTOMER NAME	none
(repeat) source-string	1	REP LODS NAME	

LOOP short-label — Loop

Operands	Bytes	Example	Flags
short-label	2	LOOP AGAIN	none

LOOPE/LOOPZ short-label — Loop if equal/Loop if zero

Operands	Bytes	Example	Flags
short-label	2	LOOPE AGAIN	none

LOOPNE/LOOPNZ short-label — Loop if not equal/Loop if not zero

Operands	Bytes	Example	Flags
short-label	2	LOOPNE AGAIN	none

LEA destination, source — Load effective address

Operands	Bytes	Example	Flags
reg16, mem16	2-4	LEA BX,[BP] [DI]	none

LES destination, source — Load pointer using ES

Operands	Bytes	Example	Flags
reg16, mem32	2-4	LES DI,[BX].TEXT_BUFF	none

MOV destination, source — Move

Operands	Bytes	Example	Flags
memory, accumulator	3	MOV ARRAY [SI], AL	none
accumulator, memory	3	MOV AX, TEMP_RESULT	
register, register	2	MOV AX, CX	
register, memory	2-4	MOV BP, STACK_TOP	
memory, register	2-4	MOV COUNT [DI], CX	
register, immediate	2-3	MOV CL, 2	
memory, immediate	3-6	MOV MASK [BX] [SI], 2CH	
seg-reg, reg16	2	MOV ES, CX	
seg-reg, mem16	2-4	MOV DS. SEGMENT_BASE	
reg16, seg-reg	2	MOV BP, SS	
memory, seg-reg	2-4	MOV [BX].SEG_SAVE, CS	

MOVS dest-string, source-string — MOVE string

Operands	Bytes	Example	Flags
dest-string. source-string	1	MOVS LINE EDIT_DATA	none
repeat) dest-string. source-string	1	REP MOVS SCREEN. BUFFER	

MOVSB/MOVSW no operands — Move string (byte/word)

Operands	Bytes	Example	Flags
none	1	MOVSB	none
(repeat) none	1	REP MOVSW	

MUL source — Multiplication, unsigned

Operands	Bytes	Example	Flags
reg8	2	MUL BL	AF=U PF=U
reg16	2	MUL CX	CF=A SF=U
mem8	2-4	MUL MONTH [SI]	OF=A ZF=U
mem16	2-4	MUL BAUD—RATE	

NEG destination — Negate

Operands	Bytes	Example	Flags
register	2	NEG AL	AF=A PF=A
memory	2-4	NEG MULTIPLIER	CF=1* SF=A
			OF=A ZF=A

*0 if destination = 0

NOP no operands — No operation			
Operands	Bytes	Example	Flags
none	1	NOP	none

NOT destination — Logical not			
Operands	Bytes	Example	Flags
register	2	NOT AX	none
memory	2-4	NOT CHARACTER	

OR destination, source — Logical inclusive OR			
Operands	Bytes	Example	Flags
register, register	2	OR AL, BL	AF=U PF=A
register, memory	2-4	OR DX, PORT ID [DI]	CF=0 SF=A
memory, register	2-4	OR FLAG BYTE. CL	OF=0 ZF=A
accumulator, immediate	2-3	OR AL, 0110110B	
register, immediate	3-4	OR CX, 01FH	
memory, immediate	3-6	OR[BX] CMD WORD, 0CFH	

OUT port, accumulator — Output byte or word			
Operands	Bytes	Example	Flags
immed8. accumulator	2	OUT 44. AX	none
DX. accumulator	1	OUT DX. AL	

POP destination — Pop word off stack			
Operands	Bytes	Example	Flags
register	1	POP DX	none
seg-reg (CS illegal)	1	POP DS	
memory	2-4	POP PARAMETER	

POPF no operands — Pop flags off stack			
Operands	Bytes	Example	Flags
none	1	POPF	AF=R PF=R
			CF=R SF=R
			DF=R TF=R
			IF=R ZF=R

PUSH source — Push word onto stack			
Operands	Bytes	Example	Flags
register	1	PUSH SI	none
seg-reg (CS legal)	1	PUSH ES	
memory	2-4	PUSH RETURN CODE [SI]	

PUSHF (no operands) – Push flags onto stack			
Operands	Bytes	Example	Flags
none	1	PUSHF	none

RCL destination, count — Rotate left through carry			
Operands	Bytes	Example	Flags
register, 1	2	RCL CX, 1	CF=A
register, CL	2	RCL AL, CL	OF=A
memory, 1	2-4	RCL ALPHA, 1	
memory, CL	2-4	RCL [BP].PARM, CL	

RCR destination, count — Rotate right through carry			
Operands	Bytes	Example	Flags
register, 1	2	RCR BX, 1	CF=A
register, CL	2	RCR BL, CL	OF=A
memory, 1	2-4	RCR [BX], STATUS, 1	
memory, CL	2-4	RCR ARRAY [DI], CL	

REP (no operands) — Repeat string operation			
Operands	Bytes	Example	Flags
none	1	REP MOVS DEST.SRCE	none

REPE/REPZ (no operands) — Repeat string operation while equal/while zero			
Operands	Bytes	Example	Flags
none	1	REPE CMPS DATA.KEY	none

REPNE/REPNZ (no operands) — Repeat string operation while not equal/not zero			
Operands	Bytes	Example	Flags
none	1	REPNE SCAS INPUT LINE	none

RET optional-pop-value — Return from procedure			
Operands	Bytes	Example	Flags
(intra-segment, no pop)	1	RET	none
(intra-segment, pop)	3	RET 4	
(inter-segment, no pop)	1	RET	
(inter-segment, pop)	3	RET 2	

ROL destination, count — Rotate left			
Operands	Bytes	Example	Flags
register, 1	2	ROL BX, 1	CF=A
register, CL	2	ROL DI, CL	OF=A
memory, 1	2-4	ROL FLAG BYTE[DI] , 1	
memory, CL	2-4	ROL ALPHA, CL	

ROR destination, count — Rotate right			
Operands	Bytes	Example	Flags
register, 1	2	ROR AL, 1	CF=A
register, CL	2	ROR BX, CL	OF=A
memory, 1	2-4	ROR PORT STATUS, 1	
memory, CL	2-4	ROR CMD WORD, CL	

SAHF (no operands) — Store AH into flags			
Operands	Bytes	Example	Flags
none	1	SAHF	AF=R SF=R CF=R ZF=R PF=R

SAL/SHL destination, count — Shift arithmetic left/Shift logical left			
Operands	Bytes	Example	Flags
register, 1	2	SAL AL, 1	CF=A
register, CL	2	SHL DI, CL	OF=A
memory, 1	2-4	SHL [BX].OVERDRAW, 1	
memory, CL	2-4	SAL STORE_COUNT, CL	

SAR destination, source — Shift arithmetic right			
Operands	Bytes	Example	Flags
register, 1	2	SAR DX, 1	AF=U PF=A
register, CL	2	SAR DI, CL	CF=A SF=A
memory, 1	2-4	SAR N BLOCKS, 1	OF=A ZF=A
memory, CL	2-4	SAR N BLOCKS, CL	

SBB destination, source — Subtract with borrow			
Operands	Bytes	Example	Flags
register, register	2	SBB BX, CX	AF=A PF=A
register, memory	2-4	SBB DI, [BX].PAYMENT	CF=A SF=A
memory, register	2-4	SSB BALANCE, AX	OF=A ZF=A
accumulator, immediate	2-3	SBB AX, 2	
register, immediate	3-4	SBB CL, 1	
memory, immediate	3-6	SBB COUNT[SI], 10	

SCAS dest-string — Scan string			
Operands	Bytes	Example	Flags
dest-string	1	SCAS INPUT_LINE	AF=A PF=A
(repeat) dest-string	1	REPNE SCAS BUFFER	CF=A SF=A
			OF=A ZF=A

SHR destination, count — Shift logical right			
Operands	Bytes	Example	Flags
register. 1	2	SHR SI. 1	CF=A
register. CL	2	SHR SI. CL	OF=A
memory. 1	2-4	SHR ID BYTE [SI][BX]. 1	
memory. CL	2-4	SHR INPUT WORD. CL	

STC no operands — Set carry flag			
Operands	Bytes	Example	Flags
none	1	STC	CF=1

STD no operand — Set direction flag			
Operands	Bytes	Example	Flags
none	1	STD	DF=1

STI (no operands) — Set interrupt enable flag			
Operands	Bytes	Example	Flags
none	1	STI	IF=1

STOS dest-string — Store byte or word string			
Operands	Bytes	Example	Flags
dest-string	1	STOS PRINT LINE	none
(repeat) dest-string	1	REP STOS DISPLAY	

SUB destination, source — Subtraction

Operands	Bytes	Example	Flags
register, register	2	SUB CX, BX	AF=A PF=A
register, memory	2-4	SUB DX, MATH_TOTAL[SI]	CF=A SF=A
memory, register	2-4	SUB [BP +2] , CL	OF=A ZF=A
accumulator, immediate	2-3	SUB AL, 10	
register, immediate	3-4	SUB SI, 5280	
memory, immediate	3-6	SUB [BP] .BALANCE, 1000	

TEST destination, source — Test or non-destructive logical AND

Operands	Bytes	Example	Flags
register, register	2	TEST SI, DI	AF=U PF=A
register, memory	2-4	TEST SI, END_COUNT	CF=0 SF=A
accumulator, immediate	2-3	TEST AL, 00100000B	OF=0 ZF=A
register, immediate	3-4	TEST BX, 0CC4H	
memory, immediate	3-6	TEST RETURN CODE, 01H	

WAIT (no operands) — Wait while TEST pin not asserted

Operands	Bytes	Example	Flags
none	1	WAIT	none

XCHG destination, source — Exchange

Operands	Bytes	Example	Flags
accumulator, reg16	1	XCHG AX, BX	none
memory, register	2-4	XCHG SEMAPHORE, AX	
register, register	2	XCHG AL, BL	

XLAT source-table — Translate

Operands	Bytes	Example	Flags
source-table	1	XLAT ASCII_TAB	none

XOR destination, source — Logical exclusive OR

Operands	Bytes	Example	Flags
register, register	2	XOR CX, BX	AF=U PF=A
register, memory	2-4	XOR CL, MASK BYTE	CF=0 SF=A
memory, register	2-4	XOR ALPHA [SI], DX	OF=0 ZF=A
accumulator, immediate	2-3	XOR AL, 01000010B	
register, immediate	3-4	XOR SI, 00C2H	
memory, immediate	3-6	XOR RETURN CODE.0D2H	

References

1. International Business Machines Corporation, *IBM-PC Computer Hardware Reference Library—BASIC,* Boca Raton, Fla., 1981, 1983 (revised).
2. Intel Corporation, *iAPX 86/88, 186/188 User's Manual,* Intel Corp., Santa Clara, Calif., 1984.
3. R. Rector and G. Alexy, *The 8086 Book*, Osborne/McGraw-Hill, Berkeley, Calif., 1980.
4. W. E. Howden, Contemporary Software Development Environments, *CACM*, May 1982.
5. P. Gilbert, *Software Design and Development*, Science Research Associates Inc., Chicago, Ill., 1983.
6. D. L. Parnas, "On the Criteria to be Used in Decomposing Systems into Modules," *CACM*, vol. 15, no. 12, 1972.
7. P. Freeman, *Software Systems Principles—A Survey*, SRA Inc., Chicago, 1975.
8. E. Horowitz (ed.), *Practical Strategies for Developing Software Systems*, Addison-Wesley, Reading, Mass., 1975.

9. E. Yourdon and L. Constantine, *Structured Design*, Prentice-Hall, Englewood Cliffs, N.J., 1979

10. W. D. Gillett and S.V. Pollack, *Introduction to Engineered Software*, Holt, Rinehart and Winston, New York, 1982.

11. M. Lipow, "Number of Faults per Line of Code," *IEEE Trans. on Software Engr.*, vol. 5, SE-8, no. 4, July 1982.

12. Intel Corporation, *iAPX 86,88 Users Manual*, Santa Clara, Calif. 1981.

13. H. H. Loomis, Jr., "Data Representation," in H. S. Stone (ed.), *Introduction to Computer Architecture*, SRA Inc., Chicago, 1975, chap. 2.

14. J. Connen et al., "A Proposed Standard for Binary Floating Point Arithmetic," *ACM SIGNUM* Newsletter, October 1979.

15. "A Proposed Standard for Binary Floating-Point Arithmetic," Draft 8.0 of IEEE Task P754, *Computer Magazine*, March 1981.

16. J. McNamara, *Technical Aspects of Data Communication*, Digital Equipment Corporation, Maynard, Mass., 1978.

17. E. Organick, *Computer System Organization—The B5700/B6700 Series*, Academic Press, New York, 1973.

18. Special Issue on Stack Machines, *Computer*, vol. 10, no. 5, May 1977.

19. S. W. Golomb, *Shift Register Sequences*, Holden-Day, San Francisco, 1967.

20. E. Horowitz and S. Sahni, *Fundamentals of Data Structures*, Computer Science Press, Potomac, Md., 1976.

21. S. P. Morse, et al., "Intel Microprocessors—8008 to 8086," *Computer*, October 1980.

22. International Business Machines Corporation, *IBM-PC Hardware Reference Library—Technical Reference*, Boca Raton, Fla., 1981, 1983 (revised).

23. International Business Machines Corporation, *IBM-PC Language Series—Macro Assembler*, Boca Raton, Fla., 1981.

24. Intel Corporation, *ASM86 Language Reference Manual*, Santa Clara, Calif., 1981.

25. S. P. Morse, *The 8086/8088 Primer*, Hayden Book Co., Rochelle Park, N.J., 1982.

26. Intel Corporation, *An Introduction to ASM86 (iAPX 86)*, Santa Clara, Calif., 1981.

27. International Business Machines Corporation, *IBM-PC Language Series—Disk Operating System*, Boca Raton, Fla., 1981, 1983 (revised).

28. P. Norton, *Inside the IBM PC*, Robert J. Brady Co., Bowie, Md., 1983.

29. M. A. Pechura, and J. D. Schoeffler, "Estimating File Access Time of Floppy Disks," Comm. of the ACM, vol. 26, num. 10, October 1983.

30. International Business Machines, "FORTRAN Compiler by Microsoft," *IBM-PC Computer Language Series*, Boca Raton, Fla., 1982.

31. International Business Machines Corporation, *IBM-PC Language Series—PASCAL Compiler*, Boca Raton, Fla., 1981.

32. G. Gordon, *System Simulation*, Prentice-Hall, Englewood Cliffs, N.J., 1969.

33. F. S. Fishman, *Concepts and Methods in Discrete Event Digital Simulation*, John Wiley and Sons, New York, 1973.

34. M. A. Franklin, "Computer Simulation," in S. V. Pollack (ed.), *Studies in Computer Science*, Math. Assoc. of America, 1982.

35. B. G. Malkiel, *A Random Walk Down Wall Street*, W. W. Norton, New York, 1973.

36. W. M. Newman and R. F. Sproull, *Interactive Computer Graphics*, McGraw-Hill Book Company, 1979.

37. J. D. Foley, *Fundamentals of Interactive Computer Graphics*, Addison-Wesley Publishing Company, Reading, Mass., 1982.

Index